Making Sense of Movies

Praise for *Making Sense of Movies: Filmmaking in the Hollywood Style*

"I very much like Stanley's style, tone, and discourse. He is far better than (other introductory text authors) in terms of making students aware of film theory and the theoretical bases of film studies. I also like his careful historicization and his attention to the topics of censorship, sound, the studio system, genre, and the classic text formula."
  —Linda Mizejewski, The Ohio State University

"For me, the best thing about *Making Sense of Movies* is its readability. It deals with a wide range of material in an intelligent, literate way. Unlike other textbooks, it covers a limited number of significant films in greater depth."
  —Arthur Fried, Plymouth State College

"Because of the stories, because of the writing, because of the problem solving examples, I think this book could be a loved piece of reading."
  —Robin Bates, St. Mary's College of Maryland

"The real strength of *Making Sense of Movies* is its conception of the 'movie idiom' . . . bridging production, history, and textual analysis."
  —Amy Villarejo, Cornell University

"The coverage of early censorship is marvelous, as good as I've read anywhere in summary form."
  —Robin Matthews, Golden West College

"I couldn't be more impressed with this book. I especially love its scope and its ability to cover a great deal of territory in a small amount of space."
  —Tom Isbell, University of Minnesota, Duluth

Making Sense of Movies

Filmmaking in the Hollywood Style

Robert Henry Stanley

Hunter College, The City University of New York

Boston Burr Ridge, IL Dubuque, IA Madison, WI New York
San Francisco St. Louis Bangkok Bogotá Caracas Kuala Lumpur
Lisbon London Madrid Mexico City Milan Montreal New Delhi
Santiago Seoul Singapore Sydney Taipei Toronto

McGraw-Hill Higher Education 🖉

A Division of The **McGraw-Hill** *Companies*

1 2 3 4 5 6 7 8 9 0 DOC/DOC 0 9 8 7 6 5 4 3 2

Library of Congress Cataloging-in-Publication Data

Stanley, Robert Henry.
   Making sense of movies : filmmaking in the Hollywood style / Robert Henry Stanley.
     p. cm.
   Includes bibliographical references and index.
   ISBN 0-07-239765-9
    1. Motion pictures—United States—History.   2. Motion pictures—Production and direction—United States—History.   I. Title.

PN1993.5.U6 S76 2003
791.43'09794'94—dc21

                                          2002023037

Sponsoring editor, Allison McNamara; production editor, Holly Paulsen; manuscript editor, Tom Briggs; design manager, Violeta Diaz; art editor, Emma Ghiselli; text and cover designer, Mark Ong; illustrators, John and Judy Waller; photo researchers, Nora Agbayani and Alexandra Ambrose; production supervisor, Richard DeVitto. The text was set in 11/12.5 Kepler by Thompson Type and printed on 45# Somerset Matte by R. R. Donnelley and Sons Company.

Cover images: Everett Collection.

Photo Credits

p. 1 Everett Collection; **p. 101** The Kobal Collection/New Line/Dark Horse; **p. 115** The Kobal Collection; **p. 140** Everett Collection; **p. 141** ©Bettman/Corbis; **p. 170** The Kobal Collection/Richee, E.R.; **p. 175** ©Bettman/Corbis; **p. 182** Courtesy of MGM CLIP+STILL; **p. 184** ©Bettman/Corbis; **p. 218** The Kobal Collection/20th Century Fox; **p. 237** Everett Collection; **p. 313** Everett Collection; **p. 316** The Kobal Collection/Edison; **p. 326** Everett Collection; **p. 327** ©Bettman/Corbis

www.mhhe.com

Brief Contents

Contents

Preface

Movies allow us to indulge our deepest wishes and hidden desires. They offer excitement without physical risk. They provide answers to questions about how we should behave that in an earlier era would have been provided by the examples of people we knew. We put ourselves in the shoes of the actors, empathizing with the characters they portray and experiencing the whole range of their emotions. Few forms of expression have been more significant than movies have in shaping our dreams, fantasies, and aspirations.

A Unified Focus—The Hollywood Style

How movies get made, who makes them, and in what context they are produced, distributed, and shown are the principal concerns of this text. The unifying focus is on the specific character types, dramatic designs, shooting strategies, and editing techniques comprised in what has come to be called the **Hollywood style.** Though by no means static or rigid, this characteristic mode of cinematic expression in the United States sets a standard against which competing forms of filmmaking must contend.

Distilled to its essence, the Hollywood style reflects the beliefs seemingly held by most moviegoers and moviemakers that screen drama should fully engage attention and interest; that filmmaking techniques should remain unobtrusive; that camera work and editing should generally provide the optimum vantage point on the unfolding action; that a central character's motives and conflicts should constitute the primary focus of interest; and that images and sounds should be integrated in ways that evoke tears, laughter, fear, and desire while at the same time keeping the storyline on a clear course toward a more or less satisfying conclusion.

Studying the Hollywood style's strengths and shortcomings as a mode of cinematic expression, the many forces that have shaped its artistic, technical, and moral parameters, and the conditions under which it achieved enormous global appeal and reach involves far more than simply matters of aesthetic appreciation and achievement. Without ignoring individual accomplishment, this orientation gives careful consideration to such factors as movie history and tradition, technical advances, character construction, acting approaches, stereotypical representations, censorship concerns, and the collaborative aspects of production.

Three-Part Structure

Broad in scope, this text provides a logical context for understanding the Hollywood style through its aesthetic, technical, historical, cultural, institutional, and theoretical development. In addition to separate sections on the technical-artistic, the historical, and the critical-cultural aspects of movies, this text weaves all three perspectives throughout all the chapters. Taken as a whole, it will provide a firm foundation for advanced film courses in such areas as screenwriting, production, genre criticism, theory, history, and cultural analysis.

Part One: Moviemaking

The first three chapters are concerned with production personnel, the standardized procedures they tend to follow, and the often exacting circumstances under which they work. These chapters take a practical, inside view of the production process, providing insights into how certain effects were created, who created them, and how they relate to a movie's overall design and intention. The emphasis in the opening chapter is on the preparations prior to filming. Chapter 2 focuses on the actual filming itself. Chapter 3 discusses the essential work done after filming is completed.

Part Two: Contexts

The chapters in Part Two place the Hollywood style in a historical context. The technical advances, cinematic innovations, and institutional imperatives that gave this mode of cinematic expression direction and dimension in the era of speechless cinema constitute Chapter 4. Chapter 5 considers the impact of talkies on the Hollywood style, and explains the operation of the studio system of production that came to dominate moviemaking in the United States during the 1930s and 1940s. In Chapter 6, the breakdown of the studio system and the emergence of new methods of producing, distributing, and exhibiting movies are the principal concerns.

Part Three: Contents

The last three chapters consider the contents and character types of movies, and the institutional and societal forces that have influenced their presentation. The salient attributes and features of specific genres, and those persistent patterns of development that movies generally have in common provide the focus of Chapter 7. The emphasis in Chapter 8 is on the interplay among character traits, actors, screen personae, and stereotypes. The final chapter looks at the effects on the Hollywood style of the growing public demands for greater movie censorship, the private constraints developed to accommodate them, and the virtual collapse of most legal and moral strictures over cinematic expression in the emerging electronic environment.

Adaptability

Each of the text's nine chapters is designed to be used for one and one-half to two weeks of class work. Subheadings further serve to make the material easily adaptable to a full-semester course. A comprehensive glossary of important concepts and terms provides reinforcement and facilitates the reordering of sections and chapters. The key terms and concepts in each chapter that appear in the glossary are set in boldface and are usually explained briefly within the same sentence of the text. For many terms and concepts, fuller explanations are provided in the glossary.

Featured Films

Analysis initially centers on a limited number of landmark or otherwise significant movies in order to concentrate on the concepts being examined. (The multitude of movies referred to in most texts too often hinders rather than helps understanding.) Among the movies considered at length are *The Birth of a Nation* (1915), *Citizen Kane* (1941), *Casablanca* (1942), *Mildred Pierce* (1945), *It's a Wonderful Life* (1946), *Out of the Past* (1948), *Shane* (1953), *Psycho* (1960), *Bonnie and Clyde* (1967), *The Godfather* (1972), *Chinatown* (1974), *Desperately Seeking Susan* (1985), *Thelma and Louise* (1991), *Malcolm X* (1992), *Schindler's List* (1993), *The Last Seduction* (1994), *Pulp Fiction* (1994), *Shakespeare in Love* (1998), *Star Wars: Episode I—The Phantom Menace* (1999), and *Traffic* (2000). Readers are encouraged to think in new ways about the movies under consideration and to apply what has been learned to other viewing experiences. The range of movies examined is expanded with each chapter. Influential foreign and nonfiction films are also analyzed in relation to the Hollywood style.

Expressive Illustrations

Still photographs, frame enlargements, diagrams, and publicity material directly related to the specific concepts under consideration are used throughout to exemplify or highlight key points. Unless otherwise indicated, all images from movies are **frame enlargements**—magnified reproductions of individual frames—presented in the same shape (aspect ratio) in which they were first shown in theatres. (Most film texts rely on **production stills**—images captured by a still photographer on the set. Although sometimes pedagogically useful, and usually clearer than frame enlargements, such stills can be misleading because actors and objects are typically arranged, lighted, and photographed in ways different from how they appear in the finished film.) In several instances, frame enlargements from consecutive shots are placed side by side to facilitate comprehension of the film techniques discussed. Captions accompanying the illustrations serve to supplement the main text.

A Jargon-Free Approach

The general writing style is informal and narrative. Although the vocabulary has not been adapted to a specific academic level, the basic concepts presented should be readily accessible to beginning college students with little background in the field of film. Some analytical terms are used because they allow a single word to express what would otherwise require a sentence, but the theoretical jargon and technical language are kept to a minimum.

Unique Coverage

All approaches to the study of film, or any other area of academic inquiry, are necessarily guided by some implicit or explicit set of assumptions that shapes the types of questions that should be asked and the kinds of evidence that can be used in answering them. You will find that this text's emphasis on the Hollywood style facilitates consideration of a wide range of theories, analyses, and research, and opens up many avenues of inquiry for further investigation.

In each of the three main parts, the interaction of forces that shaped the conventions of the Hollywood style gets far greater coverage than in most introductory books on film studies. The nuts and bolts of the production process, along with the aesthetic results of the choices made, are fully explained in a way that is readily accessible. Issues of growing importance in the discipline concerning gender, race, and ethnicity receive careful attention, as do the contributions made by women and minorities to the movie industry's development. Such increasingly significant subjects as stereotyping and censorship are also treated at length.

What is more, within each chapter are boxed asides that offer significant supplementary material. These include such topics as the use of voice-over narration in *Double Indemnity,* the writing credits dispute involving *Citizen Kane,* the mythical aspects of the western, the "sexual orientation" of the camera's gaze, and the censorship problems that plagued provocative black filmmaker Oscar Micheaux. Combining aesthetic analysis with cultural and historical insights, this detailed and comprehensive approach to the study of movies fills a substantial niche currently unoccupied in the canon of introductory film textbooks.

Acknowledgments

The writing of this text, like the making of a movie, was a collaborative endeavor. At McGraw-Hill, Allison McNamara was everything a sponsoring editor should be. Her administrative acumen, organizational skills, and gracious personality helped immensely to keep the project on a smooth course. I am also very grateful to Cynthia Ward, now a McGraw-Hill consultant, who initially recognized potential in my approach to film and helped nurture the project to publication with her highly insightful critiques and editorial suggestions. Manuscript editor Tom Briggs did a fine job of cleaning up and clarifying many details in the manuscript. John Pierce and Gary Karsten at Thompson Type were a great help with the frame enlargements. Art editor Emma Ghiselli was responsible for the skillful coordination of the art program. Production editor Holly Paulsen coordinated the production process and saw that things were completed carefully and on time. I am indebted to all these dedicated professionals.

In addition, the comments and criticisms of reviewers from colleges and universities around the country who evaluated the manuscript at various stages of the project served to clarify and strengthen my analysis. I am specifically thankful to the following people:

Doreen Bartoni, Columbia College, Chicago

Rebecca Bell-Metereau, Southwest Texas State University

Kurt Billmeyer, Northern Arizona University

Donna Davidson, College of the Canyons

Arthur Fried, Plymouth State College

Tom Isbell, University of Minnesota, Duluth

Timothy May, Yuba College

Linda Mizejewski, The Ohio State University

David Popowski, Minnesota State, Mankato

Amy Villarejo, Cornell University

Tricia Welsch, Bowdoin College

Most of the material for the text was "class-tested" through reading assignments and PowerPoint presentations in introductory and intermediate film studies courses. Computer maven Elsa Gutierrez was extremely helpful in digitizing the frame enlargements and other visual aids (a number of which appear in this text) used for the presentations. A heartfelt thank you is also due to the many wonderful students in these courses. Their questions, comments, and concerns aided me immeasurably in honing my ideas and information. Above all, I want to express my deep appreciation to my wife, Eija, and our daughter, Katri, without whose enduring love and affection this book would not have been completed.

About the Author

Dr. Robert Henry Stanley is Professor of Film and Media Studies at Hunter College of the City University of New York, where he has taught for more than thirty years. His four previous books include *The Celluloid Empire: A History of the American Movie Industry.* His professional activities have included coordinating faculty/industry seminars for the International Radio and Television Society, moderating panel discussions for movie and television professionals, and serving on the board of directors of the New York World Television Festival. He also served for many years as a judge for the International Emmy Awards of the National Academy of Television Arts and Sciences.

PART One

Moviemaking

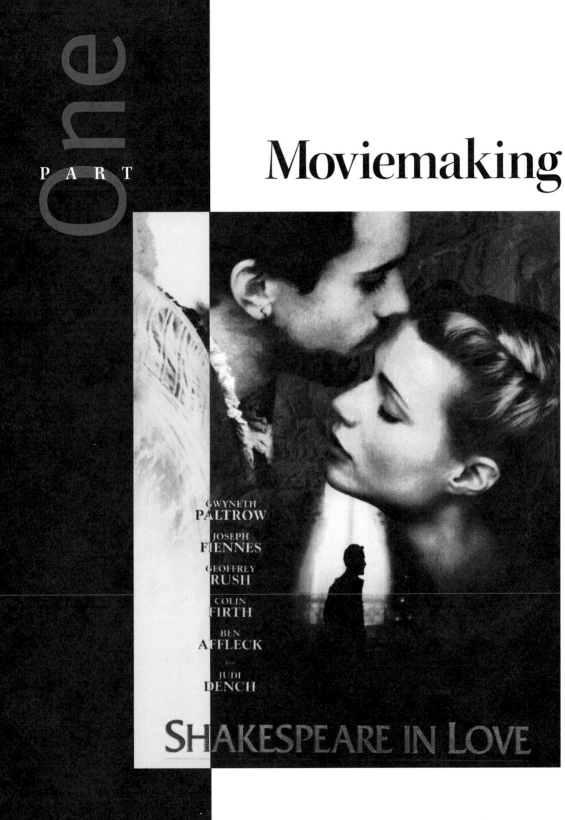

GWYNETH
PALTROW

JOSEPH
FIENNES

GEOFFREY
RUSH

COLIN
FIRTH

BEN
AFFLECK

AND

JUDI
DENCH

SHAKESPEARE IN LOVE

The Preproduction Phase

Talented moviemakers can create a world—any world—and make it seem probable and plausible. The creation of this world evolves though a complicated process requiring the coordinated efforts of dozens of artistic and technical personnel—producers, screenwriters, directors, actors, production designers, makeup artists, hairstylists, costume designers, cinematographers, camera operators, editors, sound technicians, electricians, carpenters, prop handlers, and so on. This collaborative endeavor entails three overlapping phases: **preproduction, production,** and **postproduction.**

The first phase involves all the work preparatory to the cameras rolling. This includes writing scripts, obtaining financing, designing and constructing sets, scouting locations, casting actors, testing make-up, selecting costumes, and performing scores of other tasks. The second phase, in which the actual photography or shooting takes place, is the most labor-intensive and costly stage of moviemaking. Careful planning and tight supervision generally ensure that maximum use is made of everyone involved. The final phase includes such processes as cutting and combining what has been photographed, recording the musical score, dubbing poorly reproduced dialogue, and adding sound effects. This opening chapter will look at the personnel involved in the planning of movies. Keep in mind, however, that many of these people will continue to play an active role in the project during the production phase as well.

The Producer's Role

Perhaps more than anyone else, a **producer** is likely to straddle all three phases of the production process. Under the old **studio system** of the 1930s and 1940s, in which hundreds of movies were made annually in huge complexes featuring an elaborate division of labor, legendary producers like Irving Thalberg, Darryl F. Zanuck, and Hal B. Wallis assembled and approved virtually every aspect of a movie project. This included purchasing the property (the book, play, or other work to be adapted to the screen), assigning the writers, developing the screenplay, and selecting the director, actors, and other key personnel, most of whom were under long-term contracts. During the shooting stage, they typically screened the **dailies** or **rushes** (the prints of what was photographed the day before) and provided critical comment even at the subtle levels of lighting and camera angles. They also oversaw the various elements of postproduction, helping to determine the final pace, tone, and character of the picture.

Today, the producer designation can signify something similar, or it can mean very little. (After all, what does the title mean when a movie like *Pearl Harbor* [2001] lists thirteen producers of various ranks?) Some people are, in fact, producers in name only. As a courtesy or a sign of gratitude, they are granted the rather amorphous title of executive producer, which can be bestowed on anyone from a studio executive who simply wants a screen credit to an individual who helped finance a movie project. "The producer," notes one industry analyst, "is the last remaining on-screen category for which the rules are so diffuse and the restrictions so loose that almost anyone can potentially negotiate a credit."[1]

Properly applied, the title of producer designates the prime mover behind a movie project. Bone fide producers may generate the idea themselves, or obtain the rights to a story that already exists in book, play, or magazine form; hire the director, actors, and key technical personnel; secure funding from a movie company (or "studio" as they are still called); and obtain a guarantee that the company's distributing arm will place the finished product in theatres and allot enough money to promote it effectively. Once shooting is underway, they handle such matters as placating egos, resolving conflicts, and dealing with business concerns and budgetary issues. Much of their time may be spent coping with the demands of the studio's executive cadre. When a movie is completed, they may even oversee **audience previews,** the special screenings conducted for demographically targeted groups, whose members fill out cards and answer questions about what they watched.

Producers may spend several years bringing a project to fruition. Early in 1981, after reading pal Leora Barish's debut screenplay titled *Desperately Seek-*

Madonna in *Desperately Seeking Susan* (1985). The title character is seen here freshening up after a bus ride. Publicity for the movie capitalized on Madonna's burgeoning pop icon status. One of her newly recorded songs, "Into the Groove," was even inserted into a hastily rewritten scene in which Susan gyrates around a New York club.

ing Susan, the fledgling production team of savvy insider Midge Sanford and documentary producer Sarah Pillsbury decided to develop it into a movie and sought a six-month **option.** (This common industry practice involves securing the rights to a property for a specified period by paying a percentage of its agreed-on total cost.) After securing the option and then renewing it several times, they sent the script out to over two dozen established directors. Although several filmmakers expressed interest, nothing ultimately panned out from this effort. Meanwhile, Sanford had seen *Smithereens* (1982), an unsparing character study of a punk rock groupie living by her wits on Manhattan's Lower East Side. She believed that its novice director, Susan Seidelman, possessed just the right sensibility for the project. After reading the script, the New York University film school graduate signed on to direct.

Attempting to push the project with Seidelman on board added little in the way of credibility or marketability. Apparently, not many industry insiders were familiar with her bargain-budgeted (a mere $80,000) debut feature even though it had garnered plaudits at the 1982 Cannes Film Festival. Several studios turned down the producers before they found a champion in Barbara Boyle, an executive at Orion Pictures, a thriving little studio formed in 1978 that later fell on hard times.

Eager to foster the work of women filmmakers, Boyle eventually persuaded her superiors to make the movie with Sanford and Pillsbury as producers, Barish as writer, and Seidelman as director. Under the agreed-on terms, Orion had the right to approve the budget, cast, and final script. After many conferences, compromises, and rewrites, the project won production approval. By the summer of 1984, almost four years after the producing team had initially promoted Barish's screenplay, casting for the movie finally began. Rosanna Arquette signed on in the lead role of a bored suburban housewife, and a club singer named Madonna committed to play the untidy title character, a street-smart New York up-and-comer not too far removed from the pop diva herself at the time.

Project Development

In deciding which projects to support, studio executives tend to employ a two-pronged approach—financing a combination of relatively low-budget dramas that are edgy, provocative, and character driven, and expensive pictures that will be accessible to as many people as possible. Before a big-budget feature is given the go-ahead, executives usually try to determine its potential box office appeal. Marketers, concept testers, and distributors produce tentative figures on how much it will make. If the numbers are weak, the project is likely to be dropped. The development of cheaper, more adventurous projects is generally left to subsidiaries like Miramax and New Line Cinema.

Proposals for movie projects can enter a studio's hierarchical structure at various levels. At the base of the hierarchy is the **story analyst,** who reads books, plays, scripts, and the like, and prepares synopses of the stories. Although the form of the synopsis may vary from studio to studio, the essential information provided remains the same. In addition to describing the plot and characters, story analysts generally highlight such things as the locale, era, and theme of the story, and evaluate its overall potential as a movie. If a story analyst's judgment of the material under consideration is negative, chances are no one else farther up in the studio hierarchy will read it.

Directly above the story analyst is the **story editor.** Most story editors function in more of an administrative capacity than a creative one. They supervise the story analysts and appraise their recommendations in light of studio and industry standards for success. Their role tends to be advisory, but they are usually unable to grant approval on the basis of their own determination. If they agree with a story analyst that a project is worthy of investment, they pass the material along to an executive higher in the studio hierarchy.

Next in order of ascendancy are the production executives or vice-presidents. They are charged with attracting worthwhile material to the studio, overseeing its development and production, and then turning it over to the marketing department. Like the Tim Robbins character in *The Player* (1992), they typically spend much of their day listening to "story pitches" from writers, agents, lawyers, and producers, most of which they turn down. In making an assessment, they need to know whether an actor or director with a strong track record is attached to the project or has at least expressed interest in it. They also consider how many speaking parts it entails, whether it is a costume piece, whether it will require many extras, and other such cost-related matters. When they do find a promising project, however, they are rarely able to set it in motion on their own.

This authority rests with the head of production, who picks and chooses among the proposals submitted and makes development deals. At any given time, each of the major studios has between 200 and 300 scripts in various stages of development. Only a small fraction of these will reach the shooting stage. This is especially problematic for writers working on speculation or "spec," which means they were not paid to write the material. Although spec writing may be creatively satisfying, it rarely yields any financial dividends. "Creating a script," notes a former studio executive, "is akin to entering a lottery; the chances of winning are extraordinarily remote."[2]

Superior in rank to the head of production are a series of corporate officials, any one of whom may have the power to scuttle a project at almost any stage of its development. Depending on the lines of authority, the decision to actually finance a picture may require approvals all the way up the corporate hierarchy, sometimes even including the board of directors. Decisions at this level occur behind closed doors. Whether a project is rejected because it deals with a controversial topic like nuclear power or simply because someone in the upper reaches didn't find it appealing is rarely revealed.

Risky projects are much more likely to win studio development deals and picture commitments when they have the muscle of a top **talent agency** behind them. Through their relationships with upper-echelon studio executives, agents at such formidable firms as Creative Artists, International Creative Management, William Morris, and the United Talent Agency are the major deal makers in the movie industry. In addition to handling many of the leading writers, directors, and actors, these firms represent prominent production companies and packagers, and assemble talent packages. Beyond these large, all-encompassing agencies, there are many mid-sized and small ones. The Los Angeles area alone is home to nearly three hundred talent agencies. Few movies get made without agent involvement somewhere along the way.

Screenwriting

Before the camera rolls, the basic design of a movie already exists in the screenwriter's words. These words initially take the form of a **treatment,** or outline—a narrative synopsis describing the action of the movie but containing little or no dialogue. Although having no set format, the typical treatment reads like a short story written in the present tense. It suggests the tone and flavor of the movie, and often includes a separate list of the principal characters with short descriptions. For many writers, this synopsis, generally about ten- to thirty-pages long, is the first step toward preparing a full-length **screenplay.**

A screenplay is the basic **script,** usually between 90 and 120 pages in length, with each page equivalent to about one minute of screen time. It is organized into scenes and sequences. Taking place in a single setting and within a limited period, a **scene** presents a specific unit of action that appears to be spatially and temporally continuous. Whether short or lengthy, its principal purpose is to move the story along. A **sequence** is a somewhat more slippery concept. It consists of a group of scenes linked together or unified by some common theme, time, idea, location, or action. Scenes and sequences provide the essential story structure, the relationship between the parts and the whole.

In moviemaking, the screenplay serves as a blueprint of sorts. It includes the basic idea, characterizations, and descriptions of each scene in visual and aural detail. The majority of professional screenwriters adhere to a specific format. The **dialogue,** all the words spoken within scenes, is centered on the page and indented. The name of the character speaking is centered on one line, in capital letters, followed by the dialogue on the next lines. Each new time and location is indicated by a heading in uppercase letters, such as "INTERIOR (INT.), GUEST HOUSE, AFTERNOON." Action and description are written in conventional narrative form across the page from margin to margin. The first notation to appear in the top left-hand corner is "FADE IN": (the image takes form from black). The opening of Callie Khouri's screenplay for *Thelma and Louise* (1991) shows the standard layout (the lowercase letters "b.g." stand for background, and "V.O." refers to voice-over):

FADE IN:

INT. RESTAURANT — MORNING (PRESENT DAY)

LOUISE is a waitress in a coffee shop. She is in her early-thirties, but too old to be doing this. She is very pretty and meticulously groomed, even at the end of her shift. She is slamming dirty coffee cups from the counter into a bus tray underneath the counter. It is making a lot of RACKET, which she is oblivious to. There is COUNTRY MUZAK in the b.g., which she hums along with.

INT. THELMA'S KITCHEN — MORNING

THELMA is a housewife. It's morning and she is slamming coffee cups from the breakfast table into the kitchen sink, which is full of dirty breakfast dishes and some stuff left from last night's dinner which had to "soak." She is still in her nightgown. The TV is ON in the b.g. From the kitchen, we can see an incomplete wallpapering project going on in the dining room, an obvious "do-it-yourself" attempt by Thelma.

INT. RESTAURANT — MORNING

Louise goes to the pay phone and dials a number.

INT. THELMA'S KITCHEN — MORNING

Phone RINGS. Thelma goes over to answer it.

>   THELMA
>   (hollering)
>   I got it! Hello.

INT. RESTAURANT — MORNING

>   LOUISE
>   (at pay phone)
>   I hope you're packed, little housewife,
>   'cause we are outta here tonight.

INT. THELMA'S KITCHEN — MORNING

>   THELMA
>   Well, wait now. I still have to ask
>   Darryl if I can go.

>   LOUISE (V.O.)
>   You mean you haven't asked him yet? For Christ sake,
>   Thelma, is he your husband or your father? It's just
>   two days. For God's sake, Thelma. Don't be a child.
>   Just tell him you're goin' with me, for cryin' out
>   loud. Tell him I'm havin' a nervous breakdown.

Thelma has the phone tucked under her chin, as she cuts out
coupons from the newspaper and pins them on a bulletin board
already covered with them. We see various recipes torn out
from women's magazines along the lines of "101 Ways to Cook
Pork."

>   THELMA
>   He already thinks you're out of your mind, Louise,
>   that don't carry much weight with Darryl. Are you
>   at work?

>   LOUISE (V.O.)
>   No, I'm callin' from the Playboy Mansion.

>   THELMA
>   I'll call you right back.

Three-Act Structure

Writing guru Syd Field, author of a highly influential manual, argues that most screenplays separate into three distinct acts or divisions.[3] Although not identified by name or marked by clear breaks in the action, these divisions nonetheless seem to occur in a remarkable number of screenplays. In general, the first act or major division introduces the principal characters, suggests something about their personalities, and sets up a significant problem or conflict that requires resolution. Suspenseful moments, such as questions that need answers, generally serve to stimulate interest. Toward the end of this act, perhaps twenty to thirty pages into a 120-page screenplay, there commonly occurs a major **turning** or **plot point**—an event or incident that spins the action in a new direction.

The first act of *Thelma and Louise* establishes the friendship between the title characters and reveals a great deal about their personalities and circumstances. The initial impressions of them are in the kitchen—Thelma (Geena Davis) in her untidy suburban home and Louise (Susan Sarandon) in the crowded restaurant where she works as a waitress. The two make plans to spend a weekend together but unwittingly enter a world of lecherous wolves. Once on the interstate, bullied and submissive housewife Thelma is determined to let her hair down and have some fun. She pleads with her pal to stop at a honky-tonk bar for a drink.

Before long, Thelma, drunk and giggly, is dancing with a local lothario named Harlan (Timothy Carhart). In the parking lot, despite her tearful entreaties, he begins to sexually assault her. Louise comes out, toting the gun Thelma packed for protection, and thwarts the rape attempt. However, the would-be rapist's misogynous slurs seem to spark the worn waitress's pent-up rage over past abuses (although this probable motivating factor for her extreme response only becomes apparent later). She aims the gun at him and fires a bullet directly at his chest. This marks the first major turning point and brings down the curtain on the first act.

Representing roughly half of the typical screenplay, the second act basically develops the conflict or struggle that has been established by the end of the first act. Several minor plot points may occur as protagonists strive to achieve goals and encounter various obstacles in the process. In *Thelma and Louise*, what was supposed to be a pleasant break from responsibility has plunged the terrified women into crime. They take to the road, heading west (long an emblem of male autonomy and adventure) in Louise's 1966 Thunderbird convertible. As they are dogged by deceitful men and make damaging decisions, the car becomes a place to sort things out. Their intimate talk and camaraderie lead to insights, and the journey they take is inward as well as outward.

Thelma (Geena Davis) and Louise (Susan Sarandon) take to the open road, becoming unplugged from the standard circuits that restrain women. (*Thelma and Louise* [1991])

Within a short time, they are transformed into different people. Louise, once the level-headed adult, displays all her human frailties. Thelma, once the cowed little girl, now initiates actions and makes decisions. En route to freedom and fulfillment, both women gain greater mastery of themselves and tighten their bond of friendship. While running away, they are coming closer together. But as they turn to crime for excitement, their reckless actions have disastrous repercussions. They become the targets of a huge manhunt, pursued by law enforcement officers in several states.

At the end of the second act, about 80 to 90 pages into a 120-page screenplay, another major turning point brings matters to a head and initiates the resolution in the third act. Whether a quiet moment or an action-filled event, this turning point drives the story to its climax or highest point of dramatic tension. In *Thelma and Louise,* the second major turning point occurs as the outlaw pair are driving on a moonlit highway through the imposing mesas of Monument Valley (put on the cultural map by director John Ford, who first went there in 1938 to film *Stagecoach* [1939] and subsequently returned to shoot seven more westerns). In the silence of the desert, looking at each other, they realize for the first time that there is no going back: "They're saying everything to each other in this moment, but their expressions don't change and they don't say a word. MUSIC plays on the RADIO."

The final act brings the action to its peak emotional pitch and caps off the process begun in the first act. Remaining questions are answered, conflicts or complications are resolved, and loose ends are tied up. In the last act of *Thelma and Louise,* the answer to the compelling question of what will happen to the two outlaws is provided when they literally come to the end of the road. Behind them is a small army of law enforcement agents: "More police cars have joined, and from every direction, police cars are

Thelma and Louise embrace their fate. As the still image lingers on the screen, the extended moment may elicit an array of contradictory responses: admiration for the way they choose to end the chase, feelings of futility and needless loss, a sense of the sweetness in this last flamboyant act of friendship, emotional pain over their inevitable deaths. When Callie Khouri won the Academy Award for best original screenplay, she raised the Oscar and declared, "This is the happy ending that everybody wanted." (*Thelma and Louise* [1991])

swarming across the desert, although none are in front of them. Way off in the distance, a helicopter joins the chase." At this moment, the two women become aware of their location. "What in the hell is it?" Thelma asks. "It's the goddamn Grand Canyon!" exclaims Louise, laughing and crying at the same time.

There is no escape. The police are behind them, and the Grand Canyon looms ahead. "They look at each other, look back at the wall of police cars, and then look back at each other. They smile." Rather than surrender, they decide to drive off the cliff. Louise puts the car in gear and floors it. As it sails over the edge, the image freezes. Suspended in space, the two friends seem to defy gravity. They have become free spirits.

The three-act scheme separated by turning or plot points roughly one-quarter and three-quarters of the way through the unfolding action is stressed in many standard screenwriting manuals. Although some regard it as gospel, others see it as simply a set of flexible guidelines. Whatever the case, many modern movie scribes seem to have internalized the idea of requisite plot or turning points that periodically spin the story in a new direction. Of course, what constitutes the component parts of any movie is always open to interpretation. In sampling Hollywood film fare from the 1930s to the present, one film scholar identifies a prevalent four-part pattern comprised of the setup, the complicating action, the development, and the climax. In many of the movies examined, a crucial turning point seems to occur more or less at dead center.[4]

Screenplay as Energy Source

The old maxim that a movie is only as good as its screenplay carries more than a germ of truth. Without a strong screenplay, even the most talented director is likely to falter. The screenplay provides a movie with its central source of energy. In *Schindler's List* (1993), for instance, director Steven Spielberg once again demonstrates a remarkable sense of how to place the camera and when to cut in order to obtain compelling compositions and juxtapositions on screen. Arresting images and shot sequences crop up throughout the movie (thanks in part, no doubt, to the considerable talents of cinematographer Janusz Kaminski and editor Michael Kahn). But the picture's power and poignancy owe much to Steven Zaillian's tightly constructed script, which takes a forthright approach to the horrors of the Holocaust—Nazi Germany's systematic effort to annihilate the Jewish people of Europe.

In adapting Thomas Keneally's novel for the screen, Zaillian focused on the title character, entrepreneur Oskar Schindler (Liam Neeson), with a selfless Jewish accountant, Itzhak Stern (Ben Kingsley), and an amoral Nazi, Amon Goeth (Ralph Fiennes), acting as magnetic poles for the would-be war profiteer. These three carry much of the story, but Zaillian also develops many vignettes, many scenes about people who did not survive. Through this accumulation of detail, the screenplay skillfully reveals not only the Nazi reign of terror but also the determination and resourcefulness of those who resisted.

The screenwriter's dialogue and descriptions provide the foundation on which the entire movie project is erected. Director John Madden and his talented cast and crew bring the world of Elizabethan theatre to full-bodied life in the critically acclaimed *Shakespeare in Love* (1998). Yet the essence of this paean to the power and appeal of stage drama (and by extension the cinema) resides in the strikingly inventive screenplay of Marc Norman and Tom Stoppard. The screenwriters steadfastly adhere to what little is known about Shakespeare and his early life and times. But they construct their speculative dramatic fiction on the fanciful notion that, whereas *we* are aware he will become perhaps the greatest dramatist the world has ever known, *they* in 1593 London see him only as a struggling hack, playing second fiddle to the more esteemed Christopher Marlowe.

As house writer for the Rose Theater, young Will Shakespeare (Joseph Fiennes) is working on his new play, a comedy titled *Romeo and Ethel, the Pirate's Daughter,* but has difficulty dashing off even a single page of blank verse. Neither the pressure of shaggy-toothed theatre owner Philip Henslowe (Geoffrey Rush) nor the insistence of stage-struck usurer Hugh Fennyman (Tom Wilkinson) inspires much in the way of poetry. His writer's block worsens when he catches his promiscuous paramour Rosaline (Sandra Reinton) engaging in "country matters" with another man. She is hardly the inspiration he needs to turn out the greatest love story ever told.

Young Will Shakespeare (Joseph Fiennes). After he likens his writing attempts to picking a lock with a wet herring, his doctor delicately inquires: "Tell me, are you lately humbled in the act of love?" (*Shakespeare in Love* [1998])

The beleaguered Will finds his muse in the radiant Lady Viola De Lesseps (Gwyneth Paltrow). Her passion for poetry and the theatre drives her to audition for the role of Romeo disguised as a young lad she calls Thomas Kent (women were not allowed to act in Elizabethan England). Will later spots her at a dance, is smitten, and eventually figures out that she's the "male" actor with the wispy mustache he cast as Romeo (to whom he's attracted as well). Once their ardent affair is underway, his play begins to evolve and grow, deepening into the romantic tragedy that will, of course, become *Romeo and Juliet.* During the play rehearsal sequence, the language flows seamlessly back and forth between scenes of their erotic embraces and the next scene on stage.

Faithful to the Shakespearean formula, the path of true love, alas, is strewn with pitfalls and obstacles. Will is unhappily married to Anne Hathaway and is the father of twins. Viola, for her part, cannot defy her father on the orders of Queen Elizabeth (Judi Dench) and is betrothed to the caddish but highborn Lord Wessex (Colin Firth), who plans to whisk her away to his Virginia tobacco plantation within weeks. His affaire d'amour apparently doomed, a despondent Will decides to darken the play's ending.

Cleverly crafted bits abound throughout the screenplay, such as the one involving the nasty, squinty little boy (Joe Roberts) who likes to feed live mice to stray cats and describes his idea of great theatre as "plenty of blood." He turns out to be John Webster, who will become the author of the Jacobean festival of gore *The Duchess of Malfi.* The Elizabethan version of a shrink (Antony Sher) whom Will consults to overcome his waning prowess with words has not only a couch but an hourglass to time the fifty-minute session. (While the hourglass is running, the woeful Will laments in double entendres: "It is as if my quill is broken, as if the organ of my imagination is dried up, as if the proud tower of my genius is collapsed," and so on.) When he once again takes

Al Pacino and Marlon Brando rehearse new lines written by Robert Towne for the passing-the-mantle-of-power scene. (*The Godfather* [1972])

quill to parchment, Will makes canny use of the everyday expressions he picks up while walking the London streets. "A plague on both your houses," shouts a Puritan, reviling the Rose and its rival theatre house, the Curtain.

Multiple Contributors

Scripts typically stem from many contributors. One writer might specialize in basic dramatic design, and another in dialogue or action sequences. Not only may a script pass through the hands of many writers before it is deemed ready to produce, it is also likely to be further modified while the picture is being shot. Different writers may be recruited to change a script in myriad ways—punching up the action, polishing and trimming dialogue, rearranging scenes for dramatic effect, or eliminating some segments altogether.

A person brought in to revise part or all of a script written by others is generally referred to as a **script doctor**. Robert Towne, who has mended many scripts over the years, did minor surgery on several scenes in Mario Puzo and Francis Ford Coppola's screenplay for *The Godfather* (1972). His principal assignment was to resuscitate the garden scene in which aging mob boss Don Vito Corleone (Marlon Brando) ambivalently passes the mantle of power to his youngest son, Michael (Al Pacino).

Shrouding expressions of familial respect, life philosophy, and parental aspiration in the cloak of gangland intrigue, Towne's revisions reveal the humanity of these characters and their deep affection for each other. Perhaps most moving is the old don's response when his son senses he's troubled:

"I never wanted this for you. I work my whole life—I don't apologize—to take care of my family," he explains. "And I refused to be a fool, dancing on a string held by all those . . . big shots. I don't apologize—that's my life—but I thought that . . . that when it was your time, that . . . that you would be the one to hold the strings. Senator Corleone. Governor Corleone . . . something." (Coppola acknowledged the uncredited Towne's contributions to the script when he accepted his Academy Award for best adapted screenplay.)

The producer, director, actors, agents, or anyone else who has the power to make changes may also play a role in modifying a script. David Newman and Robert Benton are the screenwriters of record for *Bonnie and Clyde* (1967). But, though not credited as a writer of the movie, its producer and star, Warren Beatty, spent many long nights with the seemingly ubiquitous Robert Towne working on pages of script. Director Susan Seidelman had a hand in shaping Leora Barish's script for *Desperately Seeking Susan,* and additional writers added romantic elements, reworked dialogue, and made structural changes. Even a screenplay like that for *Schindler's List,* which seems to reflect the distinctive voice of Steven Zaillian, underwent many revisions by other writers. Director Steven Spielberg employed several script doctors to add scenes and polish dialogue.

Robert Towne's own screenplays have been revised by others. Against Towne's wishes, director Roman Polanski made a number of significant changes in the script for *Chinatown* (1974)—although he didn't receive a screenwriting credit. Towne's ending for the movie had the enigmatic Evelyn Mulwray (Faye Dunaway), the principal female character, murdering her malevolent father (John Huston) to save their child, conceived through incest, from a fate similar to her own. Polanski decided to discard this conclusion altogether. After filming had begun, the director himself wrote the ending in which Evelyn Mulwray is killed by a policeman, and her father ends up with his incestuous clutches on the child—while the private-eye protagonist Jake Gittes (Jack Nicholson) looks on passively and powerlessly.

Multiple writers working on the same movie project became common practice under the old studio system. A dozen or more writers might have been called on to rewrite dialogue or make changes in some area of a script written by others. Still others might have further modified this work. "Writers were assigned in relays, rather as though they were pieces of sandpaper to be used up and replaced," notes an industry analyst. "Scripts resembled nothing so much as a seven-layer cake, and it often took an archaeological expedition to discover who was responsible for which layer."[5]

Some seven writers worked on the script for *Casablanca* (1942). Aeneas MacKenzie and Wally Kline were the first to undertake creating a script. They turned the unproduced play on which the movie is based, *Everybody Comes to Rick's,* into a more cinematic form and cleaned up potential censorship problems. The task of fleshing out this initial draft fell to twin brothers Julius and Philip Epstein, who were largely responsible for the dryly witty dialogue. (When a Nazi officer asks protagonist Rick Blaine's [Humphrey Bogart] opinion about the possibility of the Germans invading New York, Rick responds wryly, "Well, there are certain sections of New York, Major, that I wouldn't advise you to try to invade.")

In turn, Howard Koch lent more weight and significance to the script by providing Rick with a background of fighting for the Loyalist cause in Spain and running guns to Ethiopia. Casey Robinson, who specialized in what used to be labeled "women's pictures," added love scenes to strengthen the relationship between Rick Blaine and Ilsa Lund (Ingrid Bergman), the principal female character. Lenore Coffee also did some work on the romantic element. The Epstein twins, in turn, reworked a lot of this material. Seemingly everyone's contributions underwent revisions, so that much of precisely who wrote what remains uncertain.

Some of the movie's most memorable utterances weren't even honed by professional writers. Humphrey Bogart was apparently responsible for the catchphrase "Here's looking at you, kid." The original line was "Here's good luck to you." He is also generally credited with changing "Of all the cafes, in all the cities, in all the world, she walks into my cafe" to "Of all the gin joints, in all the towns, in all the world, she walks into mine." The movie's producer, Hal B. Wallis, is reputed to have penned Rick's closing line to Captain Louis Renault (Claude Rains) as the two walk off together into the Moroccan mist: "Louis, I think this is the beginning of a beautiful friendship."

Screen credits do not generally reflect the complexities of creating a script. At the time *Casablanca* was made, the Screen Writers Guild, the union established in 1933 to represent writers, held that a maximum of two writers or writing teams could be allowed credit on a screenplay. Even though seven writers worked on the script for the movie, only three of them got screen credit: Koch and the Epstein twins. At the Academy Awards ceremony for 1943, the three were awarded the Oscar for best screenplay. Only Koch was in attendance. In his brief acceptance speech, he made no mention of the uncredited contributions to the script.

Writers' Struggles for Recognition

Over the years, the Screen Writers Guild underwent various organizational changes and joined forces with guilds representing writers in other mediums, such as radio and television. It finally set up dual branches in 1954, as the Writers Guild of America (WGA), East and West, with the Mississippi River serving as the jurisdictional dividing line. Although this consolidated guild has won various concessions for its constituency, writers for the big screen still do not enjoy very much creative control or official recognition for the way they give shape and form to movies.

An especially sore point has been the way screen credit is apportioned. The WGA finally scored something of a victory early in 1995 when the studios agreed to assign writers the next-to-the-last credit at the beginning of a movie. That places them just after the producer and just before of the director. (In this race for recognition, the last is best, and the next-to-last is second best.) The writers have also sought to restrict the right of directors to use the phrase "A Film by . . . ," the so-called possessive credit. But they have yet to reach agreement with the studios on this issue.

Through all of its negotiations, the WGA has never been able to dismantle the assembly line system whereby several writers are assigned to work on the same movie at various stages of its development. Although it now restricts the allowable number of writers' credits to three for each movie (or double that number if writers are working as a team), often many more writers actually contribute to a given screenplay. According to some reports, the number working on intermediate drafts sometimes approaches sixty. Such writers may toil for years without ever seeing their names on the screen, a situation that has definite economic consequences for them. Among other things, screen credit means someone gets extra money, or **residuals** (compensation for the reuse of one's work), from foreign sales, basic cable, pay cable, videocassettes, and **DVDs** . (In its 2001 contract with the studios, the WGA failed to secure residuals from videocassettes and DVDs.) The fewer the credited writers, the larger the share of money they get to divide up.

The Director's Domain

How a script is translated into images and sounds constitutes, in effect, a new interpretation of what was originally written. The **director** is in charge of the day-to-day progress of this translation, attending to the preparation, staging, and enacting of scenes; to the inflections, pace, and mood of the dialogue and action; and to such matters as camera placement and movement, lighting patterns, focus, and framing. In some cases, a director's role is limited to these activities. In other instances, a director's dominion may extend to every aspect of production, from scripting to casting to final editing.

Directing in the Studio System

Under the old studio system, most directors did not enjoy much artistic freedom and had little opportunity to impress personal visions on their movies. It was not uncommon for them to be handed a script just a few days before shooting. They could pick some of their crew, but rarely could they choose other key personnel. On any given shooting day, a director of a major feature was expected to generate about two and one-half minutes of filmed material ready to be integrated into the preliminary version, or **rough cut,** of a picture.

Since failure to maintain this pace threw off the entire production schedule, discipline and order usually took priority over talent and temperament. Subservient to producers, directors could be, and frequently were, taken off a project if they failed to meet deadlines or budgets.

The status of directors in the studio hierarchy was exposed by Frank Capra, first president of the Screen Directors Guild, in an open letter to the *New York Times* published in April 1939.[6] He complained that very few directors in the industry were allowed to shoot as they wished or had any say over the way their work was edited. According to Capra, a mere half-dozen producers ruled on about 90 percent of the scripts and supervised the editing of 90 percent of the pictures. He estimated that some 80 percent of directors shot scenes exactly as they were told to, without any changes whatsoever, and that 90 percent of them had no voice in the story or the editing.

When the Screen Directors Guild (changed to the Directors Guild of America in 1960) was recognized in 1939 by the studios as the bargaining agent for directors, its members won the right to participate in casting, script development, and editing. But ultimate authority over the selection, trimming, and assembly of the hundreds of images comprised in any movie generally remained with producers and studio executives. Typically, a producer would supervise the editing until a final version of the movie won approval from the head of production—who was, as more than one industry wag has wisecracked, "Czar of all the Rushes." (Even today, very few directors enjoy the right of **final cut** for the theatrical version of a movie, although the **director's cut** of a major movie is often available on videotape and DVD.)

The conditions under which movies were made were more exacting at some studios than at others. At Warner Bros. Pictures, the emphasis was on fast and efficient production. The whole production process was tightly supervised in what amounted to a factory-like, assembly line approach to moviemaking. Costly retakes were generally avoided, and production schedules were adhered to rigidly. Producers, directors, writers, actors, cinematographers, editors, and technical staff were shuffled relentlessly from project to project. Vacations were strictly limited and could be canceled at a moment's notice.

Although certain directors could exercise some discretion, they were ordinarily kept on a tight tether. In the course of shooting *Casablanca,* director Michael Curtiz left out some lines and contributed to the addition of others. In the Paris flashback sequence, he dropped the dialogue between Ilsa and Rick written for the transition from driving down the Champs-Elysées to driving down a country road. In addition, he was instrumental in having the writers build up the character of Major Heinrich Strasser (Conrad Veidt), making him an older, more sophisticated and autocratic Gestapo official. He also suggested the insertion of some additional vignettes depicting the frustrations and anxieties of the refugees.

Michael Curtiz gives advice to Ingrid Bergman on the set for the open-market scene in *Casablanca* (1942). Although he treated her with fawning courtesy, the director typically badgered female stars and viciously berated his crew and minor players.

The movie's producer, Hal B. Wallis, greatly admired Curtiz's work. More than once, he expressed his anger at critics who said the Hungarian-born director had no personal style. He insisted that a Curtiz setup was unmistakable, "that it had a stamp as clearly marked as a Matisse."[7] But when he learned about the dropped dialogue from the flashback, Wallis let Curtiz know in no uncertain terms that he expected to be consulted before the director made any other scene changes. Wallis made all of the key decisions on the picture in conjunction with studio head Jack L. Warner.

The 1939 Screen Directors Guild agreement with the studios called for directorial credit to appear last on the screen before the actual movie started. Appearing at the end of the list of all those credited with creating a movie, the director's credit was intended to signify the person who synthesized and superseded the work of everyone else. The last may be first in the kingdom of heaven, but only in rare instances did directors enjoy a high degree of artistic freedom. Those who did frequently came from outside the studio system, bringing a strong sense of personal style and creative autonomy to their work in Hollywood. Some, like Alfred Hitchcock and Robert Siodmak, came from abroad, mainly Europe after World War II broke out; others, like Orson Welles and Elia Kazan, came from radio or stage backgrounds in New York.

A small number of established Hollywood contract directors, such as Frank Capra, John Ford, and Howard Hawks, were able to parlay past success and changing economic conditions into greater creative control under the hyphenate "producer-director." The control such filmmakers enjoyed over script development, casting, and editing, however, had more to do with their role as producers than as directors. "Such authority," as film scholar Thomas Schatz notes, "came only with commercial success and was won by filmmakers who proved not just that they had talent but that they could work profitably within the system."[8] At around the same time, several leading contract screenwriters gained greater creative freedom by achieving writer-director status. Preston Sturges led the way in 1940, followed by John Huston, Billy Wilder, and others. The ranks of "hyphenates" grew steadily during the decade.

Director as *Auteur*

The status of the director was greatly elevated as a result of developments first in France and later in the American critical community. In the 1950s, a small coterie of enthusiastic young French critics (among them such future directors as Jean-Luc Godard, François Truffaut, Claude Chabrol, Eric Rohmer, Jacques Rivette, and Alain Resnais) immersed themselves in the history of cinema through marathon screening sessions at the Cinémathèque Française, a movie theatre and resource center founded in 1936 that now operates under the aegis of the French government's Centre National du Cinéma. Because they didn't understand English well enough to be put off by contrived plots and clichéd dialogue, they were able to see the larger structures, forms, and myths of American movies. They also recognized that many Hollywood directors were much more than hacks who simply got a scheme from writers and moved it from script to screen as quickly and cheaply as possible.

Marathon viewings sharpened the critical sensibilities of these young *cinéphiles,* who argued the merits of a range of Hollywood directors in the pages of the *Cahiers du Cinéma,* an influential film journal that first appeared in 1951. Countless articles in this journal detailed how certain directors were able to present a personal vision and visual style despite the restrictions imposed upon them by the standardized assembly line techniques of the Hollywood studio system. Many of these essays suffer from arrogance and overstatement. A reader failing to recognize the genius of a favored director is clearly regarded as hopelessly benighted. Nonetheless, had it not been for the *Cahiers* critics, and their fascination with American movies, many Hollywood directors now considered cinematic artists of great ability and accomplishment may have been relegated to the scrap heap of popular cultural expression.

Andrew Sarris, then a reviewer and editor for the avant-garde journal *Film Culture* in New York, transported the analytical approach of the *Cahiers* group to the United States in the early 1960s. He translated its tactics, opinions, and polemics into what he termed the "*auteur* theory," which holds that cinema is an art of personal expression and that its great directors are to be as much esteemed as the authors of their work as any writer, composer, or painter. (Pronounced oh-TUR, *auteur* is the French word for "author.") In this approach, directors eclipse all other creative forces on a movie, including screenwriters. Coherent visual style takes priority over the substance of the script. A director expressing himself through a formulaic western can be a true *auteur* if he puts his personal imprint on the project. Another director, working with a first-rate script and cast, may be deemed a mere technician if the final film lacks an identifiable vision.

Sarris provoked much controversy and debate among film aficionados by ranking directors under such headings as "Pantheon," "Expressive Esoterica," "Less Than Meets the Eye," and "Strained Seriousness." Directors with an impressive roster of movies to their credit but no identifiable cinematic philosophy generally don't fare well in this classification system. For example, Sarris dismisses director Michael Curtiz as "lightly likable" and an "amiable technician." Although he sees *Casablanca* as Curtiz's one enduring masterpiece, he denigrates the accomplishment by calling it "the happiest of happy accidents, and the most decisive exception to the *auteur* theory."[9]

Although Sarris was careful to point out that the *auteur* approach was a first step in making sense of movies, his analytical stance served to focus critical attention almost entirely on the director. Centering analysis on a single artistic vision helped to give movies the same aesthetic legitimacy as a sonata by Mozart or a painting by Picasso. The new status enjoyed by certain Hollywood directors led critics, scholars, and students toward a wholesale reevaluation of American cinema. Beginning in the 1960s, museums mounted extensive retrospectives of the works of directors like Orson Welles, Howard Hawks, and Alfred Hitchcock; colleges increasingly incorporated the analysis of American movies into the liberal arts curriculum; and aspiring *auteurs* studied film on both the undergraduate and graduate level.

With the popularization of the *auteur* theory, which has been promoted by critics, scholars, and directors themselves, the director soon came to be widely regarded as the primary creative force in movies, the one who synthesizes, orchestrates, and guides the contributions of other production personnel. Whatever amount of creative control they may enjoy, however, directors are compelled to collaborate to some extent. They ordinarily work with scripts others have authored; they guide actors who strive to interpret characters in their own way; and they employ set designs, lighting schemes, and camera placements others have devised.

Casting Actors

Movies are a form of dramatized storytelling. Above all else, the director requires players to bring a screenplay to life. Even in this age of digital technology, when movies like *The Matrix* (1999) appear to devote much more attention to pyrotechnics than histrionics, the **actor** remains at the center of the production process. It is widely accepted by everyone involved in making a movie that, no matter how spectacular the visual display, the primary interest of viewers is in the personalities on the screen—their appearances and actions, and their effects on one another.

The **casting director** generally auditions actors and makes suggestions for filling the various roles in a movie. Those actors selected and hired will fall into one of several categories. The **principals** have the most significant speaking parts, of which two or three might be lead roles and the others supporting ones. The rest of the cast consists of minor players and extras. A **minor player** has a small speaking role or, at least, portrays a character who has a name. An **extra** adds to the background or atmosphere of a scene. Extras are hired on a daily or weekly basis and usually have no lines.

For the casting of lead roles, the casting director, or someone else involved in the project, typically brings the script to the attention of an actor's agent. The actor assesses the part in question and, if the judgment is positive, instructs the agent to negotiate a contract. It is also not uncommon for an actor to hear about a project and ask to be considered for a part. In certain circumstances, a well-established actor or even a major star will be asked to take a **screen test.** This entails making a short film or videotape of the actor reading a section of a scene in character.

Both Mario Puzo and Francis Ford Coppola wanted Marlon Brando for the role of Don Vito Corleone in *The Godfather*. However, opinions about the star were far from uniformly positive. By the late 1960s, he had developed a reputation for being difficult to direct. Moreover, most of his movies during the decade had achieved only marginal box office success. Along with other conditions, top executives at Paramount, the company in charge of production, insisted that he submit to a screen test.

Although accounts vary somewhat, Brando readily agreed to a test, which was done in the privacy of his home. In preparation, according to most versions of the story, the actor's personal makeup artist darkened his hair and combed it straight back, added shadows under his eyes to make him look older, and penciled in a thin mustache on his upper lip. As an added touch, he wadded toilet tissue into his upper and lower gums to give Brando heavy jowls. Coppola himself conducted the test with the aid of actor Salvatore Corsitto and a video camera operator. As the camera rolled, Brando, eating fruit and drinking demitasses of coffee, played an impromptu scene with Corsitto (cast as Bonasera the undertaker). Brando's performance was so powerful and persuasive that it instantly won over the studio brass.

Costume Design

In the process of translating a script into images and sounds, directors work with a wide range of creative and technical talent. The **costume designer** creates a costume plan for the entire movie, selecting or designing the clothing worn by the actors with due regard for such details as setting (place and time), weather conditions, social class status, and overall tone and mood. In making decisions about line, color, and texture—the tools of the trade—the designer must come to know the script well. All of the characters must be assessed to determine how they would be likely to dress under what circumstances.

The clothing for period pieces is typically re-created from patterns of the time or acquired from vendors and modified to suit the specific purposes of the picture. Making countless sketches, Walter Plunkett designed the 5500 individual pieces of clothing that constituted the 2000 costumes for the Civil War epic *Gone With the Wind* (1939) with an eye toward complete authenticity. Even the petticoats for the Southern ladies were made of costly Val lace. When a movie is set in modern times, the costuming of the players is usually specially designed to support their roles and serve the overall mood of the story.

Designer Ruth Carter had to costume actors over five decades for *Malcolm X* (1992). The scenes that take place in Northern Africa and the Middle East required her to be sensitive to such things as the difference between an Egyptian galabia (hooded robe) and a Saudi Arabian one. The American period clothes demanded just as much attention to detail. For scenes early in the movie, she designed several zoot suits—a flamboyant outfit that became a nationwide phenomenon in the 1940s. Initially worn by inner-city teenagers, both for vanity and as a way of shocking outsiders, the zoot suit consists of a wide-brim hat, a long suit jacket with heavily padded shoulders, and pants that balloon out below the waist but are cut very tight around the ankles. The colorful zoot suits that Malcolm (Denzel Washington) and his pal from his teenage years, Shorty (Spike Lee), wear in the Roseland Ballroom scene add to the sense of people in a frenzy—dancing, clapping, and stomping their feet.

Clothes are not mere accessories, but are key elements in the construction of screen identities. They can signify a great deal about a character. Anna Hill Johnstone, costume designer for *The Godfather*, devised garments for Don Corleone that indicated someone who wielded immense power but who

Shorty (Spike Lee) and Malcolm (Denzel Washington) in their zoot suits.
(*Malcolm X* [1992])

cared nothing about fashion. His attire simply met the minimal requirements for a given situation. For the office scenes, for instance, he was garbed in a worn, light-colored business suit with pinstripes. An ill-fitting shirt with a too-large collar, a patterned necktie twisted backwards to expose the label, and a belt worn below the loops suggest his humble origins.

The clothing characters are wearing at any given moment in a movie often suggests something about their circumstances. Costume designer Sandy Powell's garments for the lovely and cultivated Lady Viola De Lesseps in *Shakespeare in Love* make her seem sparrowlike, a delicate but willful creature that could take flight at any moment. Even her high ruffled collars don't restrict her movement; there is always something light and airy about the way they frame her face. Only in her heavy, pale-gold wedding dress—worn as she's being married to the loathsome Lord Wessex, an arrangement she is compelled by regal command and family duty to honor—does she look stiff and restricted. She even moves differently in it. She's more tentative and uncertain, and less carefree and youthful—its thick quilted bodice seems to portend the kind of bound life she likely will lead with her new husband on his Virginia tobacco plantation.

Clothing can be so expressive that even a minor adjustment affects meaning. In *Pulp Fiction* (1994), for example, the outfits of Uma Thurman's quirky character change very little, but the changes of detail are subtle and significant. For Mia Wallace's night out with Vincent Vega (John Travolta) at Jack Rabbit Slim's, costume designer Betsy Heimann dressed her in an elongated white blouse with protracted geometric cuffs, black bell-bottoms, a black bra, and gold ballet slippers (a black bob wig adds to the offbeat effect). While the oddly paired couple sit chatting in a chopped-up 1950s car body, her modest

Lady Viola De Lesseps (Gwyneth Paltrow). The elegant clothing of the Elizabethan period covered bodies that were mostly unwashed. Even someone like Lady Viola, the daughter of a wealthy merchant, would probably have bathed no more than three or four times a year. (*Shakespeare in Love* [1998])

blouse is unbuttoned once from the collar. When she appears on the dance floor, however, a second button has been undone exposing her cleavage. This area of bare flesh will become the target of the adrenalin-filled syringe intended to jump-start her heart when she overdoses on heroin.

Makeup and Hairstyling

Among the key personnel on any movie project is the **makeup artist,** who is responsible for the way actors look in a wide range of lighting situations. Makeup in movies was originally necessary to tone down the features of the players and to keep their appearances consistent. The harsh lights and type of black-and-white film stock used before the advent of talkies in the late 1920s greatly accentuated flaws in both faces and hair. Most colors translated into appropriate shades of gray, but red (including blood vessels in the face) registered as black.

Although heavy applications of theatrical makeup could compensate for this problem, features, details, and subtle changes in expression were obscured in the process. The solution came in 1914, when Russian émigré Max Factor, who had opened a wig and makeup business in Los Angeles six years earlier, invented a flexible greasepaint that masked the reds of the skin while allowing facial nuances and subtleties to show through. This enabled screen players, who were generally responsible for their own makeup, to create a more realistic-looking effect.

The makeup process gradually moved out of the hands of the players and into the control of the movie studios. The first studio makeup department

A makeover turned forty-seven-year-old Marlon Brando into an old man for his role in
The Godfather (1972).

was established in 1917 by George Westmore, an English wig maker from the Isle of Wight. All six of his sons followed him into the craft of greasepaint. By the mid-1930s, most of the major studios had a makeup department headed by a Westmore. Together, the founding father of the Westmore dynasty, along with his six sons, adorned, disguised, and altered an astonishing number of the world's most recognizable faces. Monty Westmore, the eldest of George's sons, who first made his mark plucking Rudolph Valentino's eyebrows, even managed to keep Vivien Leigh's naturally blue eyes looking emerald green throughout *Gone With the Wind*. (His name is not listed in the screen credits, as makeup artists did not receive such recognition until the early 1940s.)

Screen players of every decade have relied on experts in the latest techniques for modifying faces and follicles to create credible-looking characters. In plying their craft, makeup artists are responsible for such things as balancing flesh tones in natural and artificial lighting; painting on bruises, tattoos, and skin alterations; and making the leads look glamorous while not seeming to wear any makeup at all. Makeup effects can range from the cosmetic to the prosthetic, in which an actor's appearance is temporarily transformed.

Makeup expert Dick Smith drastically altered Marlon Brando's face when the actor played the title role of *The Godfather*. He was forty-seven years old at the time, much too young for the part of the aging Mafia leader. Smith, working with Brando's personal makeup artist, Philip Rhodes, applied a special liquid latex compound to create wrinkles of varying thickness in the actor's skin, especially around the eyes and nose. He also dyed Brando's thinning blondish hair black and touched it up with streaks of gray. A mustache, slightly discolored teeth, and some painted facial spots and shadows further heightened the illusion of age, and olive skin tones gave him a Mediterranean appearance. To complete the transformation, Smith fitted the actor with a special denture device that pushed out his lips and caused his jowls to sag. The typical makeup session lasted about one and a half hours. Another fifteen to twenty minutes was added for the scenes of the old don nearing death. And each day the painstaking process would start anew.

Equally important in creating shadings of age and personality in a character's appearance is hairstyling. The principal task of the **hairstylist** is to fashion a look consistent with the traits of each actor's character. Changes in the cut, length, and color of hair can help to make a character appear more alluring, frumpy, frazzled, mousy, or menacing. The wild locks of Glenn Close in *Fatal Attraction* (1987), for example, served to signal her character's deranged mental state.

To create a specific look, a hairstylist might work with the actor's own hair or with wigs, toupees, falls, switches, and the like. Wigs are used extensively in both period and contemporary pictures. Among other things, wigs trimmed to various lengths, along with the addition of facial hair, can suggest the passage of time for male characters out in the wild without benefit of a barber. The use of a hairpiece is also an essential element in preserving the illusion of youthful middle age for many male stars.

A distinct category of makeup and hairstyling involves the creation of certain **special effects**—striking photographic results achieved during filming. With the new urethane molding materials now available, faces and bodies can be shaped into any form imaginable. The especially gruesome look of many of the freakish creatures and monsters in recent horror and science fiction films has depended on these materials. A crowning achievement in terms of extreme alterations in appearance was special effects makeup artist Rick Baker's work in *The Nutty Professor* (1996). He helped to transform Eddie Murphy into six completely different looking characters, among them prissy exercise guru Lance Perkins and morbidly obese chemistry professor Sherman Klump. To give the latter character's body just the right bulk and jiggle, Baker used silicone, foam, and liquid-filled bladders.

To produce certain striking photographic results, an actor may be fitted with specially designed equipment before shooting commences. Special effects expert A. D. Flowers and his crew were responsible for creating the scene showing the gruesome murder of casino operator Moe Greene (Alex Rocco) in *The Godfather*. For the scene, Rocco lay on his stomach getting a massage as the hit men came into the room. After he put on a real pair of glasses, the camera stopped rolling. These were then replaced with eyeglasses rigged with special lenses and plastic tubes running down the stems. One tube contained artificial blood; the other was connected to a canister of compressed air and contained a tiny pellet. To create the gory simulation of a bullet ripping

Makeup, hairstyles, and accessories often combine to suggest a character's social status. In *Working Girl* (1988), when Tess McGill (Melanie Griffith) leaps from the secretarial pool into the upper echelons of management, she sheds her tricolor eye shadow, junk jewelry, patterned hose, and bouffant hairdo in favor of a subtler, more professional look. "If you want to get ahead in business," she decides, "you've got to have serious hair."

through his glasses and into his eye, the pellet was fired through the back of the right lens away from the actor, and then the blood in the other tube was released. Although the lens appeared to be shattering inward, it was actually blowing outward so that his eye would not in any way be damaged.

Production Design

The **art director** or **production designer** (a more encompassing title currently in use) is primarily responsible for designing and creating sets, although just what these titles mean depends on the era and the studio (or independent company). In the old studio era, an art director generally fashioned the overall look of a movie. But now that responsibility is usually given to a production designer, who then oversees one or more art directors.

The position of production designer (a title that came into general use in the 1970s) was pioneered by William Cameron Menzies, who oversaw all the visual aspects of *Gone With the Wind*. Working with artist-historian Wilbur Kurtz, he prepared an elaborate series of watercolor sketches that showed the placement of the actors and the camera angles, as well as the scenery.

ELEMENTS OF *MISE-EN-SCÈNE*

Such things as setting, costumes, and props are part of ***mise-en-scène*** (pronounced meez-on-SEN)—the French theatrical term for "staging" used by many film scholars to designate the visible elements of **meaning** operating within a movie at any given moment. Analysis of *mise-en-scène* often draws on concepts from **semiotics.** Originally concerned with spoken and written language, the semiotic enterprise now embraces all **codes of meaning**—the more or less implicit or explicit rules or social agreements within a **culture** about what stands for what, what goes with what, and what behavior is appropriate in what situation. Anything that triggers these codes is called a **sign.** A sign has physical form, refers to something beyond itself, and is recognized by someone as being meaningful. For purposes of analysis, a sign may be separated into the signifier, some object or behavior, and the signified, the thoughts, feelings, and emotions it evokes. When *Casablanca*'s Rick Blaine takes a drag on his cigarette, for instance, the signifier is the actual act or behavior and the signified is the meaning attached to this behavior. The concept of the sign compels us to see things in terms of their significance.

Stripped of its highly technical terminology, the seminal idea underpinning the semiotic method is that meanings are based on relationships of similarity and difference. The scene in which we are introduced to Rick Blaine provides an illustration of how semiotic analysis of *mise-en-scène* works. It begins with a waiter approaching a table. He is carrying a voucher. His glance off-screen makes what is outside the frame seem more interesting than what is within it. A hand extends into the frame from the left and takes the voucher. This provides a link with the next shot, which shows a strong hand scribbling across a voucher in large letters "OK. Rick." We then see a smoldering cigarette, an empty champagne glass, and a chessboard. As a hand lifts the cigarette, the camera follows the movement to reveal Rick's face for the first time as he takes a deep drag. Presiding over the gambling tables of his cafe, Rick drinks and sits by himself, playing a solitary game of chess. The solo chess game, cigarette, and champagne glass provide clues to his character. His face and body, clothing, facial expressions, gestures and movements, and speech patterns also carry connotative meanings. So do things like lighting patterns and spatial relations—who is obscured, who seems to dominate, and so on.

To analyze the possible meanings generated by the signifiers or elements in this scene, substitute one item for another in the same general category—for example, a beer mug for the champagne glass, or a cigar for the cigarette. The champagne glass and cigarette suggest a world-weary sophistication. Beer and cigars generate very different connotations. We make sense of such things as cigarettes partially in relation to the ways they differ from items in the same category (things people smoke). We also comprehend things in terms of their similarities, in the ways they seem to belong with items from other categories. The solo chess game implies cleverness and perhaps a certain aloofness, and fits well with the champagne and cigarette. A person who routinely sips champagne is not likely to play checkers for amusement or mental stimulation.

Any meaning actual audiences generate from these elements of *mise-en-scène* will invariably be constrained by time, place, age, gender, class status, and a host of

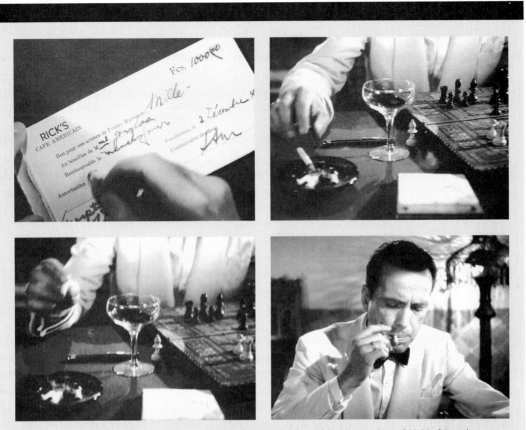

Elements of *mise-en-scène*. Focusing on these elements while withholding a view of Rick's (Humphrey Bogart) face heightens the interest the movie has already generated around him. Eavesdropping on conversations, we earlier heard Captain Renault (Claude Rains) assure Major Strasser (Conrad Veidt) that the murderer of the two German couriers carrying letters of transit would be arrested at Rick's nightclub— "Everybody comes to Rick's." We also heard Strasser's reply: "I have already heard about this cafe, and also about Mr. Rick himself." Further arousing our curiosity, we heard Carl the waiter (S. Z. Sakall) inform a woman that Rick never drinks with the customers: "Never. I have never seen it." Like one of her companions, we too may wonder: "What makes a saloonkeeper so snobbish?" (*Casablanca* [1942])

other social, psychological, and cultural factors. Very different impressions of Rick Blaine can be formed depending on one's cultural perch. Imagine, for instance, how his clothes and breath must smell as a result of all that cigarette smoking. Think about the condition of his liver and lungs. That constant sipping of champagne must have him well on the way to cirrhosis of the liver. What about the carcinogenic effects of all the cigarette smoke he inhales? However, these concerns probably never entered the minds of most moviegoers in the 1940s.

The movie's art director, Lyle Wheeler, who amassed thousands of drawings, photographs, and descriptions of the north Georgia locale that figured in the story, implemented these visualizations.

Menzies' sense of scale and scope and his meticulous attention to telling detail exerted an influence over every aspect of the movie, confounding any notion that the assessment of cinematic creativity must be focused exclusively on the director. In addition to the spectacular settings and sumptuous period details, he was largely responsible for the movie's complex color scheme, as well as its central visual metaphor of fire. Because no established Oscar category existed to recognize what he had accomplished, at the annual Academy Awards presentation dinner held early in 1940, Menzies received a special award for his outstanding achievement in the use of color for the enhancement of dramatic mood.

It is a truism of film history that many of the major studios of the 1930s retained their own special look or style. Certain elements, such as the contract players who appeared, the types of stories emphasized, and the directorial techniques employed, stamped a movie as indisputably Warner, M-G-M, or Paramount. As much as any of these factors, it was the studio's art department that fashioned the look of its pictures. The department's administrative head usually supervised all design projects.

Insisting on centralized control, M-G-M's supervising art director Cedric Gibbons, whose work ranged from the intricate and detailed backgrounds for *Dinner at Eight* (1933) to the replica of an old sailing ship in *Mutiny on the Bounty* (1935), put his visual stamp on most of the studio's output during his long reign. Some 70 percent of M-G-M's 4500 craftspeople and laborers were affected in one way or another by the work of Gibbons's department. Although his role was often largely executive and administrative, he nonetheless set the tone for the studio's sleek and elegant productions, especially its elaborate musicals. His set designs won him eleven Academy Awards between 1929 and 1956 (he even designed the Oscar statuette).

Vienna-born Hans Dreier, who held sway over Paramount's art department for thirty years, was the chief contributor to the baroque pictorial style of that studio's movies, especially during its heyday in the early 1930s. He designed several of director Josef von Sternberg's erotically charged films with Marlene Dietrich, including the highly stylized *The Scarlet Empress* (1934). But he could also produce simple, understated sets when a picture required them. His designs for *Double Indemnity* (1944) included the nouveau riche decor of a dusty Glendale villa; a cheap, sparsely furnished apartment; and a hideous Los Angeles insurance company office whose main hall consists of identical desks, blotters, lamps, and black telephones, and rows of steel filing cabinets.

Supervising art directors like Gibbons, Dreier, and RKO's Van Nest Polglase headed departments of between fifty and eighty people, including unit

The All-Risk Insurance Company's dark, cavernous main hall contains interminable rows of identical desks. Hans Drier and his associate art director, Hal Pereira, designed simple, understated sets to capture the stultifying milieu of conformity and predictability that insurance salesman Walter Neff (Fred MacMurray) attempts to escape with tragic results. (*Double Indemnity* [1944])

art directors, architects, illustrators, model makers, and set decorators. The actual work typically was done by the unit art directors assigned to specific movie projects. They commissioned sketches and architectural drawings of rooms, buildings, and facades; huge flat paintings used as backdrops; and even models of whole streets—all executed with due regard for mood, period, dramatic necessity, technical requirements, and budgetary constraints. They also oversaw the construction of these sets by crews working around the clock, six days a week, with much of the work being done on the night shift.

The art department's head typically took primary credit for a project, as Polglase did for *Citizen Kane* (1941) although his associate, Perry Ferguson, did the actual design work. The talented Ferguson, as a major study of this movie project notes, worked in close collaboration with director Orson Welles on the conception of the scenes that were then turned into sketches and set drawings by illustrators and draftsmen in the RKO art department.[10] Although Polglase's role in this endeavor was mainly managerial, his contract required that he receive the principal screen credit for the studio's movies, whether he designed them or not.

Nowadays, the person credited for set design and decor is generally the person responsible. Modern production designers approach their work in

Posters for drive-in theatre fare behind Vincent (John Travolta) and Mia (Uma Thurman) add to the ambience of Jack Rabbit Slim's—a 1950s diner-style "theme restaurant" where a Buddy Holly look-alike is the waiter and a Marilyn Monroe clone is a hostess. Even the food and beverages come with vintage celebrity labels: patrons can order a Martin and Lewis or Amos 'n' Andy milk-shake to accompany their Douglas Sirk steak, which—fittingly for a director who specialized in overwrought melodramas—comes "burnt to a crisp or bloody as hell." (*Pulp Fiction* [1994])

various ways. Some may bring a specific style to every project regardless of subject matter; others strictly adhere to the dictates of the directors with whom they work. David Wasco, who has worked several times with writer-director Quentin Tarantino, seems to adjust his aesthetic sensibilities to the requirements of the particular picture. Collaborating with his wife, set decorator Sandy Reynolds-Wasco, he designed a number of tightly contained spaces for *Pulp Fiction* that contribute to a feeling of intense confinement and claustrophobia in several scenes.

The apparent artificiality of such sets as the fantasy restaurant called Jack Rabbit Slim's, where Vincent and Mia enjoy a sizzling dance together to Chuck Berry's "You Never Can Tell," adds to the sense of absurdity sparked by the movie's jarring juxtapositions of silliness and slaughter. To heighten the mood of 1950s nostalgia specified in the script, Wasco surrounded the specially constructed elevated dance floor with six vintage convertibles and emblazoned the walls with blown-up replicas of posters for such drive-in theatre fare as *Motorcycle Gang* (1957) and *Attack of the 50-Foot Woman* (1958). In keeping with this orientation, he designed the raised dance floor's surface to resemble an automobile tachometer. On a side wall, he placed a set of video monitors that played 1950s stock footage of a Los Angeles street scene seemingly shot through a restaurant window.

The assignments of the production designer's team can get quite complicated. The **set designer** supervises actual set construction and carpentry. Things that don't move are under the domain of the **set decorator,** who arranges everything for shooting. But the **property master** gets the "action" **props**—everything that moves, is held, or is handled. Assistant to the set decorator, the **leadman** is responsible for finding and acquiring the needed furnishings. A **swing gang** or set-dressing crew actually brings all the objects back to the set. The **greensman** is in charge of dressing sets and locations with plants.

The **grip** is the all-purpose person on the set, equivalent to a stagehand on a theatrical production, who does odd jobs and various small but essential tasks. Duties might include anything from performing minor carpentry to moving and arranging set flats or equipment. The grip crew generally sets up **reflectors** (broad sheets of reflecting material strategically placed to cast either natural or artificial light into the shadowed areas of a scene) and **scrims** (the circular wire mesh screens placed in front of some lamps to soften the light and reduce its intensity). According to union rules, however, if any light-diffusing material is to be attached directly to a lamp, an electrician must do it.

Shooting Sites

Sets may be created by blocking and lighting an area of ground outdoors or by building and designing a physical environment indoors. Precisely where a movie will be made is an important decision, with numerous implications for the entire production. Many moviemakers prefer the familiar confines of a **soundstage**—a windowless, soundproofed, professional shooting environment. Approximately the size of a large barn, this facility allows, among other things, for greater control over sound, lighting, and climate.

Movies not shot on a soundstage or in a similarly controlled, artificial environment are said to be made **on location.** Of course, an "off-studio" shooting site is not necessarily the location specified in the script, the place where the events are supposedly happening. For the location shooting in *The Adventures of Robin Hood* (1938), a woodland area in Chico, California, nearly 600 miles north of Hollywood, was temporarily transformed into Sherwood Forest. Most of the movie's principal and supporting players, along with 300 extras, members of the crew, and wardrobe, hairdressing, makeup, and technical personnel, were on location there for six weeks.

During the old studio era, directors routinely shot "exterior" scenes on a soundstage. Everything in *Casablanca* was filmed at the Burbank studio of Warner Bros. Pictures except for the arrival of Major Strasser at Casablanca's airport. This scene, in which Captain Renault, in a slightly derisive tone of voice, deferentially welcomes the Nazi officer on behalf of "unoccupied France" (it is doubtful whether the indigenous population of the French colony of Morocco thought of their region as "unoccupied"), was shot at the old Metropolitan Airport in Van Nuys, California.

The concluding airport sequence was photographed entirely on a soundstage. The set was filled with fog not so much to provide atmosphere as to conceal the fact that a painted plywood cutout, creatively lit, served as the plane to Lisbon. To give the scene some sense of depth, undersized adults

Fog machines work overtime for the final airport scene in *Casablanca* (1942).

were hired to portray the mechanics swarming over the airplane, which was placed as far as possible from the main action. (An inserted shot of actual plane motors revving up provided an added element of authenticity.)

It was common practice to use preexisting or "standing" sets in a studio's inventory, especially during World War II, when the federal government placed restrictions on the use of new materials. For the scene near the beginning of *Casablanca* depicting a teeming mix of vendors, beggars, thieves, urchins, and refugees desperately seeking passage on the daily plane to neutral Lisbon, art director Carl Jules Weyl transformed a generic French street into a specifically Moorish one, with arabesques covering nearly every surface of the buildings, doorways, and gates. The Paris railway station scene in which a devastated Rick learns that Ilsa has checked out of her hotel leaving a cryptic note stating she can never see him again, was also filmed on a set designed and used for another movie and then revamped for this production.

The postwar economics provided incentives for many producers to film somewhere other than in Hollywood. When foreign governments impounded American profits, for example, the big studios sent directors and actors abroad to make movies with the blocked currency. Even when currency restrictions eased, other inducements drew filmmakers to foreign locales. Many studios set up subsidiaries in Great Britain, Italy, and France to qualify for subsidies the governments of these countries made available to local companies. Sharing costs through joint ventures with European producers provided another financial incentive to film overseas. Making movies outside the country also reduced a star's tax burden, although this advantage diminished with a 1963 change in the tax law.

The proportion of motion pictures made outside the walls of a studio complex increased greatly in the 1950s and 1960s. Director Arthur Penn filmed much of *Bonnie and Clyde* around Dallas and little Texas towns like Denton and Pilot's Point. These locations enabled production designer Dean Tavoularis to re-create the solemn, dusty atmosphere of the story's Dust Bowl setting. The bedraggled Barrow gang's bravado and deadly antics unfold against running backdrops of dried-up fields, rural clapboard seediness, and dispossessed farming families on the move.

On-location shooting was facilitated by the advent of vehicles like the "Cinemobile," which replaced a whole motorcade of trucks, trailers, and cars. Developed in the 1960s by Egyptian-born cinematographer Fouad Said, this highly mobile "location studio" contains cameras, lights, sound gear, dressing rooms, lavatories, kitchens, and wardrobe space. Some models even have a compartment for cast and technicians.

Almost every movie project entails at least some searching for locations. It is the production designer's responsibility to oversee the **location scout**'s search for locales with the feel and atmosphere the director or producer seeks to create for the movie. In his original planning for *The Godfather,* director Francis Ford Coppola wanted to film the brutal assassination of Sonny Corleone (James Caan) at real tollbooths, but problems with traffic logistics proved insurmountable. Designer Dean Tavoularis decided instead to create authentic-looking substitutes on a runway at a deserted airstrip in Long Island, New York. The undertaking entailed constructing three tollbooths, complete with curbs and lane markers. A billboard erected in the background not only added depth to the setting but also served to conceal a distant apartment complex.

Today, in the search for locations, moviemakers travel to wherever the locales and economic benefits are most attractive. Director Steven Spielberg shot on many of the actual locations of the events depicted in *Schindler's List,* including Oskar Schindler's original factory and the gates of Auschwitz. He had wanted to film on the grounds of the former concentration camp but ran into opposition. The World Jewish Congress, which administered the camp, protested to the Polish ambassador to the United States about the project. It claimed to be fearful that the director would desecrate the place by creating a "Disney version" of the Holocaust.[11] Although six other fictional features had been shot inside the camp, which along with nearby Birkenau had been commercialized with restaurants, snack bars, exhibits, and regular guided tours,

Spielberg decided not to press the matter. Instead, he had his Polish production designer, Allan Starski, build a partial replica of the camp a short distance away. The historic Auschwitz gate and some of the original barracks in the women's sector served as backgrounds. The ambitious production required Starski to design 146 settings in all for the thirty-five locations around Poland where filming took place.

To make *Saving Private Ryan* (1998), Spielberg and his five-hundred-strong production team set up shop in an abandoned British Aerospace airfield and plane factory at Hatfield, about twenty miles north of London, and pressed its large, empty hangars into use as soundstages. It was at this location that production designer Tom Sanders constructed the entire bombed-out French village featured in the movie. He first built miniatures and then carved out the places where the bombs would have hit. To create the horrific images of the harrowing twenty-four-minute Omaha Beach sequence that opens the picture, the company moved to Curracloe in County Wexford, on the east coast of Ireland. Soldiers from the Irish army were recruited to play members of the landing forces in the reenactment of the chaos and cacophony of mud, blood, vomit, agony, and death that characterized the 1944 invasion to liberate Europe.

Preparations for Filming

One of the director's most important tasks in creating a credible world is to prepare a **shooting script** (a writer or producer might participate in this process as well). A detailed shooting script facilitates control and predictability, providing the director with the technical information needed to actually photograph the movie. In addition to scene headings, descriptive material, and dialogue, it contains a breakdown of the settings, characters, dialogue, and action into the specific shots the director expects to execute.

The basic unit of any movie is the **shot**—some aspect of a scene that has been captured by the camera in a single, uninterrupted run. A version of a particular shot is called a **take.** Each time the camera motor is turned on, a take begins; when the motor stops, the take is over. A meticulous or overcautious director might do many takes before selecting one for inclusion in the final film. More commonly, scheduling and budgetary concerns compel a limited number of takes.

When composing a scene, a director usually begins by deciding how many shots will be needed and what elements will be shown in each shot. Such compositional elements as choice of setting and lighting, deployment and movement of actors, and angle and position of the camera all require meticulous planning. To achieve the nuances and details of each shot, the director may employ such techniques as central positioning of a key actor; spotlighting and variable illumination; light colors on dark fields; dark colors on light

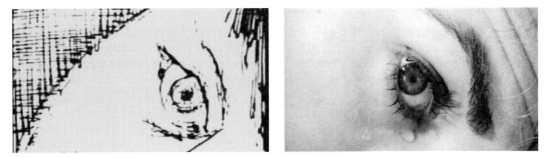

One of the many sketches Saul Bass made for the shower scene and an image from the movie itself. (*Psycho* [1960])

fields; eye-catching makeup, costumes, and gestures; arresting diagonals through the careful placement of objects or actors; movement in stillness; and stillness in movement.

To facilitate moving from script to shooting script, a **graphic artist** typically prepares a **storyboard** or series of sketches to visualize the look of each scene fragment. The end result resembles a cartoon strip. For all practical purposes, storyboards are the equivalent of a script in visual, graphic form. Properly put together, they can show exactly what bits of film will be needed to piece a scene together before going to the trouble and expense of shooting anything. A storyboard can be more or less detailed, perhaps providing cues for sound (dialogue and/or music) and for character movement.

Some directors have the details of virtually every shot depicted in storyboard form. Alfred Hitchcock prepared so carefully at the storyboard stage that he had only to realize the sketches to complete a movie. In making *Psycho* (1960), for instance, he had a cohesive picture of the entire movie laid out on storyboards before shooting began so that he could convey to his production staff exactly what he wished to accomplish. Graphic designer Saul Bass made detailed sketches for the famous scene in which real estate secretary Marion Crane (Janet Leigh), who has absconded with $40,000 of a client's money, is stabbed to death while taking a shower at a remote motel run by a strange young man named Norman Bates (Anthony Perkins). Before he began shooting, Hitchcock knew exactly where he was going to place the camera at any given instant to achieve the effect he wanted. (Bass later claimed to have directed the famous scene himself, but this fiction has been roundly refuted by others on the set at the time.[12])

Director of Photography

In establishing the photographic style or look of a movie, the director works closely with the **cinematographer** or **director of photography** (DP). This

person is responsible for such matters as the planning and execution of lighting, film stock and lens selection, and camera placement and angle. Next to
the director, the cinematographer is normally the most important person on
the set. (Those elected to the American Society of Cinematographers are permitted to have the designation ASC after their names.)

Directors and cinematographers who have developed effective professional relationships often work together on movie after movie. Screen legend
Charlie Chaplin, who began directing his own movies in 1914, collaborated
with cinematographer Rollie Totheroh for close to a quarter of a century. Director Spike Lee and cinematographer Ernest Dickerson, who met in film
school, worked together on many movies, including *Malcolm X.* (Dickerson
made the leap from director of photography to director with the gritty urban
drama *Juice* [1992].) On rare occasions, directors may double as their own cinematographers, as Steven Soderbergh did for *Traffic* (2000). His frenetic handheld camera work in this tale about the unsuccessful war the United States is
waging against drug traffickers creates a tangible sense of immediacy.

Some cinematographers tend to specialize in a particular style or approach; others become skilled at adapting to a variety of design concepts and
types of movies. Many now enjoy far greater recognition and critical acclaim
than was possible under the old studio system. In that era, the prevailing philosophy was that cinematographers were interchangeable, so that it made little difference who photographed a movie. Typically under long-term contract,
they were expected to conform to a specific style. Despite this restrictive atmosphere, a small handful got away with breaking the rules because the results they achieved were so visually compelling.

Virtuoso cinematographer Gregg Toland was under contract to the Goldwyn studio, where he was allowed far greater latitude than would have been
possible at the larger production plants. Contemptuous of what he saw as
Hollywood's stale, conservative traditions, Toland had already begun experi-
menting with the artistic possibilities offered by the major technical advances
in filmmaking during the late 1930s when he joined novice movie director
Orson Welles on *Citizen Kane.* Collaborating with the iconoclastic Welles gave
Toland unprecedented opportunities to expand on innovative cinematic
techniques he had thus far only cautiously and tentatively employed. Many of
Kane's most striking visual features represent a direct and logical extension
of the cinematographer's earlier work.

In addition to serving as the director's confidant and collaborator, the
cinematographer functions as the personnel manager and chief motivator of
the technical, behind-the-scenes crew. In most instances, cinematographers
do not touch the equipment themselves. In consultation with the director,
they decide what types of lights to use, where the lights should be placed,
how much light should enter the camera, and other such details. Support
personnel actually set up the lights, change the camera settings, and operate
the camera.

Other Support Personnel

The **gaffer** or chief electrician implements the lighting setups and oversees a crew that may number in the dozens. The **best boy** is the gaffer's top electrician. (The key grip has a best boy as well.) The best boy's responsibilities may include ordering necessary lighting equipment, keeping track of employee time cards, and doing other basic paperwork. The rest of the electricians are called juicers or lamp operators. A production with lots of lighting instruments can have scores of operators. Among other things, their tasks entail adding diffusing material to the front of a lamp and adjusting its **barn doors,** the shutterlike black metal flaps that reduce the spread of the beam. The **focus puller** adjusts the focus on the camera lens during any shot that requires it, such as a **tracking shot** (the camera travels through space forward, backward, or laterally while mounted on any one of a variety of mobile supports) or a **racking focus shot** (the sharpness of the focus shifts from the foreground to the background, or vice versa).

In moviemaking, art and economics are inseparable. The chief expense in production is time. Scenes, actors, and all other resources must be organized in such a way that they can be used in a concentrated period. Before filming begins, the **production manager** (also called an associate or line producer) prepares a detailed script "breakdown," estimating the most efficient way of scheduling and shooting each scene. Such factors as cost efficiency, accessibility of location sites, availability of actors, and weather conditions generally necessitate filming in a different order from the way scenes and individual shots will appear in the completed picture. For example, scenes taking place in the same location and with the same actors will normally be filmed together.

During filming, the production manager, who serves as the producer's representative, is generally on the set every day, attending to the technical and administrative aspects of making the movie, arranging for locales and transportation, and ensuring that extras needed for scenes are available and ready. In addition to physically running the show, this person usually signs the checks, monitored by an auditor, who makes sure the budget is adhered to and that money is being spent as it's supposed to be. In some instances, a high-powered production manager may get an executive producer credit.

Also at the shooting site each day, the **script supervisor** ensures that everything in a scene matches from shot to shot—from the actors' hair, makeup, and costumes to the arrangement of props. This person, known as a "script girl" in the old studio system, usually takes a photograph of the actors and the set, and makes sure everything is restored to that state before shooting resumes. Still, mistakes are made. In *Pulp Fiction,* for instance, when Vincent and Mia are at Jack Rabbit Slim's, he has a long drink of her milkshake and hands it back to her. However, when the camera is focused on Mia again, the glass is full. A minor mistake, but noticeable nevertheless.

The shooting phase of production brings the director, talent, and technicians together on the set or the location. The **assistant director** (AD) handles many of the more menial or routine (albeit still essential) tasks, such as calling for quiet on the set, rounding up necessary staff for shooting a scene, and maintaining an efficient work atmosphere. There may be several ADs on any movie. The **second unit director** supervises the shooting of crowd scenes, action footage, and the like that don't require the main actors (who may actually do all their work on a soundstage). The "assistant to . . ." can be anyone from a technician's helper to a director's or star's personal secretary or paramour (or both). Duties are variable.

While the crew and their units are gearing up, the actors prepare mentally and physically to perform their roles. During rehearsals and just before takes, a **dialogue coach** commonly goes over the script with the actors, making sure they know their lines and sometimes assisting with delivery. Some actors depend on additional memory aids as well. While shooting his *Godfather* scenes, for instance, Marlon Brando placed cheat sheets and cue cards just about everywhere—taped to cameras, hidden behind props, attached to other actors. He apparently even wrote lines on his hands and shirtsleeves.

When director Francis Ford Coppola confronted him about his seeming inability to learn lines, the actor denied that it was a matter of faulty memory or lack of concentration or effort. Instead, he claimed, not completely memorizing lines was an essential part of his naturalistic acting style. "Real people," he argued, "don't know what they are going to say. Their words often come as a surprise to them. That's how it should be in a movie."[13] The actor did not explain, however, just how cue cards made for spontaneity of speech and manner.

Once the camera starts to roll, everyone involved in the production process operates under the authority of the director. In the course of shooting, directors can start and stop the action at any time, call for retakes, and revise the blocking, the dialogue, or the sequence of events at will. A director may be on the set issuing commands or may supervise the action via video monitors located some distance away, as Steven Spielberg did for the recreation of the nightmarish Omaha Beach assault in *Saving Private Ryan*. The myriad ways that directors adhering to the guiding principles and priorities of the Hollywood style employ the tools and techniques of production during the principal cinematography or shooting stage to create compelling screen drama provide the focus of the next chapter.

Notes

1. Rick Lyman, "Produced by . . . Well, Just About Everybody," *The New York Times,* May 29, 2001, p. E1.
2. Peter Bart, *The Gross: The Hits, the Flops—The Summer That Ate Hollywood* (New York: St. Martin's Press, 1999), p. 67.

3. Syd Field, *Screenplay: The Foundations of Screenwriting* (New York: Dell, 1994). This manual was first published in 1979.

4. See Kristen Thompson, *Storytelling in the New Hollywood: Understanding Classical Narrative Technique* (Cambridge, MA: Harvard University Press, 1999), p. 28.

5. Aljean Harmetz, *The Making of* The Wizard of Oz (New York: Knopf, 1977), pp. 28–29.

6. Frank Capra, letter to the *New York Times,* April 2, 1939. Quoted in Frank Capra, *The Name Above the Title: An Autobiography* (New York: Macmillan, 1971), pp. 267–271.

7. Aljean Harmetz, *Round Up the Usual Suspects: The Making of* Casablanca—*Bogart, Bergman, and World War II* (New York: Hyperion, 1992), p. 64.

8. Thomas Schatz, *The Genius of the System: Hollywood Filmmaking in the Studio Era* (New York: Pantheon Books, 1988), p. 6.

9. Andrew Sarris, *The American Cinema: Directors and Directions, 1929–1968* (New York: Dutton, 1968), pp. 175–176.

10. See Robert L. Carringer, *The Making of* Citizen Kane, rev. ed. (Berkeley: University of California Press, 1996), pp. 36–42.

11. See John Baxter, *Steven Spielberg: The Unauthorized Biography* (New York: HarperCollins, 1997), p. 386.

12. See Stephen Rebello, *Alfred Hitchcock and the Making of* Psycho (New York: Harper Perennial, 1991), pp. 106–112.

13. Quoted in Peter Manso, *Brando: The Biography* (New York: Hyperion, 1994), pp. 717–718.

Principal Cinematography

Moviemakers confront countless choices about the arrangement of people and objects within any given shot, the use of color, the selection and positioning of lighting sources, the types of lenses and film employed, the movement or immobility of the camera, the duration of shots, the way shots will be joined together, and a variety of other elements that form the art of motion picture photography. Virtually every shot requires dozens of decisions. How the various tools and techniques of moviemaking are employed during the **principal cinematography**, or shooting phase, to accomplish the fundamental task of dramatizing stories is the focus of this chapter.

Tools of Moviemaking

The motion picture camera is, of course, the most important tool in the moviemaking process. It is as essential as the brush is to the painter or the instrument is to the musician. In purely technical terms, a motion picture camera is designed to record a series of images onto **film stock**, a plastic strip coated with a light-sensitive substance called an emulsion. The camera's **shutter** controls the **exposure time**, the length of time that light is allowed to fall on the film stock. To control the passage of light, the shutter opens and closes as the stock moves intermittently through the camera. When the shutter is open, the stock re-

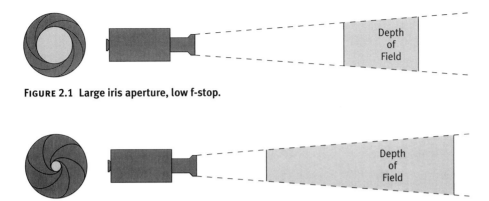

FIGURE 2.1 Large iris aperture, low f-stop.

FIGURE 2.2 Small iris aperture, high f-stop.

mains motionless; when the shutter closes, it advances to the next **frame,** the rectangular form that marks off the edges of each image. Operating at standard speed, the camera records twenty-four separate images per second.

The **lens,** or molded piece(s) of glass mounted on the front of the camera, captures patterns of light and shadow. Its **f-stop setting** and **focal length** are the primary determinants of how the scale, depth, and spatial relations of the scene being shot will be represented on the screen. Light must come through the lens aperture, or opening, to leave a photochemical impression on the film stock. The size or diameter of the lens aperture is indicated by its f-number or f-stop. The smaller the f-stop numbers, the larger the opening. A change in aperture size affects the **depth of field**—the area in which objects located at different distances from the camera remain in focus. A mechanical device called the **iris diaphragm,** made of overlapping blades, controls the amount of light passing through the lens. As the blades of the **iris** open (low f-stop), allowing more light to pass, the depth of field decreases; conversely, as they close (high f-stop), the depth of field increases. (See Figures 2.1 and 2.2.)

As an aesthetic device, **deep-focus photography** (extended depth of field), in which the foreground, middle ground, and background of a scene are in sharp focus, enables moviemakers to establish more effectively connections between characters situated within a given shot. In a scene toward the end of *Citizen Kane* (1941) that takes place in the title character's mansion, we see Kane's (Orson Welles) head in the foreground, and across the vast distance of the cavernous room, we see in the background his wife Susan (Dorothy Comingore) working on a jigsaw puzzle to alleviate her boredom. The deep-focus photography of cinematographer Gregg Toland keeps both characters in sharp focus and suggests a spatial metaphor for their emotional estrangement from each other.

Focal length refers to the distance from the center of the lens to the point at which light rays converge. It controls the size of the image formed by the

Deep-focus photography. This technique heightens the distance—social as well as physical—between Kane (Orson Welles) and Susan (Dorothy Comingore). (*Citizen Kane* [1941])

lens and the amount of the scene shown on a given size of film. A **wide-angle** (short) **lens** produces a wide horizontal field of view. It can create a sense of great size and scope by making things appear smaller and farther apart from one another. Moving objects seem to travel faster than normal if they are approaching or receding from the camera position. Objects situated close to the camera lens are enlarged and distorted. In shooting *Chinatown* (1974), cinematographer John A. Alonzo often used a wide-angle lens so that actors' elongated features looked more sinister in close-ups.

At the opposite extreme, a **telephoto** (long) **lens** flattens or compresses space. It provides a narrow horizontal field of view but magnifies and enlarges distant objects, making them appear to be the same size and quite close together. Movement seems to contract. Such distortion can be a key element in a scene. Toward the end of *The Graduate* (1967), an influential movie directed by Mike Nichols, protagonist Benjamin (Dustin Hoffman) races to arrive at the church before his girlfriend Elaine (Katherine Ross) marries someone else. In a telephoto shot, which heightens tension, he appears to be running in place, expending great effort but making little progress.

A **normal** (medium-length) **lens** closely approximates human vision. Its horizontal field of view and image magnification are about the same as if we

A wide-angle lens slightly exaggerates the facial features of Noah Cross (John Huston), *Chinatown*'s (1974) insidiously evil villain.

were standing where the camera is located. With a normal lens, relative sizes look in proportion, and relationships appear free from distortion. Movement toward or away from the camera is reproduced more or less faithfully. By using a normal lens throughout *Psycho* (1960), cinematographer John L. Russell reinforced the sensation of voyeurism that permeates the movie.

A significant advance was the development of the **zoom lens,** which has varying focal lengths that can shift from wide-angle to normal to telephoto settings (or vice versa), and anywhere in between, within a single shot. The zoom lens was available in rudimentary form by the late 1920s, and as improvements were made, directors occasionally used it to enlarge a detail for shock effect. With the advent of television, this lens was improved considerably and used primarily for covering sporting events.

As moviemakers began to shoot on location more frequently in the 1950s and 1960s, the zoom proved very handy because its focal length can be varied while shooting is in progress. This permits instantaneous "zooming in" on a detail (magnifying and flattening it as a telephoto lens does) or "zooming back" from it (demagnifying it and giving the space more volume). It is particularly useful for street scenes because the camera can be placed some distance from the performer, thereby keeping other street users unaware that filming is taking place (and so more likely to act naturally).

Film Stock

Before the director and cinematographer even consider turning on the camera, they must decide what type of film stock to use. This decision significantly affects the image on the screen—its sharpness of detail, color quality, and range of light and shadow. The earliest film stock was "orthochromatic," which meant it possessed a remarkable capacity for deep-focus photography. Most commercial moviemakers used this black-and-white stock during the "speechless" era of cinema. It was relatively sensitive to light, enabling the camera operator to adjust the lens aperture or opening to achieve greater depth of field.

In the speechless era, filming was done using very noisy arc lights for illumination. With the advent of talkies in the 1920s, however, the noise of the arc lights proved intolerable. The tungsten lights brought in to replace them, while quieter, were also much softer and less penetrating, so moviemakers switched from orthochromatic to "panchromatic" stock. Although more responsive to dimmer lights, this stock was much less sensitive to light in general. As a consequence, the camera operator had to increase the size of the lens aperture. This resulted in the diffused lighting and relatively shallow focus found in many movies of the 1930s. By the end of the decade, technical improvements in lenses, film stock, and lighting made the achievement of greater depth of field much more technically feasible.

Gauge

Film stock is available in various **gauges,** or widths. The most common gauge used in moviemaking is 35-millimeter, but movies occasionally are shot in 65-millimeter stock and then copied to 70-millimeter stock for theatrical showings. This results in projected images that are generally sharper because a wider gauge permits a wider frame, which requires less magnification to fill up the screen. However, the use of such wide-gauge film is costly, and few theatres are equipped to show it.

For budgetary or aesthetic reasons, a director may choose to shoot in a 16-millimeter format, or on videotape, and then blow up the print or transfer the tape to 35-millimeter film for distribution to theatres. Spike Lee shot his 1996 film *Get on the Bus,* a fictional account of a group traveling to that year's Million Man March in Washington, DC, on super-16-millimeter and then transferred it to the standard gauge. Among other things, this enhanced the gritty realism of the images. The smaller, less obtrusive super-16 camera also allowed him to move about more readily and to capture subtle facial expressions of the actors in motion that might have otherwise been missed. (Lee photographed *Bamboozled* [2000] entirely with ultralight digital video cameras, which gives this satire about media stereotyping of blacks a look that effectively emphasizes its television setting.)

Speed

Film stock can be manufactured with various sensitivities to light. Such sensitivity is categorized in terms of **speed.** A film's speed is determined by the fineness, density, and size of its grain, the light-sensitive particles in the film emulsion. This emulsion is composed of a solution of silver halide crystals suspended in a gelatin substance. When these crystals are struck by light—that is, exposed—their properties change. Further changes occur when they are subjected to chemical developers.

High-speed or fast film stock is more suitable for shooting in low-light situations but can produce a grainy effect (the scene is seemingly flaked with jiggling salt and pepper). Grain can be a nuisance if this effect is not required. Lower-speed or slow film stocks produce a cleaner image but require more light for proper exposure. Recent developments in film stock and lenses have allowed high-speed qualities to be retained while reducing the amount of grain. Once film stock has been exposed, it is usually referred to simply as film; a specific length of exposed film is called **footage.**

Color

Moviemakers also have the option to shoot with color or with monochrome (black-and-white) film stock. Prior to the 1950s, it was considerably more expensive to make a color feature than a monochrome one. The Technicolor Corporation had a virtual monopoly over the color system used by all the major studios. Its three-strip process recorded separate red, green, and blue images on different negatives. A special "beam-splitter" camera was required, and it could only be leased, not purchased outright. The studios also had to hire Technicolor's cameramen and color consultants to work with their art directors and set designers. Color negatives were processed and printed behind closed doors, which gave the company a great deal of control over the aesthetic uses to which color was put.

Technicolor filming added about 50 percent to the cost of a feature, but the results could be quite stunning. Working with the fairly new three-color process for *The Adventures of Robin Hood* (1938), cinematographers Tony Gaudio and Sol Polito achieved extraordinary photographic effects. Their use of muted greens and browns and vivid touches of scarlet give the movie the look of a Renaissance painting. By the end of the 1940s, about 15 percent, or forty features per year, of the total output of the eight major studios were Technicolor releases. The process was used mainly for musicals, fantasies, and epics.

The use of inferior color processes such as Cinecolor could reduce costs and increase control. Many westerns of the late 1940s and early 1950s were shot this way. But the Technicolor monopoly wasn't seriously challenged until the 1950s, when the major studios started using Eastman Kodak's competing single-strip Eastmancolor film, which was compatible with a standard 35-millimeter camera. (Although cheaper and more flexible, the Eastmancolor prints didn't hold their color value for very long.) Color emulsions became progressively faster, more sensitive, and more flexible, allowing quality color film to be competitive with monochrome.

Since the late 1960s, most films have been shot in color unless a moviemaker is striving for a particular effect. Director Steven Spielberg's decision to shoot *Schindler's List* (1993) in gritty monochrome gives the movie an atmosphere of veracity similar to 1940s newsreel footage. The two color sequences that partly frame the story suggest quite different time periods and serve as a distancing device to contain the central narrative about the horrors of the Holocaust. The opening establishes an aura of rich tradition through the use of warm colors. In an old-world setting, a European family lights candles and recites the prayers that precede the Sabbath. As one image blurs into another, the candles burn down until only one is left aflame. In a coda, shot in a faded color scheme that suggests the passage of time, some of the actual survivors (now some fifty years older), accompanied by the actors who portrayed them in the movie, place flowers and commemorative stones on the grave of the real Schindler in a cemetery near Jerusalem.

Lighting Sources

The camera, the lens, the film stock, and all the other tools and materials of cinematography provide the means to record and shape patterns of light and shadow. Light is needed to register an image on film, but it plays a much more complex role than merely that. In addition to providing general illumination, lighting serves to underline mood and meaning, enhance the perception of depth, fix the time of day the action takes place (daytime, twilight, nighttime, and so on), and direct attention to important elements within a scene.

There are two basic kinds of lighting sources: available light and artificial light. Available light includes "natural" light such as sunlight, skylight, firelight, and whatever lighting sources are a given part of an existing setting, such as streetlights or car headlights. The color properties of natural lighting change constantly, from the warm reddish cast of sunrise and sunset, or the ominous grayish-green preceding a thunderstorm, to the bright, flat, bluish light of the noontime sun. The intensity of natural light also ranges from the brilliance of noon, to the dimness of the long, darkened shadows of evening, to the cold, shallow light of the moon.

Spots and Floods

Artificial lighting, in contrast, has fixed properties that are highly predictable and consistent. It falls into two broad categories: the **spotlight,** with its harsh, focused beam, and the **floodlight,** with its soft, diffuse quality. The former usually illuminates small concentrated areas, whereas the latter casts an even beam of light over a fairly large area. (However, many spotlights have a variable beam width that can be adjusted to cover either a small or a large area.) Both types come in varying sizes and intensities, ranging from the great

10,000-watt brutes, which can illuminate large areas, to the tiny "inkies," the 100-watt spots that light the eyes of star players.

During the old studio era, stars were usually lit in ways that made their faces appear to emanate rather than reflect light. This effect was reinforced by the fact that such facial lighting usually had no identifiable source in a scene. Veteran cinematographer Arthur Edeson, one of the cofounders in 1919 of the American Society of Cinematographers (ASC), used techniques of **star lighting** in *Casablanca* (1942) to enhance the appearance of Swedish-born Ingrid Bergman, who plays Ilsa Lund, the principal female love interest in the movie. Soft lighting accentuates her cheekbones, and delicate shading of her high forehead directs attention to her expressive eyes. Whenever the camera closes tightly on her face, filters, makeup, and subtle lighting effects combine to make her appear to be as submissive as she is seductive.

Sets are typically illuminated with dozens of spots and floods in various sizes and shapes, although the trend seems to be toward lighting schemes that are less elaborate and easier to manage. The highly light-sensitive film stocks in use today make it possible to illuminate a scene—in color or in black and white—at a much lower light intensity. In addition, small, lightweight lamps are now available that emit the same intensity of light as comparable heavy studio lighting equipment.

Three-Point Lighting

The different types of lights are frequently categorized according to their primary function. The standard setup is generally referred to as **three-point lighting.** Although this entails dozens of actual lights, not just three, they are situated in ways to suggest three basic sources. The main source of illumination is called the **key light,** which creates the effect of light coming from a specific direction. Usually situated at a forty-five-degree angle to the camera-subject axis, it provides bright, hard beams of light that cast harsh shadows.

To soften the hard edge of these shadows, more diffuse illumination, called **fill light,** is usually placed on the opposite side of the key light. To a large degree, the intensity of the fill light relative to the key light determines the dramatic quality of the shadows. If the fill light is close in terms of intensity to the key light, the shadows will be light. If the fill is much lower than the key, the shadows will be deeper. **Backlight** is usually placed above and on the opposite side of the subject from the camera. It ordinarily functions to define depth by sharply distinguishing actors or objects from the background, and it can produce a bright edge or halo on an actor's hair and shoulders.

Although generally of lesser importance, backlight can be central to certain scenes. When such illumination predominates, and no light falls on the camera side of the subject, it can generate a sense of mystery or fear by producing shadowy, spectral-like figures. For example, in *Psycho's* famous shower

stabbing scene, cinematographer John L. Russell deployed backlighting inde-
pendently of frontal illumination to conceal the identity of the killer, creating
a silhouetted figure whose shape is outlined with light but whose face and
body are in shadow.

The standard three-point lighting setup is usually supplemented with **set
lights,** which produce all those shadows and highlights in the background of
a shot. In addition to increasing visual interest, this layer of illumination can
provide a meaningful sense of time and place to a setting. It can also simulate
realistic elements, such as daylight filtering through curtains. The play of
light and shadow can, in fact, become part of the set design itself.

Creating with Light and Dark

The overall proportion of light to dark in a scene is an essential element in
creating mood and atmosphere, and can be adjusted to achieve effects ranging from **high-key** to **low-key lighting.** The terms "high" and "low" in this
context refer to the ratio of fill light to key light. Thus high-key lighting has a
high ratio of fill light and produces a brightly lit image with little contrast between the darks and lights. This effect, which often implies cheerfulness and
gaiety, is generally employed in musicals and comedies.

With low-key lighting, there is high contrast within the image between
light and dark areas. This effect often serves to heighten tension and contribute to a sense of despair or mystery. Cinematographer Arthur Edeson employed low-key lighting to reinforce the downbeat dialogue in *Casablanca*
during the scene in which Ilsa returns to Rick's cafe and belatedly tries to tell
him something of her past. Having heard it all before, to the tune of "a tinny
piano in the parlor downstairs," an embittered Rick lashes out at her. "Who
was it you left me for? Was it Laszlo—or were there others in between? Or
aren't you the kind that tells?" In visual contrast to the shadowed Rick's verbal portrait of promiscuity, her brightly lit white outfit and the shawl framing
her sculptured facial features give her an aura of eternal virginity.

Control of lighting contrast can create striking visual effects. A low ratio
of fill to key light can infuse a scene with an unsettling sense of anxiety, agitation, and apprehension—perhaps of someone or something lurking just beyond the glare of a solitary street lamp. Hinting at the hidden, the unknown,
and the sinister, such lighting patterns can produce a visual effect approximating and inducing awareness of the dark inner recesses of the mind.

The evocative power of darkness can contribute to mood and meaning in
myriad ways. There are many instances in movies in which the lights that are
not turned on are as significant as those that are. Reducing or eliminating fill-
lights can produce ominously stark patterns of light and dark. Spotlights can
be positioned in ways that generate scary or menacing shadows on an actor's
face. **Under lighting,** in which light comes up from below a subject, casts

Low-key lighting. Ilsa (Ingrid Bergman) exudes an aura of eternal virginity. (*Casablanca* [1942])

shadows upward and creates a ghoulish look. In photographing *The Godfather* (1972), cinematographer Gordon Willis used **top lighting,** which shines down from directly above the subject, to make Marlon Brando's eyes look like dark sockets—inscrutable, unnatural, and a little frightening.

Shifting patterns of light and shadow carry strong emotional and symbolic overtones, which can be exploited within a single shot or from scene to scene. Contrasts between light and dark can set a mood even before any action has occurred. Within a single shot, one character may be modeled in bright tones and another in shadows or dark tones to suggest something about their traits or their emotional or dramatic situations. When the title character of *Citizen Kane* leans over and out of the spotlight to sign his "Declaration of Principles" for a newspaper he has recently acquired, as his colleagues look on, his silhouetted form serves to undercut this supposedly high-minded moment. In fact, he later abandons these principles.

Cinematographer Janusz Kaminski employs stark lighting contrasts in *Schindler's List* to emphasize character traits, intensify emotional moments, and convey a sense of personal and cosmic chaos. At the nightclub where Oskar Schindler (Liam Neeson) sizes up the high German officials who will eventually help him, close-ups of his watchful eyes are accentuated by intense

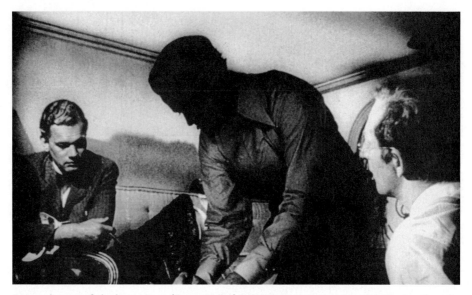

Expressive use of shadows. Kane (Orson Welles) is in silhouette as he signs the "Declaration of Principles" for the newspaper he has recently taken over. (*Citizen Kane* [1941])

key lighting while the rest of his face falls into shadow. (At the same time, his face is sculptured through lighting and makeup to create a glamorous sheen.) A burst of camera flashbulbs accompanies rapid cuts as he scrutinizes his surroundings like an animal in search of prey. Later in the movie, when the Jewish women employed in Schindler's factory are mistakenly routed to Auschwitz, rapid flashes of bright sunlight coming through the slats of the otherwise darkened freight car reflect the growing terror in one of these women's eyes as she spots a boy near the tracks sadistically slashing his finger across his throat.

Noir Lighting

Perhaps more than any other single factor, it is the visual style of the lighting that provides the thread uniting *film noir,* or "dark cinema." The low-key illumination in such movies as *Double Indemnity* (1944), *Woman in the Window* (1944), *Murder My Sweet* (1944), *Detour* (1945), *The Killers* (1946), *The Big Sleep* (1946), *Night and the City* (1950), *On Dangerous Ground* (1951), and *The Big Heat* (1953) contributes to an atmosphere permeated by a sense of paranoia, claustrophobia, and despair. The action typically takes place in the dark, shadowy worlds of shabby train stations, dimly lit cocktail lounges, remote hilltop mansions, and rundown hotel rooms lit with flashing neon signs.

Interior sets are usually dark, with foreboding shadow patterns from Venetian blinds often lacing the walls. Spotlights are placed in every conceivable position. One may be located below or high above the actors to produce

Kick lighting of Lee Marvin in *The Big Heat* (1953) suggests there may be something sinister about his character.

unnatural shadows and strange facial expressions. Or it may be moved behind and to one side of an actor—using what is called a **kick light**—to make the actor's face look sinister or mysterious. The first shot of Lee Marvin in *The Big Heat* is lit in this manner. The odd play of light and dark makes him appear frightening and ready to erupt into violence. The restricted depth of field and the turn of his head toward the camera enhance this effect.

The absence of floodlights produces areas of total blackness and peculiar patterns of light and dark. Actors may play a scene completely shrouded in deep shadows, or they may be silhouetted against an illuminated background. Exterior scenes frequently suggest some primordial darkness, an effect achieved by "night-for-night" shooting—night scenes that are actually shot at night, producing a jet-black sky and sharp contrasts. Prior to the emergence of what has come to be called *film noir*, night scenes were generally photographed in daylight—a technique known as "day-for-night" shooting. To create the illusion of night, cinematographers placed filters over the lens to restrict the amount of light entering the camera. The effect produced was one of moderate contrast, with the sky rendered a grayish color.

The taxonomy of *film noir* is often said to begin with *The Maltese Falcon* (1941) and culminate with *Touch of Evil* (1958). The quiet **chiaroscuro** (the moody interplay of light and shadow) and occasional oblique camera angles

NOIR LIGHTING IN *OUT OF THE PAST*

The aura of *film noir* is perhaps best exemplified by those movies featuring a slightly disreputable "hard-boiled" private eye. The basic ingredients include a seductive *femme fatale*; a flashback structure; a first-person narration involving murder, duplicity and sexual obsession; a complex chiaroscuro lighting pattern; and a downbeat denouement. A liberal amount of male sexual anxiety is usually sprinkled throughout as well.

These ingredients blend together especially well in the *noir*-ishly romantic *Out of the Past* (1947), which derives some of its most captivating moments from lighting effects that are simultaneously sinister and sensuous. The protagonist, Jeff (Robert Mitchum), is a former Manhattan private investigator who has forsaken the fascinations of the city for the serenity of small-town life. But like many ill-fated *noir* protagonists, he cannot escape the consequences of his past actions.

Out of his past comes one last assignment, which will draw him into a complicated criminal scheme that results in his death. While he drives with his reserved, virtuous fiancée Ann (Virginia Huston) to meet crooked gambler Whit Sterling (Kirk Douglas), the doomed ex-detective reveals through a first-person narrative structure, employing voice-over and flashback, the circumstances of his earlier fall from grace.

The balefully compelling ambience created by the movie's director, Jacques Tourneur, and cinematographer, Nicholas Muscaraca, who also worked together on such highly atmospheric horror films as *Cat People* (1942), serves as a veritable textbook of what have come to be regarded as *noir* lighting techniques. As the world-weary Jeff works his way through a serpentine plot involving brutal killings and unscrupulous

females, the stress is on tone and mood: the murky moral milieu he inhabits and the ways in which it affects him, particularly in relation to sexual obsession.

The flashback begins in an apartment in New York City where Jeff is hired by Sterling to locate his mistress, Kathie Moffat (Jane Greer), who, after shooting him, has vanished with $40,000 of his money. The setting is dark and forbidding. Below-eye-level key lights, ostensibly from a table lamp, throw high shadows on the walls and lend a gothic quality to the faces of the characters, saturating the scene with a hint of menace. Even picture frames and furniture are lit in ways that give them ominous dark shadows.

In many of the scenes that follow, the rich tonal qualities of the black-and-white imagery serve to accentuate shifting moods and emotions. Jeff traces Kathie to Acapulco, where he stakes out a tawdry cantina, convinced that she will eventually turn up. He soon sees her silhouetted figure as she strolls in from the sun-drenched plaza. Wearing a white dress and matching hat, she seems to have materialized out of the

A subtle air of menace permeates the scene in which Whit Sterling (Kirk Douglas) hires Jeff (Robert Mitchum) to find his wayward mistress. (*Out of the Past* [1947])

The sensuous play of light and shadow on Kathie's (Jane Greer) face suggests unfathomable depths.
(*Out of the Past* [1947])

brightness. This impression is reinforced by his voice-over comment on her arrival— "And then I saw her . . . coming out of the sun." It invests her with an almost ethereal essence (as does his similarly sentimental romanticizing of her second entrance: "And then she walked in out of the moonlight— smiling"). But her otherworldly quality will turn out to be more demonic than divine.

Jeff's account of their ensuing romance suggests some nocturnal trance. "I never saw her in the daytime," he explains. "We seemed to live by night. What was left of the day went away like a pack of cigarettes you smoked." In an intensely erotic scene at Kathie's bungalow, the chiaroscuro lighting carries a strong sexual charge. Giggling like

anxious adolescents, they dash inside from a torrential downpour. The interior is dimly lit, with most of the illumination coming from the side and back, and a solitary lamp seemingly casts high shadows on the wall. As she roughly dries his hair with a towel, shadows sensuously play across her face. After she puts on a phonograph record, he takes the towel and begins to dry her hair. The music mixes with the sound of rain hammering on the window. Kissing her on the neck, he tosses the towel, knocking the lamp to the floor.

When the light goes out, there is a swirl of music, and the camera drifts toward the front door, which is blown open by a gust of
(continued on next page)

Noir Lighting in *Out of the Past* (Continued)

wind. Then there is a cut to the veranda outside, with the camera tracking and panning a bit in the backlit rain. A cut back to the interior of the bungalow follows, with a silhouetted Jeff walking over to shut the door. The back lighting seems to come from the moon shining through a pair of French windows, although it is still raining heavily. As they discuss running off together, Kathie is illuminated from the side and back so that part of her face is submerged in deep shadow. Soft frontal lighting delicately shades her upper bosom and low-cut white blouse.

They move up to San Francisco and hide out successfully until Jeff's former partner, Jack Fisher (Steve Brodie), now in the employ of Whit Sterling, spots him at the racetrack. Jeff tries to shake Fisher from his tail,

but the gumshoe follows Kathie instead. Chiaroscuro lighting is used to sinister effect in the cabin scene in which Jeff and Fisher slug it out as Kathie looks on. A shot rings out and the ex-partner falls to the floor. Jeff turns to see her standing calmly, a smoking gun in her hand. She flees the murder scene, leaving behind her bankbook. As Jeff opens it, a close-up shows a deposit of $40,000.

The long flashback ends as Jeff and Ann reach Whit Sterling's retreat. The remainder of the movie takes place in the present as Jeff is seduced anew by Kathie and becomes entangled in a web of deception. In the climactic scene, she shoots him in the groin just before a hail of police bullets cut them both down.

of the first film in the cycle are inflated to elaborate and sometimes grotesque proportions in the final one. The latter's looming and restless camera, extreme deep-focus compositions, barrage of tilted and disfiguring angles, distorting lenses, and complex patterns of darkness and light constitute a summary—albeit an overheated one—of what were by 1958 the visual conventions of the *noir* style. Although these two movies provide convenient frames for the "classic" *noir* period, many critics and historians regard *film noir* as part of a larger cycle that began before 1941 and continues to the present. The label "neo-*noir*" is often applied to more recent downbeat crime thrillers like *Chinatown* (1974), *Body Heat* (1981), and *The Last Seduction* (1994).

Color and Light

Color photography also can affect the emotional tone or atmosphere of a movie in subtle ways. Moviemakers can draw upon a rich palette of colors to set the overall mood of a scene, convey psychological states, or evoke a sense of nostalgia or a period feeling. Light sources and images are generally thought of as being warm or warmer as they move toward red (the reddish glow of candlelight) and as being cool or colder as they move toward blue (the bluish cast of fluorescent lamps).

Director Spike Lee employed changing patterns of color and light intensity in *Malcolm X* (1992) to convey the different moods of the title character's life. Working with cinematographer Ernest Dickerson, he bathed the early

Lighting for sinister effect. Pugilist Butch Coolidge (Bruce Willis) seems to be having an audience with the devil. (*Pulp Fiction* [1994])

Boston street scenes of the movie in a mellow, sepia-toned sunlit glow and then shifted to a colder, more bluish hue for the scenes in prison. When Malcolm (Denzel Washington) becomes a Muslim, the images are very stark. The clarity is considerably softened during his journeys to Mecca and the Sahara. In many of the key moments of his life as a public figure, the color photography is interspersed with black-and-white, quasi-documentary footage.

The color and intensity of light can be controlled in various ways to achieve specific moods and meanings. Quentin Tarantino and his cinematographer, Andrzej Sekula, used red light to sinister effect during the mostly static scene in *Pulp Fiction* (1994) at a nightclub owned by crime boss Marsellus Wallace (Ving Rhames). As the scene begins, struggling boxer Butch Coolidge (Bruce Willis) seems to be having an audience with the devil. The camera remains fixed on the pugilist's partially shadowed face as a disembodied voice (not yet identified as Marsellus's) states with brutal frankness that his career in the ring is nearing its end. Throughout most of the scene, everything is bathed in a red glare of light causing the background objects and scenery to bleed into one another, suggesting that the boxer has descended into hell. The way the scarlet aura infuses the cavernous room also serves as an evocative metaphor for the "heat" put on Butch to take a dive in the fifth round of an upcoming match in exchange for a bribe he would be unwise to reject.

Serving as his own cinematographer, director Steven Soderbergh uses different color tints, film stock, and lens coatings to give each of the three main storylines of *Traffic* (2000) a distinctive look and feel. Tijuana and its environs are rendered in jaundiced yellows and burnt browns as two local policemen (Benicio Del Toro and Jacob Vargas) get caught up in a web of cruelty, corruption, and betrayal. Steely blues and grays predominate when the focus is on a Cincinnati judge (Michael Douglas) newly appointed as the federal drug czar or on his teenage daughter's (Erika Christensen) descent into drug addiction.

The stress is on bright primary colors in the deceptively dangerous San Diego suburbs as two Drug Enforcement Administration agents (Don Cheadle and Luis Guzman) apprehend a narcotics kingpin (Steven Bauer), whose pampered and very pregnant wife (Catherine Zeta-Jones) proves just as capable of drug trafficking as her incarcerated spouse. Throughout this complexly constructed movie, the contrasting textures and color schemes of the different locales help identify the shifting scenarios.

Framing the Image

Movie images are framed, or confined, within specific boundaries. The shape of the film frame is fixed by convention. Almost every movie prior to the early 1950s was shot in a format of 1.33:1—that is, roughly four units of width for every three units of height. This gives the frame a slightly rectangular shape (a square would have a format of 1:1). Working within the dimensions of this **aspect ratio** (the relationship of the image's width to its height), directors usually employed lighting, focus, camera angle and distance, actor movement, set design, and costuming in ways that kept the principal object of interest at any given moment in the foreground near the center of the frame.

The convention of centering is grounded in the nature of human vision. Unless trained in other ways, the convergent focal planes of the eye seek out a vanishing point lying directly ahead. This tendency to look toward the center of an image has been reinforced over hundreds of years by the tradition of **perspective** that originated in the drawings and paintings of early fifteenth-century Europe. Prior to the Renaissance, European artists commonly represented people and objects according to their relative status in the world at large. Religious figures like the Christ child and the Virgin Mary were usually shown as having much greater stature than mere mortals (a God's-eye view of the world, as it were). The new style of painting simulated the way the human eye sees people and objects when viewed from a single vantage point. Artists suggested depth or distance by making closer objects and figures larger and more detailed than distant ones, by placing objects and figures in overlapping planes so that the closer ones partially block the more distant ones from view, and, most uniquely, by having sight lines recede and converge toward the back of the image on the canvas.

In this latter technique, called linear perspective, sight lines also seem to come together in the imaginary space in front of the canvas, a space that is filled by the gaze of the spectator. The composition in such paintings appears to contain a number of sightlines moving toward a limitless horizon found at the very rear and center of the image. Since the camera lens records images according to the same optical principles operating in these paintings, moviemakers are able to use this process of centering and convergence to focus our attention on key aspects of a scene. (Of course, camera lenses can be altered, and each type of lens renders the scale, depth, and spatial relations of a scene in different ways.)

Careful composition utilizing centering techniques to great advantage is evident in the lengthy shot in *Citizen Kane* in which Mrs. Kane (Agnes Moorehead) signs her son Charles (Billy Swan) over to Walter Thatcher (George Coulouris), the eastern banker who will act as his guardian. It begins with a medium shot through the open window of the boardinghouse showing the child playing with his sled in the snow; then the camera pulls back rapidly to reveal Mrs. Kane looking out the window and calling to her son. The camera continues to pull up and back as Mrs. Kane turns around, and then reveals the eastern banker. The camera tracks backward in front of them as they move to the other side of the room, talking about signing the papers that will give the banker custody of young Charles.

As the camera moves back, the boy remains visible and audible through the window. As Mrs. Kane and the banker continue to move toward the opposite end of the room, Charles's father (Harry Shannon) is revealed on the left side of the frame. Weakly arguing that the child should be allowed to stay, he remains slightly behind his wife as she and the banker approach the table on which the papers are located.

While they move to the table, the boy playing in the snow is temporarily blocked out. Mrs. Kane sits erectly at the extreme right of the frame, flanked by the banker. On the other side of the frame, to the left of the window, stands Charles's father. Between these two groupings of adults, almost in the center of the image, young Charles—the object of their discussion—can again be seen through the window. He is in sharp focus, as are the documents that will determine his future. They are on the table at the very front of the frame, in a direct visual line with the boy. When Thatcher indicates that the parents will receive $50,000 per year, the father ceases his weak protest, moves to the window, and closes it. The sound of Charles's play is stilled, his future sealed.

After some experimentation during the 1950s, the movie industry settled on a standardized aspect ratio of 1.85:1 for 35-millimeter projection. Despite this shift to a more rectangular shape, however, the impulse of the director and the cinematographer—and the tendency of viewers as well—is to focus on the center the frame. Very few directors lavish much attention on the edges of the frame, although they tend to avoid placing the primary figure of interest in the exact center—especially in medium and long shots. When elements within the frame are evenly balanced, the composition appears stable but relatively flat. Of course, whether a particular composition is balanced or unbalanced depends on the desired effect.

Some directors play with the centering tendency for dramatic effect. Roman Polanski's recurring deep-focus shots in *Chinatown* often serve to undercut the cocky, tough-guy demeanor of private eye J. J. Gittes (Jack Nicholson). In his scenes with police officers and civic officials, Gittes is typically boxed in

Centering in *Citizen Kane* (1941). Cinematographer Gregg Toland shot this scene with a wide-angle lens that, together with fast film stock, a high f-stop setting, and more intense lighting than was normal on a studio set, makes everything within the camera's field of view clearly visible—in the background and foreground, and in between.

or pushed to the edges of the frame. This "decentering" suggests his ultimate impotence in the face of forces he doesn't fully comprehend.

Shooting Schemes

In order to efface the camera's presence, directors working within the conventions of Hollywood tend to avoid extremes, shooting at eye level or slight deviations from it for purposes of dramatic construction or exposition. At the same time, they typically utilize a wide range of shots to provide many vantage points and peak emotional involvement. A specific shot can be identified in various ways. One distinguishing factor is duration. Shots may be as short as a fraction of a second or as long as several minutes. A shot of long duration—called a **long take**—allows for the interplay among a group of characters in real time and space. Combining shots of shorter duration focuses audience attention more fully, brings out otherwise buried meaning, allows for greater control over pacing, and evokes strong emotional responses.

Shots may also be described in terms of the camera's angle (high, low, eye-level, and so on.) in relation to the subject, by virtue of the camera's movement, and according to their content. A **two-shot** contains two people, a three-shot three people, and so forth. The apparent distance between the camera and the subject being filmed also distinguishes shots. If a person or object appears extremely close, the shot is called an **extreme close-up.** When they seem very far away, it is referred to as an **extreme long shot.** In between lie a wide range of possible subject-distance relationships.

The human figure usually provides the chief standard for categorizing apparent camera-subject distance, although the distinctions among the various kinds of shots are hardly precise or consistently employed. In an extreme long shot, a person might be visible, but the setting clearly dominates. The same person may be about half the height of the frame in a **long shot,** but the setting receives the strongest emphasis. This is usually distinguished from a **full shot,** which includes the entire body but not much else. A medium long shot reveals about three-fourths of the person, whereas a **medium shot** shows the person from roughly the waist up, with only incidental background in view. A medium close-up shows the person from the shoulders up, and a **close-up** shows only the head. An extreme close-up reveals only a small part of the face, such as the lips or an eye.

Camera-to-subject distances ranging from the panoramic to the extremely close create many dramatic possibilities not achievable on the stage. The long shot is ideal for showing relationships among characters or between characters and their environment. In the classic western *Shane* (1953), for instance, director George Stevens uses a panoramic (extreme long) shot to show a small group of settlers at a funeral dwarfed by the vast landscape of the Grand Tetons. We get a clear sense of the isolation of the community and the inhospitality of the terrain.

The close-up is especially effective for conveying emotion. It allows the smallest reaction of a player to be seen—the slightest quirk of the lips, the tiniest lift of the eyebrow or droop of the shoulders, even the almost imperceptible tensing of the muscles. Through close-ups early on in *Bonnie and Clyde* (1967), director Arthur Penn provides us with an intimate, not to mention extremely erotic, glimpse of one of the title characters. After a short series of still photographs outlining the childhoods of the outlaw pair, the movie proper begins with a screen-filling extreme close-up of a moist pair of slightly separated lips. Subsequent shots reveal a bored, sexually frustrated Bonnie Parker (Faye Dunaway). A particularly arresting close-up of Bonnie pressing her face against the bars of her bed frame clearly communicates her sense of being caged and suggests her intense sexual frustration.

Point of View

In addition to the distance/closeness dynamic, shots also may be described with reference to the points of view they provide. Many different perspectives

Bonnie's (Faye Dunaway) lips nearly fill the frame in the opening shot proper of *Bonnie and Clyde* (1967).

can be presented in a movie, ranging on a continuum from the objective to the subjective. With the **objective point of view,** individuals, events, and locations are shown neutrally, and not from any character's vantage point. They may be presented in a distant wide-angle view, approximating how we might see them on a stage, or in varying degrees of closeness. With the **subjective point of view,** the camera is situated to suggest something shown from the established angle of vision of a character in the previous shot. Subjective shots can also suggest the physical or psychological state of a character. Blurred images, for example, might signal the point of view of someone who has just been hit over the head.

A subjective point-of-view shot is typically joined together with two objective shots to suggest the vantage point of a specific character: an objective shot of the character looking at something, a subjective shot of what the character sees, and then an objective shot of the character again reacting to what was seen. The prelude to the shower stabbing in *Psycho,* in which Norman Bates (Anthony Perkins) peers through a peephole in the wall to watch Marion Crane (Janet Leigh) as she undresses, involves this standard shot combination.

As the scene unfolds, Norman approaches a picture on the wall. We hardly have time to register that it is a depiction of the biblical story about a woman molested by voyeurs whose passions are aroused when they spy on her as she prepares to bathe. After Norman quietly removes the picture, the three shots follow: a medium close-up of him looking through the peephole, a medium shot suggesting his view of Marion undressing (a circle of darkness around her simulates the peephole), and a "tight" or extreme close-up

Norman (Anthony Perkins) removes a painting of *Susana and the Elders*. (*Psycho* [1960])

of his unblinking eye peering through the peephole. Through the combination of these three shots, his eye becomes our eye as we, too, spy on Marion disrobing. Our complicity in his voyeurism is heightened by the use of a "normal" or 50-millimeter lens on the camera—which provided the closest approximation to human vision technically possible on the 35-millimeter cameras of the day.

Movies with too many subjective point-of-view shots usually disrupt the dramatic illusion. In *Lady in the Lake* (1946), for example, director Robert Montgomery tries to simulate a first-person perspective throughout. Almost everything is shot from the point of view of the narrator-protagonist Philip Marlowe (played by Montgomery himself). Marlowe addresses the audience directly at the beginning and end. In the rest of the movie, he is seen only when his reflection is caught in mirrors. At one point, a female character (Audrey Totter) kisses Marlowe. Her face—lips apart—fills the screen.

What is perhaps most distracting in this movie is the way the camera is deployed to simulate where Marlowe is supposedly looking. This distraction stems from the inability of camera movement and the lens itself to duplicate the properties of human vision. Although we have a wide field of vision, we keep only a small proportion—as little as two degrees—of what we can see in focus at any given moment. The rest of our vision is increasingly blurred as we get nearer to the periphery of our focus. We compensate for this limitation by constantly moving our eyes in different directions. As we do this, the things in our field of vision go in and out of focus. In contrast, when the camera moves vertically or horizontally, the lens keeps all objects in the same plane in focus at the same time.

The standard point-of-view shot combination.
(*Psycho* [1960])

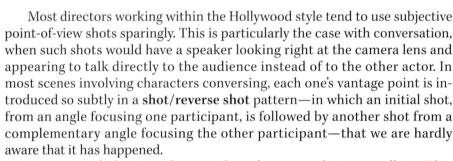

Most directors working within the Hollywood style tend to use subjective point-of-view shots sparingly. This is particularly the case with conversation, when such shots would have a speaker looking right at the camera lens and appearing to talk directly to the audience instead of to the other actor. In most scenes involving characters conversing, each one's vantage point is introduced so subtly in a **shot/reverse shot** pattern—in which an initial shot, from an angle focusing one participant, is followed by another shot from a complementary angle focusing the other participant—that we are hardly aware that it has happened.

A scene might begin with a two-shot of a man and woman talking. This would be followed by a medium **over-the-shoulder shot** of the man alone, then a similar shot of the woman, and then a nearly frontal close-up of the man speaking slightly to one side of the camera. This latter shot actually represents the point of view of the woman, so the scene has moved from an objective to a more or less subjective point of view. The next shot might be a similar frontal close-up of the woman, thereby shifting from the vantage point of one character to that of the other.

This may be followed by a series of nearly frontal shots alternating between the two characters. For economy purposes, these shots would be filmed of out of sequence and spliced together during editing. There is no need to change setups each time an actor speaks; the whole conversation would take place with the camera looking first over one actor's shoulder and then over or in the vicinity of the other actor's shoulder.

Because the camera is, in effect, our surrogate, the shot/reverse shot pattern in the typical conversation scene puts us in the position of one character as the other is speaking, making the expressions on each of their faces much easier to read than if they were shot in profile. Such camera positioning also tends to implicate us in what the characters are saying to each other. This is likely to encourage our emotional involvement with them, especially if the process is repeated in the movie with the same speakers.

Director Francis Ford Coppola used relatively straight subjective point-of-view shots in *The Godfather* at two key moments to narrow viewers' perspective to that of one of the protagonists. In the movie's dramatic opening, a petitioner (Salvatore Corsitto) speaks almost directly to the camera ("I believe in America . . ."). He is tightly framed against a totally dark background. The camera gradually pulls back to reveal Don Corleone (Marlon Brando) as the addressee of the petition. Thus we begin the movie firmly planted in the powerful don's position. Some forty minutes later, we assume Michael Corleone's (Al Pacino) point of view when he visits his wounded father at the hospital.

Subjective point-of-view shots can also be used in conversation scenes to achieve an eerie effect. In *The Silence of the Lambs* (1991), director Jonathan Demme cannily shot the mental and verbal sparring between FBI trainee Clarice Starling (Jodie Foster) and cunningly droll serial killer Hannibal "the Cannibal" Lector (Anthony Hopkins) by having the two at times talk directly to the camera. The psychopathic Lector stares straight at the camera lens as he utters the famous line: "A census taker once tried to test me. I ate his liver with some fava beans and a nice Chianti."

Early on in *GoodFellas* (1990), director Martin Scorsese playfully exposes the artifice of subjective point-of-view shots. As we are introduced to protagonist Henry Hill's (Ray Liotta) fellow hoodlums, his point of view is suggested through a long tracking shot (in which the camera moves forward, backward, or laterally while mounted on any one of a variety of mobile supports). He talks to us, and we seem to see what he sees as the camera moves diagonally from right to left across a crowded nightclub, pausing to show various characters responding to his off-screen presence. At the end of this long take, Scorsese disrupts expectations by having Henry emerge from the left side of the frame, rather than from where the camera is positioned.

Establishing Shots

A standard arrangement of shots, especially common in the 1930s and 1940s, begins with an **establishing shot** that sets up the parameters of the situation and location or otherwise introduces the scene within which the subsequent action will take place. Closer and more particularized shots follow, with an

This frame enlargement is the beginning of the innovative establishing shot that opens the story proper of *Malcolm X* (1992).

occasional return to a long shot to reestablish the context. This pattern, which may be repeated for each new scene, creates points of reference that introduce the action a step at a time.

Director Spike Lee and cinematographer Ernest Dickerson open the story proper of *Malcolm X* with an especially innovative establishing shot (captured in a long take with the use of a handheld camera and crane). It begins with a view of a giant billboard for Coca-Cola above an elevated train station. The camera swoops in below the station to a period re-creation of a vibrant street scene in the Roxbury section of Boston during the World War II years. It then comes down tighter until it holds on a pair of two-toned shoes being shined. The familiar figure of Lee, playing the title character's flamboyantly dressed sidekick Shorty, leaps up from the shoeshine stand and struts across the street like a peacock, arms sashaying in tempo at his side.

Some modern moviemakers eschew the customary establishing shot altogether. Director Quentin Tarantino, for instance, begins the opening scene of *Pulp Fiction* without an establishing shot. Although the *mise-en-scène* signifies that the petty thieves discussing their life in crime are seated in the booth of a diner, its location is neither specified nor suggested. It is simply any and every diner, an artifact of American mass culture. There are, in fact, few visual hints as to the specific suburban setting. The general geographic area becomes apparent only when a character refers to "our man in Inglewood," which is a city near Los Angeles International Airport.

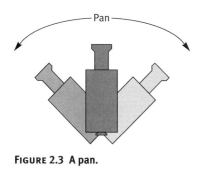

FIGURE 2.3 A pan.

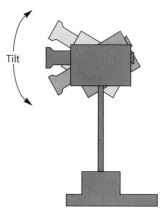

FIGURE 2.4 A tilt.

Camera Movement

Much of a movie's visual complexity comes from a kind of "double movement"—of the camera and the subject being photographed. A movie camera can readily be moved in myriad ways. It is useful to distinguish between camera movement on a fixed base and movement involving actual transportation of the camera from one place to another. In a strict sense, the former is not movement but a series of gestures the camera can make along fixed axes of rotation.

These gestures consist primarily of panning and tilting. In a **pan,** the camera rotates from left to right (or the reverse) on its vertical axis to varying degrees to reveal what lies before the lens on either side. (See Figure 2.3.) A **tilt** entails moving the camera up or down on its horizontal axis—usually smoothly and subtly as not to distract. (See Figure 2.4.) When the camera is in close-up on a face, for instance, a slight lateral swivel may be employed to emphasize the direction of a glance.

To facilitate fluid movements from one place to another, the camera can be mounted on tracks or attached to a platform on wheels called a **dolly.** As the camera moves along a vertical or horizontal line (or a vector of some sort), the subject being photographed may be either stationary or mobile. A variety of effects can be created through dolly or tracking movements. A **dolly-in** can generate a sense of curiosity gratified, as well as a feeling of spatial intrusion as we enter an area previously only observed. A **dolly-out,** in contrast, often suggests a sense of leave-taking, escape, or abandonment. A zoom lens can mimic the effect of forward or backward camera movements, but there are significant differences between the two techniques. Zooming in or out magnifies or shrinks all objects evenly. The effect is somewhat similar to that achieved in looking through binoculars. The moving camera, in contrast, provides a series of changing spatial relationships.

Camera movement can take place during or between shots, enabling the director to change the vantage point of a scene from a close-up to an extreme long shot. As the camera moves in, it not only singles out something by excluding other things but also changes its scale so that it appears larger and occupies more screen space. As the camera pulls back, the view becomes increasingly more expansive so that everything appears smaller. This process of exclusion or inclusion through camera movement can serve as a forceful indicator of what is important in a scene at any given moment.

An image can be changed within a single shot to heighten dramatic intensity and interest simply by moving the camera in, out, and around the action, as director Orson Welles did in the opening sequence of *Touch of Evil*. The shot begins with a close-up of hands setting a timer on an explosive device. The camera pulls back to reveal a shadowy figure running and placing the device in the trunk of a flashy convertible, which is parked on a street in a seedy Mexican border town. The figure flees the scene as a couple appears, gets into the car, and drives off. Now the camera follows the action, gliding alongside and ahead of the car as it passes a border checkpoint. Suddenly, the car explodes. The forebodingly dark night; the street with its flashing neon signs, tawdry hotels and strip joints, and swarming crowds; the sense of heat and tension—all are brought to life in complex detail in less than three minutes of screen time.

This entire opening sequence was filmed in a single long take from a camera mounted on a **crane,** a vehicle equipped with a mechanical arm or boom at whose end is a camera platform that can be lifted and moved fluidly through space. The use of a crane makes possible otherwise unobtainable camera angles and shots. The camera can move in and out or up and down as though on an elevator. Depending on the speed of movement and the specific context, the effect of crane shots can be soothing, exhilarating, or tension producing.

Crane shots can also be extraordinarily eloquent, lending added poignancy to an already affecting scene. A stunning crane shot in *Gone With the Wind* (1939) enlarges our view of the open-air, makeshift military hospital at Atlanta's railroad depot where Scarlett O'Hara (Vivien Leigh), seemingly insensitive and indifferent to the human suffering that surrounds her, searches for Dr. Meade (Harry Davenport) to help in the delivery of Melanie Wilkes's (Olivia de Havilland) baby. As the camera slowly pulls up and back, it reveals countless rows of wounded and dying Confederate soldiers. It finally comes to a stop with a close-up of a torn and tattered Confederate flag waving over the human carnage. Since a standard moviemaking crane at the time had only a 25-foot reach, an extended 90-foot construction crane was rented from a

The camera comes to a stop on a close-up of a Confederate flag waving over the human carnage. (*Gone With the Wind* [1939])

shipyard to capture the full scope of the scene. Weighing 120 tons, it was pulled by a flatbed truck down a concrete ramp expressly constructed so the camera platform could move up and away with utter smoothness. After several rehearsals, the shot was done in one take.

Cameras have become much lighter in weight and trimmer in design, making them more portable and easier to maneuver. A device called a **Steadicam**—consisting of a lightweight frame, torsion arm, movie camera, and small video monitor—can be attached by harness to an operator's body, making possible movements similar to those achieved with a dolly. (Its makers won a technical Oscar in 1977.) The operator can walk or even run up stairs with the camera while maintaining an extremely steady image. In addition to increased mobility, a Steadicam (and similar devices) permits much faster setups and shots in tight quarters where a dolly can't fit. It is especially useful for filming in rugged terrain.

In many situations, it may be desirable or necessary for the camera operator to actually hold the equipment. A handheld camera can be moved in, out, around, or up and down at will. The thrill and often perverse fun of

French *Nouvelle Vague* (New Wave) films, so influential in the United States during the 1960s, owe much to the emergence of lightweight, handheld cameras that enabled the director and cinematographer to change the focus of the lens as the action unfolded.

Director Jean-Luc Godard's 1960 crime romp *Breathless,* about an amoral thug (Jean-Paul Belmondo) on the run who is finally betrayed by his American paramour (Jean Seberg), was one of the first films to make extensive use of the nervous, jerky images created by a freely moving camera. The portability of the equipment allowed Godard and his cinematographer, Raoul Coutard, to move about the streets of Paris and Marseilles with relative ease, contributing to a sense of spontaneity and improvisation. To achieve the long take of Seberg and Belmondo walking on the Champs Elysées, Coutard sat in a wheelchair holding the camera while Godard pulled him along ahead of the actors. (The entire movie was shot without sound equipment and dubbed in postproduction.)

A handheld camera can serve any number of thematic and aesthetic purposes. Shaky images usually confer a sense of immediacy and authenticity, especially if the events depicted are unpredictable and dangerous to the participants. Frantic camera movements function throughout *Schindler's List* to convey the daily terror and unrelieved confusion, the feeling that anything can happen at any given moment, that it's all so arbitrary. When an S.S. soldier shouting "Your card, Jew" stops Itzhak Stern (Ben Kingsley), the frenetic camera and rapid cuts reinforce the sense of how fast-paced life is, and how quickly it can be taken away. Director Steven Spielberg and cinematographer Janusz Kaminski employed a similar visual style in *Saving Private Ryan* (1998). Nearly 50 percent of its total footage involved the use of handheld camera techniques.

Camera Angles

Our perspective changes every time the composition of the frame changes, whether by moving the camera, adjusting the lens, or altering the angle or position of the camera relative to the subject. **Camera angles** can range from a **bird's-eye view** (directly above) to a **worm's-eye view** (directly below). The camera is pointed down at the subject in a **high-angle shot,** up at the subject in a **low-angle shot,** and directly at the subject in an **eye-level shot.** Such camera angles can be employed to enhance a range of feelings. They often convey attitude, giving us a sense of what the subject feels in relation to the surrounding people or objects. The greater the angle, the more a feeling is intensified.

In general, low-angle shots generate in us a sense of weakness, impotency, and diminution. The subject is imbued with an air of dominance, power, or authority. Perhaps this reaction is related to childhood memories of looking up at parents and other authority figures. Conversely, when the camera is

Phyllis Dietrichson (Barbara Stanwyck) enjoys visual dominance over Walter Neff
(Fred MacMurray). (*Double Indemnity* [1944])

aimed downward, our point of view is that of a tall person, and the subject is
diminished in stature and put in a subordinate position. Again, resonance of
past experiences and responses may be struck to create this effect.

The angle of the camera often determines which character dominates the
frame at any given moment. The first glimpse of Phyllis Dietrichson (Barbara
Stanwyck), the *femme fatale* of *Double Indemnity* (1944), is from insurance
salesman Walter Neff's (Fred MacMurray) point of view as he looks up at her
standing at the top of the stairs draped in nothing but a bath towel. This is
followed by a high-angle shot of him so that she has visual dominance.
Quickly describing his errand, he looks her up and down, and they begin the
first of several rounds of erotic sparring. Soon she will dominate not only the
framing but his life as well.

Of course, particular effects always depend on context. The subject is ordinarily diminished in stature when the camera is aimed downward, but there
are some notable exceptions to this facile generalization. One of the most politically potent images in the history of cinema was shot from an extremely
high angle. It occurs in German director Leni Riefenstal's *Triumph of the Will*
(1935), a record and celebration of the 1934 Nazi Party rally in Nuremberg. The
centerpiece of the film, a sequence paying tribute to those Germans who died
in World War I, begins with an extreme long shot of three figures entering the
huge stadium where the ceremonies are to take place. They walk along the
corridor created by column after column of ordered and anonymous Nazi followers. This long shot of the stadium is followed by a closer shot clearly identifying the figures as the Nazi leader Adolf Hitler and two of his cohorts. In the
light of such exceptions, the best one can say with some confidence is that an
extremely angled shot (whether overhead or very low) usually indicates that a
certain attitude toward the subject photographed is being encouraged.

An extreme long shot of Adolf Hitler and his cohorts. Working with a crew of 172, Leni Riefenstal situated cameras on ramps, ladders, and towers to glorify the Nazi party and deify its leader through the power of cinematic expression. (*Triumph of the Will* [1935])

Sometimes very high angling of the camera may be used for concealment. Alfred Hitchcock employed an extreme high-angle shot in *Psycho* to hide the identity of the murderer without appearing to do so during the scene in which Milton Arbogast (Martin Balsam), a private investigator hired by missing secretary Marion Crane's (Janet Leigh) employer, returns to the Bates Motel in an attempt to meet the proprietor's mysterious mother. He enters the front door of the old Victorian house on the hill and slowly climbs the steep staircase. The high angle of the camera makes him appear vulnerable. There is a cut to a crack of light appearing on the floor through the slowly opening door of a room. The camera shifts back to Arbogast as he continues his ascent and then to an extreme overhead shot as he reaches the landing. This bird's-eye view camouflages the identity of the knife-wielding figure who dashes out of the room and strikes Arbogast full in the face.

Camera Setups

Multiple **camera setups** are usually employed for the separate shots comprised in most scenes. Each new setup may involve changes in the lighting scheme, the deployment and movement of actors, the angle and position of the camera (and possibly lenses and filters), and the placement of microphones. Because of the amount of time and organization entailed in these activities, shots requiring the same basic setup are typically filmed together, even though they may appear in different parts of the scene. The simplest of scenes can involve intricate camera setups that are quite time consuming to execute. The scene in *Psycho* in which a highway patrolman (Mort Mills) questions errant secretary Marion Crane, after he finds her sleeping on the front seat of her parked car along a deserted roadside, takes up less than three minutes of screen time. Yet shooting it entailed eleven separate camera setups (Figures 2.5 and 2.6).

Each of the thirty-five shots resulting from these setups serves some specific expository or dramatic purpose. Setup A provides a conventional establishing shot (1). Lasting twenty-three seconds, this shot shows Marion's car parked by the telegraph pole. Then another vehicle, clearly recognizable as a patrol car, comes into view from frame right, drives past the first car, stops, and then reverses to park behind it. In setup B, the camera was placed at a low angle adjacent to the front door of the secretary's car, facing the patrolman who gets out of his own car (2). As he walks toward the camera, the morning sun is behind him so that he casts a long shadow. His silhouetted form makes him appear somewhat threatening. In setup C, the camera has not moved far from its previous position (B), but it is now turned toward the car and raised up to frame a section of it as the patrolman comes into view and stoops to look through the front side window (3). In setup D, the camera frames the secretary through the side window (4). She is asleep on the front seat.

The setup (C) for shot 5 is the same one used for shot 3. Although this shot lasts only two seconds, there is a slight reframing as the patrolman knocks on the window. His knocking action carries over to the next shot (6), which was created from the same setup (D) as shot 4. As Marion awakens and sits up, the camera reframes slightly to show her startled reaction on seeing the patrolman.

In setup E, the camera was placed inside the car for shot 7. The policeman's face nearly fills the frame, and his dark glasses and grim expression add to the tension. Shot 8, showing the nervous secretary trying to start her car, is a repetition of setup D. Her action motivates the patrolman to move from beside the rear car door to the position he takes up in shot 9. A new camera setup (F) was established to record this movement.

The verbal exchange between Marion and the patrolman that follows comprises of eighteen shots, yet they required only two camera setups. Nine shots taken from setup G show her in close-up. These are interspersed with nine tight shots of him taken from setup E (which was also used for shot 7).

The camera positioning for setup G captures her from the general vicinity where the policeman has been established standing. In contrast, its placement in setup E captures him from precisely the vantage point established for her. Standing near the car, he looks down at her while she must look

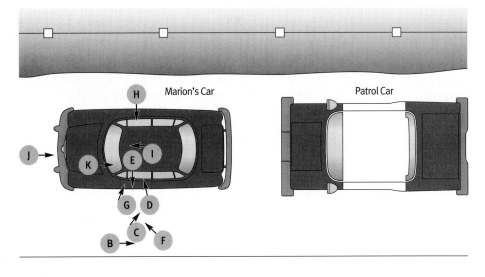

FIGURE 2.5 Camera positions in *Psycho*.

Camera Set-Ups	A	B	C	D	E	F	G	H	I	J	K
Shot Numbers	1	2	3 5	4 6 8	7 11 13 15 17 19 21 23 25 27	9 34	10 12 14 16 18 20 22 24 26	28 33	29 32	30	31 35

FIGURE 2.6 Camera setups and shot numbers in *Psycho*.

up at him from her seated position inside the car. The effect of filming the two characters in this way is to heighten her sense of anxiety as he interrogates her.

A new camera setup (H) from the passenger's side of the car was employed for shot 28, which reveals Marion rummaging through her handbag for her driver's license. Her back is turned to conceal from him the envelope containing the stolen money. The patrolman is seen hovering menacingly

Setup A.

Setup B.

Setup D.

Setup E.

Setup G.

Setup H.

Setup I.

Setup K.

behind her, attempting to peer over her shoulder. After she hands him the license, he moves toward the front of the car.

His movement is continued in Shot 29, which shows him framed by the front windshield as he checks the license plate against the number on the driver's license. As in the previous shot, this entailed a new camera setup (I). Another new camera setup (J) was required for the next shot (30), which provides a full-frame view of the Arizona license plate (the significance of which will become apparent in the next scene). Shot 31 was likewise taken from a new setup (K). Apparently positioned on the hood of the car, the camera frames Marion in a medium close shot through the front windshield. Shot 32 is from the same camera position as shot 29, only this time looking toward the secretary, not the license plate.

The final three shots of the scene were done from camera setups used for earlier shots. In shot 33 (setup H), the patrolman is seen from inside the car as he moves toward the driver's side. His movement is picked up in shot 34 (setup F), in which he returns Marion's license. The front windshield once again frames her in the scene's final shot (setup K). As she puts the license and money back into her handbag, the patrolman can be seen in the background through the rearview window walking toward and then getting into his patrol car. When she drives off, his car can be seen following hers.

While costly and protracted, this system of shooting allows for a great deal of stylistic flexibility. Each fragment of a scene can be set up, rehearsed, and shot separately using a single camera. The participants can be framed in intimate close-ups and illuminated in ways that enhance their appearance. Any error in performance or recording can be easily remedied through a retake of a single shot of short duration. Using several cameras simultaneously would create a need for more uniform illumination, resulting in a kind of flat, low-contrast lighting effect, as opposed to the more molded, high-contrast lighting possible with single-camera setups. Moreover, errors made during lengthy shots with multiple cameras are much more difficult to rectify.

Cut to the Close

The elements of script, acting, lighting, and camera work all come together in the postproduction phase. Only when images and sounds are combined into a coherent whole—with actions and reactions, tempo and rhythm—is a movie fully realized. The next chapter looks at what happens when the shooting stops and the cutting commences. The focus is on how editors, sound technicians, composers, conductors, and other key personnel orchestrate such elements as reverse-angle shots, musical scores, and editing patterns in ways designed to achieve peak emotional involvement in a movie while at the same time concealing the complex apparatus underlying the final product.

The Postproduction Phase

Perhaps more than any other factor, it is the integration of sounds and images that determines the final pace, tone, and character of a movie. When mistakes are made during filming or when scenes fall short of expectations, directors frequently find consolation in the prayerful utterance "Don't worry, we'll fix it in postproduction." This is especially the case now that digital technologies allow so many more things to be done after the principal cinematography is completed. According to movie industry folklore, the proper mix of images and sounds has made many otherwise mediocre movies good and, occasionally, even turned a good movie into a great one. The final stage of the production process is the focus of this chapter.

The Editing Process

As the technical coordinator of postproduction activities, the **film editor** monitors the work of the various departments to see that all visual and aural values are uniform and consistent. Once these things are assured, the editor's primary responsibility is to select, order, trim, and splice together the various film shots into a credible and coherent rough cut. In creating this preliminary assembly of shots, scenes, and sequences, the editor is concerned with such matters as the proper way to make a smooth cut, the appropriate dramatic length of a piece of film, the way

Bonnie (Faye Dunaway) comes to a violent end. This scene's slow-motion aesthetics and rapid-cut editing quickly became part of the Hollywood style's visual lexicon. (*Bonnie and Clyde* [1967])

the interplay of cuts contributes to the desired tempo and rhythm, and the manner in which the selection of the right camera angle and point of view can generate a specific emotional tone. Judicious editing techniques can do much to intensify the drama, heighten the humor, or quicken the pace of the action.

Although the work of film editors theoretically begins with the completion of the principal cinematography, in actual practice they often consult with the director and other key production personnel throughout the moviemaking process. This is especially the case for complicated scenes and sequences. The complex final scene of *Bonnie and Clyde* (1967), in which the title characters are brutally ambushed on a quiet country road, required the coordinated efforts of director Arthur Penn, cinematographer Burnett Guffy, editor Dede Allen, and producer-star Warren Beatty (who was intimately involved in every aspect of the movie from the outset). To film this short scene, Penn and Guffy placed four cameras side-by-side, each running at a different speed. The differing speeds allowed Allen to select footage with varying rates of **slow motion** (produced by operating the camera at a higher-than-normal speed) and combine it with images of the action shot at normal speed.

From the point at which a flock of startled birds abruptly flies off, signaling the onset of the ambush, to the final image in the movie, after the gunfire has ceased, the scene takes up fifty-four seconds of screen time and contains fifty-one separate shots. The most rapid cutting occurs as the two outlaws, aware they are about to be killed, exchange glances that reveal panic, affection, and perhaps a sense of resignation. In just four seconds, nine separate images flash onto the screen. Then a barrage of bullets riddles the couple. The kinetic and intense rhythm of the shot changes creates an almost balletic effect as their bodies writhe convulsively.

The Kuleshov Effect

The power of editing to shape viewers' perceptions is something Russian filmmaker and teacher Lev Kuleshov reportedly demonstrated in one of his many experiments during the early 1920s at a film college in Moscow. According to one of his most prominent pupils, the great filmmaker V. I. Pudovkin, Kuleshov obtained a close-up from an old film in which a perfectly expressionless actor glanced off-screen.[1] He then inserted identical prints of this close-up with three successive images: one from the actor's face to a bowl of soup, another from his face to a little girl playing with a teddy bear, and a third from his face to a coffin containing a woman's corpse. When shown the experimental reel, people naturally assumed that, each time the film cut from the actor's face to one of the three images, it was revealing what he was observing at that moment. Not only were they unable to discern that each cut of the actor was identical, they are said to have praised his "performance"—his look of hunger at the bowl of soup, his delight on seeing the child, his grief over the dead woman.

Several critics have noted the imprecise way this experiment is described and have questioned its validity.[2] Moreover, the original footage no longer survives, and there is no corroborating evidence that it ever actually existed. Although the experiment may be a bit of cinematic folklore, the so-called **Kuleshov effect** is nonetheless a useful concept in film analysis. It encapsulates what anyone who has ever worked an editing table knows: a wide range of meanings and nuances can be created from the juxtaposition of fragments of time and space captured on film.

Of course, many of the effects created during editing have to be anticipated in the script and implemented during shooting in order for the editor to bring them to fruition in postproduction. Regardless of the original intent, however, once the action is captured on film, it begins to take on a life of its own. Freed from the confines of real space and time, things not only look different from the way they did during the principal cinematography but also begin to suggest new meanings or new ways of shaping originally intended meanings. Even in those situations in which the editor's role might seem to be minimal, decisions still must be made about how to join separate shots. The film editor has the best perspective from which to determine how the scene fragments should be assembled for maximum emotional impact.

Sometimes the entire structure of a scene is altered in the editing room. The incomplete script for *The Godfather* (1972) called for the baptism of

Michael Corleone's (Al Pacino) godchild to be followed by the systematic assassination of the Corleone family's enemies. Some of this footage was completed before director Francis Ford Coppola went on location to shoot the Sicilian portion of the movie. Before departing, the director reportedly said to editor Peter Zinner, "Why don't you try and see what you can come up with using whatever you have? I will shoot the rest when I return from Italy."[3] Zinner cast aside the incomplete script and integrated the baptism and the murders, with the voice of the priest presiding over the sacred ritual running continuously. He also added organ music to the combined footage. In the process, he created a rough cut for what became one of the most magnificent sequences in movie history.

Effacing Editing Within Scenes

Combining selected bits and pieces of action captured on film into a coherent whole encompasses two different forms of organization: editing within a scene and editing from scene to scene. The primary goal of editing within a scene is to create a sense of continuous space and time so that the action unfolds without any apparent interruption or intervention. The process for accomplishing this is called **continuity editing.** But this commonly used term is somewhat misleading in that more than merely editing is involved. Directors must employ specific shooting strategies during the principal cinematography to ensure that editors have the necessary footage to create a smooth, logical flow from shot to shot within a scene.

The 180-Degree System

Central to continuity editing is the **180-degree system.** With this strategy of shooting and editing, the space of a scene is constructed along what is called the 180-degree line or axis of action. This facilitates the breakdown of the scene into smaller units without confusing the audience about the spatial relationships being depicted at any given moment. During a conversation scene, for instance, the direction of the line can be anywhere the director chooses, but it is usually the line of sight between the two characters conversing. Once the line is determined, a working space of 180 degrees is established. Any shots obtained within that space will be consistent with each other. If the camera were to cross the imaginary axis of action, the speakers would reverse positions when the combined shots were projected on the screen (Figure 3.1.).

Other Techniques of Continuity Editing

Additional components of continuity editing involve "matching" successive shots with ongoing action, graphic similarities, connecting glances, or

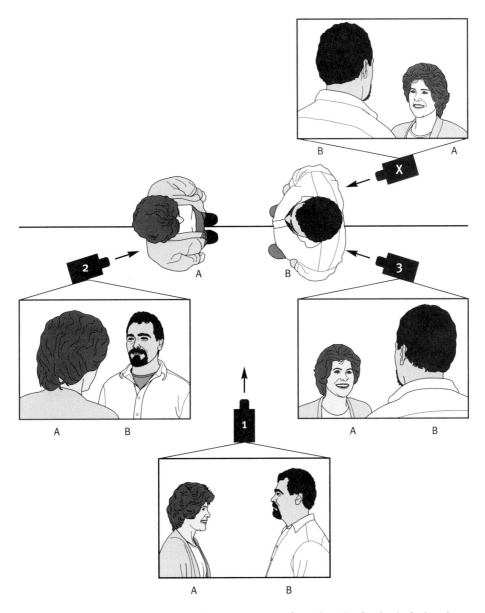

FIGURE 3.1 Bird's-eye view of a man and a woman conversing. The axis of action is the imaginary line connecting the two of them. In photographing them under the 180-degree system, the camera can be put at any point as long as it stays on the same side of the line. A typical series of shots would be: (camera position 1) a medium shot of them together; (camera position 2) a shot over the woman's shoulder, focusing on the man; (camera position 3) a shot over the man's shoulder, focusing on the woman. In each of these three shots, the two people remain in the same positions in the frame relative to each other (she is always on the left, and he is always on the right). If photographed from the other side of the axis of action (camera position X), they would appear to have reversed positions when the shots were combined and projected.

Match on action. A bumptious banker (Gregory Gaye) tries to gain entry into the gambling room of Rick's Cafe Americain in *Casablanca* (1942). The second shot, taken from inside the room, picks up his movement from the first as he attempts to push past Abdul the doorman (Dan Seymour).

common sounds. In a **graphic match,** actors, objects, and other compositional factors retain their approximate positions in the frame from shot to shot. **Eyeline matches,** in which the separate glances of the speakers connect, let the audience know whom each speaker is looking at and talking to even when they are not shown together on the screen. A **match on action** continues a physical action from one shot to the next without any disorienting jumps. (Common sounds from shot to shot further help to conceal cuts.)

The effectiveness of matching depends on its smoothness. If there are noticeable jumps in the flow of events from one shot to another, the events lose their rhythmic continuity, and the action may even seem to leap about in time. Such unnatural motion ordinarily results when two discontinuous pieces of footage shot from the same camera angle are joined together. To avoid this problem, an editor tries to make matches in which there is a definite change in the angle of vision. As a rule, joining shots taken from camera angles varying by at least thirty degrees—the so-called **thirty-degree rule**—creates the impression of an undisturbed flow of events because such a shift seems logically motivated. Of course, the suggestion that a change from one shot to another serves some dramatic purpose can only be made if the editor has the necessary footage available in the first place.

Reverse-Angle Cutting

A key component of continuity editing is **reverse-angle cutting,** in which the second of two shots joined together reverses the field of view of the first by more than ninety degrees. The two separate shots generally adhere to the 180-degree system and are typically connected visually by an eyeline match, involving viewers in the eye contacts of the characters and, ultimately, in their verbal exchanges as well. The degree to which this common cutting pattern is employed varies from director to director and from period to period. Historically, it reached its peak exploitation in the 1940s.[4] In *Casablanca* (1942), a prime exemplar of how movies were typically filmed and edited in the studio era, fully 50 percent of the shot transitions involve reverse-angle cutting.

The scene introducing protagonist Rick Blaine (Humphrey Bogart) illustrates how this cutting pattern typically operates. In the first shot that we actually see him, he is playing a solitary game of chess. Providing a spatial layout of the room, the next shot reverses the angle. The camera is now behind Rick, who is in the foreground, and the entrance to the casino is visible in the background. This shot sets the 180-degree axis as a diagonal connecting Rick and the doorman, who is pausing in the entrance with a couple. The next shot is a closer view of the doorman looking to Rick for approval. Another guest appears at the door. The next shot reverses the angle as Rick signals his disapproval. This is followed by three medium shots of a rumpus at the door. Rick then appears at the doorway to deal with the Deutschbank representative trying to bully his way into the gambling room. The cutting now goes into a brief series of reverse-angle shots as Rick and the banker exchange words. Spatial and temporal continuity is conveyed across shots through eyeline matches and jaunty piano music.

While generally showing what we need to see at any given moment, reverse-angle cutting requires us to fill in the gaps between shots by making implicit connections and drawing inferences, mentally driving the drama forward. As we concentrate on the meaning of the combined images, we are diverted from examining the means by which they were constructed. Thus actions on the screen are rendered more real and inevitable, while the dozens of decisions that were made about such matters as actor deployment, camera placement and focus, and lighting, are to varying degrees concealed.

Linking Separate Scenes

Editing from scene to scene provides the fundamental structure of the movie as a whole. The ways of linking scenes range from the purely linear to the convoluted. The 1945 melodrama *Mildred Pierce,* which is examined at length in Chapter Seven, opens in the present, with a murder. Two lengthy flashbacks follow, motivated by the title character speaking to a detective and separated by a brief return to the present. Then the events of the previous evening are retold in a third flashback, after which the film reverts to the present, now the morning of a new day.

For the most part, the scenes in *The Godfather* are edited chronologically in a linear structure. In contrast, the intricate editing patterns of *The Godfather Part II* (1974) allow the events of Vito Corleone's (Robert DeNiro) rise and his

Reverse-angle cutting in *Casablanca* (1942). From left to right, the first five images are from consecutive shots. In the final image, after a ruckus at the door, Rick joins Abdul and the banker. This establishes a new 180-degree axis as Rick and the banker exchange words in a brief series of reverse-angle shots.

son Michael's (Al Pacino) fall to unfold in tandem, alternating from one to the other in forty-year leaps so that developments in each character's life in effect comment on the other's. In the complexly structured drug war drama

Traffic (2000), several loosely linked vignettes are deftly cut together to create a tragic cinematic portrait of the greed, corruption, economic inequity, and boredom behind the multibillion-dollar narcotics trade and the largely futile battle being waged against it.

Separate scenes are typically connected through straight cuts, fades, or dissolves. A **cut** is an instantaneous change from one image to another. In a **fade,** an image gradually goes to black (fade out) or takes form from black (fade in). Fades often signify a **temporal ellipsis**—a break in time designed to compress narrative duration and heighten drama. There are three such ellipses in the "horse head" sequence of *The Godfather,* in which Don Corleone's *consigliore,* or legal counselor, Tom Hagen (Robert Duvall) secures a major movie role for singer Johnny Fontaine (Al Martino) by making a studio executive "an offer he can't refuse." Hagen meets with Jack Woltz (John Marley), powerful head of Woltz International Studios, who rudely refuses a request to cast the singer in an upcoming picture. Hagen calmly informs the studio head that he can expect a call from him.

After Hagen departs, Woltz tells an underling to find out for whom the lawyer works. At this point, there is a break in time, signaled by momentary darkness as one image fades out and another fades in. After this temporal ellipsis, Hagen visits the movie magnate's mansion, where he's treated with greater deference because, we soon learn, Woltz now understands that the lawyer is in the employ of Don Corleone. Despite Woltz's initial deference, however, he angrily informs Hagen that Fontaine will never work for his studio. It seems the singer, "with his olive-oil voice and guinea charm," seduced one of his protégées.

After another ellipsis, the scene shifts to the exterior of Woltz's mansion and then to his bedroom, where he is sleeping. Woltz awakens to discover the bloody severed head of his prize racehorse that he had proudly showed off to Hagen earlier that evening. He emits a loud, piercing cry, which continues over an exterior view of his mansion. The clear inference is that Hagen ordered someone to sever the horse's head and place it in the magnate's bed as he slept. The causal chain of events is capped in the next scene. Following another fade, Don Corleone is seen presiding over a meeting. A brief reference to a garland of flowers displayed in his office confirms that Johnny Fontaine sent it on the occasion of his assuming the movie role.

Movies entail two basic time frames: the time of the action, events, and relationships depicted, and the time it takes to depict them. The first temporal scheme is necessarily transformed to fit the second. In this regard, a primary function of temporal ellipses is to condense the running time of a movie to two or three hours. In *Psycho* (1960), for instance, after absconding with money entrusted to her, Marion Crane's (Janet Leigh) car journey takes a day and a night, but only a few minutes of it is shown. The scene of her waking in the car soon after sunrise suggests that she has been traveling overnight.

A temporal ellipsis in *The Maltese Falcon* (1941). Audiences were allowed to decide what, if anything, happened during the fade following Sam's (Humphrey Bogart) kiss. Instead of such subtle suggestion, a movie these days would be more likely to show a couple heatedly groping each other.

Temporal ellipses serve other practical purposes as well. They proved especially expedient under the old studio system because explicit sex scenes could not be shown. An omission of time in *The Maltese Falcon* (1941), for example, subtly suggests that private eye Sam Spade (Humphrey Bogart) has become sexually intimate with his alluring client Brigid O'Shaughnessy (Mary Astor). As he leans over to kiss her, he notices through the window that his apartment is being watched. A fade-out as the scene shifts to the street suggests that they will remain together for the night. This impression is reinforced some time later when Spade comes to work. As he opens the door to his inner office, Brigid rushes to him, calls him darling, and explains that her apartment was searched the night before.

With a **dissolve** (also called a lap or overlapping dissolve), one image gradually fades out while another begins to appear so that at a certain point the two images are superimposed. A dissolve often signals a **flashback,** in which the narrative time is disrupted to recall earlier events. For example, a flashback introduced by a dissolve occurs in *Casablanca* when a distraught Rick reflects back on his love affair with Ilsa (Ingrid Bergman) in Paris before the

A superimposition suggests we are seeing Rick's recollections of Paris. (*Casablanca* [1942])

German invasion. He is hunched numbly over a whiskey glass, with a half-empty bottle of bourbon close at hand. The nearby airport beacon intermittently breaks the darkness. His sidekick Sam (Dooley Wilson) is playing the piano. Musing about America, Rick says with sudden vehemence: "Of all the gin joints, in all the towns, in all the world, she walks into mine!" At Rick's command, Sam plays "As Time Goes By"—"You played it for her," growls Rick, "and you can play it for me." There is a cut to a medium close-up of Rick as he pours a drink. The camera moves in, filling the frame with his face. Gradually, his image blurs as the outline of the Arc de Triomphe in Paris comes into sharper relief, and he and Ilsa are shown driving along the Champs-Elysées.

Various editing techniques can be employed to condense time and events. When the scene shifts to Paris before the Nazi invasion, the whirlwind courtship of Rick and Ilsa is captured through **montage editing**, which involves the cutting together of very brief shots to form a scene or sequence: driving in an open car through the French countryside, taking a boat ride down the Seine River, drinking champagne at Ilsa's hotel room (as they touch glasses, Rick says, "Here's looking at you, kid."), dancing in a Paris nightclub under a glittering, rotating mirrored ball. This editing technique is used again while they are at their favorite bistro, La Belle Aurore. After Sam has played "As Time Goes By" and Rick once again toasts Ilsa, Gestapo loudspeakers in the street interrupt them, announcing the imminent arrival of the Germans. The Nazi onslaught is then represented through a quick montage of news clips.

The temporal duration of events can also be suggested through the use of a technique called a **swish pan** (also called a flash pan, zip pan, or **wipe**), which creates a blurring sidewise motion across the screen. In *Citizen Kane* (1941), the disintegration of the title character's first marriage over the course of nine years is convincingly compressed into a series of brief breakfast scenes punctuated by swish pans. The passage of time is also reflected in the couple's positioning (they are gradually seated farther apart from each other at the table) and in their overall appearance. With each breakfast episode, the lighting and background music become more somber. By the end of the sequence, which lasts slightly more than two minutes, they are sitting in stony silence, reading rival newspapers. The camera pulls back to reveal that they are situated at opposite ends of a very long table.

Parallel Editing

Editing from scene to scene moves the story along, creates suspense, and constructs the causal logic of the events. Separate scenes can also be intercut to suggest that they are happening simultaneously. The dramatic power of this **parallel editing** is apparent in the baptism sequence in *The Godfather*. This is the sequence in which Michael Corleone (Al Pacino) serves as godfather for his nephew while enemies of the Corleone family are being systematically eliminated at various locations. The five-minute sequence, which contains sixty-seven separate shots, begins with a long shot of the interior of the cathedral in which the baby is being baptized. The action starts slowly, with shots of the service and of preparations for the murders interspersed. Sounds of organ music, Latin prayers, and the intermittent cries of the baby continue uninterrupted across the disparate scene fragments.

The pace of the crosscutting begins to accelerate following a close-up of Michael Corleone at the moment when he must declare his own faith and answer on behalf of the baby (the infant Sofia Coppola in her first screen role). After he professes his belief in God, Jesus, the Holy Ghost, and the Holy Catholic Church, the exorcism ritual and the calculated killings commence. Crosscutting between the church and the crime scenes continues as the priest asks: "Michael Francis Rizzi, do you renounce Satan?" Shot of an elevator door opening as the church organ sounds a loud arpeggio. The passengers are blasted with a shotgun. Shot of Michael responding on behalf of the infant: "I do renounce him." Another loud arpeggio provides musical punctuation.

Parallel editing reveals two baptisms—one in water, the other in blood. (*The Godfather* [1972])

The camera cuts to a massage room. As the intended victim puts on his glasses, a bullet penetrates his eye. Another shot of the church interior follows. The camera focuses on Michael as the priest continues: "And all his works?" Shot of a man trapped in a revolving door. Again gunfire eliminates an enemy of the Corleone family. Shot of Michael responding: "I do renounce them." The sound of the organ stops abruptly. Shot of a man and woman in bed. Machine gun bullets rip them apart. Shot of Michael as the priest asks: "And all his pomps?" Once again, he responds affirmatively. Shot of a courthouse. Two men are murdered on the street, and a third is shot in the back as he flees up the courthouse steps. All through the killings, the roar of gunfire and the cries of the dying are intermingled with the sounds of the sacred service.

The killings concluded, at least for the time being, we return to the church for the completion of the holy ritual of exorcism, purification, and acceptance. "Michael Francis Rizzi wilt thou be baptized?" inquires the priest. Michael Corleone softly answers: "I will." Following each mention of a member of the Holy Trinity, the priest pours water on the baby's head. This is the moment of the actual baptism. As the priest intones in Latin, we see flashes of the murder victims. We then return to the interior of the church one last time, where the priest bids the baby to go in peace and the organ music stops. The camera slowly tracks toward Michael Corleone's face, etched by candlelight. There is no sign of emotion or remorse. His baptism in blood is complete.

Cutting back and forth between the situations of Roberta (Rosanna Arquette) and Susan (Madonna) suggests the clash of a number of conflicting values: conventional versus unconventional, bourgeois versus antibourgeois, suburban versus urban, married versus unmarried, fidelity versus promiscuity, security versus autonomy, restriction versus libertinism. (*Desperately Seeking Susan* [1985])

The opening scenes of *Desperately Seeking Susan* (1985) combine parallel editing with *mise-en-scène* and music to highlight the stark differences in the lifestyles of the principal characters, Roberta (Rosanna Arquette) and Susan (Madonna). In a parody of middle-class suburbia, we first see Roberta in an antiseptic beauty salon in Fort Lee, New Jersey, which is just across the Hudson River from Manhattan. The girlish romanticism of "It's in His Kiss" provides a musical backdrop. An assembly line of women in protective smocks is submitting to manicures, hairstyling, and the like. The pink tones of the salon's decor suffuse the scene. Roberta's conventional lifestyle is suggested by her expressed desire not to have anything "weird" done to her hair.

As she and her sister-in-law sit under white-domed hair dryers, Roberta reads aloud a classified ad in the personals indicating the time and place someone named Susan can rendezvous with whoever is desperately seeking her. Roberta's comments reveal that she has been following this relationship for some time. Her enthusiasm for the word "desperate" suggests that she is ripe for some unusual or exciting experience.

After she circles the ad, the scene shifts to Susan in Atlantic City, New Jersey. The insistent sounds of "Urgent," an unsentimental rock-'n'-roll song, suggest we're entering a very different world. There is a brief establishing shot of the locale, followed by a cut to the interior of a hotel room. As the camera slowly tracks back from the curtain-covered window, we see Susan lying on the floor taking her own picture. Unlike the situation at the beauty salon, symbols of excess and unrestrained pursuits are in evidence everywhere. The entire room is in disarray, and Susan herself is attired in a bizarre black outfit that brings to mind nothing of suburban life. Despite these stark contrasts, the link between her and Roberta is made when she draws a large heart around the same ad. She then steals money and unusual-looking earrings from her sleeping male companion, packs her things, and departs—catching the eye of a sinister-looking character who is just getting off the elevator.

We return to Roberta's world. A shot of her upscale town house is followed by a cut to its interior, where a birthday party is in progress. Once again, signs of suburban malaise abound. A bland Carly Simon song is playing on the stereo. A close-up of a plate of meticulously arranged hors d'oeuvres fills the screen. One woman is wearing the same dress as Roberta; another is looking to meet a doctor. The full extent of Roberta's limited domestic horizons becomes apparent when her boorish husband calls a halt to this merriment so everyone can watch him in a television commercial for his bathroom spa business.

As an obviously bored Roberta walks out on to the balcony, the last line of the commercial can be heard in the background: "Come to Gary's Oasis, where all your fantasies can come true." A subjective point-of-view shot provides a stunning glimpse at the George Washington Bridge linking New Jersey and New York. As Roberta looks out at the bridge's lighted spires, the sound track goes up-tempo, and the scene shifts to a bus arriving in Manhattan. It carries Susan and the purloined earrings. Soon Roberta herself will bus across the bridge to meet Susan and begin an adventurous (albeit highly improbable) new life involving amnesia, identity switching, and a murder mystery.

Visual Effects

Most moviemaking entails at least some **visual effects,** which, in the argot of industry, are different from special effects. In general, the latter are generated during principal photography, with eyeglasses exploding, cars crashing, and water gushing. Visual effects, in contrast, come alive in the relative calm and economy of postproduction, with **glass shots,** miniatures, stop-motion animation, optical printers, and computer-generated imagery (CGI). (In actual practice, the phases of production are not nearly as distinct as this division might imply.) When a scene is too risky or too costly, the visual effects specialists often come to the rescue by working their own brand of movie magic.

Visual effects are as old as the movie industry itself, although early on they were created "in-camera" rather than in a laboratory. One of the more basic types of effects involved the use of **matte shots,** in which a portion of the frame is matted or blanked out and another picture substituted for that part of the frame. Early filmmakers were able to create matte shots in-camera by covering part of the lens with a mask while filming or by placing a sheet of glass with a blacked-out area between the camera and the scene to prevent a portion of the film from being exposed. The camera operator then rewound the film, and shot again with the mask removed and the previously exposed area covered, thus combining two images in one shot.

As early as 1903, Edwin S. Porter used in-camera matte photography for *The Great Train Robbery,* shooting with the same piece of film twice—once with the first matte and then with the second that obscured the area covered by the first. For example, when bandits break into a train car, moving images can be seen through its open sliding side door. To achieve the impression of a moving train, Porter first photographed the background scenery with a partially masked lens so that the surrounding area was left unexposed on the film. He then rewound the film in the camera, masked the portion already exposed, and shot the action on the mock train car set.

The photographic technology of the **optical printer** revolutionized visual effects in the 1920s. This device consisted of a camera and a projector running in sync with lenses facing each other. Two or more pieces of film, each showing different picture elements, were run through the projector side of the printer. The camera side filmed these layered elements as a single, **composite** image. (In the 1990s, digital composites became commonplace. Multiple film images are scanned into the computer, combined digitally, and then transferred to a single piece of film.) Throughout the decade, the techniques for melding separate images became increasingly more intricate and inventive.

Animated Models

Faster-speed film, improved lights and lenses, and more versatile cameras enabled ever greater technical sophistication. The sophistication visual effects had achieved by the early 1930s is evident in Willis O'Brien's work for *King Kong* (1933), codirected by former expeditionary filmmakers Merian C. Cooper and Ernest B. Schoedsack. A pioneer in the field of animation, O'Brien had first used animated three-dimensional models to represent prehistoric life in the 1917 production of *The Dinosaur and the Missing Link.* That film had a running time of five minutes and took almost two months to complete. The "missing link" was an apelike creature that proved to be the prototype of O'Brien's most famous creation, the mighty Kong—an eighteen-inch-high model that became the eighth wonder of the world.

Marcel Delgado, who had worked with O'Brien on *The Lost World* (1925), one of the first features to use animated models, constructed all the figures used in the tabletop animation for *King Kong.* For the 6 eighteen-inch models of Kong, each of which weighed almost ten pounds, Delgado used a metal skeleton with ball-and-socket joints, which he padded with foam rubber and cotton and covered with pruned rabbit skins to simulate fur. Some of the models of the prehistoric animals, which averaged $2\frac{1}{2}$ to 3 feet in length, were fitted with rubber bladders to give them a realistic-looking breathing effect. Appropriately scaled models of the human performers were also made. And a full-sized foot, hand, and bust of Kong were built for close-up shots. The bust had a face $6\frac{1}{2}$ feet wide, ears a foot long, and a chest some 36 feet across.

Three men huddled inside to operate the eighty-six motors powering the facial and head movements. A series of levers enabled the men to operate the eyes, mouth, lips, nose, ears, and even the eyebrows, all of which were activated by compressed air. These facial components were molded and manipulated to create the illusion of personality and psychological depth.

A painstaking process known as **stop-motion animation** was used to bring the models of Kong and the other prehistoric creatures to cinematic life. They were photographed exposing only one-sixteenth of a foot of film at a time. After each slight movement, the camera was stopped and the models repositioned. When the processed film was projected in sequence, the inanimate models gave the illusion of being alive. Although the models are generally kept in proper perspective, Kong appears to be about 18 feet tall in his Jurassic jungle habitat and 24 feet tall when he runs amok through Manhattan, peering into apartment windows, hurling automobiles, and disrupting mass transit.

Several of the animation sequences entail quite complex interactions. The brutal fight between Kong and a tyrannosaur, lasting nearly three minutes, contains thirty-one cuts and involved several camera setups. Cooper directed the scene by showing the two animators some holds and moves he knew from his boxing and wrestling experiences. After throwing a few punches at his taller opponent's large head, Kong tries to topple the small-limbed creature by grasping its leg, and the two somersault together. The giant ape finally emerges victorious after jumping onto the dinosaur's back and cracking its jaw.

Projection Systems

The live actors in *King Kong* were combined with the animated models through the use of matte shots and **rear projection.** The latter technique (also called back projection) generally entails staging action in front of a translucent screen behind which a filmed background is projected. The camera then records the combined image of the foreground and background. For example, previously photographed images of the animated struggle between Kong and tyrannosaur models were projected behind female lead Fay Wray as she sat perched in a full-sized tree. As Kong appears to bump against the tree, it topples to the ground, seemingly pinning her beneath its trunk (Figure 3.2.).

For some scenes, O'Brien and his technical team used a tiny rear projection screen (made of surgical rubber sheeting) built right into a miniature set. There is, for example, a skillfully executed scene in which the Kong model seemingly reaches over the edge of a cliff to grope for male lead Bruce Cabot, who is hiding in the hollow of a cave below. The actor was actually filmed earlier in a full-sized cave set, and the images were then projected from the rear onto a small screen just beyond the opening of the cave on the miniature set.

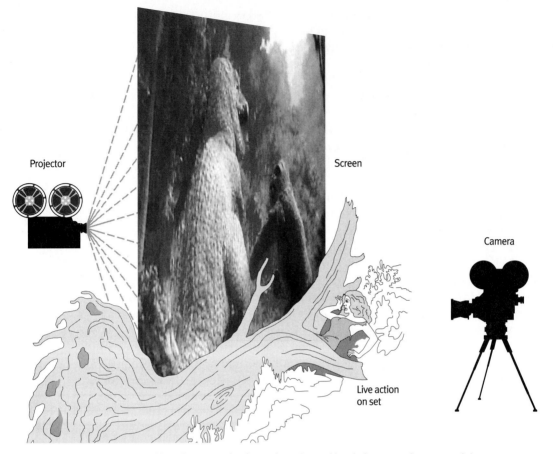

Projector

Screen

Camera

Live action
on set

FIGURE 3.2 Full-scale rear projection. The animated battle between the two models was projected behind Fray Wray, who cowers in the lower right-hand corner. (*King Kong* [1933])

As each frame of Kong's actions was photographed, the film of the actor was
moved ahead one frame, giving the illusion of a normal-sized man trying to
avoid being grabbed by a huge ape (Figure 3.3.). (A close-up of the actor inter-
acting with the large mechanical hand was integrated into the scene so that
the ape appears to reach behind him.)

In a similarly created scene, Kong seems to remove some of Fay Wray's
clothes, intimating an interspecies sexual violation. Appearing to hold her in
his huge paw, he slowly peels off the flimsy garments. (Composer Max
Steiner's enigmatic four-note musical motif, played on a solo violin with
strings backing, subtly suggests the oversized simian's perplexity and en-
thrallment as he inquisitively sniffs his fingers after touching her.) To achieve
this effect, she was filmed alone in the constructed hand, with hidden draw-
strings used to pull off some of her clothes. This footage was then projected

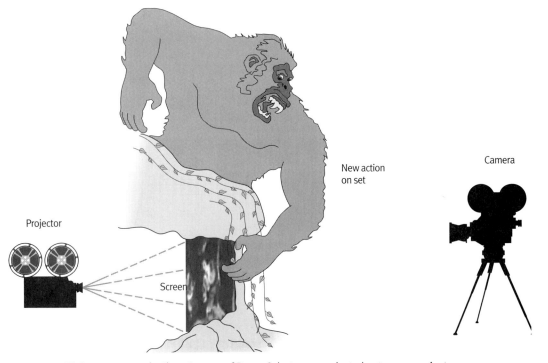

FIGURE 3.3 Miniature rear projection. Images of Bruce Cabot were projected onto a screen just inside the cave on the set. The film of the actor was advanced as the Kong model was shot. (*King Kong* [1933])

on a tiny rear projection screen one frame at a time, and the Kong model's motions in front were animated to correspond with the partial disrobing. This short scene alone is said to have taken twenty-three hours to film. The entire movie took over a year to make.

Earlier movies employed full-scale rear projection, but it did not become a well-established process until the making of *King Kong*. The very first rear projection screens were made of sandblasted glass. The part of the image near the center of these fragile screens, which exposed actors and crew to peril from breakage, photographed brighter than the parts around the edges. The flexible, cellulose screen used for the full-scale rear projection in *King Kong* reduced this "hot spot" by 50 percent while providing better white highlights and more intense blacks. (Sidney Saunders, who invented the new screen, received a special award from the Academy of Motion Picture Arts and Sciences.) Around the same time, the redesign of the optics of rear projectors made satisfactory projection possible on large screen surfaces.

Throughout the 1930s and 1940s, full-scale rear projection was commonly used to give the effect of characters riding in a car, train, or other moving vehicle. The scene in *Casablanca* in which Rick and Ilsa drive out of Paris

Humphrey Bogart and Ingrid Bergman were actually sitting in a mock-up convertible on a sound-stage. (*Casablanca* [1942])

into the countryside was created using this process. The two actors were photographed sitting in a mock-up convertible while a receding landscape was projected behind them (the background dissolves into another scene while the car and its occupants remain in focus).

Rear projection was also used in the scene on the terrace in which Captain Renault (Claude Rains) attempts to probe Rick's past but makes little progress. (How did Rick end up in Casablanca? He came for the waters. "Waters? What waters?" asks the puzzled captain. "We are in the desert." Rick responds wryly, "I was misinformed.") The airplane ascending in the background appears as if it is going to scrape their heads because this technique produced a rather shallow, flat-looking image.

In the 1960s, when color virtually replaced black-and-white photography, rear projection fell into disuse. Shooting in color requires a greater amount of light on the subject, which tends to wash out the rear-projected image. It also makes it more difficult to match the foreground and background because a color image provides greater visual detail than a monochrome one.

A system of **front projection** that produces a brighter projected image and a greater sense of depth was perfected for director Stanley Kubrick's *2001: A Space Odyssey* (1968). Utilizing a highly reflective screen against which live action is filmed, it requires a more complicated setup of camera and projector than its predecessor. An image from a slide or movie projector is transmitted to this screen using a half-silvered mirror set at a forty-five-degree angle in front of the camera so that the actors and objects in the foreground cast no visible shadows on the projected background. The overall lighting is adjusted so that it is just bright enough to wash out traces of the transmitted image that unavoidably fall on the actors and set.

Today the preferred method for melding foreground action with a background scene shot elsewhere involves something called **blue-screen photography.** Replacing front projection when color film began to dominate the industry, this difficult and exacting process entails filming live action against a background of deep blue (or sometimes green). Deep blue works best for most production situations because it can be easily blocked out without doing damage to the color composition of the images. The moving outline of the action is then removed from the film of the desired background in laboratory printing (a process that often involves use of digital imaging systems). After additional lab work, these images of the live action are printed back into the constantly shifting blank area that was created in the background footage. The flight of mild-mannered Clark Kent's (Christopher Reeve) alter ego through the steel-and-glass canyons of Metropolis in *Superman* (1978) was created in this manner.

Scaled-Down Sets

The use of **miniatures**—small-scale models used to simulate buildings, vehicles, creatures, and so on—has long been integral to the creation of visual effects. The Roman epic *Ben-Hur, a Tale of Christ* (1925), with its fierce chariot race, marked a breakthrough in the use of scaled-down sets in ways that make them appear normal sized. Only the lower part of the Antioch Coliseum replica, where the charioteers fly around the track at breakneck speeds, was built to scale; the upper tiers, including thousands of tiny figures to simulate spectators, were done in miniature and suspended in front of the camera.

To provide the appropriate environment for the animated models in *King Kong*, technicians constructed lavish and intricate miniature sets on tabletops. The use of glass paintings as many as three levels deep, with the miniature sets between the panes, created the illusion of depth. The ghostly mansion glimpsed above a crested iron gate in the opening of *Citizen Kane* was similarly created through a series of paintings that were combined with three-dimensional miniatures in the foreground. (Bernard Herrmann's score greatly enhances the use of this technique. Underneath the images, he quotes Rachmaninoff's "Isle of the Dead," a funereal tone poem inspired by Arnold Bocklin's once-famous painting of the same title.)

Scaled-down sets are a practical way to pull off the kinds of explosions that seem particularly prevalent in recent summer releases. The widespread

The partial coliseum replica for *Ben-Hur* (1925) was constructed in Culver City, California, at a cost of $300,000. In addition to the simulated spectators, some 3300 extras filled the seats of the mammoth set as forty-two strategically placed cameras filmed the race. Special camera-equipped cars sped before the twelve chariots drawn by forty-eight horses as they careened around the track. A pit dug into the ground permitted a camera operator to photograph the chariots thundering over him.

destruction that takes place in *Independence Day* (1996) required scores of intricately constructed miniatures. The production's model-making team, led by Michael Joyce, had to replicate such landmarks as the Statue of Liberty, the Empire State Building, the White House, the Capitol Building, the Washington Monument, and the Lincoln Memorial—all of which were eventually blown to bits. Joyce and his team also built model interior sets for close-up shots of the various settings during the demolition. These included such details as miniature chairs, desks, computers, telephones, and even coffeemakers. A special remote-controlled camera, swathed in flame-retardant material, captured the explosions.

Digital Dazzle

Visual effects are becoming ever more stunning through the application of digital technology that turns cinematic material of all kinds into the zeros and ones of computer language. The capabilities of the computer—the juggler at the heart of the digital revolution—and **computer-generated imagery**

Jim Carrey in a computer-generated image from *The Mask* (1994). The visual effects in movies such as this mark a new era and threshold of visual-effects achievement.

(also called computer graphics, computer animation, and digital animation) make it possible for moviemakers to create and control film images in ways ranging from the mundane to the miraculous.

Computer manipulation can eliminate scratches, remove objects, correct continuity errors, and even create wholly fabricated characters and settings. Many of the complex, visually striking images in *Titanic* (1997) were conceived with a computer. The digitized water looks like real water, and the computer-generated figures look like actual human beings falling to their deaths from the severed ship's nearly vertical stern. The vast ocean in *The Perfect Storm* (2000), with its sweeping waves and swirling cloud cover, is a computer creation as well.

Computer mavens are constantly pushing the parameters of digital expression with software that can re-create anything from the crest of a huge sea wave to some vanished historical epoch. All sorts of things that never were can likewise be imagined on a computer. Through a complicated process called **morphing** (a term adapted from the word *metamorphosis*), the shape and general appearance of images can be altered at will by scanning filmed frames into a computer and manipulating the individual picture units—called **pixels** in computer parlance. First used in the fantasy-adventure *Willow* (1988) and the underwater saga *The Abyss* (1989), morphing was significantly refined in *Terminator 2: Judgment Day* (1991), in which a cyborg from the future constantly changes shape. In the course of the movie, he changes from a patch of linoleum floor into a prison guard, grows a sword out of his arm, and even turns from a policeman into a housewife.

Morphing makes possible all sorts of effects with live actors that were previously impossible. Achieving some of the more bizarre images in *The Mask* (1994) required building a wire frame model of bulging eyes and tongue in a computer; adding light, color, and texture; animating the model; and then electronically blending it with the live-action image of Jim Carrey. In this way, the comedic actor's already elastic face and body were stretched in every conceivable direction, creating stunning visual images inspired by the manic 1940s cartoons of Tex Avery.

Many of the most talked-about visual effects in *Forrest Gump* (1994) were created by computer as well. For the scene in which the title character (played by Tom Hanks) meets with John F. Kennedy, filmed images of Hanks shot against a deep blue screen were digitized and combined with archival footage of the long-dead president. Kennedy's amused response to the fictional Gump was accomplished by manipulating the brightness of the pixels around the president's lips so that he appears to be mouthing the words created by a contemporary screenwriter.

Sound Editing

A movie is edited in two stages. After a rough cut is completed, the sound experts take over. Their job is to create a vivid, consistent, convincing sound environment. To accomplish this, they break down the rough sound track, separating out the sounds so that they can be re-recorded later to smooth differences in sound quality. Getting just the right sound can be as exacting a task as getting just the right image. Ordinarily, every element of sound is assessed, and if it doesn't "ring right," it is modified or replaced.

Dialogue and Voice-Over Narration

The various sound elements can be divided into three broad categories: speech, ambient noise, and music. The two basic types of speech in movies are dialogue and **voice-over narration.** Even though dialogue (all the spoken language in a scene) is recorded on the set, it may later be replaced—or looped—by the automatic dialogue replacement or **ADR editor.** The actors are brought in to re-record their lines. Microphones are set up in front of a large screen, and the movie is cut so actors see only that portion they have to work on. This usually involves one or two lines at a time. The lines to be replaced are played back so that the actors can get an idea of the rhythm.

Looping replaces dialogue marred by such things as on-set noise, previously undetected flubs, and inappropriate inflections. It is also used when directors are not satisfied with a particular line reading and want another interpretation. The director may even want a different voice entirely—a proce-dure called **revoicing**—in which case all of an actor's lines will be redone. If the craggy, worn voices of the fresh-faced flyboys in the black-and-white pro-logue of *Space Cowboys* (2000) have an uncanny familiarity, it is probably be-cause they belong to the movie's aged stars James Garner, Donald Sutherland, Tommy Lee Jones, and—perhaps most recognizably—Clint Eastwood, who also directed.

Because so many movies nowadays are shot on location, looping has be-come a major part of production. Cars honking, a plane flying overhead, a city bus backfiring—all conspire to muffle lines. The ADR editor also loops alternative lines of dialogue to eliminate language that would not be permit-ted on broadcast television, where the movie will eventually be shown. Any-where from 40 to 90 percent of the dialogue of a movie may be looped.

The second type of speech found in movies, voice-over narration, can be from an anonymous source or a character in the story. Such narration, which is generally limited to information not supplied directly in the action or dia-logue, may stress a particular viewpoint or provide impartial commentary. The opening sequence of *Casablanca*, for example, employs anonymous voice-over narration to establish the general time, place, and political milieu in which the dramatic action will unfold. As long lines of the displaced trudge wearily along, superimposed on a revolving globe, a doom-laden voice ex-plains that, as a result of World War II, refugees are streaming from all cor-ners of Europe toward the freedom of the New World via a circuitous route that takes them through the port city of Casablanca in French Morocco. Lou Marcelle, a local radio announcer, intoned the weighty narration: "With the coming of the Second World War, many eyes in imprisoned Europe turned hopefully or desperately toward the freedom of the Americas." It was done after editor Owen Marks had assembled a rough cut of the picture.

Ambient Noise

A seemingly immutable rule of sound recording is that clearly captured voices usually result in poorly recorded background sounds. As a consequence, much of the barely audible ambient noise of a locale picked up during shoot-ing is replaced with **sound effects.** Whole sound settings are created, layer by layer. Ambient or atmospheric sounds can be provided by special libraries of sound clips or created in a sound studio. Some facilities use computer-based audio to create specific sound effects from "digital samplers"—recordings of various sounds that can be changed to something else. Sound characteristics like pitch, volume, and timbre can be electronically manipulated in myriad ways, so that a door slamming becomes an explosion, or birds chirping be-come a scream of terror.

Sound effects may also be produced in a specially equipped studio called a Foley room (named after Jack Foley, a pioneer in postproduction sound).

VOICE-OVER IN *DOUBLE INDEMNITY*

Character voice-overs are commonly employed in those movies labeled *film noir*. In such pictures as *Double Indemnity* (1944), *Murder My Sweet* (1944), *The Postman Always Rings Twice* (1946), *Dead Reckoning* (1947), and *Out of the Past* (1947), voice-over narration is intrinsic to setting the mood and providing an interpretation of the dramatic events. The periodic voice-overs of the central male character in *Double Indemnity* (directed by Billy Wilder from a script he co-wrote with Raymond Chandler) are effectively combined with his within-scene commentary to provide a verbal account of his thought processes and reactions to events.

The movie begins in the early hours of morning with a sporty little 1938 Dodge Coupe driving erratically along dark, rain-soaked city streets. After running a red light and barely avoiding a collision with a newspaper delivery truck, it lurches to a halt in front of an office building. A shadowy figure, soon revealed to be Walter Neff (Fred MacMurray), staggers out and makes his way into the building. The night guard and the elevator operator greet him. Taking the elevator to the twelfth floor, he haltingly moves along the corridor to his office.

Once settled at his desk, lamp and Dictaphone switched on and cigarette lit, he begins a wry and weary explanation of his current circumstance in the form of an interoffice memo. It is addressed to a close colleague, Barton Keyes (Edward G. Robinson), the canny head of the claims department at the insurance company where he works as a salesman. When he starts telling his story, he says flatly: "I suppose you'll call this a confession when you hear it. Well, I don't like the word 'confession.' I just want to set you right about something you couldn't see . . ." But he also seems to be talking to himself in a soliloquy of sorts, perhaps trying to make sense of why he murdered a client and how he got caught up in a web of sexual duplicity. "I killed him for money—and for a woman," he laments. "I didn't get the money, and I didn't get the woman. It all started . . ."

As the events unfold in flashback, with periodic voice-over narration, it is revealed that a seductive and ruthless housewife named Phyllis Dietrichson (Barbara Stanwyck) beguiled him. His sexual interest was aroused when, on a routine house call concerning an automobile insurance renewal, he first glimpsed her at the top of the stairs, clad in nothing but a towel, and they engaged in a sexually suggestive verbal exchange. ("I'd hate to think of you getting a smashed fender or something while you're

A **Foley artist** can create all sorts of sound simulations—footsteps approaching, doors closing, guns firing, glass breaking, clothes rustling, wind blowing through the trees, and so on. These effects are often produced by ingenious means, such as rattling a piece of sheet metal to simulate the sound of a thunderstorm. Many dubbing studios have removable floor panels above different kinds of surfaces (gravel, dirt, wood, concrete), which produce various sounds of footsteps when walked on. Personnel called Foley walkers watch the movie being projected onto a large screen and perform the actions needed to provide synchronous sound for the movement of the actors.

The function of sound effects is primarily to lend mood and feeling to a scene. They can also be used in subtle ways to heighten tension. In *The God-*

not, uh, fully covered," he says, looking her up and down. "I know what you mean," she retorts. "I've been sunbathing.")

While he's waiting for her to dress and descend, we hear his voice-over comments about the Spanish-style villa's cheerless interior. They function to reinforce and complement the mood and meaning generated by the *mise-en-scène*. "The living room was still stuffy from last night's cigars," he notes. "The windows were closed, and the sunshine coming in through the Venetian blinds showed up the dust in the air." (The dusty effect was the work of cinematographer John Seitz, who used finely ground aluminum fillings to reflect the shafts of waning sunlight entering through the blinds.) His reference to the lingering cigar smell subtly hints at the suffocating relationship the brassy blond Phyllis has with her boorish husband (Tom Powers), initially revealed in a framed photograph next to one of his daughter (Jean Heather) from his first marriage. The notable absence of any photographs of the current Mrs. Dietrichson provides another indication of familial disharmony.

After Phyllis put on some clothes, still buttoning the front of her dress as she descended the stairs, the two continued to engage in flirtatious double entendres.

In a voice-over, Walter Neff (Fred MacMurray) questions "How could I know that murder can sometimes smell like honeysuckle?" (*Double Indemnity* [1944])

When he expressed a sudden disinterest in meeting her husband, she cautioned him that because he was going well over the state's speed limit she might have to whack him over the knuckles. In the course of their erotic sparring, she tentatively broached the topic of accident insurance. In a voice-over, as we see him driving back to the office, he recalls that the smell of honeysuckle permeated the street near her house and suggests that because of his infatuation he failed to grasp the significance of her interest in this kind of coverage. "How could I know," he asks rhetorically, "that murder can sometimes smell like honeysuckle? Maybe you would have known, Keyes, the minute she mentioned accident insurance. But I didn't. I felt like a million."

father, for instance, three claps of thunder intensify Michael Corleone's confrontation with the police after he averts an attack on his hospitalized father. The first occurs as police officers grab Michael, the second when the corrupt police captain approaches him, and the third as the camera captures the captain's reaction after punching Michael in the face.

The heightened tension and horror of *Psycho*'s famous shower scene owes much to the judicious integration of images and sound effects. Actual shooting of the scene took about seven days. After the rough assembly of the movie was completed by veteran editor George Tomasini, composer Bernard Herrmann persuaded director Alfred Hitchcock to add screeching violins and slash-and-chop string chords to the sound track.

The scene begins with Marion Crane (Janet Leigh) slipping out of her robe and stepping into the shower. We hear her unwrapping the soap and turning on the water. There's a brief shot of the spray from the showerhead. The camera then lingers on her as she offers herself up to the water, closing her eyes and stretching out her long neck. Through the translucent curtain, we see the bathroom door open and a silhouetted figure enter. The curtain is pulled aside, revealing what appears to be a woman wielding an enormous knife.

Suddenly, the scene erupts into violence. The knife plunges down, violin strings shriek, and we see some twenty-eight separate images in the next twenty-two seconds as the attacker continues to slash at Marion. Shots of the knife rising and falling are intercut with images of her screaming lips, flailing arms, and twisting torso. An overhead view shows her trying to turn away from her attacker as she shields her breasts. Slashing sounds and birdlike cries serve to intensify the mood. The savagery seems out of all proportion to everything that has gone before. Except for a fleeting instance in which the knife touches her skin, however, the brutal attack is not actually graphically depicted. We create the violence in our heads from the fragmented images and shrieking violins.

After the attacker flees and Marion is losing consciousness, the shrieking violins stop and bass strings are heard. Sliding down the wall of the shower, she grabs hold of the curtain. The music slows and ceases, leaving only the patter of the water. As the curtain hooks snap in succession, she pitches forward onto the floor. The camera then follows her blood as it is washed away by the water, moving in for a tight close-up of the drain. The image of water mixed with blood spiraling down the drain dissolves into a tight close-up of her lifeless-looking eye.

Musical Score

Music is an essential part of most movies. The **musical composer** usually comes into the moviemaking process in the late stages of editing. In consultation with the director and others, the composer compiles cue sheets that list directly where music will go and how long it will run. The composer writes the **score** but usually does not orchestrate it personally. Music can serve any number of purposes. It often accompanies the opening titles and credits to help set the tone for what will follow. *Psycho*'s titles and credits are superimposed over an abstract pattern of intersecting horizontal and vertical lines, set against a musical backdrop of pulsing, frantic violin sounds.

The atmosphere of most movies owes much to the music. At the beginning of a scene, it can establish mood or suggest something about what is taking place. It often plays over the establishing shot of a scene and is faded down as dialogue begins. Within scenes, it can substitute for dialogue and contribute to a sense of continuity. Between scenes, it can act as a bridge.

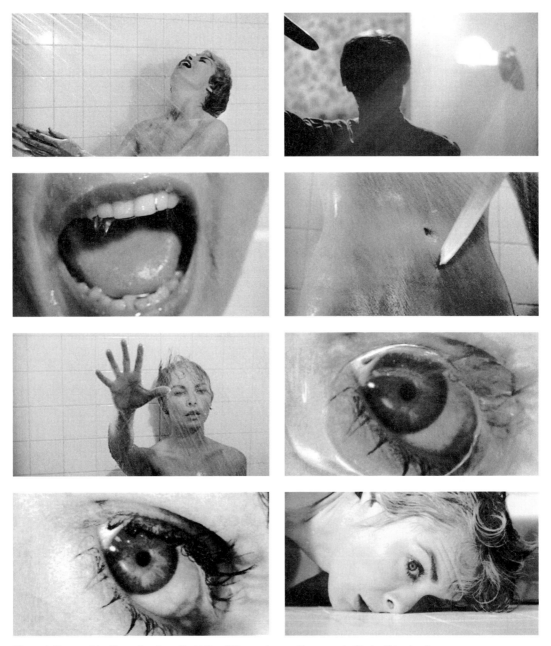

Through the combination of well-crafted bits of film and evocative sound effects, this simple
scene, in which a woman takes a shower, is stabbed, and slumps down the side of the tub,
is transformed into a visual and aural montage of seemingly savage, almost visceral violence.
(*Psycho* [1960])

When played over the closing credits, it can sustain the mood of the final scene or recapture an earlier emotional quality.

Depending on the desired effect, music can be used to either reinforce the overall mood of a scene or contrast with it. When West Indian Archie (Delroy Lindo) and his henchmen come to abduct and murder the title character (Denzel Washington) in the nightclub scene in *Malcolm X* (1992), ousting him from his table while Billie Holiday (Miki Howard) performs "Big Stuff," Malcolm wants to wait until she finishes singing before departing with them. Though he is hustled out before the song ends, her voice lingers ironically on the sound track as he frantically flees from his would-be killers.

To a large degree, music helps determine the extent of our involvement in any movie and can often evoke strong emotional responses. Musical composer Max Steiner used "As Time Goes By," written in 1931 by Herman Hupfeld, as the centerpiece of *Casablanca's* complicated score. From the time Ilsa presses Sam to play the song ("Play it once for old time's sake. . . . Play it, Sam. Play 'As Time Goes By'"), it is a pervasive presence in the movie, presaging events, heightening emotion, and fusing past and present. Steiner greatly enlarged and enriched the song, using it to convey a wide range of feelings. As Rick sits in his darkened nightclub hunched over a glass and half-empty bottle of whiskey, the song becomes idyllic and ethereal, setting the mood for the flashback to Paris depicting Rick and Ilsa's romantic interlude. There, as the couple talks about the Germans marching into Paris, the tone of the song turns dark and ominous. The musical strains suggest bittersweet resignation when the scene shifts back to the present. As Rick says goodbye to Ilsa at the airport in the movie's climactic scene, the tone is transformed emotionally from one of sweetness and nostalgia to one of sorrow and loss. It then takes on elements of tragedy as Ilsa turns her back and walks off with her husband toward the plane that will take her away from Rick forever.

Steiner's score for *Casablanca* is an intricate weave of several musical strands. The French national anthem, the "Marseillaise," is used almost as much as "As Time Goes By" and similarly serves to underscore the mood of the story. Throughout the movie, the composer creates a musical duel of sorts between the "Marseillaise" (named in 1792 for soldiers from Marseilles who sang it on their march to defend Paris against the Prussians) and both "Deutschland Uber Alles" ("Germany Above All Things") and "Wacht am Rhein" ("Watch on the Rhine"). The latter piece was written in 1840 when France was threatening to annex part of the Rhineland. It had been popular in Germany ever since the Franco-Prussian War of 1870.

Near the beginning of the movie, the ominous strains of the German national anthem can be heard faintly as a police official intones over the radio that German couriers carrying important official documents have been murdered and orders the roundup of all suspicious characters. A suspect fleeing the police is shot down before a poster of Marshall Philippe Petain, dictator-

Nazi fraternizer Yvonne (Madeleine LeBeau), her voice heard above the rest of the singing, is overcome with patriotic feelings. (*Casablanca* [1942])

ial leader of Vichy France. As police pry papers bearing the Cross of Lorraine (symbol of the Free French Organization, headed by General Charles de Gaulle) from the dead suspect's hand, the "Marseillaise" begins to play on the sound track. The sad-sounding anthem soon fades as other suspects are herded into the station house, which bears the tarnished motto "*Liberté, Egalité, Fraternité.*" In the film's finale, "Deutschland Uber Alles" subtly shifts into the French national anthem as the fatally shot Major Strasser (Conrad Veidt) falls to the floor of the airport hangar. A triumphant-sounding "Marseillaise" accompanies Rick Blaine and Louis Renault (Claude Rains) as they head for the Free French garrison in Brazzaville.

Even the most cynical moviegoer is likely to have moist eyes during the scene in *Casablanca* in which the bellicose lyrics of the "Marseillaise" are sung (the stirring orchestral arrangement and choral singing serve to conceal the bloodthirsty sentiments). At the cafe and gambling house where much of the action takes place, a group of Nazis gathers around a piano to sing a rousing rendition of "Wacht am Rhein." (In actuality, this song had fallen out of favor with the Nazi party, but a German publisher controlled the copyright for its "Horst Wessel" anthem.) Hearing the hated song, fugitive Resistance leader Victor Laszlo (Paul Henreid) directs the band to play the "Marseillaise."

As Rick nods approval, most of the cafe's patrons take up the musical call to arms and join in the harmonic fray. Camera close-ups capture tears streaming down the cheeks of patriots and erstwhile collaborators alike as they sing about drenching French fields with the "tainted blood" of foreigners ("*Qu'un sang impur abreuve nos sillons!*").

The mounting exhilaration of the patrons soon overwhelms the Nazis, who subside into glum silence. When the anthem ends to loud applause, an outraged Major Strasser orders the Vichy Prefect of Police Captain Louis Renault to close down the cafe under any pretext. The intense musical interlude concludes on a note of levity. "I'm shocked," cries the charmingly corrupt French official, "shocked to find gambling is going on in here!" As he's ordering everyone out, a croupier hands him his winnings.

Music helps to set the pace of the action, communicates mood, serves as a substitute for dialogue, sustains tension, and gives a sense of dramatic continuity. The musical score of *Bonnie and Clyde* often contributes to a comic as well as nostalgic effect. In the movie's opening, grainy, sepia-toned snapshots of the pair are accompanied by the sounds of hand-cranked phonographic music from the 1930s (Rudy Vallee singing "Deep Night"). Soon after the title characters first meet, they walk along the street talking like sophomoric kids, Clyde (Warren Beatty) bragging that he once hacked off two toes to get off a work detail in state prison. He shows Bonnie (Faye Dunaway) a large handgun, which he holds over his crotch (we soon learn his bravado compensates for sexual impotence). After hesitatingly stroking the barrel in a manner that suggests repressed excitement, she dares him in a sexually loaded line: "But you wouldn't have the gumption to use it." He then robs a grocery store with the weapon to impress her.

As they zoom down the road in a stolen car, their errant actions are undercut by the strains of banjo bluegrass music on the sound track (Lester Flatt and Earl Scruggs playing "Foggy Mountain Breakdown"). When they ineptly stick up a bank that "failed three weeks ago" and is devoid of funds, an embarrassed Clyde has the bank teller explain to Bonnie that there is no money. She finds the situation hilarious and laughs loudly as they speed off to the tune of a jaunty, honky-tonk banjo song ("We got a dollar ninety-eight and you're laughin'"). The musical score often supports tone and attitude, but sometimes it works against them as the scenes shift unexpectedly from slapstick to brutal violence to intense lyricism.

The infinite flexibility and variability of music allows for the evocation of a wide range of moods and feelings. Veteran composer Nino Rota used both original material and excerpts from a score he wrote for an Italian production to create *The Godfather*'s hauntingly evocative musical score. From the movie's opening "Godfather Waltz," performed on a single trumpet, to the richly orchestrated arrangement accompanying the closing credits, the score is interlaced with intricate melodies and passages associated with different moods and characters.

The jaunty music of the wedding sequence and the nostalgic waltz to which Don Corleone and his wife dance (both composed by Carmine Coppola, the director's father) stand in sharp contrast to the edgy piano chords that heighten tension in several scenes. A short eleven-note piece for flute, piano, and clarinet serves as the musical motif for Michael's rise to power in the Corleone family. Early in the baptism sequence, a solo organ modulates through a series of major chords. As scenes showing preparations for the killings are intermingled with ones showing the sacred service, the tone becomes slightly more ominous through the modulation to a minor chord. The sounds of the organ gradually metamorphose into the passacaglia from Johann Sebastian Bach's Passacaglia and Fugue in G Minor, a rather morose work that sets the mood for the multiple murders that follow.

Film scholars conventionally use the term *diegesis* (pronounced dia-GEE-sis), the ancient Greek word for "recounted story," to refer to everything that belongs to the fictional world of the movie—that nonexistent place that is fabricated out of temporal and spatial fragments. This term is frequently applied in its adjective form, diegetic (pronounced dia-JET-ik). Characters, action, and dialogue are diegetic, whereas music, voice-overs, and other such devices are often nondiegetic. At various times, the music in *The Godfather* has a diegetic source, such as the band accompanying Johnny Fontaine (Al Martino) as he sings "I Have But One Heart" at a wedding. At other times, the songs are nondiegetic, having no apparent source within a scene.

Nothing is inherently diegetic or nondiegetic. Music is diegetic if played by a character but nondiegetic if performed off-screen, separate from the storyline. On several occasions, the music in *The Godfather* shifts seamlessly from a nondiegetic to a diegetic source. Not from any apparent in-scene source, "Have Yourself a Merry Little Christmas" is used to help establish the setting in front of a department store when Michael and Kay (Diane Keaton) are shopping. When the scene shifts to Luca Brasi (Lenny Montana) putting on his bullet-proof vest, the source of the song becomes diegetic, playing scratchily on the radio in his apartment.

The scene in *Pulp Fiction* (1994) in which boxer Butch Coolidge (Bruce Willis) agrees that his "ass goes down" in the fifth round of an upcoming fight is anchored by Al Green's "Let's Stay Together" playing on the sound track. The music is nondiegetically cued in with the title card "Vincent Vega and Marsellus Wallace's Wife" and provides a placid underlay for mobster Marsellus's (Ving Rhames) intimidating monologue informing the aging pugilist that his boxing days are almost over. It is not until a cut to the bartender opening the door that the music's shift to diegetic status becomes evident. When he steps outside to greet Jules (Samuel L. Jackson) and Vincent (John Travolta), the ambient sound diminishes. As they enter the nightclub, the volume increases, suggesting that the source of the music is somewhere inside.

Assembling the Movie

The **supervising sound editor** oversees such matters as the dubbing of dialogue and the placement of music. Additional "editors" participating in this process may include, among others, the dialogue editor, sound effects editor, music editor, music editorial consultant, assistant editor, and apprentice editor. Building up layers of sounds on separate tracks, each of which is carefully synchronized to specific frames of the movie, creates the overall composition and structure of the sound track. The actual number of separate tracks can range from only a few to thirty or forty.

The **sound mixer** combines the separate voice, music, and effects tracks into a single master track. When the film negative is cut in accordance with the final print, this master sound track is synchronized with it. The **color timer** adjusts the final print, working closely with the director of photography to ensure that the look and mood of the movie are consistent with the director's intentions from shot to shot. Image contrast, density, and color balance are among the variables adjusted. The **negative cutter** matches the actual camera negative with the cut of the film provided by the editor, who assembles a temporary work print that's usually full of scratches and splices. A positive print is then struck from this negative and is used to make a handful of negative prints. Hundreds of positive prints are made from these negatives for distribution to theatres.

The Way of Frescoes

The digital wizardry of the computer is increasingly being used in the editing process. Camera takes are scanned into a computer, where they can be selected, arranged, trimmed, and joined together more easily than when working with film. Once transformed into digital data, film footage may also be more readily integrated with music, special sound effects, and digital creations like the aquatic cities in *Star Wars Episode I: The Phantom Menace* (1999). Only about 5 percent of this movie's 130 minutes is free of digital enhancements. Real characters and digital ones, actual landscapes and imaginary places—all are seamlessly blended together. One of the unresolved problems with digital editing is that the film image is so rich in detail. To store the thousands of takes done during the typical movie project requires enormous hard disk space. Nonetheless, as surely as Anakin Skywalker points the way into the future of *Star Wars,* digital editing heralds the threshold of a new era of electronic cinema.

In some significant ways, as acclaimed sound-mix editor Walter Murch has suggested, the shift in moviemaking from celluloid to digital technology resembles the transformation in fifteenth-century European artwork from frescoes to oil colors on canvas instead of wooden panels.[5] Creating a fresco—

such as Michelangelo's famed ceiling in the Sistine Chapel—involved a painstaking process of staining fresh, moist plaster with pigments that bonded chemically with the mixture. A wide range of factors had to be controlled in this expensive collaborative endeavor, which involved extensive personnel and various interlocking technologies.

With the advent of oil colors on canvas, the artists of the Renaissance were freer to paint wherever and whenever they wished. Whereas fresco production precluded the possibility of the artist making any revisions, those working with oil on canvas could paint at will over areas they didn't like. Corrections could be made directly on the painting in the course of execution. Still-wet areas could be scraped off; if already dry, they could be painted over, completely covered by a new layer of opaque color. As a result, the process of painting became more open and flexible, and artists were no longer as dependent on teams of assistants. This gave them more control over every technical aspect of their work.

The movie industry may well be on the threshold of a breakthrough comparable to the shift from fresco to oil on canvas, one that could bring drastic changes to the entire production process. With advances in digital technology, a single person will be better able to control the disparate components of moviemaking. The digital moviemaker of the not-too-distant future will in all likelihood have the technical capacity to create and combine compelling images and sounds without the aid of myriad technicians and craftspeople while working with equipment whose speed will make traditional techniques seem archaic.

Even with the entire panoply of digital dazzle now on the horizon, the basic conventions of the Hollywood style are likely to remain largely intact. Developed over decades of trial and error, they have proved to allow considerable leeway for individual choice and invention. The historical context in which this dynamic cinematic idiom emerged and assumed global implications is the focus of the next chapter.

Notes

1. See Vsevolod Pudovkin, "On Film Technique," in *Film Technique and Film Acting: The Cinema Writings of V. I. Pudovkin,* trans. Ivor Montagu (New York: Bonanza, 1949), p. 140.
2. See, for example, V. F. Perkins, *Film as Film* (Harmondsworth, England: Penguin Books, 1972), p. 106.
3. See "The Editor with Peter Zinner," in Roy Paul Madsen, *Working Cinema: Learning from the Masters* (Belmont, CA: Wadsworth, 1990), p. 283.
4. See Barry Salt, *Film Style and Technology: History and Analysis,* 2nd ed. (London: Starwood, 1992), pp. 236–238.
5. Walter Murch, "A Digital Cinema of the Mind? Could Be," *The New York Times,* May 2, 1999, Section 2A.

PART TWO

Contexts

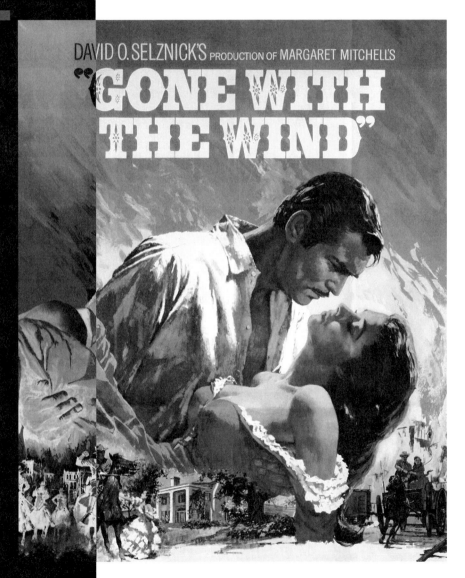

The Speechless Era

Amovie constitutes a separate reality of sorts, one full of seemingly living images. Those who reside in this alternate reality can command a great deal of our psychic energy and attention. We often become deeply involved in their fates, and their actions can affect our thoughts and feelings about everything from fashion to fascism. The factors that contributed to the creation of compelling cinematic realities prior to the advent of talkies are the concern of this chapter. The focus is on the evolution of the Hollywood style and on the emergence of Hollywood itself as one of the world's great symbol centers.

Technical Antecedents

The technical roots of moviemaking trace back to the Renaissance in fifteenth-century Europe. Around the time Johannes Gutenberg's invention of printing from movable type was causing a stir in Germany, an innovation of another sort was becoming a source of wonder in Italy. Someone had discovered that, if on a sunny day you sit in a darkened room illuminated only by the light coming through a pinhole on one wall, you see on the opposite wall an upside-down image of the outside world—a landscape, a bustling street, a passing carriage.

This visual marvel, described in Leonardo da Vinci's unpublished notes, functioned at first as a kind of amusement. Fitting a lens or molded piece of glass into the pinhole sharpened the rays of light. A group of people in a darkened room, watching the images on a wall thrown by a beam of light slicing through the darkness, must have resembled patrons in a movie theatre. Although the "moving picture" was upside down, it was far more detailed than could be achieved by drawing or painting.

By the 1600s, the lens was being put on one side of a sealed box or dark chamber—called a *camera obscura*—instead of on a wall. The use of mirrors made it possible to present the image right side up on a drawing board with paper. Soon artists were using this device to solve problems of linear perspective—the representation in a drawing or painting of parallel lines as converging in order to give the illusion of depth and distance. By tracing the image with a pen, the artist was able to create a detailed scene on a two-dimensional surface that gave the illusion of three-dimensional objects and depth relationships.

The next step was to preserve the camera image directly without the help of a tracing pencil. The darkening of certain silver compounds when exposed to light had been observed as early as the seventeenth century. But the problem of how to halt this reaction so that the image would not darken completely seemed intractable. The combination of chemical and optical principles necessary to preserve images had to await a flash of genius, as well as the social and political transformations of the late eighteenth and early nineteenth centuries that gave rise to an expanding middle class with the desire to spend money on pictures, especially family portraits. Prior to that time, only the rich had been able to afford such things.

In the late 1820s, French chemist Joseph Niépce and Parisian set designer and showman Louis Daguerre formed a working alliance to develop a method for preserving images. A few years later, Niépce died, but Daguerre, nearing a solution, carried on. By 1839, he had produced a workable system of photography, which he unabashedly called the daguerreotype. The exposure time required was about fifteen minutes, and the prints themselves were positive and therefore not reproducible. However, advances by others soon reduced the exposure time and made it possible for any number of copies to be made.

As the photographic process improved, there were simultaneous efforts in Europe and the United States to capture movement with a camera. A major technical problem was solved by an American minister, Hannibal Goodwin, who in 1887 invented a transparent and pliable celluloid (a derivative of carbohydrate cellulose) film roll that could hold a coating of chemicals sensitive to light. Advances by American entrepreneur George Eastman (later of Eastman Kodak) in the next few years led to the mass manufacture and marketing of celluloid roll film on what would soon become an international scale. (In 1913, the courts concluded that Eastman had infringed on Goodwin's patents.)

Recording Motion

By the end of the nineteenth century, almost all the technical concepts for capturing a permanent record of motion had been discovered, or were about to be discovered, somewhere in the world. The real breakthrough occurred in the West Orange, New Jersey, laboratory of inventor and entrepreneur Thomas Alva Edison, who wanted to provide a visual accessory to the phonograph he had invented in 1877. He assigned his assistant, William Kennedy Laurie Dickson, a young Scotsman who had come from London some years earlier, to the task of recording and reproducing things in motion in a way that was inexpensive, practical, and convenient.

Dickson's experiments with celluloid soon resulted in a major contribution to motion picture technology—the perforation of the filmstrip at equidistant intervals so that toothed gears could pull it smoothly past the lens of a camera. Utilizing this innovation, he devised the first camera that was effectively able to capture and record motion, for which the "wizard" Edison took full credit (his legal right as employer). Called the **Kinetograph,** this unwieldy, battery-driven machine weighed about 500 pounds and resembled an upright piano in size and shape. It was for all practical purposes immobile.

Another problem was the lack of sufficient artificial light, which didn't become available for filmmaking until about 1904. To provide illumination for filming, Edison had a new building constructed in 1893 at his plant in West Orange. This oblong-shaped structure was officially named the Kinetoscope Theatre, but its staff dubbed it the "Black Maria" because it resembled the police patrol wagons of the time with that nickname. It had both a sloping roof, hinged to permit utilization of natural light, and a pivot-mounted foundation—enabling the rotation of the building to follow the sun. The interior decor was funereal in the extreme. To ensure maximum contrasts, the walls were covered with black tar paper, and a stage at one end of the single large room was also draped in black. Little about this somber setting suggested that film would become the signature art of our age.

Edison applied for United States patents on his motion picture apparatus in 1891 but unaccountably neglected to spend the $150 necessary for international control. After studying the workings of his equipment, the Lumière brothers, Louis and Auguste, who operated a factory for the manufacture of photographic equipment in Lyon, France, developed a hand-cranked combination camera-projector in 1894 that ran perforated 35-millimeter film. (Most historians now agree that Louis alone was largely responsible for its actual design and construction.) It weighed around sixteen pounds, giving it the distinct advantage of portability, and was built to operate at a speed of sixteen frames per second. (This became the standard until the advent of talkies, when the number of frames per second was increased to twenty-four to accommodate the sound track.) But the actual rate at which shooting occurred

Edison's movie studio, constructed in early 1893, was nicknamed "Black Maria."

could vary greatly, especially because most cameras weren't equipped with speed indicators until the 1920s.

The most important innovation of the Lumière camera unit was its shutter and claw mechanism. The film stopped for a split second in front of the lens, an individual image was exposed, and then the shutter closed and the claw advanced the film. German inventor Oskar Messter's addition in 1896 of a "Maltese cross" device to this transport mechanism allowed the film to move smoothly through the camera in regular increments. Soon after the turn of the century, the basic tools for recording moving images were in place— flexible and durable celluloid film, artificial lighting adequate for indoor and nighttime shooting, and relatively portable camera equipment capable of capturing the subtleties and nuances of movement.

Leisure Time Entertainment

The American cinema made its debut in a United States that was increasingly characterized by industrialization, immigration, and urbanization. As increased efficiency in agriculture reduced the need for farmhands, millions of Americans seeking employment moved from rural areas into large cities. People were pouring in from Europe as well to work in the newly created factories where goods were now mass manufactured. Between 1870 and 1900, the population of the United States almost doubled, from roughly 40 million to 76 million, and most of the growth occurred in urban areas. Some fifty-eight cities had populations of more than a half-million by 1890. During the first three decades of the new century, the population grew by another 47 million, nearly two-thirds as much as it had grown in the 125 years prior to 1900.

With the shift from a rural-agrarian to an urban-industrial society came higher wages and greater leisure time—time not taken up by work or other social obligations. Although the average weekly work hours in cities dropped substantially in the latter half of the nineteenth century, the nature of work itself was becoming increasingly dull, routinized, and mechanistic. These unsatisfying working conditions, coupled with expanded leisure time, created new business opportunities to fill the idle hours in people's often humdrum lives with commercial entertainment.

By the 1840s, promoters and producers of live theatre in the rapidly growing cities of the Northeast discovered that they could pack huge playhouses if they staged a wide range of inexpensive entertainment fare. Theatre capacities soon soared from a few hundred to thousands. As the expanding American population migrated westward, facilitated by cheaper and faster railroad transportation, troupes of traveling players were quick to follow. Popular stage entertainment became commonplace in Philadelphia, Chicago, and other major urban areas. By the 1880s, booking offices based in New York were sending entire dramatic and musical productions on the road. With the appearance of moving pictures toward the turn of the century, the plots, characters, themes, situations, and devices of popular theatre—with all of its emotionalism, sentimentality, and moralizing—seemed to cry out for cinematic expression.

Early Efforts at Moviemaking

Almost from the outset, the wide circulation of films started an ongoing international exchange of styles and techniques that makes it nearly impossible to identify precisely who was responsible for what innovation—especially since relatively few early films have survived. Moreover, the co-opting of film ideas was common practice. But whether established by innovator or imitator, virtually every advance in forging a cinematic style with global reach and appeal has been designed to make something more compelling—an event, an idea, an emotion.

The first films were fairly literal in conception. The Edison studio's initial output consisted primarily of trained animal acts, dancers, sports figures, circus performers, and vaudeville stars. Boxer Jim Corbett, muscleman Eugene Sandow, and sharpshooter Annie Oakley were among the celebrities of the day who ferried across the Hudson River from New York to New Jersey to achieve celluloid immortality. In France, pioneer filmmaker Louis Lumière was using his portable camera to capture such madcap adventures as a train arriving at a station and workers leaving the factory.

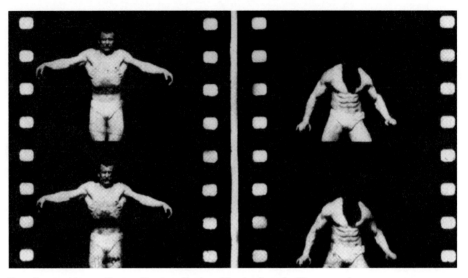

Prussian muscleman Eugene Sandow displays his physique for the camera's gaze.

Within a short time, films were being embellished with special effects—techniques for achieving unusual or striking photographic results during production. Edison employee Alfred Clark's half-minute film *The Execution of Mary, Queen of Scots* (1895) featured a beheading. This effect was achieved by stopping the camera after the doomed monarch (played by a man) rested her (his) head on the block and just as the executioner was about to strike. The actor was replaced with a dummy and the shooting resumed as the ax descended. This ability to stop the action and start it again without any apparent temporal break would prove to be one of the key elements in shaping the stylistic conventions of movies.

French filmmaker Georges Méliès, a magician and Paris theatre owner, made much of this stop-start technique in his efforts to achieve special effects not possible on the stage. Clever optical illusions, fantasy interlaced with humor, and an emphasis on parody, absurdity, and theatrics made his cinematic work distinctive. Between 1896 and 1912, he turned out some 500 films (fewer than two-thirds of which survive) ranging in length from less than a minute to ten or fifteen minutes. In the process of bringing the theatrical world of magic, pantomime, and spectacle to the screen, he took the first tentative steps toward establishing the techniques of film narrative, although his plots were often merely a flimsy framework for the display of special effects.

For all his inventiveness, Méliès remained bound by the traditions of the theatre. Still very much the stage creator, he shaped his screen narratives for a motionless camera, making the film frame equivalent to the proscenium arch (the curved structure that frames a traditional theatre stage). Changes in time and space coincided precisely with changes in scene. As a substitute for opening and closing curtains, he frequently joined scenes by dissolves, the blurring of one image into another (which he achieved by cranking the film back a bit and shooting the opening of the next scene over the ending of the current one). His actors made entrances and exits much as they would have on stage, and their performances adhered to the exaggerated histrionics of the day.

Méliès's most successful and influential film was *A Trip to the Moon,* which has a running time of about fourteen minutes at the standard silent speed. In this 1902 parody, loosely based on a Jules Verne story, he employed a detailed scenario, a sizable cast of professional actors (including himself as the chief scientist), elaborate costumes, and highly stylized props and sets to lampoon scientific assumptions of the day. The film is filled with such clever cinematic tricks as moon creatures that disappear into puffs of smoke when scientists whack them with their umbrellas. But each of its thirty separate scenes were captured in a single, uninterrupted run of a stationary camera from a fixed point of view, that of a theatregoer sitting in the orchestra center. In addition to the cuts used to achieve optical illusions, editing occurs between scenes rather than within them. The process of combining separately photographed scene fragments into a coherent whole remained for other filmmakers to realize.

A New Cinematic Mode of Expression

Although Méliès did little to advance a distinct cinematic mode of expression, his work nevertheless had a strong impression on other filmmakers. One of those influenced by the Frenchman's films was Edwin S. Porter, an Edison studio mechanic and projectionist who made big strides in the use of editing techniques to heighten dramatic effect. At the turn of the century, Porter turned out a number of short, groundbreaking films. In his most significant effort, *The Great Train Robbery* (1903), he cinematically unfolded a western tale of banditry and retribution. This innovative little film, which runs just over twelve minutes, consists of fourteen separate shots—aspects of scenes that have been captured by the camera in a single, uninterrupted run. The actions contained in each shot were themselves dramatically incomplete.

Porter's decision to cut between his scenes without playing them out was the beginning of a truly cinematic language. It established that the basic unit of meaning would be the shot rather than the scene. By taking scene fragments filmed at different times and places and splicing them together, Porter was able to visually transport viewers back and forth from the train, to the telegraph office, to a dance hall, and then back to the outlaws on horseback. To

Exhibitors had the option of presenting this close view of one of the bandits firing his pistol toward the camera at either the beginning or the end of *The Great Train Robbery* (1903).

keep the horsemen in view as they rode off, he broke with the usual fixed-angle position, moving the camera vertically and horizontally to follow the action.

Porter himself seemed unaware of the importance of his own accomplishments, and he soon regressed to more primitively conceived productions. Neither he nor the majority of his American contemporaries apparently recognized the potential his work had revealed. As a result, important cinematic possibilities initially went unnoticed. At the end of *The Great Train Robbery*, for example, Porter attached a piece of film unrelated to the rest of the story. It shows a fairly close view of a bandit firing his pistol point-blank at the camera. That a close-up or medium shot could be integrated into the unfolding action to help dramatize a story more fully apparently never occurred to Porter. This narrative strategy would have to wait for more inventive minds.

A group of filmmakers clustered around the seaside resort town of Brighton, England, (most notably Robert Paul, George Albert Smith, James Williamson, and Cecil Hepworth) was making rapid progress in refining the grammar and syntax of the evolving movie language—what to shoot, how to shoot it, and how to combine the various shots. They experimented with apparent camera-subject distance, placing the camera so that it approximated the position of a character, breaking scenes into shots of varying duration,

The movement of *Rescued by Rover*'s (1905) canine hero continues from one shot to the next.

matching action from separate shots, and developing other such cinematic procedures that have since become standard practice.

James Williamson was perhaps the first person to discover the basics of how to create a subjective point of view, a combination of shots that suggests the angle of vision or psychological state of a character. In his innovative 1901 film *A Big Swallow,* a man apparently upset about having his picture taken seems to consume not only a camera but also its operator. The short scene comprises just three shots: the irate man approaching the camera with his gaping mouth gradually filling the frame, the photographer and his camera toppling into darkness, and the irate man seemingly munching on both as he makes his retreat.

One of the most influential films from the "Brighton School" was Cecil Hepworth's *Rescued by Rover* (1905), a simple tale of a dog that rescues a stolen baby. The shooting and editing of the sequence in which the canine hero seeks out the baby, and then guides the infant's distraught father back to where it's being held, shows remarkable inventiveness. To mark the dog's progress toward and away from the kidnapper's lair, Hepworth used the same camera positioning. He then combined the separate shots to map out a coherent dramatic flow. Although hardly great drama, the sequence has both fluid continuity and visual energy.

From Peep Shows to Nickelodeons

Films were initially shown in a viewing machine called the **Kinetoscope,** which was devised by Edison employee William Dickson. It consisted of a large cabinet containing batteries, a light, and a motor that turned a fifty-foot loop of film at about forty-six frames per second. Through an eyepiece at the top of the cabinet, one spectator at a time could peer or "peep" at the flickering shadows on the strip as it moved rapidly along the sprockets. Except for the hums and groans of the machinery, the film passed before the spectator's eyes in silence.

In April 1894, when the first Kinetoscope or "peep show" parlor opened on lower Broadway in New York City, enthusiastic crowds waited all day and far into the night to see the "pictures that moved." By the end of that year, parlors were springing up all over the country. They ordinarily contained five separate coin-operated viewing mechanisms. For the total price of a quarter, the equivalent of a skilled worker's hourly wage, patrons could move from machine to machine to watch five different films, each lasting less than a minute.

Even as peep show parlors proliferated, many people were working on ways to project filmic images onto a big screen so that they could be watched by many people simultaneously rather than by only one at a time. Inventors and innovators like Louis and Auguste Lumière, Thomas Armat and Francis Jenkins, and Orville and Woodville Latham (with the help of Edison's former assistant, William Dickson) perfected projection devices, which were used to show films in such venues as vaudeville houses, town halls, fairgrounds, and amusement parks. The demand for projectors was on, and the supply kept pace.

Edison and his backers financed the manufacture and sale of a projection unit developed by Armat and Jenkins that incorporated the intermittent movement of film, a sprocket providing a small loop before and after the film gate to relax film tension, and a shutter device designed to give the screen long periods of illumination and relatively short periods of darkness. Called the Vitascope, this apparatus was promoted as the wizard Edison's newest invention. It made its debut in April 1896, at the Koster & Bial's Music Hall in the Herald Square area of New York City.

Soon after the turn of the century, when film pioneers turned to dramatizing stories, makeshift theatres began to appear in cities across the nation. Cigar stores, restaurants, pawn shops, and skating rinks were converted into movie houses that, for a brief period, charged a nickel for admission—hence the name **nickelodeon,** which combines the price of admission with the Greek word for theatre. The conversions initially occurred primarily in congested tenement districts. But studies of cities like Boston and New York suggest that movie houses soon spread to established entertainment centers.[1] Many theatre operators launched campaigns to lure the family trade. A pianist generally accompanied this silent film fare, but in the plushier venues, a violinist and other instrumentsalists also sometimes played. Film programs were frequently supplemented with sing-alongs, variety acts, and illustrated lectures.

The growth of movie houses, which began in earnest in 1905, was nothing short of spectacular. By 1910, some 10,000 or so had sprung up in cities and towns across the nation, and gross receipts for that year alone reached into the millions of dollars. An estimated 26 million people from all strata of society attended on a weekly basis. "Inside the new movie houses, particularly in the downtown areas," as a study of early cinema notes, "an Italian carpenter ... might sit in an orchestra seat next to a native-born white-collar salesman or a Jewish immigrant housewife—in short next to anyone who shared with him a sometimes secret passion for what might flicker across the screen."[2]

As the industry expanded, intermediaries emerged between producers and exhibitors. These "distributors" worked out of "film exchanges," buying or leasing films from producers and renting them to exhibitors. The first such exchange was organized in 1902 in San Francisco. Within five years, more than 125 film exchanges were in operation, serving all areas of the country. Thus the tripartite structure of the movie industry evolved—production (the actual making of movies), **distribution** (the marketing and delivery of them to theatres), and **exhibition** (the business of presenting them to the public).

Patent Disputes

Control over the movie industry became increasingly more centralized and concentrated as the century unfolded. The most powerful companies sought domination through patent rights. (A patent is a grant made by the federal government that confers upon the creator of an invention the sole right to make, use, and sell that invention for a period of seventeen years (twenty since 1995). After that time, the invention enters the public domain, and anyone can use it without recompense.) Two companies, Edison and Biograph (the later formed by William Dickson and his associates), controlled most of the key patents for movies and were fierce rivals in the battle for dominance at the box office.

Competition and litigation eventually threatened to exhaust the resources of both companies. By December 1908, they decided to join forces with Vitagraph and Armat, two other makers of cameras and projection equipment, to organize the Motion Picture Patents Company (MPPC), which was designed to control all three phases of the nascent movie industry: production, distribution, and exhibition. Its licensees included the American production companies Biograph, Edison, Essanay, Lubin, Selig, and Vitagraph; the French firm Pathé Freres; and Kleine Optical, a U.S. importer of foreign films and equipment.

To control production, the MPPC entered into an exclusive agreement with the Eastman Kodak Company, the country's sole manufacturer of raw film stock. To control exhibition, it organized its own distribution operation. Only licensed theatres were permitted to show the movies made by its members. The major beneficiaries from this attempt to dominate all aspects of the movie industry were the Edison and Biograph companies, both of which received several hundred thousand dollars annually in royalties.

Although seemingly quite formidable, this complex organization was unable to eliminate competition. Of the 9000 or so movie theatres in operation around the country by 1910, only about half were licensed. The many unlicensed theatres provided outlets for the scores of independent film companies that sprang up in the months following the patent trust's formation. Independent producers soon were turning out hundreds of films, usually using patented equipment without permission and obtaining their film stock from a French firm. The MPPC tried to shut down these operations through court injunctions and hired thugs, but the independents gradually gained in strength. In 1911 the threat of antitrust prosecution forced the MPPC to abandon its exclusivity arrangement with Kodak. By 1914, inefficiency, internal dissension, and reluctance to change had rendered the patents trust almost wholly ineffectual; three years later, the courts declared it legally dead.

The Movie Moguls

The movie industry eventually came under the control of some of those same independent producers and exhibitors who had challenged the authority of the patents trust. These were the legendary "movie moguls," a term that came into use about 1915 to describe the public image of these enterprising immigrants—part grand potentate, part barbarian invader. Born in small towns like Laupheim in Germany, Ricse in Hungary, and Krasmashhilz in Poland, and in the ghettos of Kiev and Minsk and Warsaw, they rose from such modest occupations as furrier, haberdasher, trolley bus driver, and junk dealer to reign over celluloid empires.

Among the most ambitious of this group was former garment worker William Fox, who sought to crown himself supreme ruler of movieland and who almost accomplished this grandiose goal. Raised in the tenements of New York's Lower East Side, the Hungarian-born Fox had already become a formidable figure in exhibition and distribution by 1915. That year he entered the production side of motion pictures as well. He and his associates formed Fox Film, which was soon turning out mostly low-budget films featuring second-string stars and heavily promoted screen novices. Few would have predicted that aggressive expansion would ultimately catapult this modest operation into a corporate aggregation of staggering proportions.

The Fox studio's biggest star of the speechless era was western hero Tom Mix. In his simple frontier adventures, rough-and-tumble Tom invariably chose soda pop over whiskey, never let a cigarette touch his lips, and clearly preferred the companionship of his "wonder horse" Tony to members of the opposite sex. Villains were typically subdued by elaborate lasso work or clever horsemanship rather than through more violent means. His highly popular cowboy sagas helped fill Fox Film's coffers for over a decade before talkies put a damper on his screen career.

Another central figure in shaping the character and structure of the modern movie industry was Adolph Zukor, an impoverished immigrant from Hungary who, after succeeding as a furrier, diversified his interests to include penny arcades, nickelodeons, and—eventually—a chain of movie theatres. Zukor first made his mark in production in 1912 with the formation (in partnership with Broadway impresario Daniel Frohman) of the Famous Players Film Company, which initially produced pictures starring well-known Broadway performers. When several of the stage actors proved unsuitable for the unique demands of the screen, Zukor developed his own stable of stars, who honed their craft on a studio back lot.

In 1916, Zukor teamed up with Jesse L. Lasky, a vaudeville manager who with his brother-in-law, Samuel Goldfish, a successful glove salesman, had formed the Jesse L. Lasky Feature Picture Company two years earlier. Lasky and Zukor took over Paramount Pictures Exchange, which had been handling distribution of their movies, merging it with their own operation to form Famous Players–Lasky Corporation (later changed to Paramount Pictures). To assure a steady outlet for its pictures, the new company's distribution arm adopted a policy known as **block booking.** Under this system of distribution, exhibitors were required to contract for the rental of some or all of a studio's output rather than for only a single picture. Through such aggressive practices and policies, Paramount soon moved to the front ranks of the movie industry.

In the new organizational structure, Zukor served as president, Lasky as vice president in charge of production, and Goldfish as chairman of the board. But conflict erupted posthaste between Zukor and Goldfish. With Lasky's support, Zukor forced the former glove salesman to sell his interest in the newly merged firm. Soon after his ouster, Goldfish joined forces with vaudeville producer Edgar Selwyn to found Goldwyn Pictures Corporation. The Polish-born Goldfish, his odd name the result of an immigration official's error, so liked the title of the new company that he eventually legally changed his name to Goldwyn.

After being dislodged from Goldwyn Pictures in a power play in 1922, he went on to establish himself as one of the most profitable and prolific independent producers in the industry. Although inarticulate and uncultured, crude and uncouth—at least according to his detractors—he became known for the good taste and attention to detail that he brought to his pictures.

To make certain one and all knew they were *his* pictures, he insisted on having his name appear at the very end of the opening credits, upending the emerging tradition that the director got the final billing.

Picture Palaces

As the movie industry expanded, actual cinemas gradually replaced the old nickelodeons. Many of these new structures were designed to delight average moviegoers seeking surcease from the daily grind. Between 1914 and 1922, some 4000 new movie theatres were built across the United States. New York City witnessed the opening of such palatial facilities as the 2460-seat Regent (1913), the 3500-seat Strand (1914), and the 5300-seat Capitol (1919)—all at various times managed by an imaginative exhibitor named Samuel "Roxy" Rothefal. The interiors of these "picture palaces" included gargoyles, intricate frescoes, copies of Greek statues, elaborate fountains, marble floors, and thick carpets. Ushers were attired in resplendent uniforms. Film presentations were supplemented with symphony orchestras, a mélange of song and ballet, and live variety acts. Rothefal was also responsible for running the Roxy (1927) and Radio City Music Hall (1933)—that lasting monument to art deco.

The trappings of the 6200-seat Roxy theatre, located at 50th Street and 7th Avenue in Manhattan, were so plush that Cole Porter, in his song "You're the Top," rhymed "steppes of Russia" with "pants on a Roxy usher." No theatrical structure in the world could equal its stage and proscenium arch in size. A cyclorama of immense proportions served to diffuse sound. The orchestra pit provided ample space for over a hundred musicians to play their instruments. A tower of twenty-one chimes soaring above the grand organ console weighed 10,000 pounds. Sixteen operators working various shifts throughout the day and evening ran the battery of projection machines. A small army of ushers under the charge of an ex-marine escorted patrons to their seats. An imposing five-story rotunda could accommodate 2500 people waiting to enter the theatre proper. When you pass through the Roxy's portals, enthused a contemporary observer, "you step magically from the drab world of confusion and cares into a fairy palace whose presiding genius entertains you royally with all the fine allurements that art, science, and music can offer."[3]

On the West Coast, Sid Grauman constructed Grauman's Egyptian Theatre on Hollywood Boulevard in 1922. It seated 1760 people, who were escorted by twenty-eight usherettes attired in Egyptian-style costumes. Gilt sphinxes framed the proscenium. A beaded Bedouin wearing a striped robe and carrying a spear strode across the parapet before each performance. Five years later, Grauman opened his Chinese Theatre. Its motif included objets

The famous Roxy Rotunda. Ushers were never to call it a "lobby." Twelve huge marble columns supported the dome from which hung a twenty-foot chandelier. The huge oval rug on its polished, honey-colored marble floor weighed over two tons.

d'art, draperies, and statues imported from Asia. In the Midwest, theatre tycoon Barney Balaban, with his four brothers and brother-in-law Samuel Katz, operated a string of large, ornate movie palaces with grandiose names like the Valencia, the Riviera, and the Granada.

The atmosphere of fantasy was often carefully planned, as Samuel Katz, who in the mid-1920s took charge of Paramount's theatre operations, explained to a group of students at the Harvard Business School. After the location has been determined, he noted, "a study of the community is made, a study of the existing theatres, and from that we determine the type of architecture that ought to go with a particular theatre. If the community already has a theatre in the style of French Renaissance or Italian Renaissance we will probably take an entirely different type for the architecture of our theatre so as to make it distinctive."[4] Thousands of new cinemas appeared across the country. In most of them, an attempt was made to suggest at least some element of luxury and glamour, even if it consisted only of a stucco facade and a chandelier-lit foyer.

RACIAL SEGREGATION AT THE MOVIES

Even the most opulent of the movie emporiums ostensibly were accessible to anyone with the price of admission. However, although theatre operators proclaimed their doors open to one and all, not all patrons received the same greeting. Anecdotal evidence and oral histories suggest that the rich might have rubbed elbows with the poor in picture palaces, but that in varying degrees blacks and other people of color were often made to feel less than welcome. A palpable "whites only" attitude seemed to permeate the atmosphere of many of these palaces. Both theatre personnel and a goodly number of patrons were inclined to glare at any black or other person of color who sought to "step magically from the drab world of confusion and cares into a fairy palace."

In the North, where segregation was illegal, blacks couldn't be denied entry to a downtown theatre, but they tended to be cautious about calling undue attention to themselves, apparently realizing that they were often regarded as interlopers. "My mother made sure my appearance and that of my sisters was acceptable," recalls a black woman. "We were told not to argue with the ticket taker, who would act as if he didn't want us there, and we weren't to say anything uncalled for."[5]

In the Deep South, blacks typically were completely excluded from theatres attended by whites or were admitted through a special entrance leading to a blacks-only balcony, which typically had a small number of seats. Ticket takers were inclined to direct black patrons upstairs even when other parts of the theatre were practically empty. Another way of segregating audiences was for a theatre to be open exclusively for whites during the day and evening, and to provide a midnight screening for blacks.

Throughout most of the United States, racially segregated moviegoing experiences often resulted from residential patterns. People tended to frequent neighborhood theatres, and blacks generally lived in a separate part of town from whites. Such segregated viewing became more pronounced as movie houses in predominantly

Hollywood, the Movie Capital

Early American films were made primarily in the eastern United States. But the little village of Hollywood, incorporated as a municipality in 1903 and annexed by the city of Los Angeles seven years later, gradually became the hub around which most production activity centered. The first moviemakers to set up shop in the Los Angeles area were members of the MPPC. As early as 1907, a director from the Selig Company of Chicago shot some water scenes for an adventure film at the nearby Pacific Ocean. Two years later, the Selig crew returned, establishing headquarters in a converted Chinese laundry in the downtown district. Not long after, Colonel William Selig relocated his entire company to the city. Then, in 1910, Biograph director D. W. Griffith began a policy of taking his filming crew and players to the area for the winter months. The following year, Vitagraph set up a branch of its company in the coastal community of Santa Monica; later, it moved its studio facility to Hollywood.

This "dream palace" catered to black movie patrons.

black neighborhoods proliferated. Most of these local theatres, the vast majority of which were owned by whites, were hardly comparable downtown picture palaces catering to Caucasians.

The elaborate system of distribution and exhibition that developed in the movie industry contributed to discrimination against blacks and other ghettoized minorities as well. It became standard practice for a movie to open first in the downtown picture palaces, most of which were owned by the major movie companies. This ensured that they would receive the bulk of box office revenues. After showing in "first-run" theatres, a movie would move to neighborhood houses on the outskirts of a city, and then to outlets in rural areas and urban ghettos. It would ordinarily play in only one place in any particular area, which also favored the large studio-owned theatres.

As a movie moved through successive runs, "clearances" of between seven and thirty days were observed, during which time it would be unavailable. This practice protected each tier of theatres from the cheaper admission prices of potential competitors further down in the hierarchal structure. No matter how prosperous, those theatres in predominantly black neighborhoods would receive the movie in its final runs. In big cities, a movie could run for many months, and at times for more than a year, before it became accessible to black audiences.

Scores of moviemakers soon settled in or around Hollywood, where clement weather and the unique geography of adjacent ocean, deserts, forests, and mountain ranges provided the ideal setting for moviemaking. But sunshine and topography weren't the only inducements in the region. Movie companies were shifting from shorts to full-length features and erecting elaborate outdoor sets. This necessitated hiring many more laborers and skilled craftspeople of all kinds, and Los Angeles had an ample supply of electricians, carpenters, technicians, dressmakers, and other specialized workers eager for employment. Moreover, it was the nation's leading open-shop, nonunion city. Labor costs there ranged from 20 to 50 percent below those in New York.

The ready supply of skilled, relatively low-cost labor in Los Angeles, coupled with the availability of large expanses of inexpensive land in the surrounding area, facilitated the construction of sprawling studio facilities. One-time haberdasher Carl Laemmle, a producer operating outside the patents trust, set the standard. In March 1915, on a 230-acre tract in the San Fernando Valley, ten miles out of the city on El Camino Real, the German-born Laemmle officiated at the opening of Universal City, a new municipality founded for the sole purpose of making movies. This self-sufficient enclave eventually had its own police department, fire brigade, railroad, bus system, post office, hospital, reservoir, zoo, and educational facilities. Two restaurants were equipped to serve 1200 patrons a day. Dotted along the streets were a blacksmith shop, garages, mills, tailoring facilities, and apothecaries. The most impressive feature was a 300-foot-long open-air stage with muslin diffusers stretched overhead to soften the California sunlight.

That same year, a developer named Harry Culver offered free land to anyone who would build a production facility in a new city he was naming for himself about eleven miles southwest of downtown Los Angeles. Director-turned-producer Thomas Harper Ince, who had been operating his Inceville studio in the Santa Ynez Canyon near Hollywood, took advantage of the offer and snapped up sixteen acres near a dusty road that became Washington Boulevard. On this parcel of parched shrubbery, he constructed a modest but recognizably modern studio complex, complete with five glass-enclosed shooting stages, office buildings, workshops, and dressing rooms.

A top director in his own right, Ince was at his best supervising the work of others. By 1914, he had turned almost exclusively to producing pictures. Unlike many of his contemporaries, he recognized the importance of good writing and was largely responsible for developing the detailed and thorough shooting script (a written breakdown of individual shots) that became common practice in Hollywood. His principal writer was C. Gardner Sullivan, who effectively used titling to deepen and intensify what actors, lighting, and set design conveyed. Sullivan wrote scripts for granite-visaged western star William S. Hart that stressed character over action. He also is generally credited with introducing the soon-to-be hallowed concept of the "good badman"—the borderline blackguard who is redeemed by the love of a virtuous woman.

Ince initiated the system of production whereby the staff was divided into units, with each responsible for a set of films. Each unit was headed by a production manager, who supervised the filming from a detailed shooting script approved by Ince in its final form. In overseeing every phase of a movie project, Ince stressed sound organization, careful preparation, thorough execution, and economical editing. The westerns and action pictures he produced were always tautly edited and adhered to a clear-cut style and tight dramatic structure. Authority over the final cut or sequence of shots in a movie was his alone. Anything that didn't advance the progress of the plot was mercilessly discarded. If he thought a movie wandered, he would recut footage, rearrange scenes, and change its meaning in order to make it more compelling. His innovative production procedures served as the prototype for the Hollywood studio system that was to dominate moviemaking in the coming decades.

By the time his new production plant was ready, Ince and his company had joined with directors Mack Sennett and D. W. Griffith in an ill-fated ven-

A poster promotes *The Square Deal Man* (1917), a typical William S. Hart western.

ture called the Triangle Film Corporation. Under the title of "director general," each reigned over his own production unit. Together they covered most of the main forms of moviemaking. Sennett specialized in slapstick comedies, Griffith in melodrama and eye-catching display, and Ince in action films—usually with a frontier setting. When Triangle expired in 1918, the Culver City studio facility that had been its home was bought and expanded by Goldwyn Pictures. (It eventually became the fabled Metro-Goldwyn-Mayer [M-G-M] lot.)

Many of the shoestring movie firms that set up shop in Hollywood were located in offices on a block along Beachwood Drive near Sunset Boulevard known as "Poverty Row." The most successful producer to emerge from this seedy side of town was Harry Cohn, who, with his brother Jack and an associate, formed a company in 1920 that became Columbia Pictures. The tyrannical

Harry Cohn eventually enjoyed unprecedented power in his company, serving as both president and production chief, the only movie mogul to hold both positions simultaneously. Under his operating philosophy, which seemed to mirror fascist dictator Benito Mussolini's (whose portrait adorned his office wall), Columbia became a national production and distribution organization of the first rank by the end of the decade.

Most movie production gradually shifted to the Los Angeles area. Although a number of facilities sprang up in outlying communities, the favorite location for studios was the suburb of Hollywood. The very name soon stood for the American movie industry in general. It also became associated in the public mind with the lavish lifestyles of the stars—their glamorous parties, designer clothes, sleek automobiles, and palatial homes located in nearby Beverly Hills or posh communities along the Santa Monica beachfront.

The Rise of Star Power

Stars as Box Office Attractions

Movie firms initially were reluctant to promote their players or even to give them screen credit, perhaps fearful that they might demand higher salaries for their services. This proved to be a shortsighted policy. Copyright titles between 1907 and 1908 suggest that over the course of that single-year period fictional fare all but eclipsed nonfictional forms (travelogues, newsreels, and the like). This same period saw the output of comedies, melodramas, adventure stories, and similar kinds of screen drama increase from 17 to 66 percent of all films produced.[6] This proliferation of narrative-dramatic forms made the screen actor an essential component of the production process. It was clearly a propitious time for film producers to promote players, something theatrical impresarios had been doing for decades.

Vitagraph was one of the first of the patent trust members to exploit the profit potential of screen players.[7] It featured its leading female player, Florence Turner, in lobby card displays and even arranged for her to make personal appearances at movie theatres. The first of these, in April 1910, was in Saratoga Park, Brooklyn, where she gave a "naive and fetching little speech" to an adoring audience. The personal appearances of the "Vitagraph Girl," as she was called, were enormously successful. Taking notice in June 1910, the *New York Dramatic Mirror* wrote a story on her titled "A Motion Picture Star," perhaps the first time the phrase came into the public consciousness. The company soon sent other players on the road as well. Some 1600 people turned out to see Maurice Costello, its major male player, when he appeared at a Brooklyn auditorium in November 1910.

Independent producers were quick to grasp that such promotions could greatly enhance profit margins. An unbilled Biograph player named Florence

Lawrence was very popular with moviegoers. The enterprising Carl Laemmle, seeing glimmers of gold in the starlight emanating from her screen image, lured Lawrence to his production company with a lucrative contract offer. Shortly after signing her, he launched one of the first successful "publicity buildups" in the movie industry; it would hardly be the last. Players soon began to be known by their names, and both profits and salaries started to spiral upward.

Some stars achieved almost mythic status. Charlie Chaplin's rare gift of mime, physical agility, and subtle shades of characterization made him the silent screen's most successful comedic star. He was already a major English music hall performer by 1913 when he joined Mack Sennett's Keystone Studio, which specialized in slapstick comedies whose loose plots were little more than a pretext for the characters to smash cars and heads, engage in marital squabbles, and call the zany Keystone Kops. Character logic and dramatic structure were usually sacrificed to the rapid-fire visual humor of pie-throwing bouts, frenetic car chases, and last-minute rescues.

In his first film, *Making a Living* (1914), Chaplin played a typical English dandy in a manner that did not bode well for his screen potential. But his prospects brightened considerably with his next film, *Kid Auto Races at Venice* (1914), in which he began to assume the attire of the "Little Tramp" character that would make him world famous—oversized shoes, baggy trousers, ill-fitting waistcoat, derby hat, and cane. A cropped, brushlike mustache added a final touch of absurdity (much as it did years later for Adolf Hitler). With each new screen appearance, his Little Tramp characterization grew more deft and precise, coming to epitomize the inner tragedy of the poor soul—comic, anguished, mute, frustrated, buffeted by fate—who aroused a unique combination of sympathy and laughter.

During his year at Keystone, Chaplin made thirty-four short films and one feature-length comedy, *Tillie's Punctured Romance* (1914). Writing and directing most of his later pictures, he revolutionized movie comedy, transforming it from knockabout farce into a subtle art form. After leaving Sennett, he worked for several film companies. Each new contract gave him greater autonomy and increased income. He soon enjoyed a degree of creative freedom that few other writers, actors, or directors could hope for in the movie industry at the time.

The popularity and drawing power of stars permitted studios to set high film rental prices and helped to stabilize production output. Most movie companies eventually hired publicists to stimulate and satisfy the growing demands of moviegoers for information about their screen idols. A vast network of coaches, publicity agents, talent agents, lawyers, and producers developed to publicize both the pictures and the personal lives of the stars who appeared in them.

The alleged off-screen antics of the stars soon became as fascinating as the feats and foibles of the characters they played in the movies. Magazines

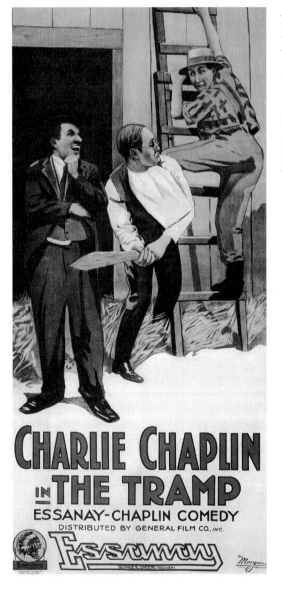

A poster promotes *The Tramp* (1915), named for the trademark character that Charlie Chaplin originally improvised for a single film. By 1916 Chaplin's rare gift of mime and his seemingly limitless imagination earned him $10,000 a week plus a $150,000 bonus, a total of $670,000 a year—an especially impressive figure considering that income taxes at the time were negligible and the dollar was worth at least four or five times its current value.

devoted to movie industry gossip and personalities became required reading for many movie fans. Screen players often became closely identified with the characters they played, especially when this connection was promoted through the marriage of publicity and publication.

The link between actors and the characters they played was strengthened by feature-length films, which became the industry standard between 1912 and 1914. More complex dramatic narratives began to be constructed around the traits and motivations of certain characters. This invariably made the actors portraying these characters seem all the more interesting and important. Actor appeal was further enhanced by the shooting strategies employed. As actors became central to story progression, their bodies, and most notably their faces, figured more frequently in close shots. With their magnified faces filling the screen, they seemed even more fascinating, stepping up demands for tidbits about their personal lives. Publicists were pleased to provide them, even if it meant making things up.

Star Personae

Leading players were carefully nurtured and sustained through role assignments and coordinated publicity campaigns. They often assumed specific public images, or **personae** (an ancient Greek theatrical term referring to the masks actors wore to convey various emotions), that reinforced the roles they played. The persona and the person behind the mask could be closely connected or bear few similarities beyond physical attributes.

In cultivating Tom Mix's persona, Fox's publicity department stressed his cowboy credentials. Born in Mix Run, Pennsylvania, he migrated westward at an early age in search of adventure. His various jobs before riding the cinematic range included serving as a sheriff, deputy U.S. marshal, and Texas Ranger. Although the Fox publicity machine exaggerated his achievements beyond what anyone could realistically cram into a single lifetime, there was no doubt about his ruggedness, courage, horsemanship, or facility with a lasso. When his film career was shot down by sound, he continued to show off his equine skills in Tom Mix's Circus, which toured the world throughout the 1930s.

Sometimes a star's background was totally fabricated to fit a screen image. When demure Theodosia Goodman was cast as a sexual predator in Fox's *A Fool There Was* (1915), based on Rudyard Kipling's poem *The Vampire,* she assumed the name Theda Bara (an anagram of "Arab death"). Although the daughter of a Cincinnati tailor, she was promoted as the possessor of profoundly occult powers, born on the desert sands in the shadow of the Sphinx, the child of a French artist by his Arabian mistress. When the movie scored big at the box office, Bara became internationally famous as the Vamp, an especially sinful subtype of the *femme fatale*—an unscrupulous, seductive woman who uses her wiles to entrap and exploit unwitting men with the promise of unbridled passion. Her rejoinder to some hapless victim, "Kiss me, my fool!"(on a title card in the movie), became one of the nation's most repeated catchphrases.

To reinforce her screen image, Bara exaggerated her pallor by wearing indigo eye makeup; surrounded herself with symbols of desert mysticism, such as skulls and crossbones and glass balls; was served by "Nubian slaves"; and

Publicity shots of Theda Bara highlighted her baleful eroticism.

received the press while stroking a serpent in a darkened parlor permeated with tuberoses and incense. She received $75 a week for her first starring role. Some four years and forty features later, playing such notorious destroyers of men as Carmen, Madame Du Barry, Salome, and Cleopatra, she was earning $4000 a week.

The Allure of Stardom

Hollywood's emergent royalty basked in an ambience of glamour and extravagance. The lavishness of Tom Mix's lifestyle, for example, rivaled that of a rajah. After roaming the sagebrush, the cowboy star returned home to a sprawling Beverly Hills mansion where his English butler greeted him at the front door. If chasing culprits around the studio back lot all day had raised a sweat, he could cool off in his huge sunken bathtub or take a dip in his spacious swimming pool. Then he could slip into one of his many white linen suits, pull on a pair of fancy boots from his unique collection, and affix his favorite belt buckle—the one with the letters *T.M.* embossed in glittering diamonds. If nothing special was planned, he might give the uniformed chauffeur a night off and drive his custom-built limousine himself.

The imposing Hollywood sign on Mount Lee, long a beacon to aspiring screen thespians, was first erected as "Hollywoodland" in 1923 to herald a real estate development (the last four letters were removed in 1949). Worn from time, weather, and vandalism, the original structure was replaced in 1978. The current sign stands 50 feet high, stretches 450 feet across, and weighs 450,000 pounds.

The once sleepy hamlet of Hollywood soon stood as the prime exemplar of a culture in which personality and appearance were increasingly seen as projects to be undertaken. Even when the artifice of a screen persona was revealed, it didn't seem to diminish the allure of stardom. Rather, it invited movie fans to draw parallels to their own less glamorous lives and to consider the possibilities of transformation. Did screen lover Rudolph Valentino really once work as a waiter and a gardener? Was comic actor Roscoe "Fatty" Arbuckle actually a plumber's assistant before he soared to stardom? How did Brooklyn-born Clara Bow become the quintessential flapper? Can bobbed hair and cupid-bow lips possibly be the secret of her screen success? Is a beauty contest victory the key that will open studio gates?

Anything seemed possible in this new Promised Land by the Pacific. Hollywood became a magnet that attracted young people from across the country and around the world. Because acting didn't appear to require any special skills or ability, hopefuls could easily imagine themselves strutting across the silver screen. Unlike most other professions, the way movie players made their living was on full public display. "The visual evidence of the films," noted one industry analyst, "offers the waitress a chance to compare herself to the movie queen; it gives the shoe clerk a chance to match himself against the matinee idol. It provokes the thought, 'Say, I could do that . . .' No other industry presents so simple an invitation to the ego."[8]

Young women in particular were drawn to Hollywood by visions of fame and fortune in the movies. Thousands of Eliza Dolittles descended on the movie colony in search of a Henry Higgins who could transform them from street urchins into aristocrats. With the right coaching and cosmetics, even the most humble could hope to succeed. Why not take a stab at stardom? Perhaps they might possess the special brand of personal magnetism that seems to exert an inexorable pull on the camera. Weren't studios always searching for this elusive, difficult-to-define inner force?

Every once in a while—through some combination of charisma, chance, and calculation—an aspiring performer would attain stardom. But most ended up sorely disappointed. Unable to find work, encountering repeated rejection or exploitation, many eventually departed in despair. Stories about the pitfalls of pursuing an acting career circulated in the popular press. Movie magazines regularly ran features describing the hard work and years of sacrifice required in the movie business. Melodramas such as *A Girl's Folly* (1917), *Mary of the Movies* (1923), *Broken Hearts of Hollywood* (1926), and *Stranded* (1927) served as cautionary tales about the unscrupulous men who preyed on the star-struck girls. Yet countless young people continued to migrate westward each year in search of stardom. Still today Hollywood exerts a strong magnetic pull.

The public obsession with Hollywood was not lost on the stars themselves, many of whom demanded increasingly greater remuneration for their services. Among the highest paid were Charlie Chaplin, Mary Pickford, and Douglas Fairbanks. Pickford rivaled even the great Chaplin in popularity. Her screen image embodied the ideals of Victorian virtue, and she was promoted as "America's Sweetheart," a symbol of wholesomeness and girlish innocence. Fairbanks was the silent screen's leading adventure hero. "Dashing Doug," as he was often called, gave off a sense of controlled energy that many described as electric. He was famous for his jaunty smile, remarkable physical dexterity, and penchant for swashbuckling screen romance.

United Artists

The movies of Chaplin, Pickford, and Fairbanks were so financially successful worldwide that the three stars were able to join with D. W. Griffith in 1919 to

Douglas Fairbanks, Mary Pickford, Charlie Chaplin, and D. W. Griffith joined forces to form United Artists. Upon learning of their new company, one industry wag quipped: "So the lunatics have taken over the asylum."

form their own company, appropriately named United Artists. Western star William S. Hart had been part of the initial negotiations, but he pulled out when Adolph Zukor offered him $200,000 a picture. The aggressive Zukor would later encourage Griffith, beset by financial reversals and dismayed by the way his movies were being distributed, to withdraw as well with a deal to direct three pictures for Paramount at $250,000 each.

United Artists functioned as a domestic and international distributor that rented and publicized the pictures of its owners, all of whom retained control over their own production activities. It had no actors under contract, did not produce any movies, and owned no production facilities. (Some of the individual owners, however, maintained studios. For example, Mary Pickford and Douglas Fairbanks, who were married soon after United Artists was incorporated, operated a studio on Santa Monica Boulevard.) Each of the four founders signed agreements that, upon completion of their respective contracts with other distributors, gave United Artists the exclusive right to release their movies for five years.

The number of movies supplied by the founding members proved insufficient to maintain United Artists' enormous overhead, so other independent producers were invited to release their movies through the company. In late 1924, its owners hired tough-minded Russian immigrant Joseph M. Schenck (whose brother Nicholas would later head Loew's Inc.) to manage the entire operation. Within a short time, he brought into the company fold such silent-screen immortals as his wife, Norma Talmadge; his brother-in-law, Buster Keaton; and the enormously popular Gloria Swanson. He also lured several producers who would make a considerable mark on the movie industry, among them Samuel Goldwyn and Walt Disney.

Hollywood in Wartime

Stars of the first magnitude like Chaplin, Pickford, and Fairbanks were among the most potent weapons in the government's promotional arsenal during World War I, which the United States entered in April 1917. They appeared in short films and made personal appearances around the country to promote the sale of Liberty Bonds, raising millions of dollars for the government's war chest. They were also pictured regularly in newspapers and magazines engaged in such activities as working in their gardens, knitting for servicemen, and donating items like ambulances to the American Red Cross. Even photos of the Vamp, Theda Bara, had "buy a bond and help the cause of humanity" stamped across them before they were sent out to fans. Such highly publicized acts of patriotism turned many stars into home-front heroes and no doubt added to the box office appeal of their pictures.

Classified as an essential industry, Hollywood helped the war effort in myriad ways. The War Activities Committee of the National Association of the Motion Picture Industry (NAMPI), a trade association set up in July 1916, worked with government agencies to promote everything from food conservation to the sale of war bonds. Theatre managers across the country showed short, government-sponsored instructional films about such matters as beef and wheat conservation, accommodated recruiting stations in their lobbies, acted as collection centers for things like the peach pits used in gas mask filters, provided music for the singing of such patriotic songs as "Over There," and encouraged patrons to purchase Liberty Bonds and War Savings Stamps.

Many of NAMPI's activities were coordinated through the Committee on Public Information (CPI), created by executive order in April 1917 to foster unity and loyalty on the domestic front. The CPI's projects promoting patriotism included sponsorship of 75,000 speakers—mostly small-town businessmen, lawyers, and other professionals. They gave tens of thousands of four-minute speeches in over 5000 American cities and towns as part of a massive effort to generate support for the "war to end all wars" and "to make the world safe for democracy."

Movie theatres nationwide, which were allowed to remain open even on that day of the week when other businesses had to close to conserve fuel, provided a forum for these "four-minute men" to champion the war effort and condemn the heresy of antiwar protest. At a movie house in Portland, Maine, for example, a local bank manager, serving as a lieutenant in this carefully synchronized national mission, urged patrons to report anyone who spread misleading stories, asked misleading questions, or belittled efforts to win the war. "Give all the details you can, with the names of witnesses if possible," he exhorted. "Show the Hun that we can beat him at his own game."[9] The same rallying cry for increased vigilance and exposure echoed in countless cinemas across the country.

The conflict raging in Europe seemed to demand a single-minded devotion on the American home front to the immense task of converting the peacetime economy and consciousness to the stringent requirements of war. Protestations against the war could result in harsh punishment. Under the Espionage and Sedition Acts of 1917 and 1918, more than 2000 federal prosecutions took place, with almost any antiwar sentiment being a potential source of government suspicion. Calling the military draft unconstitutional, criticizing the war bond drive, even stating that the war was in opposition to the teachings of Christ—all became a crime.

The surging nationalistic fervor aided the activities of the many xenophobic societies that sprang up around the country. Equating any sign of social or intellectual nonconformity with disloyalty, these zealous flag-wavers hounded dissenters and convinced many legislators and law enforcement agencies that patriotism demanded such measures as banning use of the German language, deporting alien radicals, and suppressing immigrant associations of all sorts. In this repressive political climate, patriotism was the practical course of action.

Whatever its motives, Hollywood heartily embraced the home-front campaign to win hearts and minds, turning out a series of patriotic sagas and virulent anti-German features. However, it took the industry time to gear up its prowar production apparatus. Estimates based on trade journal listings suggest that only about 14 percent of the 568 available films during the nineteen months of American involvement were war-related, and half of these were newsreels and documentaries.[10] Although the overall percentage of war-related movies was rather small, their influence on the way many Americans came to regard the enemy—albeit impossible to determine with any certainty—was undoubtedly far-reaching.

Jingoistic pictures like *The Claws of the Hun* (1918), *The Hun Within* (1918), *The Prussian Cur* (1918), *Outwitting the Hun* (1918), and *The Kaiser,*

Beast of Berlin (1918) painted a portrait of the Germans as evil incarnate. In *Till I Come Back You* (1918), Belgian children are shipped to Germany to work in munitions factories, where they are whipped and starved into submission. A purported "inside look" at the atrocities of Prussian prison camps is provided by *My Four Years in Germany* (1918). In *Hearts of the World* (1918), a once-idyllic French village is occupied by depraved Prussians who plunder and rape at will. Perhaps the most virulent example of this hate-the-Hun propaganda was *The Heart of Humanity* (1918), in which Eric von Stroheim plays a German military officer who, in the process of trying to rape a young mother, tosses her baby out of an upstairs window.

Such movies contributed to a climate of hysteria and blind hate in which everything German came under assault. The German names for food were eliminated (sauerkraut became "liberty cabbage"); German musicians, actors, and writers were shunned (the music of Bach and Beethoven was withdrawn from the programming of civic orchestras); and Americans of German descent who did not change their names were subject to persecution. Although the vast majority of Germans living in the United States had no responsibility whatsoever for the war, all the vials of wrath produced against their country of origin were poured upon them.

Worldwide Distribution

With most of Europe's production centers severely hobbled by the war, the American movie industry had an unprecedented opportunity to market its products abroad. This effort was aided by the Committee on Public Information, which used the broad appeal of American movies to ensure that German film fare was banned from the cinemas of Europe's neutral nations. Authorities in countries like Sweden, Norway, Holland, and Switzerland were told that Hollywood's products would not be provided to any cinema that showed German films. The vast majority of exhibitors in these neutral nations quickly fell in line, apparently reluctant to lose out on the latest Chaplin or Pickford picture. Within a short time, German films virtually vanished from their screens.

Between 1916 and 1918, the focal point of worldwide movie distribution gradually shifted from London to New York, and anticipated foreign revenue became an important component in the calculation of production costs. Companies like Fox Film, Famous Players–Lasky, Goldwyn Pictures, and Universal, which had established outlets in Europe before the war, managed to blanket most of the globe with their regional distribution networks. By the time capital was once again available abroad for local production, Hollywood had gained dominance in the field.

In the prosperous 1920s, the American movie industry rode the crest of worldwide enterprise. In Germany, for example, most moviegoers were probably watching Hollywood films during the 1920s (even early in the decade since quota restrictions established in 1921 were not fully enforced). The Dawes Plan of 1924, under which the United States, in partnership with other nations, provided loans to stabilize the German economy (plagued by hyper-inflation), made it cheaper in many instances for distributors to secure films from abroad rather than finance production in Germany. A new quota policy set in 1925 allowed German distributors to release one foreign film for each German picture they had handled in the previous year. But even if this regulation were strictly enforced, half of the films shown could be imported.

As it did in many countries, Hollywood flooded Germany with its movies, most of which had been amortized in the home market and thus could be rented abroad cheaply. By the end of 1925, according to one estimate, over 40 percent of the movies screened in Germany were of American origin.[11] Bolstered by block booking and low rental rates, American movies also proved their potency in the Far East, Latin America, and parts of Africa. As the American movie industry shifted from a domestic- to a global-scale operation, its idiom of cinematic expression developed enormous reach, appeal, and influence.

The Griffith Legacy

The American moviemaker who had the greatest influence abroad during the era of speechless cinema was D. W. Griffith. The expressive Hollywood style owes much to him. In welding together the techniques developed by others, he gradually created a distinctively cinematic art form, one that freed screen drama from its stage moorings. With each new film project, he increased the complexity and variety of movements within shots. Eventually, he became a master of such compositional elements as setting and lighting, deployment of actors, and angle and position of the camera.

During rehearsal and production, Griffith stressed subtlety and natural expressiveness in performance, insisting that his actors speak clearly and with feeling even though there was no sound equipment to record their voices. He disparaged physical exaggeration and sought screen players who could "express every single feeling in the entire gamut of emotions" as if they were involved in real-life experiences.[12] He required his actors to respond to such techniques as the delineation of character through close-ups and the building of tempos in short scenes.

Working in close conjunction with cinematographer Billy Bitzer, Griffith put his camera in the middle of the action, taking close-ups and angle shots with an eye toward cutting and editing. He built separate shots into scenes, the scenes into sequences (a group of scenes linked together or unified by some common component), and the sequences into a swift, cohesive dramatic narrative. He crosscut between scenes to show parallel action and create suspense. He altered the chronological order of events to indicate a remembered incident or antecedent causal factors. Between 1908 and 1915, he completed 451 films of varying lengths, in the process gaining acceptance of movies as a form of enacted storytelling with enormous power and reach.

More than any other director of his time, Griffith clearly demonstrated the capacity of the motion picture to provide a coherent and compelling screen drama from disparate pieces of time and space. The dramatic power, eloquence, and vigor of his 1915 Civil War epic *The Birth of a Nation* constitutes a significant milestone in the evolution of moviemaking, although the cinematic dazzle is undeniably dimmed by its rabid racism (see Chapter Eight). Based on southern clergyman Thomas E. Dixon Jr.'s highly controversial novel and play *The Clansman,* the movie dramatizes a fictional account of the Old South, the Civil War, the Reconstruction period, and the emergence of the Ku Klux Klan—a white supremacist group formed soon after the war ended that imposed a reign of terror on former slaves.

In terms of conceptual scale, acting, sets, and technical devices, there simply had never been a movie like this before. Griffith used no shooting script, creating all the details and nuances of the screen epic as he went along. He employed hundreds of people to construct huge, elaborate indoor sets. Prior to shooting, he held six weeks of rehearsal, not a common practice at the time. Shooting itself took nine weeks, a remarkable schedule given that most movies were cranked out in one or two. The more than 1500 separate shots took three months to edit. The scene depicting the assassination of Abraham Lincoln alone comprises fifty-five shots, some lasting only a few seconds.

The three-hour movie combines sweeping, epic events with intimate moments of joy and sorrow. The mixture of the private and sentimental with the remote and impersonal is especially effective in the war scenes. Griffith's depiction of Union General William Sherman's vengeful "march to the sea" begins with everything blacked out save for a circular area in which we see a weeping woman and her children huddled near the ruins of a home on a hilltop. As this **iris,** or circular mask, opens out to reveal the full screen, the camera pans slowly to the right, showing a column of troops far below wreaking havoc throughout the countryside, and we understand the cause of her sorrow. The Union siege of Petersburg, South Carolina, is represented in ferocious detail. The Confederate battalion sweeps in from the left, the Union from the right. The two otherwise indistinguishable sides collide head-on in the field. Through long shots, medium shots, and close-ups, we see the men in trenches, the shelling, the bloody hand-to-hand combat, the human slaughter, and the harvest of death. The title card "War's Peace" accompanying a close-up of dead bodies extends the feeling conveyed by the devastation.

To accompany theatrical showings, Griffith, in collaboration with composer Joseph Carl Briel, synthesized an orchestral score from the music of

The title "War's Peace" is followed by an image of the dead bodies from both sides. This shot is repeated in slightly different versions after broad views of the fighting still in progress. (*The Birth of a Nation* [1915])

classical composers like Beethoven, Liszt, and Wagner, along with American folk music and period songs, such as "Dixie" and "Marching Through Georgia." Individual melodies suggested different times and locations. Most of the leading characters were assigned musical motifs. The depictions of battle were supported by such stirring pieces as Tchaikovsky's "1812 Overture." Edvard Grieg's "In the Hall of the Mountain King" lent excitement to the climactic and triumphant ride of the Ku Klux Klan. When the movie premiered at Clune's Auditorium in Los Angeles, with the original title *The Clansman,* a forty-piece orchestra and a large chorus accompanied it.

Russian Montage

Other filmmakers both in America and abroad absorbed many of the techniques Griffith refined. A contraband print of his 1916 epic *Intolerance,* which integrates a modern story of class hatred and the miscarriage of justice with three stories of intolerance from three different historical periods, made its way to Lev Kuleshov's film workshop in Moscow. There, a circle of young Bolshevik filmmakers was especially interested in the use of editing to convey emotion, thought, and revolutionary fervor. Because of budgetary constraints, the curriculum centered on the dissection, analysis, and discussion of films already made. Scenes and sequences from *Intolerance* were torn apart and rearranged incessantly to see whether more potent effects could be achieved from different juxtapositions.

When a print of Griffith's *The Birth of a Nation* reached the workshop, it was reportedly screened so often that it eventually fell apart. Kuleshov and his students spent months studying how the American director integrated the hundreds of separate shots in this cinematic tour de force. They used the French word **montage** to refer to the way a film is spliced together or "mounted." The term is virtually synonymous with editing, but it connotes more an act of "creation" than simply one of "combination." (Hollywood later appropriated the term to describe the piecing together of snippets of action to convey a great deal of information in a short time.)

Workshop member V. I. Pudovkin later credited Griffith with greatly influencing his own cinematic work. A chemist-turned-filmmaker, Pudovkin adapted the American director's shooting and editing techniques to the small dramas of everyday life. In the opening scene of his first dramatic feature, *Mother* (1926), which centers on hardships that befall a young worker and his mother during the time of the aborted 1905 revolution in Russia, the title character intercepts her nasty, drunken husband as he steps on a stool to grab a cherished old clock so he can pawn it. A flurry of quick cuts follows as she tries to wrest him away from his quarry. We see her weary but determined face, her hands gripping his thighs, his contorted expression as he struggles to free himself, their startled son sitting up in bed, the husband's snarling features, the stool tipping, the clock being ripped from the wall, and a piece of its inner mechanism rolling across the room. As the intense cutting ceases, the camera focuses on the husband stretched out on the floor.

Pudovkin's techniques for letting the parts speak for the whole would become a standard practice in the American movie industry. So, too, would his use of shot linkages to show thought processes, which are especially effective in the scenes after the son is arrested and sentenced to prison in a rigged trial. To represent the young man's anticipation of being set free, the director intercut tight shots of his smiling face and nervous hands with images of birds splashing in a village pond, of children laughing, and of a thawing mountain stream, its sparkling waters freed from winter confinement. In subsequent films, Pudovkin refined and polished techniques for revealing complex feelings and emotions through the juxtaposition of images. His astute shooting and editing methods were to have a strong influence on Hollywood film practices.

Griffith also influenced another Moscow workshop alumnus, Sergei Eisenstein, although the great Russian director's work departs significantly from the stress on personal drama characteristic of the idiom of cinematic expression taking root in the United States. In such pictures as *Strike* (1924), *The Battleship Potemkin* (1925), and *Ten Days That Shook the World* (1928), he replaces the traditional individual protagonist with a collective one. The Russian people, the disenfranchised masses, are the true heroes. Through motion pictures, Eisenstien symbolically represents their struggles so that one significant event epitomizes an entire social movement or phenomenon.

Eisenstein identified various kinds of montage, all which could be used simultaneously within any sequence. He spoke of "metric montage" to indicate the sense of beat that is created from cut to cut regardless of the content, "rhythmic montage" to indicate the movement within shots, and "tonal montage" to indicate the play of light and shadow, the characteristic emotional *feel* of the piece. He also explored what he called "intellectual montage," in which images unrelated in space or time are combined to evoke an idea. Cutting from a character to a peacock to symbolize the character's pride is an example of this kind of montage.

Of all Eisenstein's editing theories, the most significant is the concept of "dialectical montage," through which he sought to establish a cinematic language based upon psychological association and stimulation having little or nothing to do with narrative logic. Rather than subordinate style to story, he strove to develop a system of montage that operated according to Marxist dialectical principles. Each shot was conceived of as a thesis that, when placed next to another shot of opposing visual content (the antithesis of the first shot), produces a synthesis (a synthetic idea or impression).

Eisenstein wrote widely in books and articles about his theories of film construction, but it is his films that most brilliantly demonstrate the power of montage to jolt an audience to heightened awareness. His stunning camera work and careful editing is especially evident in the Odessa steps massacre in *The Battleship Potemkin*. By the time this horrifying scene begins, the sailors aboard the armored cruiser have mutinied and are anchored in the Ukrainian port city of Odessa. Many of the townspeople have gathered on the stone steps leading down to the harbor to cheer the sailors.

The scene is upbeat, festive, and full of movement, with parasols twirling, people laughing, hands waving, and boats sailing out to the cruiser with food for the mutineers. The camera singles out some of the townspeople—a white-bloused woman with dark bobbed hair, a matronly woman wearing a pince-nez, an ardent young man in wire-rimmed glasses, a mother urging her young son to wave at the mutinous crew, a dark-clad mother with a baby carriage, a legless man scooting along the steps. Each will achieve greater focus in the ensuing massacre.

There is little hint of the carnage to come. The title card "Suddenly" serves as a detonator of sorts. It is followed by a woman's shadowed face, her head jerking, her dark hair swirling, as she reacts in horror at what she witnesses. Through a series of **jump cuts**—mismatched shots that create a sense of abrupt spatial and temporal changes—her head yanks back again and again. The camera captures additional faces in the crowd freezing in fear. The legless man pushes away frantically on his hands, followed by other terrified citizens. All at once, everyone is dashing madly in one direction, toward the

Shadows of the advancing soldiers stretch ominously across her as a woman carrying an unconscious boy mouths the words "My child is hurt." (*The Battleship Potemkin* [1925])

camera, including a lady with a parasol. The entire screen fills up with its white, beribboned fabric.

The source of the townspeople's terror is soon revealed. A row of white-jacketed militiamen, rifles thrust forward, bayonets fixed, begins to move relentlessly down the steps, their long, stark shadows advancing ahead of them. They kill without hesitation or apparent remorse, firing on everyone from old women to young boys. Interspersed with individual incidents of brutality are shots of the fleeing townspeople and the advancing line of faceless militiamen firing into them. The average length of each shot is about two seconds. The rapid pacing and abrupt cutting, along with the chaotic movement and conflicting compositions, serve to heighten the sense of shock and horror.

As the troops descend, the small boy who waved at the ship falls down, his face bloodied. One small group kneels in prayer. An individual appeals for mercy but is shot down. Amidst cut upon cut of people running and falling, a soldier's boot crushes the injured child's hand. His mother's agonized face fills the screen. Clutching him in her arms, she begins to ascend the corpse-strewn steps. The shadows of advancing militiamen stretch ominously across her just before she and her child are gunned down.

The bloodshed culminates with a cut to the young mother hurriedly pushing her baby carriage across a landing to get her infant out of harm's way. As she is pierced by a bullet and stumbles, the carriage begins to roll down the steps. A collage of rapid cuts follows. We see the baby within the carriage as it careens out of control. As the militia advances, people continue to scurry in panic. Arriving at the bottom of the steps, they are trampled, beaten, and butchered by mounted Cossacks wielding sabers. We see the descending carriage from overhead with the baby's face in focus. We see the dying mother gasping her last breath, the carriage wheels spinning, the baby crying, the steps littered with bodies, and the woman with the pince-nez, looking bloodied and bedraggled.

As citizens are gunned down or hacked to death, the young man in wire-rimmed glasses looks up and screams in terror. The baby carriage continues to careen down the seemingly endless stairs. A close-up shows the jackbooted feet of the militiamen, who pause over a heap of fallen people whose hands reach up in supplication. Smoke drifts across the screen following a burst of rifle fire. The chaos ends as it started in a series of violent jump cuts. A frenzied young Cossack slashes his saber down again and again. His target is the elderly woman wearing the pince-nez. Her face fills the frame as blood gushes out of her right eye.

The cutting pattern marks out every conceivable contrast: between light and dark, between rounded and angular shapes, between high and low angles, between close and full shots, and between the methodical descent of the militia and the chaotic flight of the panicked crowd. Virtually every angle and every element are exploited to heighten and prolong the sense of relentless terror. Subjective time, the way it must have felt to be there, replaces natural time. By the middle of the massacre, when it seems everyone should be dead or have reached the bottom of the stone steps, the entire cycle of fleeing and killing appears to start anew. (This stunning sequence has been parodied or imitated in American movies ranging from Woody Allen's *Bananas* [1971] to Brian De Palma's *The Untouchables* [1987].)

The great Russian filmmaker's refusal to accept the restrictive tenets of his country's propagandists brought him into repeated conflicts with political authorities. His work is primarily aesthetic, and only secondarily political. His striking techniques for stretching or accelerating film time, his handling of large crowd scenes, his stunning use of montage, and his ability to extract every symbolic significance of social contrast gave a new luster to moviemaking and greatly influenced serious students of cinema in this country.

German Influences

Hollywood's aesthetic parameters were expanded by the inflow of many European cinematic currents. The burgeoning of artistic expression in Germany following the First World War, misanthropic and disillusioned but nevertheless striking and effective, was also evident in films. Among the many films probing the emotions and tensions of the postwar generation, *The Cabinet of Dr. Caligari* (1919), a highly stylized treatment of madness and evil, is one of the great achievements.

The effectiveness and importance of *Caligari* owes much to the stridently painted scenery and distorted designs of Hermann Warm, Walter Röhrig, and Walter Reimann. Through acutely angled shapes and sharp geometric figures highlighted by bizarre shadows painted a deep black, they created a nightmarish atmosphere steeped in an ambience of anxiety and terror—malformed doors, windows, and street lamps; jutting parapets, serpentine alleyways, and twisted house fronts that lean toward one another; and multilevel stages with platforms placed at peculiar angles. Costumes, props, and makeup are all similarly highly stylized. The extreme stylization of the *mise-en-scène* is echoed in the performances as well, with the actors often exhibiting jerky or dancelike movements. Most of the film was photographed in medium long shots that allow the surrounding decor to be fully seen and require the viewer's eye to study the entire frame.

The warped and out-of-joint images of the film's inner story about a sinister doctor who controls a somnambulist serial killer (Conrad Veidt, who later in his career played *Casablanca*'s Major Strasser) turn out to be the product of the twisted mind of its narrator, a patient at an insane asylum. But the film offers no normal world to offset this paranoid vision. The opening and closing scenes that frame the inner story are set in a hallucinatory landscape as well. (The film's director, Robert Wiene, added these framing scenes, much to the chagrin of its screenwriters, Carl Mayer and Hans Janowitz.)

Although a unique cinematic achievement, *The Cabinet of Dr. Caligari* also marked the immersion of a small but influential contingent of German filmmakers into the ferment of **expressionism,** an artistic movement that began in Europe around the turn of the century. In theatre, film, and the visual arts, this rather imprecise but useful category incorporates works that entail the use of violent distortion to represent intense emotions, especially terror, pathos, or agony. Among the more notable expressionist films produced in Germany during the early 1920s are *The Golem* (1920), based on a medieval Jewish legend about a gigantic clay statue that becomes a raging monster; *Nosferatu* (1922), an unauthorized adaptation of Bram Stoker's 1897 novel *Dracula*; and *Warning Shadows* (1923), in which the figures in a shadow play come to life and act out the secret passions of guests at a dinner party.

The legacy of German expressionism is reflected a wide range of Hollywood movies produced in the late 1920s and early 1930s. It is especially apparent in many horror films of the early talkies era. Such gothic tales of fear as *Dracula* (1931), *Frankenstein* (1931), *The Old Dark House* (1932), *The Invisible Man* (1933), *Mark of the Vampire* (1935), and *The Bride of Frankenstein*

The vampire Nosferatu. Whereas *Caligari*'s creators depended principally on production design for expressionistic effect, the approach taken in *Nosferatu* (1922) is much more cinematic, relying on camera angles, lighting, and editing. The vampire title character (Max Schreck), for example, is made all the more monstrous and sinister-looking through extreme low-angle shots.

(1935) feature eerie lighting, lifeless forests, fog-bound swamps, crumbling castles, torch-wielding villagers, demented scientists, and monstrous creatures that resonate with echoes of German expressionism. James Whale, under contract to Universal, directed several of these still often scary and unsettling screen classics. Before he began shooting *Frankenstein,* the British-born Whale reportedly watched such expressionist fare as *The Cabinet of Dr. Caligari* and *The Golem* for inspiration.

German expressionism is frequently cited as the progenitor of a *noir* sensibility as well. Although some similarities are apparent, the movies classified as *film noir* involve mostly naturalistic urban settings, carefully lighted and shot in ways that infuse mundane realities with an air of the sinister. Moreover, many of the *noir* directors and cinematographers invoked to support some ancestral relationship have no association with expressionist filmmaking. Further negating the alleged connection is the fact that most of the German craftsmen, technicians, and directors fleeing economic hardship or Nazi oppression found refuge in Hollywood by the mid-1930s, which leaves a wide gap between their arrival and the advent of *film noir.*

The former doorman enjoys a feast. This "happy ending" is wholly out of key with the unrelieved grimness that has gone before. It may have been tacked on to enhance the movie's foreign appeal, especially in the United States. (*The Last Laugh* [1924])

By the close of 1924, the macabre fantasies of the expressionist movement were beginning to fade before more mundane cinematic concerns. A number of German films focused on the oppressiveness of lower-middle-class life. Among the most influential of these was *The Last Laugh* (1924), whose realistic elements assume darkly symbolic overtones as the action unfolds. Its central character (Emil Jannings) gradually loses his mind when he is demoted from senior doorman to lavatory attendant because of advancing age. His status-conscious tenement house neighbors, previously in awe of his sparkling doorman's uniform, now gossip behind his back and taunt him. He's even rejected by his own family. Just when he seems to be at the lowest point of his life, a wealthy American unknowingly wills a fortune to him. Having the last laugh, as the film's only title card suggests, the now rich former doorman enjoys a huge feast in the dining room of the hotel where he had been humiliated.

This simple tale assumes a more complex narrative structure through innovative camera movements and subjective point-of-view shots. Working from a script by Carl Mayer, director F. W. Murnau begins the film with a striking shot of the bustling hotel lobby taken from a descending elevator. When the gates open, the camera glides across the floor to the revolving doors,

The camera takes an elevator ride. (*The Last Laugh* [1924])

where it pauses to focus on the rainy night. The proud old doorman is escorting patrons in and out of cabs under the cover of his big umbrella. Behind him is a broad city street filled with cars and buses and with pedestrians scurrying to get out of the rain. In the next shots, the camera joins him outside, where his struggle with a heavy trunk convinces the hotel manager that he is too old for the job. When he's notified of his demotion to lavatory attendant, a shot from his established point of view shows the manager's letter. It then blurs so that the words can no longer be read. As he descends into dementia, the thrusting spires of the urban landscape dissolve into towers of light and movement that seem to mock his reduced stature.

Throughout the film, the camera plays an integral role in suggesting the old man's shifting moods and emotions as it accompanies him through city streets, into the courtyard of his gloomy tenement dwelling, and down a long, dark corridor in the hotel where he works. In the absence of modern dollies and cranes, the film's Czech-born cinematographer, Karl Freund, achieved smooth camera movements through the use of bicycles, fire engine ladders, and overhead cables. To simulate the old man's point of view after consuming too much alcohol, Freund strapped a lightweight camera to his own chest and stumbled dizzily around the set of a bedroom. The film enjoyed great

A collage of malicious laughing faces reflects the demoted doorman's demented state of mind at the height of his despair. (*The Last Laugh* [1924])

critical acclaim in the United States, and many Hollywood directors and cinematographers were quick to emulate the way its innovative camerawork contributed to characterization.

Consolidation

The evolving idiom of the Hollywood style assumed direction and dimensions in a movie industry that was becoming increasingly centralized and concentrated. Companies expanded both horizontally—absorbing their competitors—and vertically—gaining the capacity to produce, distribute, and exhibit movies under a single corporate umbrella. Famous Players–Lasky, which changed to Paramount Publix in 1925 and which a decade later became simply Paramount Pictures, had set the consolidation process in motion during the war years. Adolph Zukor's policy of high rental rates and block booking prompted several theatre circuits in 1917 to form their own distribution channel, First National. To secure its position, the new company signed up several major screen stars to produce their own movies. Zukor, in turn, began to acquire theatre chains to control access to the markets for his movies. By the mid-1920s, Paramount had acquired substantial interests in nearly 400 theatres in both the United States and Canada.

The move toward ever-greater consolidation often came at the expense of the smaller, unaffiliated enterprises. Marcus Loew, an enterprising exhibitor, bought a nearly moribund production company called Metro Pictures in 1920 and, four years later, added the Goldwyn Pictures Corporation and the L. B. Mayer Company. The resultant Metro-Goldwyn-Mayer (M-G-M), Loew's production subsidiary, became the crown jewel of the movie industry. Mayer headed the studio facilities in Culver City, and Loew oversaw the parent corporation's exhibition and distribution empire from New York. (After Loew's death in 1927, Nicholas Schenck ascended to the presidency of Loew's Inc.)

The European Exodus

The big Hollywood studios attracted a steady flow of fresh talent from around the world. The migration of many German filmmakers to the movie colony had an especially salutary effect on American cinematic craftsmanship. In the postwar period, many independent German production firms folded. Those that survived found it increasingly difficult to borrow money from German banks. When the nationally subsidized UFA (*Universum Film Aktiengesellschaft*) conglomerate began to founder, Paramount and M-G-M seized the opportunity to subordinate their chief continental competitor by signing contracts with it. In exchange for financing UFA's debt, the two American studios gained the power to direct its policy and intensify their appropriation of its leading artists and technicians.

Scores of UFA employees emigrated to the United States, finding work in a variety of studios. Cinematographer Karl Freund, for instance, was initially under contract to Universal, where he photographed the highly atmospheric *Dracula* for director Tod Browning and also directed eight movies himself, among them *The Mummy* (1932). He later moved to M-G-M, where his cinematography for *The Good Earth* (1936) won him an Academy Award. (In the early 1950s, he pioneered a multiple-camera technique of film production for the *I Love Lucy* television series.)

Although many UFA émigrés became frustrated with the American studio production process and returned to Germany (some only to return later as refugees when Adolf Hitler came to power), a significant number settled in the southern California movie colony, carving out careers for themselves. Among the most successful was Budapest-born director Mihály Kertész, who had already made sixty-two silent movies before migrating to America. Under the name Michael Curtiz, he directed another hundred for Warner Bros. Pictures between 1927 and 1960—an eclectic mix of melodramas, swashbucklers, horror tales, westerns, and gangster films.

Paramount's photographic style was particularly affected by the large influx of UFA artists and technicians, which helped to make it in many ways the most conspicuously continental of the Hollywood studios. During the 1920s and 1930s, the company employed many directors, cinematographers, and craftspeople who had honed their skills while working for UFA. German modes of lighting, set design, and camera work are evident in scores of its pictures.

Like every other Hollywood studio, Paramount churned out the usual quota of undistinguished westerns, comedies, melodramas, and adventures. But many of its movies had a certain salacious savoir faire not often apparent in the output of most of its competitors. One of its most influential directors was UFA alumnus Ernst Lubitsch, whose drawing-room comedies set the standard for the symbolic use of detail to suggest sexual activity that would otherwise have been taboo on American screens. The irony, elegance, and sophistication he invested in his movies became known throughout Hollywood as "the Lubitsch touch." In the mid-1930s, the Berlin-born director actually assumed the mantle of Paramount's production chief for a while.

Paramount even hired Sergei Eisenstein to prepare a screen adaptation of Theodore Dreiser's *An American Tragedy,* an indictment of the crass materialistic values that drive a young man to seek success no matter what the consequences. The idea was that it would be the director's first Hollywood film. Eisenstein wrote a script with an associate, but up-and-coming studio executive David O. Selznick, though he found it extremely moving, argued that making it into a film was a bad commercial risk. "When I had finished it, I was so depressed I wanted to reach for the bourbon bottle," he said in a memo to Paramount's production chief. "As entertainment I don't think it has one chance in a hundred."[13] The studio decided to drop the project—or, at any rate, to drop the famous Russian director. (Josef von Sternberg, a European who had learned to give Hollywood what it expected, directed a decidedly different version of *An American Tragedy* in 1931.)

Innovations from abroad were invariably adapted to the American movie industry's prevailing idiom, whose parameters had become fairly fixed by the early 1920s. Most artists and artisans in Hollywood's ateliers increasingly saw themselves as "bound by rules that set stringent limits on individual innovations." They generally agreed that "telling a story is the basic formal concern," that "realism" was always to be aimed for, and that "artifice" should be concealed through unobtrusive filmmaking techniques and a stress on continuity of action. In addition, it was established that the stories themselves should be "comprehensible and unambiguous" and should possess "a fundamental appeal that transcends class and nation."[14]

These guiding principles, which prevail to the present, proved themselves able to accommodate both great art and works of inferior quality. Virtually all phases and aspects of production saw steady improvement and refinement during the 1920s. But the greater skill and subtlety evident in screenwriting, acting, directing, set design, photography, and editing techniques was briefly annulled by the shift from speechless cinema to talking pictures. The next chapter considers the impact of talkies on the idiom of the Hollywood film and traces the evolution of the studio system of production that came to dominate moviemaking in the United States.

Notes

1. See Russell Merritt, "Nickelodeon Theatres, 1905–1914: Building an Audience for the Movies," in Tino Balio, ed., *The American Film Industry,* rev. ed. (Madison: University of Wisconsin Press, 1985), pp. 83–102; and Robert C. Allen, "Motion Picture Exhibition in Manhattan: Beyond the Nickelodeon," *Cinema Journal,* Spring 1979, pp. 2–15.
2. Charles Musser, *The Emergence of Cinema: The American Screen to 1907* (Berkeley: University of California Press, 1990), p. 494.
3. Jack Alicoate, "The Romance of the Roxy," in Ben M. Hall, ed., *The Golden Age of the Movie Palace* (New York: Potter, 1961), p. 82.
4. Quoted in Joseph P. Kennedy, *The Story of Films* (Chicago: Shaw, 1927), p. 265.
5. Sharon Scott, "Imitation of Life," *AFI Report,* 4, 2 (May 1973), p. 8. Quoted in Douglas Gomery, "Movie Theatres for Black Americans," in *Shared Pleasures: A History of Movie Presentation in the United States* (Madison: University of Wisconsin Press, 1992), p. 157.
6. These figures are cited in Robert C. Allen, *Vaudeville and Film 1895–1915: A Study in Media Interaction* (New York: Arno Press, 1980), pp. 213–214.
7. See Anthony Slide, *The Big V: A History of the Vitagraph Company* (Metuchen, NJ: Scarecrow Press, 1976), pp. 34–40.
8. Leo C. Rosten, *Hollywood: The Movie Colony, the Movie Makers* (New York: Harcourt, Brace, 1941), p. 13.
9. Quoted in Stuart Ewen, *PR! A Social History of Spin* (New York: Basic Books, 1996), p. 103.
10. Leslie Midkiff DeBauche, *Reel Patriotism: The Movies and World War I* (Madison: University of Wisconsin Press, 1997), p. 38.
11. Reported in Kristen Thompson and David Bordwell, *Film History: An Introduction* (New York: McGraw-Hill, 1994), p. 120.
12. D. W. Griffith, "What I Demand of Movie Stars," *Motion Picture Classic,* February 1917, p. 40.
13. Quoted in Rudy Behlmer, ed., *Memo from David O. Selznick* (New York: Viking Press, 1972), p. 26.
14. See David Bordwell, "The Classical Hollywood Style 1917–60," in David Bordwell, Janet Staiger, and Kristin Thompson, eds. *The Classical Hollywood Cinema: Film Style & Mode of Production to 1960* (New York: Columbia University Press, 1985), p. 3.

The Studio Era

The Hollywood style came into full flower during the great Studio Era of the 1930s and 1940s. Huge industrial complexes employing an elaborate division of labor churned out hundreds of movies every year. A handful of companies not only produced most of these movies but also distributed them for exhibition in their own theatre chains. All through this period, neighborhood movie houses were attracting Americans in far larger numbers than either libraries or legitimate theatres. Millions went to "the movies" at least twice a week regardless of what appeared on the screen. This chapter looks at the policies, priorities, personalities, and production practices that influenced the characteristic form of movies made in the United States from the advent of talkies to the end of the Second World War.

The Arrival of Sound

Few developments affected moviemaking more than talking pictures, which were the result of a long process of technical experiments and entrepreneurial efforts. As early as 1895, Thomas Edison had attempted to market a combination of his viewing machine and phonograph called the Kinetophone. But the music, heard through ear tubes, seldom related to the images it was accompanying. Few were sold, and the system was soon shelved. In the ensuing years, a number of unsuccessful phonograph-linked sound systems appeared on the market. The earliest ones used wax cylinders, and the later ones disks. All had varying degrees of difficulty with synchronization and amplification. The brevity of the disk format made it especially difficult to apply to feature-length films.

Lee de Forest, a pioneer in radio technology, developed a method of recording sound directly on the film itself, which he publicly unveiled in 1923 at the Rialto and Rivoli theatres in New York City. Despite this system's highly sophisticated design, which solved the problem of amplification, de Forest's attempts to secure financial backing met with repeated failure. At this time, sound technology of any sort was likely to generate little more than mild curiosity from studio chieftains and their financial backers.

Already realizing hefty profits from speechless cinema, the movie industry had no economic incentive to invest the many thousands of dollars necessary for construction of new sound production facilities and the installation and utilization of sound equipment in theatres. The major studios had other solid economic reasons for not shifting from speechless cinema to talkies. They would be stuck with a large library of silent pictures representing millions of dollars in investment and would not be able to compete in the international market as effectively with sound movies as they did with silent ones with their easily exchangeable titling.

Any diminution of the vast overseas market for American movies was of special significance because of the substantial revenue they generated. To exploit the lucrative film export trade, silent film titles had been translated into dozens of languages, including Arabic, Armenian, Chinese, Croatian, Estonian, Finnish, Flemish, Gaelic, Greek, Hebrew, Hindi, Javanese, Korean, Latvian, Malay, Serbian, Syrian, and Ukrainian. With the addition of spoken dialogue would come all sorts of translating, subtitling, and **dubbing** problems. This would allow lagging European firms to revitalize their studio operations and achieve a certain degree of independence, especially since many governments were already taking measures by the latter half of the 1920s to reduce imports, such as placing quotas on exhibition requiring a certain percentage of screen time annually for indigenous film fare.

The Boom in Broadcasting

A strong impetus for the conversion to sound pictures came from the boom in broadcasting. Soon after the first radio station began sending out its signal on a regular basis in 1920, seemingly everyone wanted to get on the broadcast bandwagon. Department stores, hotels, churches, newspapers, colleges, and business corporations all applied for licenses. New stations were springing up on a daily basis throughout the nation. At the same time, radio receiving sets were fast becoming a household fixture. An estimated 5 million homes were equipped to receive broadcast signals by 1926; some 21 million more remained to be supplied.[1]

The birth that year of the formidable National Broadcasting Company (NBC), which soon would provide radio programming nationwide, virtually assured that most of the remaining homes would buy a set. The new network was the progeny of a giant electronics consortium consisting of Radio Corporation of America (RCA), General Electric (GE), and Westinghouse. This was not a bloodline to be taken lightly by the movie industry, especially because that same year saw a precipitous drop in theatre attendance. Soon after its emergence, the infant NBC had two radio networks in operation, each with a powerful lineup of stations across the country.

The interconnection of stations and the centralization of programming coincided with the general consolidation and standardization of goods and services nationwide. Radio broadcasting provided an extremely effective means of promoting standardized products of all sorts. The makers of canned soups, packaged desserts, cigarettes, brand-name coffee, and other mass-produced items were soon lining up to sponsor shows. Access to the airwaves went to the highest bidder in a process that resembled an auction block. The huge revenues this generated enabled producers to offer programs and performers that kept listeners riveted to their radio sets.

Radio's resounding financial success made the economic climate in the movie industry more conducive to the promotion of sound conversion. Already at the summit of the broadcasting system, RCA and its corporate companions seized the opportunity to get a foothold in Hollywood as well. Why not? The same vacuum tubes, microphones, amplifiers, and loudspeakers that were used in broadcast transmission and reception could also be used to bring voices, music, and sound effects to the silent screen. In the fall of 1926, RCA attempted to market a sound-on-film system developed by GE. Its initial overtures to the major studios met with some success, but negotiations stalled when the system suffered frequent breakdowns.

Investment in Sound

At around the same time, American Telephone and Telegraph (AT&T), which for a short time belonged to the RCA consortium and which continued to share patents for electronic equipment with RCA through cross-licensing agreements, was promoting a sound-on-disc system synchronized with the unrolling picture film. The company's Bell Laboratories had developed it. Like RCA, AT&T sought to sell Hollywood on the idea of converting to sound pictures. When the major studios failed to sign up for its system, the telephone giant pursued converts lower in the industry hierarchy.

Warner Bros. Pictures, incorporated in 1923, was the first company to respond favorably to AT&T's advances. Although hardly in the industry's front ranks, it was clearly a studio on the rise. The four brothers in charge of the company—Samuel, Harry, Albert, and Jack—were the sons of impoverished

Polish immigrants from Krasmashiltz, near the Russian border, who had eventually settled in Youngstown, Ohio. The three older brothers, along with eleven-year-old Jack, had begun in the movie business modestly, opening a nickelodeon in 1903, renting films to other nickelodeons a few years later, and becoming shoestring producers in 1917.

After the First World War, the brothers bought forty acres of a ranch on Sunset Boulevard in Hollywood and built studio facilities to expand their production activities. The mainstay of the Warner studio's financial structure in the 1920s was a German shepherd named Rin Tin Tin, whose canine exploits made him one of the biggest box office attractions of the American silent screen. It also enjoyed the histrionic talents of the eminent stage actor John Barrymore. In the spring of 1925, Warners purchased the ailing Vitagraph Company (sole survivor of the ill-fated patents trust), which had a nationwide distribution operation and two well-equipped studios—one in Brooklyn and the other in Hollywood.

Once Warner Bros. signed on for the sound-on-disc system, AT&T's manufacturing subsidiary, Western Electric, quickly installed sound reproduction and recording equipment in the studio's Brooklyn operation. A corporation called Vitaphone was formed early in 1926 with the express purpose of marketing the sound apparatus. Western Electric granted this new concern an exclusive contract to record and reproduce sound movies on its equipment. Some 70 percent of Vitaphone's stock was owned by Warner, which had agreed to finance the entire venture.

To capitalize on its investment, Warners decided to delay the release of an already completed silent film titled *Don Juan*, starring John Barrymore as the philanderer who finds love, so that a musical score played by the New York Philharmonic could be synchronized to the action. Along with several sound film shorts, one of which featured industry spokesperson Will Hays extolling the virtues of sound pictures, *Don Juan* premiered in August 1926 at the Warner Theatre in New York City. Among the enthusiastic audience were such industry leaders as Adolph Zukor and William Fox.

Other successful synchronized sound shorts and features followed. By the end of 1926, Vitaphone had won contracts to install nearly a hundred systems, mostly in the East. But the big breakthrough came in the fall of the following year with the New York premiere of *The Jazz Singer*, based on a successful Broadway play about a cantor's son who enters show business. The movie starred popular songster Al Jolson (reportedly paid $100,000 plus a percentage of the profits for his services). After singing his first song, "Dirty Hands, Dirty Face," Jolson utters the prophetic words "Wait a minute. Wait a minute. You ain't heard nothing yet." He continues to speak, introducing his next song, "Toot, Toot, Tootsie." Midway through the picture, he engages in a conversation with his screen mother, played by Eugenie Besserer. This brief verbal exchange in the natural voices of the performers made an otherwise

A billboard promotes *Don Juan* (1926), which premiered at the "refrigerated" (air-conditioned) Warner Theatre in New York City on August 6, 1926.

mediocre movie memorable. Produced at a cost of about $500,000, *The Jazz Singer* broke box office records almost everywhere it played.

Before the end of decade, the era of speechless cinema was over. Employing complicated maneuvers, Western Electric managed to terminate its exclusive contract with Warner and, through a newly created subsidiary called ERPI (Electrical Research Products, Inc.), began to license all comers. By mid-1928, such formidable production companies as Paramount, M-G-M, and Universal had become ERPI licensees. Several smaller companies soon fell in line as well. By the close of the next year, over 37 percent of sound-equipped theatres in the country had Western Electric installations.

To secure a leading role for itself in the sound pictures, RCA joined with GE and Westinghouse in the spring of 1928 to form a sound-equipment marketing company called RCA Photophone (its optical sound system eventually became the industry standard). It had earlier bought a substantial block of stock in Film Booking Offices (FBO), a small movie company that had studios in California and thirty-five exchanges throughout the United States. A short time later, it gained controlling interest of Keith-Albee Orpheum, a vaudeville chain that had fallen on hard times.

In October 1928, FBO and the vaudeville chain were merged with RCA Photophone to create Radio-Keith-Orpheum, a new holding company with assets in excess of $80 million. Its principal production subsidiary, RKO Radio

A contemporary poster promotes *The Jazz Singer* (1927), the movie that sounded the death knell for speechless cinema.

Pictures, quickly became one of the major players in the movie industry. Although the studio fell on hard times during the Depression, its trademark of the blinking radio tower atop a spinning globe nonetheless introduced some of Hollywood's most unique and memorable movies, among them such classics as *King Kong* (1933) and *Citizen Kane* (1941).

Stylistic Setbacks

When the movies first began to "speak," sound technicians from the broadcasting and telephone industries, most of whom had little or no knowledge of moviemaking, exercised a great deal of authority over production. "The sound man at that time had been supreme god on the set," states cinematographer Hal Mohr, who photographed *The Jazz Singer*. "If he said 'You have to move

A poster for *King Kong* **(1933).** A massive publicity campaign helped to generate interest in the movie, which played simultaneously at the Roxy Theatre and Radio City Music Hall in New York City. It was one of the first movies to be promoted on the rival medium of radio. Over their radios, listeners heard, "King Kong is coming! A monster! All-powerful! Beating down all weapons, smashing all barriers! You won't believe your eyes! Here he comes . . . listen!" A great roar followed.

that light there,' then the light disappeared; or if he said 'I want that microphone down here,' that's where the microphone was placed, despite the fact that an actor had to deliver the lines and we had to photograph him."[2]

This short but dictatorial reign of the sound technician contributed to a general loss of stylistic flexibility, resulting in a brief setback in the steady advance of aesthetic achievement in moviemaking. "Most talkies seemed bare and clumsy by comparison with the dazzling inventions of the late silent cinema," notes film scholar David Bordwell. "Acting styles often coarsened, camera positions became far more limited, editing options were reduced."[3] By all accounts, it simply was not possible early on to make a sound picture that even approached the artistic quality of a silent one.

Ironically, silence was required for sound. Since cameras whirred when in operation, they were placed in glass-fronted soundproof booths. Housing both camera apparatus and operator, these bulky contraptions were facetiously dubbed "ice-boxes" because that's what they resembled and because, inside, they were extremely hot. Soon the booths would be equipped with wheels and rails to make them more mobile. However, although this permitted some mobility, camera movements tended to be slow and ponderous. In most tracking shots, the camera followed a straight path with little or no lateral or vertical variation. Some films from this period do show unimpeded panning and tilting, but the shots in most cases were taken with an unsynchronized camera, with the sound laid under them in editing.

Directors were compelled to stage the action to accommodate the requirements of sound recording. Intimate close-ups were difficult to achieve because the bulky camera booths could not be put in close proximity to the actor, and their thick glass reduced the photographic capacity of long lenses. This made the action seem more remote and less involving. Shooting was confined within the four walls and ceiling of a soundstage, because the weight and bulk of the camera booths precluded the possibility of shooting outside a studio. The vacuum tube microphones were also heavy and hard to move, and were sensitive in only one direction. Actors had to speak their lines from relatively static positions into potted plants and table lamps without turning their heads.

Recording on wax discs required each take to be made with a full ten-minute roll of film. Retakes were resorted to only under the most dire circumstances. To preserve the changes in framing essential to continuity cutting, scenes were often shot with multiple cameras, enabling the action to be captured from different angles using lenses of varying focal lengths. Because each fragment of a scene was not set up, rehearsed, and shot separately using a single camera, any error in performance or recording required that the entire action be started all over again. Using several cameras simultaneously created a need for more uniform illumination, resulting in a kind of flat, low-contrast lighting effect, as opposed to the more molded, high-contrast lighting possible with single-camera setups.

The Fall of the Silent Stars

Talkies took an especially terrible toll on silent-screen stars. Some of moviedom's most magnetic personalities lost their electrical charge the moment they attempted to speak into a microphone. Romantic leading man John Gilbert was one of the most famous casualties of the sound revolution. Hollywood legend to the contrary, his speaking voice was a pleasant enough tenor. But it was not very rich in nuance and recorded as slightly high-pitched (baritones faired better than tenors with the early sound equipment). He made his speaking debut in M-G-M's all-star extravaganza *Hollywood Revue of 1929,* in which he credibly performed the balcony scene from *Romeo and Juliet* with Norma Shearer.

Quintessential flapper Clara Bow. Her already stellar career got a big boost in 1927, when she starred in the movie *It,* from a story and script by English author Elinor Glyn. Bow thence became known as the "It" girl, the designation defined by Glyn as "an inner magic, an animal magnetism."

Gilbert's career took a dive after he starred in *His Glorious Night* (1929), directed by actor Lionel Barrymore, who was suffering from debilitating arthritis. The previously adored romantic star's not quite husky enough voice, coupled with a silly script and the ailing Barrymore's diminished capacity, resulted in an unmitigated cinematic disaster. In Gilbert's first speech, when he uttered the words "I love you, I love you, I love you," his mouth and nose came together almost like a bird's beak. It was steadily downhill from there. He made nine more talking pictures between 1929 and 1934, none of them big box office successes, and seemed to have lost self-confidence, drinking ever more heavily. Late in 1935, he suffered a mild heart attack while swimming and never recovered his health. He died early the following year of heart failure.

Several silent stars fell victim to the tyranny of talkies because they didn't have voices to match their screen personae. Aided by Paramount's publicity machine and slick productions, Clara Bow, born into a desperately poor and brutal Brooklyn family, was molded into the quintessential Hollywood flapper—sexy, rebellious, and worldly-wise—in movies like *It* (1927). But she came to grief in trying to transfer her screen image to her private life. Already plagued by sex scandals and nervous breakdowns, she proved unable to meet the challenge of the microphone. The less-than-mellifluous sounds emanating from her cupid-bow lips were neither magical nor magnetic. (Her later years were plagued by severe psychiatric problems.)

The enormously popular Talmadge sisters were also unable to come to terms with sound. Norma Talmadge, who made her film debut with Vitagraph in 1910, saw her long career came to an abrupt end on the sound stage. After playing the long-suffering heroine in scores of tearful melodramas, her first entry into talkies—*DuBarry, Woman of Passion* (1930)—revealed her decidedly Brooklynese diction. She soon retired from the screen to live off her considerable fortune. Her younger sister Constance, whose specialty was sophisticated comedy, did likewise without making a single talkie. For both of them, it apparently was simply too late to start over.

Elocution experts suddenly found themselves in great demand as scores of screen players panicked. Except for those few with extensive stage training, most would need voice tests and diction lessons. The sound barrier proved to be especially difficult for actors from other countries to surmount. Many were simply unable to perform effectively in an alien tongue. The thick accent of Mexican-born Ramon Novarro, who had starred in such silent-screen classics as *Ben-Hur, a Tale of Christ* (1925), quickly sent his career into a tailspin (although he later bounced back as a character actor). Exotic French leading lady Renée Adorée, who counted among her credits such high-powered pictures as *The Big Parade* (1925), suffered much the same fate. Her glitter was gone well before she succumbed to tuberculosis in 1933.

Some actors with foreign accents triumphed in the transition from silent movies to talkies. As Greta Garbo, Swedish-born Greta Gustafsson had soared to stardom in the 1920s primarily playing slightly neurotic temptresses who bring about their own downfall. Her love scenes with John Gilbert in such romantic melodramas as *Flesh and the Devil* (1927) and *A Woman of Affairs* (1928) scorched the silent screen. While her costar's career collapsed, she rose to even greater heights in the sound era. Her throaty intonations added to the air of elegance, sensitivity, and restless reserve she brought to her characters.

Hollywood's royal couple, Mary Pickford and Douglas Fairbanks, decided to combat the threat of sound by combining their drawing power and costarring in *The Taming of the Shrew* (1929). He clearly had a persona that fit the bill for the swaggering, self-confident Petruchio, but his voice came through the microphone an octave or two higher than normal; and she was badly miscast as the shrewish, mercurial Kate. The production itself, adapted and directed by Sam Taylor, was stagy and poorly paced. Released just as the stock market crashed, it flopped at the box office. Perhaps its most memorable and amusing aspect is a now legendary credit: "By William Shakespeare, with additional dialogue by Sam Taylor."

Clarence Brown directs Greta Garbo and John Gilbert in *A Woman of Affairs* (1928), in which the two actors play former lovers who have a night of illicit sex (her wedding ring slips off her finger and falls to the floor as they couple).

This was the couple's only costarring appearance. Although both made additional sound movies, none came close to their silent-screen successes. (Fairbanks's son and namesake became a star of both film and television.) Whether their screen demise was the result of talkies or would have come in any case is difficult to tell. By 1930, Pickford was thirty-seven and Fairbanks was ten years older. Even celluloid icons tarnish over time.

Charlie Chaplin, the couple's United Artists business partner, managed to weather the sound storm largely by ignoring it. During the 1930s, he released just two movies. He was already working on the first of these, *City Lights* (1931), when sound disrupted the movie industry. After weighing his options, he decided not to compromise his pantomime with dialogue. He continued shooting it as a silent film, adding synchronized sound effects and his own musical score in postproduction. The result is a poignant, sentimental comedy of mime and characterization in which Chaplin's tramp character falls in love with a blind flower girl and goes through a series of misadventures in order to raise money for the operation that will restore her sight. The movie is filled with funny bits such as the swallowed whistle that emits peculiar sounds at an elegant cocktail party.

His second picture of the decade, *Modern Times* (1936), has the tramp character in a series of comic confrontations with the machinery of a factory assembly line as he struggles to maintain his sanity in a completely mechanized world. Chaplin again wrote a musical score—bouncy, jaunty tunes for the comic sequences and a lushly romantic violin melody for the tender ones—and added several amusing sound effects—for instance, giving factory machines a hum and whir. In addition, he used synchronized speech of sorts for two sequences. In one, the factory president's booming voice, slightly distorted by an echo effect, emanates from a television screen as Chaplin's tramp sneaks a smoke in a gleaming white, sterile lavatory. In the other, the resilient tramp, working as a nightclub waiter after being fired from the factory, sings a gibberish song when his shirt cuffs containing the actual lyrics fly off. But this comical attack on the social ills of the machine age was the last time Chaplin thumbed his nose at talkies. His remaining pictures all depend on conversation and speeches.

Hard Times for Female Filmmakers

With few exceptions, female filmmakers did not fare well in the sound revolution. In its early years, the movie industry had opened its doors wide to women, and a significant number held positions of some power as writers, editors, and directors. The first notable woman to occupy the director's chair in Hollywood was Lois Weber, who was as well known as D. W. Griffith in the mid-1910s. Working with her husband, W. Phillips Smalley, she not only directed but also wrote scenarios and title cards, acted, designed sets and costumes, edited, and even developed negatives. Together, the couple turned out dozens of short and feature films for a succession of small production companies.

A one-time street corner evangelist and missionary worker in the poorer sections of Pittsburgh, Weber frequently used the film medium as a forum for severe moralizing. She attacked prejudice in *The Jew's Christmas* (1913), religious intolerance in *Hypocrites* (1914), child labor in *Shoes* (1916), and capital punishment in *The People vs. John Doe* (1916). Although unwilling to ally herself with any special interest groups, she made several movies that focused on the social and moral problems women faced. For example, she wrote and codirected (with husband Phillips Smalley) *Where Are My Children?* (1916), that deals with the still-controversial subject of abortion. While making a strong case for the importance of educating women about birth control, it mounts an unequivocal attack on the use of abortion to avoid child-bearing.

By 1916, Weber was a top salaried director at Universal, earning $5000 a week. She formed her own production company the following year, and three years later, she signed a five-picture contract with Famous Players–Lasky at $50,000 apiece. In the early 1920s, however, her films began to fail at the box office. Among her surviving pictures from this period is *Too Wise Wives* (1921), a satire about marital relationships that she produced, wrote, and directed.

(It was made while her own marriage to collaborator Phillips Smalley was falling apart.) Although it contains some droll social observations, it is burdened by stilted acting, verbose titling, and a static camera style. By mid-decade, Weber had lost her company and suffered a breakdown. An attempted comeback in 1926 met with little success. During her directorial career, which ended in 1934, she is estimated to have made between 200 and 400 films—although fewer than 50 of them still exist. She died in 1939, alone, penniless, and largely forgotten.

With the advent of sound, most female directors faded away. During the 1930s, Dorothy Arzner was the only woman director in Hollywood to produce a substantial body of work. Starting out as a script typist, she became a skilled editor before turning to directing in 1927. Over the next sixteen or so years, she directed seventeen movies, including Paramount's first talking feature, *The Wild Party* (1929), in which Clara Bow was cast as a sexy college coed despite her unrefined diction and harsh nasal tones.

Leaving Paramount in 1932 to go freelance, Arzner subsequently directed movies at several major studios. Among her directorial efforts that have attracted latter-day attention for their supposed nascent feminist slant are *Christopher Strong* (1933), whose pregnant aviatrix protagonist (Katherine Hepburn) crashes her plane to protect her married lover from scandal, and *Dance, Girl, Dance* (1940), in which an aspiring-ballerina-turned-burlesque-dancer (Maureen O'Hara) berates the men ogling her gyrations. After the soft-spoken and self-effacing Arzner retired from Hollywood in 1943, mainstream movie directing remained for decades an almost exclusively male enclave. (In the early 1950s, British-born film star Ida Lupino directed a handful of low-budget movies.)

Adverse Effects on Women Writers

Women writers were also adversely affected by the advent of talkies. From the 1910s to the early 1930s, according to various accounts, women constituted about a quarter of the screenwriters employed in the movie industry and had a major hand in half of all films produced. Of course, just who was responsible for what is often impossible to determine. The division of labor at most studios was fairly rigid by the 1920s, and enforced collaboration was the rule in all aspects of the production process. A team of writers typically developed stories in stages, from the early treatment describing the action but containing little or no dialogue to the last-minute reworking, polishing, and revising before the completed scenario went into production.

The highest-paid writer toiling in this assembly line was Frances Marion, a former newspaper reporter and magazine illustrator. Arriving in Hollywood in 1913, she was employed as an actress when Lois Weber, who had a reputation for nurturing new talent, offered her a job. She became the prominent

Frances Marion in her army uniform. In 1918 she gave up her $50,000-a-year salary as a scenario writer to serve as a government war correspondent.

director's protégée and quickly demonstrated skill in all stages of production. Her career really took off in 1916 when she began writing scenarios for Mary Pickford, who became part of her close network of fiercely loyal female friends, which included other successful writers for the screen such as Adela Rogers St. Johns, Anita Loos, and Bess Meredyth. Reflecting back on her career, Marion once remarked: "I hope my story shows one thing—how many women gave me real aid when I stood at the crossroads. Too many women go around these days saying women in important positions don't help their own sex, but that was never my experience. The list is endless, believe me."[4]

After a hiatus as a war correspondent in France (1918–1919), Marion returned to the movie colony and within a few short years enjoyed enormous success. By 1928, she was earning $3000 per week as head of the story department at M-G-M. Until the mid-1930s, no writer for the screen—male or female—could match her paycheck or enjoyed as much acclaim. Despite her achievements, however, she had to prove herself again and again to male superiors such as Louis B. Mayer, who apparently never completely accepted women in prominent positions on the dark side of the camera.

A gifted scenarist, prized for her ability to create compelling characters, Marion collaborated with virtually every major silent director from Maurice Tourneur to John Ford. She drafted hit films for a pantheon of silent screen stars: Marie Dressler in *Tillie Wakes Up* (1917), Douglas Fairbanks in *He Comes Up Smiling* (1918), Mary Pickford in *Pollyanna* (1920), Norma Talmadge in *The Lady* (1925), Rudolph Valentino in *The Son of the Sheik* (1926), Lillian Gish in *The Scarlet Letter* (1926), and Greta Garbo in *Love* (1927). With the arrival of talkies, her assignments included adapting Eugene O'Neill's 1921 Pulitzer Prize–winning play *Anna Christie* for the sound debut of Garbo, who immortalized the title character's first line (straight from the original play): "Gimme a whiskey—ginger ale on the side. And don't be stingy, baby."

Marion is credited with turning out over 300 scripts during her career. She also won the second and third Oscars ever awarded for screenwriting— for *The Big House* (1930) and *The Champ* (1931). But by the latter half of the 1930s, this pioneering writer for the screen was clearly on a downward trajectory. Although she remained on M-G-M's payroll until 1946, most of her professional time was devoted to doctoring the scripts of other writers.

Scribes from the East

Once talkies took hold, the studios replaced many of their silent-screen scenarists with writers imported from the East Coast. Failed playwrights, frustrated novelists, out-of-work reporters, and even literary luminaries flocked to Hollywood seeking fortune if not fame. Among those migrating westward were members of the famed Round Table, journalists and playwrights who met weekly over lunch at the Algonquin Hotel in Manhattan to trade in well-publicized witticisms. Although they often mocked movies, the Algonquin group found the lure of Hollywood lucre irresistible.

The "gold rush" started late in 1926 when recent Hollywood arrival Herman Mankiewicz, missing his caustic luncheon cronies, sent a now-famous telegram to Ben Hecht: "WILL YOU ACCEPT THREE HUNDRED PER WEEK TO WORK FOR PARAMOUNT PICTURES? ALL EXPENSES PAID. THE THREE HUNDRED IS PEANUTS. MILLIONS ARE TO BE GRABBED OUT HERE AND YOUR ONLY COMPETITION IS IDIOTS. DON'T LET THIS GET AROUND." The word did get around, spread mostly by the mischievous Mankiewicz himself. When Hecht took up residence in Tinseltown, as the movie capital was derisively called, his buddy Mank decided to give him a crash course in writing for the screen: "I want to point out to you that in a novel a hero can lay ten girls and marry a virgin for a finish," he noted among other things. "In a movie this is not allowed. The hero, as well as the heroine, has to be a virgin. The villain can lay anybody he wants, have as much fun as he wants cheating and stealing, getting rich and whipping the servants. But you have to shoot him in the end."[5] The astute Hecht apparently caught on quickly. By the mid-1930s, he had eclipsed Frances Marion for the title of "Hollywood's highest paid screenwriter."

Several celebrated scribes turned out to have a flair for scriptwriting and stayed on in Hollywood to make both big money and lasting contributions to cinematic art. Others found the indignity of toiling on a literary assembly line too much to bear. More than a few, although often scornful of the studio system, succumbed to demons that had little to do with the demands of martinet moguls or dictatorial directors. Some, like the great novelist F. Scott Fitzgerald, simply had neither the talent nor the temperament for writing movie scripts. Despite several sojourns in Hollywood, Fitzgerald received screen credit on only one movie—a 1938 adaptation of *Three Comrades,* Eric Maria Remarque's celebrated novel about three young men in Germany in the wake of the First World War.

The New Studio Order

Spoken dialogue came to movies only months before the Great Depression enveloped the United States and much of the rest of the world. The concentration of capital necessary for the conversion to sound, coupled with the economic crisis gripping the nation, led to corporate upheaval in many movie companies and to a reordering of the entire industry. When the dust had settled, eight companies dominated the industry. The Big Five—those involved in all three phases of the movie industry (production, distribution, exhibition)—were Loew's–M-G-M, Warner Bros. Pictures, Paramount, Fox Film (20th Century–Fox in 1935), and RKO. The Little Three included Universal, Columbia, and United Artists. Of these, Universal and Columbia were producers-distributors, and United Artists was solely a distributor. Although the production facilities of these companies were centered in and around Hollywood, their administrative offices were located in New York City, close to the center of finance.

The expense involved in converting to sound movies had made the major companies much more dependent on their sources of financing, particularly the banking interests of the Morgans and Rockefellers. Financial control of several enterprises had, in fact, slipped out of the hands of the old movie moguls and into those of their backers. William Fox, for instance, was divested of his company in 1930. Wall Street's grip tightened further early in the decade, when slumping box office receipts put several major movie firms in financial disarray, forcing them to submit to or fight off receivership and bankruptcy.

Some foes of high finance's dealings in the movie industry turned to the works of the at-once revered and reviled German political philosopher Karl

NONFICTION FILMS

Many elements of the Hollywood style can be found in the documentary, a cinematic form that came into its own in the 1920s and 1930s. As with most fictional films, mainstream documentaries are constructed from the basic building blocks of Hollywood moviemaking—close-ups, point-of view shots, striking angles, continuity editing, graphic matches, and so on. In the shooting phase, documentary filmmakers invariably make choices about such matters as camera positioning, lens adjustments, and lighting sources, which anticipate a certain presentation of the material in the final film. After shooting is completed, as in movies, the raw footage is ordered, reshaped, and placed in narrative form to give it purpose and perspective. Though just about anything might be captured by the camera, the documentary is not merely a recording of some "reality" but a *way* of representing it.

The leading documentary filmmaker of the post–World War I period was American director Robert Flaherty, whose exotic travelogues seemed at first to fit nicely into the Hollywood system. In shooting *Nanook of the North* (1922), which enjoyed great commercial success, Flaherty was not content merely to record the Inuit Eskimos of northern Canada engaged in everyday activities. Instead, he sought to "dramatize" aspects of their culture he was familiar with from his earlier travels into the Hudson Bay area. Toward this end, he showed Eskimos hunting seals with harpoons instead of using the guns they had adopted for this activity. A low-angle shot of the title character with harpoon in hand, captured at the moment of greatest concentration and focused

An Eskimo hunter is presented as a towering figure against a backdrop of land and sky. (*Nanook of the North* [1922])

strength, turns him into a monumental figure, towering against a backdrop of land and sky.

Flaherty seemed set on capturing a sense of some earlier nobility, filtered through the memories of his subjects. What he created instead, as one film analyst aptly puts it, "are travelogues to places that never were."[6] After the success of *Nanook*, Jesse Lasky of Famous Players–Lasky offered Flaherty the opportunity to go anywhere in the world to shoot his next documentary. He chose the South Seas, where he spent almost three years making *Moana* (1926), an idyll about the coming of age of a Samoan boy. Here again, Flaherty seemed determined to revive the past through the distorting lens of memory, as well as the camera. He encouraged the natives to discard the clothes of the missionaries and traders in favor of the traditional siapos they had once worn. For the climax of the film, he staged a

Marx to understand the implications of this involvement. The revolutionary nineteenth-century thinker argued that members of the ruling classes, who owned the means of production, were able to justify their own wealth and ritual tattooing ceremony involving painful needlework that had all but been abolished through missionary influence.

For the most part, *Moana* lacks the movie idiom's stress on conflict and the intensity of incident and feeling. The kind of struggle for survival that had made Nanook so compelling hardly existed on Samoa, a tropical paradise abundant in natural resources. In place of a Nanook-like conflict, Flaherty had to settle for the re-creation of a traditional wedding ceremony. When the film opened in New York City at the Rialto Theatre, it was billed as "The Love-Life of a South Seas Siren." But viewers anticipating sexual titillation were surely disappointed. The subterfuge ensured a box office fizzle, which virtually ended Flaherty's association with the big American studios.

Flaherty returned to form a few years later with the British production *Man of Aran* (1934), whose scenes he framed, filmed, and edited in ways that heightened their emotional appeal. The focus was on a family grappling with the forces of nature as it tries to wrest a living from the sea surrounding the small, rocky, and bleak island of Aran, which lies off the western coast of Ireland. The arresting figures of the family, the perilous maneuvers of their small open boat navigating mountainous waves, the intensity of their hunt for a huge shark, and the splendor of sea, sky, and towering cliffs of their small island—all combine to create a thrilling "real-life" drama of stoic and noble people struggling to survive against great odds, and succeeding in their endeavors. Sound effects such as the roar of wind and waves were mixed with snippets of dialogue in postproduction to heighten the dramatic effect.

Like Flaherty's earlier efforts, *Man of Aran* reflects a nostalgic yearning for some simpler, more physical, preindustrial world. The actual conditions of everyday life on Aran had little relationship to the struggles against the forces of nature depicted in the film. (Flaherty hired an expert to instruct the islanders in the use of harpoons and in the process exposed them to much danger.) At the time it was made, Europe and the United States were mired in a severe economic depression, and most people on this tiny island lived in abject poverty. Many families were, in fact, evicted from their homes by local police acting under orders from absentee landlords in Ireland or England. To make their lot in life even worse, like their Protestant and Catholic counterparts on the mainland, the islanders were plagued by religious conflict.

Hailed as a great cinematic achievement, *Man of Aran* won first prize at the Venice Film Festival. But many in the burgeoning documentary movement criticized the film for its lack of social context. Despite its undeniable craftsmanship, it seemed a "reactionary return to the heroic."[7] This should have endeared it to Hollywood, but by this time the fictional feature was entrenched as the movie industry flagship, leaving all other cinematic forms far behind in its wake. The documentary in the United States developed an identity primarily as an educational, noncommercial endeavor, one usually requiring the financial backing of corporations, government agencies, or philanthropic groups to cover costs.

privilege in the face of social inequity and injustice because ideas widely circulating in society represented the class relationships of capitalism as being the natural scheme of things. Scattered throughout Marx's writings are indications about how systematic analysis of the way such ideas are produced and distributed should proceed.

One of the most influential passages appears in *The German Ideology* of 1845, an early work written jointly with his lifelong friend and collaborator Friedrich Engels when Marx was in his late twenties. "The class which has the means of material production at its disposal," they argued, "has control at the same time over the means of mental production, so that thereby, generally speaking, the ideas of those who lack the means of mental production are subject to it."[8] This proposition opens up several possible avenues for empirical investigation. These include the connection between ownership and control, the relations between producers and owners, the process through which ideas favorable to the already powerful make their way into movies, and the dynamics of reception involved as audience members adopt these ideas as their own.

Marxist-inspired studies of the movie industry in the 1930s tended to take such passages as accepted doctrine rather than as guidelines, and they focused only on the issue of ownership of the means of production. Using elaborate charts and detailed financial data, two British analysts showed how, through control of sound recording systems and ownership of the major studios, "the most powerful financial groups in the United States, if not the capitalist world" had created a concentration of control nearly as complete as the old patents trust. "Whether the movies will regain their former financial success," they ominously concluded, "ultimately depends on whether the Morgans and the Rockefellers will find it in their interest in the increasing change in American life to provide the masses with the type of pictures that alone will induce them to flock to their cinemas."[9]

Although it provided a useful analysis of potential sources of control over the process of moviemaking, this study said nothing about how such control might actually work. Nor did it give any indication of why financiers would want to make movies that "the masses" find unappealing. There is little reason to doubt that for financier and studio executive alike the ability to make money was the principal yardstick of success—as much money as possible. The path to profit was in the production of movies with broad audience appeal. If the alliance with Wall Street left any permanent mark on the creative aspects of production, it was to make adherence to the conventions of the Hollywood style all the more axiomatic.

Supervisory Structure

In many ways, Hollywood was a community unto itself. The heads of the major studios maneuvered to balance demands from the New York executives for a steady supply of easily salable films at the lowest possible cost with pressures from the moviemakers in Hollywood for productions that were often costly and sometimes controversial. But the businessmen and bankers on the East Coast—a three-day train journey away—often could do little to influence the moviemaking activities of their own companies.

Each studio functioned like a small fiefdom ruled by a feudal lord whose power over his charges was absolute. His ultimate weapon was to banish one of his minions from the manor. Since production was "institutionalized"— built into the rules and routines of the moviemaking process—most day-to-day decision making swirled at levels below him, requiring only his occasional benediction. Rigid organization and tight production schedules allowed most studios to operate smoothly and efficiently. Virtually every aspect of production functioned effectively in an interlocking structure.

Each major studio made between forty and fifty feature films a year. To turn out that many movies required an immense staff. Most production personnel were kept under contract, including producers, directors, screenwriters, cinematographers, art directors, costume designers, sound recording experts, and other technical staff. Contracts were drawn and signed for long terms, typically tying creative personnel to the studio for seven years. However, the options on the contract were renewed at six-month intervals. And at any renewal point, an option might be "dropped"—meaning the employee was out of work. In this environment, tension was often high, and the interest of less established personnel was oriented toward ensuring that an option would be picked up for another six months. While under contract, an employee could not quit to join another studio, refuse to work on an assigned project, or renegotiate for increased compensation. Salary increase increments and any bonuses were predetermined at the time of signing.

During the early 1930s, in particular, even the lot of high-paid stars was not an easy one. They typically worked six days a week and were expected to be at the studio early in the morning and to stay well into the night when needed. If they refused to play a role, they were suspended without pay, and when they returned to work, the time away was added to their contracts. In addition to the heavy work schedules, they were required to attend studio publicity functions and to promote their own pictures. Their personal appearance was regulated as well, including such matters as hairstyle, body weight, and choice of clothing.

Contracts usually allowed for stars to be loaned out or rented to other studios. The lending studio generally received about 75 percent more than the star's actual salary to compensate for its temporary loss. The borrowing studio benefited from the star's services without incurring the cost of a long-term contract. "The star system of the 1930s," as movie industry analyst Alexander Walker puts it, "gradually took on the reality, if not the appearance, of a star serfdom. Glamour was its camouflage and fame its dazzling illusion. But behind the grandeur of being a movie star in these years lay all the gradations of servitude."[10]

The famous M-G-M trademark was inherited from Goldwyn Pictures. Louis B. Mayer replaced its pictured lion with footage of a real one roaring. When talkies arrived, three separate lions were recorded to create the three-part lion roar.

Production Units

The way the production process evolved in this era is exemplified by M-G-M, the largest and most prolific of the major studios. Its trademark was Leo the Lion, with his head enhaloed by a scroll proclaiming the Latin *Ars Gratia Artis* (roughly, "Art for Art's Sake"). But the entire operation functioned like a well-oiled machine. With its stable of over a hundred stars and featured players, large roster of specialists (screenwriters, lighting experts, set designers, makeup artists, hairstylists, cameramen, and so on), and cadre of competent directors, the studio was able to turn out an average of one feature every nine days or so along with assorted shorts of various kinds.

The lion presided over a production plant running at full capacity. Inside its high walls could be found most of the essentials of a large city. At its height, the studio complex contained twenty-nine soundstages and a hundred-acre back lot that could be photographed as anything from a prison courtyard to the jungles of Central Africa. A village, several town squares, city streets, a park, and an authentic looking waterfront were among the vast assortment of permanent outdoor sets. Some 3000 craftspeople, technicians, and laborers were on the payroll. The wardrobe department alone employed over 170 milliners, seamstresses, tailors, and the like. Dresses routinely cost from $500 to $1500. The extensive research library could provide a writer or set designer with such esoteric information as the number of stars in a U.S. flag flying over a western outpost in the 1880s.

The head of the studio operations, Louis B. Mayer, was in charge of business matters, deciding how much should be spent, who should be hired and fired, and what policy would be. Second in command was production chief Irving Thalberg (the model for Monroe Stahr in F. Scott Fitzgerald's *The Last Tycoon*). Most M-G-M pictures of the late 1920s and early 1930s bore Thalberg's imprint if not his name. (A self-effacing company man, he rarely allowed his name on any of the many movies under his supervision.) He was committed to maintaining studio authority over the careers of stars, directors, and writers alike, and he displayed little tolerance for unruly ambition or expressions of individual style. To make sure the production apparatus ran as smoothly as possible, his managerial team watched over every project and apprised him of any delays or deviations.

The complexity of sound production, however, soon made Thalberg's method of control unwieldy. Suffering from a weak heart, he would end each day in a state of exhaustion. (He succumbed to pneumonia in 1936 at age 37). In the spring of 1933, while Thalberg was on an extended vacation, Mayer reorganized the studio operations into separate, relatively autonomous production units. Under this new system, which became the industry standard, individual producers had responsibility for their own productions. They chose scripts, actors, and directors from those available at any given time. These production units tended to form around the studio's star players.

The importance and profitability of stars like Clark Gable, under contract to M-G-M since 1930, can be seen in the studio's loan-out practices. When David O. Selznick of Selznick International, set up in 1935 to make Technicolor features, produced *Gone With the Wind* (1939), he decided he wanted Gable to play the pivotal role of Rhett Butler. Louis B. Mayer (Selznick's father-in-law at the time) agreed to lend his prize star only on the condition that M-G-M be given the distribution rights to the movie and half the profits. In addition to Gable, the studio put up half the estimated production cost of $2.5 million. Although the actual cost of the movie exceeded $4 million, M-G-M provided no additional funds.

Gable got a $100,000 bonus for playing Rhett Butler. It was money well spent considering that *Gone With the Wind* became the biggest box office success in history, selling more tickets than any other movie ever made. M-G-M eventually gained sole ownership of the movie, which continued to make money for the studio for the next several decades. When it was technically

Production still of Clark Gable and Vivien Leigh in *Gone With the Wind* (1939). During the 1930s, Gable was the "king of Hollywood"—at least according to the M-G-M publicity department.

renovated in 1967 for large-screen, 70-mm projection, with enhanced color and stereophonic sound, it once again demonstrated its enormous drawing power. (The NBC television network paid a reported $5 million for its November 1976 two-part presentation of the picture.) By the dawn of the new millennium, according to a ranking of "all-time" hits, it had earned $972.9 million (adjusted for inflation).[11]

The Development of Guilds

Working conditions in Hollywood were often a source of strife. In an effort to promote greater intra-industry harmony, the major studios established the Academy of Motion Picture Arts and Sciences in 1927. This high-minded organization had five branches representing the major divisions of moviemaking—producers, writers, directors, actors, and technicians—and membership was by invitation only. Now associated with the awarding of Oscars, the Academy then functioned, in effect, as a company union, representing creative talent in negotiations with the studios. For example, the "writers division" handled disputes over screen credits, money, and other such matters. When the advent of sound brought an influx of Broadway dramatists to Hollywood, the position of screenwriters was greatly strengthened. But for a time at least, they seemed content to have the Academy handle their disputes with the studios.

In the harsh economic climate of the early 1930s, however, it was inevitable that the Academy's policies would come under attack. To reduce costs and avert wholesale dismissals, producers, working through the Academy, devised a plan for reducing salaries for an eight-week period. Although the plan received general endorsement, it was not popular. When some of the studios refused to restore full salaries at the end of the salary waiver period, many members of the Academy felt betrayed.

The screenwriters were the first to defect from the Academy's ranks. In April 1933, the Screen Writers Guild (SWG), which had been loosely organized thirteen years earlier, was revived. Screen actors were the next to leave the Academy. In July 1933, eighteen actors incorporated the Screen Actors Guild (SAG), and within three months, many of the industry's biggest stars had joined. Following the lead of the writers and actors, directors defected from the ranks of the Academy as well. Early in 1936, seventy-five directors formed the Screen Directors Guild. They organized partly in response to rumors that the studios were about to institute a system whereby several directors would routinely be assigned to a single film, a fate that had already befallen the writers. After a prolonged and acrimonious struggle, each of the guilds eventually won recognition from the studios.

Antitrust Action

As the 1930s came to a close, Hollywood faced a challenge from the federal government to its economic structure that, in the decade to come, would lead to a fundamental realignment of the studio system. In 1938, after five years of intensive investigation, the U.S. Department of Justice filed an antitrust suit against the eight major movie companies charging them with monopolistic trade practices. A delegation of movie industry attorneys met with President Franklin Delano Roosevelt in an attempt to quash the suit, but the architect of the New Deal was unsympathetic. He referred the entire matter to his attorney general.

In November 1940, the government filed an amended and supplemental complaint charging the Big Five (Loew's–M-G-M, Warner Bros. Pictures, Paramount, RKO, and 20th Century–Fox) with combining and conspiring to restrain trade unreasonably and with monopolizing the production, distribution, and exhibition of motion pictures. The Little Three (Universal, Columbia, and United Artists), in turn, were charged with illegally conspiring with the Big Five to restrain trade and curtail competition.

The remedies sought in the Justice Department's petition included the elimination of such distribution practices as block booking and **blind**

CITIZEN KANE WRITING CREDITS DISPUTE

In an agreement with the major studios in October 1940, the members of the Screen Writers Guild (SWG) won the right to arbitrate among themselves on the assignment of screen credit. One of the first credit disputes the SWG was asked to resolve concerned the script for *Citizen Kane* (1941). Precisely who was responsible for what in this script is still in dispute. The probable sequence of events leading to its creation begins with veteran screenwriter Herman J. Mankiewicz being hired in 1939 to develop some scripts for Orson Welles's CBS network radio program, the *Campbell Playhouse,* the name given to his *Mercury Theatre on the Air* after it gained a sponsor. Able to produce penetrating dialogue almost on demand, Mankiewicz was put on the payroll at $200 a week, with all the writing credits going to Welles.

When *Mercury*'s broadcast a year earlier about a mythical invasion by Martians caused nationwide panic, the twenty-three-year-old Welles caught the eye of the movie industry. So self-confident was the "boy wonder," and so devoted to stage and radio work, that he was able to hold out until RKO Radio

Pictures offered him an unprecedented contract to write, direct, produce, and perform in two movies. The deal gave him the kind of creative carte blanche most of the old pros working in Hollywood would have killed for. As long as the studio initially approved a project, no alteration whatsoever could be made without his approval. After his effort to adapt Joseph Conrad's *Heart of Darkness* was shelved, Welles discussed with Mankiewicz the idea of a movie modeled on powerful press baron William Randolph Hearst's life, which would be presented from several different viewpoints (who originated this idea remains in dispute).

With the idea established, the enormously creative but self-destructive Mankiewicz, who had been a guest of Hearst and his mistress Marion Davies at their opulent West Coast castle in San Simeon, went into retreat at a ranch in the high desert country near Victorville, California, to draft a script. Mercury coproducer John Houseman was in attendance to edit as well as to ensure that the barely reformed alcoholic writer remained sober. With assistance from

---

bidding, in which exhibitors contracted for the rental of movies without seeing them. But most unsettling to the Big Five was the government lawyers' request for the divorcement of production and distribution from exhibition. This would have meant that they no longer had guaranteed outlets for their movies. Negotiations for a settlement intensified as soon as the case went to trial in federal court. As a result, the government and the Big Five became parties to a "consent decree"—a legal maneuver in which an accused corporation admits nothing but promises not to do it again. The suit against the Little Three was delayed since they did not own any theatres.

Under the consent decree, the Big Five agreed to modify certain trade practices. Among other things, block booking was limited to five pictures, blind bidding was curtailed by requiring trade shows at which new movies would be presented for consideration, and the forced rental of short films as a condition of obtaining features was abolished. With minor restrictions, the

Houseman (just how much is also in dispute), Mankiewicz wrote a rather unfocused three-hundred-plus-page draft that was weak on characterization and so blatantly biographical that it almost seemed to invite a libel suit. (RKO eventually paid Ferdinand Lundberg, author of the 1936 biography *Imperial Hearst,* a substantial amount of money as an out-of-court settlement in a plagiarism suit.)

Welles then reworked, sharpened, and condensed this material to 160 or so pages, removing a great deal of the biographical detail. Revised pages were passed back and forth between Welles and Mankiewicz, with each modifying and refining the other's work. All apparently went well until, in August 1940, Welles told gossip columnist Louella Parsons that he wrote *Citizen Kane*'s script. It was a casual remark and perhaps misquoted. However, Mankiewicz was outraged when he read it even though he had agreed to forgo any claim to screen credit.

In the view of a Welles biographer, the actual source of Mankiewicz's ire was his realization, after first seeing footage from *Citizen Kane,* that it was going to become a "magnificent" picture, albeit one the audience might not fully understand.[12] He had apparently had a much more visually conventional movie in mind. In shooting the movie, director Welles employed extreme low-angle shots, stark contrasts of light and dark, and vast in-depth perspectives to reveal complex social and psychological relationships. He also made unconventional use of music, disembodied voices, overlapping dialogue, and other such techniques he had first honed in radio. In the process, *Citizen Kane* became the work not of a wordsmith but of a master of images and sounds.

Apparently fearful of being denied any screen credit, Mankiewicz lodged a complaint with the SWG claiming sole credit for the creation of the script. In consultation with RKO, Welles and Mankiewicz eventually agreed to share screen credit. After being assured of prior billing over Welles as author, a still-vexed Mankiewicz withdrew his complaint with the SWG. At the Academy Awards in 1941, he and Welles won the Oscar for best original screenplay. Neither one was on hand to pick up the statuette, and the two never worked together again.

Big Five were permitted to remain in the exhibition business and retain ownership of movie theatres. The ominous shadow of war had begun to fall over Europe and Asia, and the government apparently did not want to disrupt a major industry at a time of international crisis. However, it did reserve the right at the end of a three-year period to seek further restrictions if it felt the decree had not proved effective.

Prelude to War

Moviemakers generally avoided any topics touching on international politics. As the threat of Nazism mounted, however, some studios undertook projects that were decidedly political in orientation. Warner Bros. Pictures led the way with its 1939 release *Confessions of a Nazi Spy,* an exposé of the subversive activities of the German-American Bund, a Manhattan-based organization

A poster promotes *Confessions of a Nazi Spy* (1939), the Warner studio's prewar cinematic salvo against Nazism.

whose members carried out propaganda and espionage activities mainly on the East Coast of the United States.

Based on actual evidence presented at the trial of eighteen accused spies, the movie reflected the strong anti-Nazi sentiments of its director, Anatole Litvak, and star Paul Lukas, who were German émigrés, as well as its writers, Milton Krims and John Wexley, and another star, Edward G. Robinson, who were active in Hollywood's anti-Nazi movement. It gained an added aura of authenticity through judicious use of actual newsreel footage of the notorious 1938 German-American Bund rally in Madison Square Garden, during which opponents who spoke out were abruptly removed and beaten by the organization's uniformed thugs.

Although the movie may appear in hindsight to be rather tame, it raised a storm of controversy at the time of its release. The German consulate filed an official complaint, charging that it was part of a broad U.S. conspiracy. Fritz Kuhn of the German-American Bund threatened the Warner studio with a $5-million lawsuit, and German diplomatic forces openly worked to suppress the movie, in the United States and abroad. When it was shown in a predominantly German-American section of Milwaukee, an irate band of pro-Nazi sympathizers burned the theatre to the ground. Eighteen Latin American and European nations banned the movie outright. Within the countries of the British Empire, however, it was shown without a single cut.

After war broke out in Europe in 1939 and the continental market closed, Hollywood released a flock of anti-Nazi features. A naive American reporter discovers a traitorous plot against England in *Foreign Correspondent* (1940). In the final scene, as bombs fall all around, he exhorts the United States in a radio broadcast from a London studio to prepare itself for an expansion of the war. The vicissitudes of a German middle-class family divided in its loyalties when the Nazi regime comes to power are chronicled in *The Mortal Storm* (1940). *Four Sons* (1940) depicts the dissolution of a Sudetenland family during the Nazi occupation of the former Czechoslovakia. In *The Man I Married* (1940), the fanaticism of the Nazis is seen through the eyes of an American woman who visits Germany in 1938 with her German-American husband and their small son. A British big-game hunter in *Man Hunt* (1941) stalks Adolf Hitler to his Berchtesgaden retreat just for sport. He aligns the Nazi fuehrer in his telescopic sight but fails to shoot since he had deliberately neglected to load his rifle.

Perhaps the most provocative anti-Nazi picture of the period was *The Great Dictator* (1940), a seriocomic representation of the Hitler mythology in which Charlie Chaplin played a dual role, appearing both as a humble Jewish barber and as Adenoid Hynkel, the ranting, posturing dictator of Tomania. Their paths cross toward the end of the movie when the barber, mistaken for the dictator, takes his place before the microphones. During the six-minute oration, which is packed with political doubles entendres, he urges, "Soldiers! Don't give yourselves to these brutes . . . who drill you—diet you—treat you like cattle and use you for canon fodder." Within the dramatic fiction, of course, he is addressing the citizens of Tomania, but his words are aimed directly at the movie audience. To those attuned to the comic actor's leftist political affinities, phrases like "canon fodder" must have carried clear echoes of the communist charge that President Franklin D. Roosevelt was planning to sacrifice American lives to defend British imperialism.

Those who accused Chaplin of warmongering apparently missed this connection. Along with the rest of Hollywood's anti-Nazi movies, *The Great Dictator* drew the ire of isolationist groups like the America First Committee, which believed that the European nations should fight their own battles. One of its senatorial supporters, Republican Gerald Nye of North Dakota, warned in a national radio speech broadcast from St. Louis that the movies "have become the most gigantic engines of propaganda in existence to rouse war fever in America and plunge the nation to her destruction." He went on to list the heads of the major movie companies, stressing their Jewish surnames, and noting that "in each of these companies there are a number of production directors, many of whom come from Russia, Hungary, Germany, and the Balkan countries." Are you ready, he demanded, "to send your boys to bleed and die in Europe to make the world safe for this industry and its financial backers?"[13]

The isolationist outcry culminated in hearings before a Senate subcommittee investigating war propaganda in movies.[14] The fiery senator from North Dakota led the offensive, referring to the movies he considered interventionist in orientation as vicious propaganda. But when pressed, Nye was unable to recall even the names, let alone the plots, of the pictures he wanted the committee to condemn. It turned out that he hadn't seen most of the movies he excoriated. Other isolationist opponents of Hollywood proved equally ill informed.

Wendell Wilkie, the defeated but highly popular and respected Republican presidential candidate in 1940, represented the movie industry. In presenting the industry's case, the perpetually rumpled Wilkie readily conceded that its leading executives were unequivocally opposed to the Nazi dictatorship in Germany. He calculated that only 50 of the 1100 Hollywood movies produced in the two years since the outbreak of the European war had war-related themes. Some of these 50, he gladly admitted, did portray Nazism as a cruel, lustful, ruthless, and cynical force. By claiming that they were accurate representations of a terrifying regime, he effectively wrapped the industry in a star-spangled cloak of patriotic service.

Industry executives who testified before the subcommittee tended to follow much the same line. The most telling was Fox studio head Darryl F. Zanuck, who began by pointedly mentioning his deep Methodist roots in Wahoo, Nebraska. He argued forcefully that Hollywood pictures were powerful sales vehicles for the American way of life, not only to America but to the entire world. They sold it so strongly, he asserted, that the first thing the dictators who took over Italy and Germany did was to ban them. When he finished speaking, the Senate gallery erupted in applause. Everything that followed was anticlimatic. The subcommittee did not meet again prior to the Japanese attack on the drowsy American naval base at Pearl Harbor in Hawaii, which rendered the matter moot.

Hollywood Goes to War

Once the country was officially at war, the government quickly proclaimed movies an "essential industry," much like coal and steel production, shipbuilding, and food processing. Although movies were hardly the first line of defense, they helped mobilize the home front. Exhibitors and producers alike were more than willing to cooperate with the government on most matters concerning the war. The local movie house once again proved to be a propitious place for disseminating information, bolstering morale, promoting the sale of war bonds, collecting scrap rubber and other scarce materials, and soliciting money for charities like China Relief and Red Cross.

Propaganda Shorts

Some 16,000 movie houses around the country were committed to the exhibition of U.S. government **propaganda** (messages deliberately designed to influence attitudes and beliefs toward some predetermined end) shorts on a wide range of subjects. Federal agencies produced several short films designed to sell war bonds by instilling feelings of fear and loathing toward the Japanese. A particularly nasty example of this type of propaganda is called *Justice* (1943), in which Japanese soldiers are shown tossing babies with their bayonets. (This scene was shot in the old Paramount studios in Astoria, New York, which had been taken over by the military during the war.) Such staged scenes were combined with actual footage of the aftermath of the Japanese attack on China. In the closing segment, a narrator intones: "Every tank kills a Jap. . . . How about it, folks, have you killed a Jap soldier today?" (Recent research suggests that the actual brutality of Japanese soldiers in China may have far exceeded what was depicted in American propaganda films.[15])

Films like this provide some insight into the atmosphere of the time that permitted the relocation of some 120,000 Japanese Americans—two-thirds of them U.S. citizens—to internment camps in such desolate places as Heart Mountain, Wyoming; Minidoka, Idaho; and Topaz, Utah. The federal government attempted to justify these internment camps in a propaganda piece titled *Japanese Relocation* (1942). Images of huddled families with belongings in tow belie the narrator's assurances that this forced relocation was being done "with real consideration for the people involved."

Indiscriminate acts of violence against Asians in general became commonplace during the war. Chinese people in particular were singled out for abuse. To "dispel some of the confusion," shortly after Pearl Harbor, *Life* magazine ran a photo essay on "How to Tell the Japs from the Chinese."[16] Mug shots of a representative of each group, accompanied by arrows and asides, served to highlight the distinctions. Comparisons were made between such features as the Japanese model's massively boned head and face, and flat, pug nose (which betray his "aboriginal antecedents") and the Chinese representative's longer, more delicately boned visage and finely bridged nose. One wonders for whom this lesson in physiognomy was intended. Certainly bomber pilots and soldiers in the field had no need for such instruction. Perhaps it was for the hooligans who were harassing (not to mention attacking) people of both Japanese and Chinese ancestry.

At the height of the conflict, about 50 percent of the screen time devoted to shorts went to the war effort. The government-produced films were shown every other week. On alternating weeks, the major studios provided short films on a wide range of war-related matters under the heading *America Speaks*. M-G-M's *Mr. Blabbermouth* stressed the danger of careless talk in wartime. The need to conserve food and materials was highlighted in Paramount's

Letter from Bataan. In Disney's animated *Out of the Frying Pan into the Firing Line,* Minnie Mouse offers some bacon drippings to Pluto but is interrupted by a radio voice informing her that kitchen fat can be converted into the glycerin needed for cannon shells. Columbia's *Men Working Together* began with a war poster coming to life and continued by portraying the unity of purpose between men on the battlefield and those on the home-front assembly lines. These shorts were made without recompense from the government.

Disney's Image Arsenal

Film shorts stressing supposed Nazi traits became a specialty of the Disney studio. Its animation apparatus operated in high gear, turning out film fare of incalculable value to the American government's war effort. In *Der Fuehrer's Face* (1942), Disney employed familiar images and symbols to ridicule the regimentation of German life under the Nazis. The irascible Donald Duck dreams that he is in Nutzi Land. He lives in a house that bears a striking resemblance to Adolf Hitler. Everywhere in sight are swastikas: on the dial of the alarm clock, on the walls of his humble dwelling, and even in the shape of the shrubbery around it. He is abruptly awakened by a bayonet-toting martinet. "Up *dumkopf*!" he roars, "you will have the privilege of working twenty-eight hours a day for the fuehrer." After a hurried breakfast of ersatz food (the bread loaf is made of wood), Donald marches to his job at a munitions factory weighted down by a big bass drum marked with the Nazi insignia. Along the way, he passes a fire hydrant shaped liked a swastika.

In the course of the day spent screwing down bomb casings, the distraught duck goes berserk, and a close-up of his face rotates and explodes into a surreal nightmare world in which images of him are pounded as they move down the conveyor belt. Following another explosion, dozens of his images fall, settling finally into his sleeping form. When he awakens with a start, still half asleep, Donald sees the shadow of an outstretched arm and starts to respond with a "*Heil*" but then perceives that it is actually the arm of a miniature Statue of Liberty. The film seemingly concludes with his heartfelt expression of appreciation that he is a citizen of the United States. However, the closing iris opens again just long enough to show a close-up of Hitler getting hit in the face with an overripe tomato.

Despite humorous elements, the overall tone of many Disney shorts is decidedly somber and grim. In *Education for Death* (1943), adapted from a 1941 book of the same title by Gregor Ziemer, the focus is on the indoctrination of a German lad named Hans as he grows from young school boy into an adult soldier. At elementary school, young Hans is taught a Nazi version of the Sleeping Beauty story in which the Wicked Witch is Democracy, the Prince is Hitler (clad in an armor suit), and the slumbering figure he awakens is Germania—an obese, overly amorous Brünnhilde (the goddess of composer

A distraught Donald makes his way to his job at a Nazi munitions plant. The cartoon short was originally supposed to be called *Donald Duck in Nutzi Land*. A hit recording by Spike Jones and his City Slickers of its robust theme song ridiculing Adolf Hitler, "Der Fuehrer's Face," written by Oliver Wallace, persuaded Disney executives to give the song title to the film as well. (*Der Fuehrer's Face* [1942])

Richard Wagner's Ring cycle operas), who bears a striking resemblance to German field marshal and Nazi party leader Hermann Goering.

In another classroom sequence, a Nazi instructor uses the parable of the wolf and the rabbit to illustrate that the world belongs to the strong. When Hans shows sympathy for the rabbit, he is swiftly punished and subjected to reeducation. After a montage of book burnings, smashed church windows, and Bibles dissolves into *Mein Kampf* (*My Struggle*), Hitler's autobiographical account of his philosophy and plans for conquest, the film concludes with a chilling sequence in which marching children are gradually transformed into goose-stepping Nazis. Wearing blinders and manacles, they finally dissolve into rows and rows of gravesites.

The Treasury Department enlisted Donald Duck's help to remind people to pay their taxes. The Tax Revenue Act of 1942 put many people on the tax rolls for the first time. There were no mechanisms in those days for withholding income tax from people's salaries before they were paid. Workers had to be encouraged to put some money aside for the quarterly payment of taxes.

In Disney's *The New Spirit* (1942), an eight-minute short, Donald Duck is shown listening to the radio, with the American flag literally waving in the pupils of his eyes. In a patriotic fervor, he beseeches the radio to tell him how to aid the war effort. At first, the answer ("By paying your taxes") enrages the web-footed patriot; but, when he is informed of the power of his taxes to purchase armaments ("taxes to beat the Axis"), he gladly sets about calculating his income tax. Working as an actor, Donald has earned $2501 (Walt's studio was notorious for its low pay and long working hours). He finds that he owes $13 in taxes (he has three dependents—his adopted nephews) and immediately rushes to the nation's capital with his contribution in hand.

The short was so successful in getting people to pay their taxes that Disney was commissioned to make a sequel. (An estimated 26 million people saw *The New Spirit,* and 37 percent of them reported, in a Gallup poll, that it had an effect on their willingness to pay taxes.[17]) Called *The Spirit of 1943,* it presents Donald Duck as the typical worker on payday. His mind is divided into two personalities: the gentle, thrifty Scotsman and the irresponsible, "zoot-suited" spendthrift. Although a nationwide phenomenon in the 1940s, popular with poor black and white youths in the large cities, the look featuring a wide-brimmed hat, baggy but tight-cuffed trousers, and an oversized jacket with heavily padded shoulders was most closely associated in the national consciousness with the Mexican teenagers—or *pachucos,* as they were called—of Los Angeles.

During World War II, long-standing prejudice against Mexicans coalesced into hatred of the zoot-suiters. Around the time the Disney studio was producing this short, there were widely publicized clashes between sailors stationed in southern California and the Mexican teenagers. When a sailor was knifed by a zoot-suiter, naval personnel went on a rampage, beating up anyone who was wearing the hated clothing. The Los Angeles City Council responded by passing an ordinance forbidding the wearing of zoot suits within city limits.

Playing on this kind of adverse publicity, the zoot-suited spendthrift in *The Spirit of 1943* is associated with the Nazi cause. He and the Scotsman engage in a tug-of-war over Donald, one exhorting him to spend his money frivolously and the other beseeching him to save it so he can pay his taxes ("thanks to Hitler and Hirohito taxes are higher than ever before"). Both lose their grip and fly in the opposite direction. To stress what each symbolizes, the Scotsman smashes into a wall whose plaster falls away to reveal lines of red bricks and white mortar and a window of stars on a blue field in a composition that suggests an American flag. In sharp contrast, the zoot-suited spendthrift hurtles into the Idle Hour Club, whose swinging doors are in the shape of a swastika. When he emerges, his bow tie is shaped like the Nazi insignia as well, and he blows swastika-shaped smoke rings. He also sports a Hitler-like mustache and forelock. Rather than succumbing to his entreaties, Donald smacks him back into the nightclub, its door shattering into a large V for victory. After the enlightened duck pays his taxes, a narrator explains over animated visuals of American guns, airplanes, and ships destroying the enemy how the money will serve to bury the Axis powers and preserve democracy.

Features Depicting the Enemy

The huge investments, production capacity, and output of the movie industry became an integral part of the nation's image arsenal, although the primary aim of the major studios continued to be profit, not propaganda. Most attempts in feature films to influence people or events tended to be incidental to the entertainment. According to a survey of industry releases between December 1941 and August 1945, roughly three out of every ten features had content related to the war.[18] The total release was 1313, and only 374 were war-oriented.

For the most part, wartime movies depicted the Japanese as inhumanly cruel and sadistic. In *Behind the Rising Sun* (1943), whose setting is the Sino-Japanese War of the 1930s, Japanese soldiers toss babies into the air and bayonet them, molest women and insert needles under their fingernails, and string men up by the wrists until the blood vessels in their arms burst. In several wartime movies, there were calls for the total annihilation of Japan. Facing torture and death at the hands of the insidiously evil Japanese character played by Hawaiian-Chinese actor Richard Loo in *The Purple Heart* (1944), the American protagonist (Dana Andrews) cries defiantly, "It won't be finished until your dirty little empire is wiped off the face of the earth."

In depicting Germans, Hollywood's emphasis tended to be on Nazi characteristics in particular rather than on those of the population as a whole. Screen Nazis typically spoke with thick guttural accents, shouted "*schweinhund*" at the slightest provocation, and religiously said "*heil* Hitler" when greeting one another with kicking boot heels and outstretched right arms. They seemed to derive particular pleasure from tormenting old people and brutalizing attractive young women. At the end of *Hitler's Children* (1943), for example, the heroine (Bonita Granville) is subjected to a ritualistic flogging for refusing to produce future Aryan-pure followers for the fuehrer. As other young women watch, she is forced to kneel, her hands are tied to the base of a flagpole, and the back of her blouse is ripped open. After the first few lashes, the man she loves (Tim Holt) interrupts the flagellation, an action that brings death to both of them.

Series Characters' Role in the Fray

Several popular characters were enlisted in the cinematic war effort. Columbia's contributions included the irrepressible Blondie, a comic strip character

In *Sherlock Holmes and the Voice of Terror* (1942), Holmes (Basil Rathbone, right) and Watson (Nigel Bruce, left), shown in this production still, battle to save England from a Nazi invasion.

brought to life on the screen by Penny Singleton in over two dozen films. In *Blondie for Victory* (1942), Blondie organizes her neighbors into Housewives for America, replete with uniforms and civil defense apparatus. The final entry in this studio's Ellery Queen mystery series, *Enemy Agents Meet Ellery Queen* (1942), had the famed fictional sleuth (played by William Gargan) facing a formidable Nazi spy ring.

Universal updated Sir Arthur Conan Doyle's "The Adventures of the Dancing Men" to pit Sherlock Holmes (Basil Rathbone) and Dr. Watson (Nigel Bruce) against the Nazis in *Sherlock Holmes and the Secret Weapon* (1942). The brilliant "consulting detective" and his faithful friend also battled Nazi sabotage and terror tactics in *Sherlock Holmes and the Voice of Terror* (1942). This latter film ends with a stirring ode by Holmes to England's plight: "There's an east wind coming, . . . such a wind as never blew on England yet. It will be cold and bitter, Watson, and a good many of us may wither before its blast. But it's God's own wind, nonetheless, and a cleaner, better, stronger land will lie in the sunshine when the storm has cleared." (The lines were taken from the final passage of Doyle's "His Last Bow," in which an elderly Holmes comes out of retirement to aid his country.)

Noble Wartime Allies

Hollywood turned out movies depicting America's wartime allies as peace-loving foes of tyranny and fascism. Several films stressed the courage and fortitude of the British people under fire. In M-G-M's *Mrs. Miniver* (1942), the war disrupts the tranquil way of life in a small English town. Entire middle-class families, housewives, humble shopkeepers, and those to the manor born all become valiant fighters on the home front. The title character, played by Greer Garson, even manages to capture a downed Nazi flyer.

Many of the major studios also produced paeans to Russian strength and resilience under fire. In Warner Bros.'s *Mission to Moscow* (1943), a semidocumentary starring Walter Huston, the tenacity and intelligence of the former Soviet Union's leadership is stressed. Based on the memoirs of Joseph E. Davies, once the American ambassador to the Soviet Union, this misguided movie glosses over Josef Stalin's bloody political purges, treats his 1939 alliance with Hitler as a purely tactical maneuver to buy time, and even justifies Russia's invasion of Finland as part of some vague master strategy. It also suggests that the United States Senate was a hotbed of profiteering isolationists. (In the movie, one member of this august legislative body asserts, "Not only can we do business with Hitler but we can make a nice profit doing so.")

The Motion Picture Bureau

Throughout the war years, movies were made under the watchful eye of government bureaucrats. Soon after the United States entered the fighting, President Roosevelt established the Office of War Information (OWI), which incorporated the information activities of a number of prewar agencies. Having a domestic and an overseas branch, the new agency's mandate was to promote public understanding of the war, coordinate government information activities, and act as liaison with the various mass media. A Bureau of Motion Pictures was put in place to oversee government filmmaking and deal with the movie industry. Among other services, it supplied moviemakers with the special information needed for the production of war-related film fare.

The motion picture bureau tried to influence movie content as well by analyzing and evaluating projects, suggesting story subjects and plot lines, and exerting pressure on the industry to secure cooperation. But its requests to see scripts prior to production initially met with strong opposition from the major studios. The bureau also raised the wrath of a conservative coalition of Republicans and southern Democrats that regarded the OWI and its subsidiaries as imprudently pro-Roosevelt and perilously liberal if not leftist. Thus, in 1943, an increasingly hostile Congress cut off almost all funding for the OWI's domestic operations.

All the same, the motion picture bureau still enjoyed considerable economic leverage to shape the output of the movie industry. Its advisory authority was augmented by another wartime agency, the Office of Censorship, which was empowered to bar the export of movies deemed detrimental to the war effort. In an effort to fortify foreign distribution dividends, most of the major studios eventually acceded to the bureau's request to see scripts prior to production. From mid-1943 until the end of the war, according to one scholarly account, "OWI exerted an influence over an American mass medium never equaled before or since by a government agency."[19]

Government policy affected what went on behind the scenes, as well as what appeared on the screen. The War Production Board, a federal agency formed in January 1942 to set priorities for the nation's industrial and economic resources, limited the material costs of set construction to $5000, about one-tenth the amount spent on major movie projects in the prewar period. It also imposed a sharp cutback in the use of raw film stock, primarily so the government would have an adequate supply for its own shorts and features. This limitation led to more careful preproduction planning and to fewer takes during principal cinematography. The number of movie prints in circulation was also reduced.

The End of an Era

Although burdened by labor and material shortages and by government constraints, Hollywood prospered during the Second World War. In the immediate postwar period, industry leaders looked to the future with seemingly justified optimism. Some estimates put average weekly attendance in 1946 at an all-time high of 90 million, and profits soared to a record $120 million. But the boom proved to be short-lived. As box office revenues began to plummet, the major studios slashed production schedules and allowed long-term contracts with producers, directors, actors, and technicians to lapse. An atmosphere of disquiet and anxiety pervaded Hollywood. The most foreboding factor was the specter of television, which loomed ominously on the horizon. Over the next several decades, the entire movie industry would undergo substantial structural and operational changes. These changes are the concern of the next chapter.

Notes

1. See Eric Barnouw, *A Tower in Babel: A History of Broadcasting in the United States,* Vol. I (New York: Oxford University Press, 1966), p. 186.
2. Quoted in Evan William Cameron, ed., in *Sound and the Cinema* (New York: Redgrave, 1980), p. 72.

3. David Bordwell, *On the History of Style* (Cambridge, MA: Harvard University Press, 1997), pp. 36–37.

4. Quoted in Cari Beauchamp, *Without Lying Down: Frances Marion and the Powerful Women of Early Hollywood* (New York: Scribner, 1997), p. 370. (The title of this insightful biography comes from Marion's quip that she spent her life "searching for a man to look up to without lying down.")

5. Quoted in Ben Hecht, *A Child of the Century* (New York: Signet, 1955), p. 447.

6. Richard Barsam, *Nonfiction Film: A Critical History,* rev. ed. (Bloomington: Indiana University Press, 1992), p. 49.

7. Quoted in Eric Barnouw, *Documentary: A History of the Non-Fiction Film* (New York: Oxford University Press, 1974), p. 98.

8. Karl Marx and Friedrich Engels, *The German Ideology,* trans. R. Pascal (New York: International Publishers, 1947), p. 39.

9. F. D. Klingender and Stuart Legg, *Money Behind the Screen* (London: Lawrence & Wishart, 1937), p. 79.

10. Alexander Walker, *Stardom: The Hollywood Phenomenon* (New York: Stein & Day, 1970), p. 240.

11. "An All-Time Hit Parade," Outlook 2000, *The New York Times,* December 20, 1999, p. C42.

12. See Barbara Leaming, *Orson Welles: A Biography* (New York: Viking Press, 1985), p. 245.

13. Gerald P. Nye, "War Propaganda: Our Madness Increases As Our Emergency Shrinks," *Vital Speeches,* 7 (September 1941), pp. 720–723.

14. U.S. Congress, Senate Subcommittee of the Committee on Interstate Commerce, *Propaganda in Motion Pictures,* 77th Congress, 1st Session, September 9–26, 1941 (Washington, DC: Government Printing Office, 1942).

15. See Iris Chang, *The Rape of Nanking: The Forgotten Holocaust of World War II* (New York: Basic Books, 1997).

16. "How to Tell the Japs from the Chinese," *Life,* December 22, 1941, p. 81.

17. Cited in "Walt Disney: Great Teacher," *Fortune,* August 1942, p. 94.

18. See Dorothy B. Jones, "The Hollywood War Film," *Hollywood Quarterly,* 1 (October 1945), p. 2.

19. Clayton R. Koppes and Geogory D. Black, "What to Show the World: The Office of War Information and Hollywood 1942–1945," *The Journal of American History,* 64 (1977), p.103.

The Electronic Era

For most of us in the United States—child or adult, male or female—there comes a point each day when we seat ourselves before the television set, click the remote control, and—like modern-day Aladdins—say, "Entertain me." Time and again, we turn to television for comfort, diversion, and even enlightenment. Its influences resonate in our collective psyches. We carry around in our heads images of stars, snatches of dialogue, and remembered moments from countless commercials, sitcoms, crime shows, quiz programs, and soap operas. Although the occasional trip to a movie theatre provides surcease from the daily routine, television has become a pervasive presence in our lives.

The rise of television following the Second World War doubtlessly helped to transform the entire American movie industry. Although clearly the most significant influence from the 1950s onward, television was but one of several factors affecting the production, distribution, and exhibition of movies. This chapter considers a range of developments that contributed to a fundamental change in the basic character and structure of the American cinema from the postwar period to the present.

The Decline of Urban Theatres

When television burst onto the American scene in the postwar years, many observers blamed it for sending box office revenues into a free fall. Movie houses certainly fell on hard times soon after the war ended, but competition from television was hardly the prime cause of their economic woes. Movie attendance had, in fact, started tumbling in 1947. And it continued to fall sharply over the next few years even though the explosive growth of the television industry had been forestalled by the actions of the Federal Communications Commission (FCC), which instituted a "freeze" in 1948 on all further allocations of television channels so that it could study signal interference problems.

At the time the FCC took this action, some 108 stations had been authorized to go on the air, and fewer than fifty were already in operation. During the freeze period, which lasted until July 1952, only twenty-four cities had two or more stations. New York and Los Angeles each had seven stations up and running. But major metropolises like Houston, Kansas City, Milwaukee, Pittsburgh, and St. Louis could boast of only one station, and eleven large cities had no television service whatsoever.

Although many theatres did close permanently in cities well saturated with television, a series of social upheavals that transformed postwar American society probably damaged the movie business more than did the arrival of this new electronic competitor. One key factor, the baby boom, meant that millions of young couples were staying home in the evening to look after their offspring. This deprived movie theatres of a significant portion of their most loyal patrons—people under the age of thirty.

The Shift to Suburbia

Adding to the sharp drop in attendance, such leisure pursuits as gardening, bowling, miniature golf, do-it-yourself projects, or simply going for a drive (new-car sales soared after the war) became extremely popular in the postwar period. This was especially so for the many families that fled from decaying city centers to the newly built suburbs, where a surge in housing sales was spurred by the ready availability of government-insured mortgages that featured small down payments and low interest rates.

Developer William J. Levitt ignited the suburban housing boom (everything but the movie business seemed to be booming in the postwar period). On a thousand acres of farmland near Hempstead, Long Island, some twenty miles from Manhattan, he and his architect brother Alfred mass-produced four-and-a-half-room houses on 60-by-100-foot lots that could be purchased for as little as $7900; later, an expanded ranch-style house sold for $9500. In the beginning, they even threw in a free television set as an incentive to buy.

The Levitts also constructed look-alike housing complexes on sites in New Jersey and Pennsylvania. Other builders soon followed their lead. By the mid-1950s, over 3000 acres a day nationwide were being bulldozed for housing complexes, shopping centers, and other suburban construction projects. Few movie theatres initially existed in the suburban communities springing up around the country, but their recently settled residents showed little inclination to make the trek back to the downtown cinemas for their evening's entertainment.

Drive-In Theatres

The massive migration to suburbia ushered in the age of the **drive-in theatre**—a venue specifically designed for showing movies on outdoor screens that patrons view from their cars. The first one had opened for business in Camden, New Jersey, on June 6, 1933. Others soon followed. By 1942 there were almost a hundred drive-ins scattered across twenty-seven states. It wasn't until the postwar period, however, that drive-ins really spread across the country—from fewer than 1000 in 1948, to nearly 5000 a decade later.

Built mostly on large, inexpensive tracts of land, and requiring only modest outlays of capital for the construction of a screen, projection booth, and sound system, drive-ins generally proved to be profitable for their owners (primarily small, independent exhibition chains). And with the baby boom in full force by the late 1940s and early 1950s, young families flocked to the drive-ins. Although the actual viewing experience lacked the intimacy of an indoor theatre, and the sound quality of the in-car speakers was poor, these outdoor theatres offered patrons a casual and convenient alternative to traditional venues. Parents didn't have to hire a babysitter, dress up, or drive into town; children could come in their pajamas; the entire family was able to spend a relatively noncostly evening watching movies under a star-lit canopy; and, of course, parking was not a problem.

As drive-ins grew in size and number, many operators added playgrounds, train and pony rides, miniature golf courses, and cafeteria-style concession stands able to provide fast-food dinners and snacks to hundreds of children and adults during the ten-minute intermissions that became standard practice. (A clock counting down the time to the beginning of the second movie typically was featured on the large screen.) More than a few even offered laundry facilities, permitting people to complete a household chore and enjoy an evening out at the same time. The grounds usually were opened well before sundown so parents could bring their youngsters early to enjoy the facilities.

In the later-evening hours, the relative seclusion of the drive-in provided a private place for teenagers to engage in activity of another sort. Special teen-targeted late-show double features became the norm by the close of the 1950s. While drive-ins prospered, however, urban theatres closed at the rate of two a day. Between 1948 and 1958, the period drive-ins enjoyed their greatest growth, over 5000 indoor movie houses went out of business.

Opening night at the nation's first drive-in theatre. An usher stands ready to escort patrons who stray from the well-lighted path.

Targeting Teenagers

By the mid-1950s most moviemakers were attuned to teenagers, whose numbers had grown to about 13 million. The "teenager" as a cultural and economic phenomenon was the unintended product of educators who wanted to protect immigrant children from the lure of the streets and of union leaders who pushed for child labor laws to tighten the job market and boost wages. Before the depression, as a recent study explains, working-class children became adults with no definite intermediary stage, typically dropping out of high school in the first or second year.[1] A diploma was a clear mark of membership in the middle class. By the dawn of the 1940s, however, high school had become a nearly universal experience, an entitlement parents came to expect for their children regardless of economic or social status.

As high schools became widely accepted places of preparation for adult life, most youngsters experienced a lengthy period of adolescence before becoming productive members of society. This unique transitional phase between childhood and adulthood, amplified by growing economic prosperity and accelerated birth rates during and after the war, set the stage for the

A collage of releases by American International Pictures. Before its demise in 1980, American International Pictures had thrived by exploiting the teenage market. The company would occasionally release movies of some artistic merit, such as *Cooley High* (1975), a $750,000 production based on the work of black writer Eric Monte that provided a sensitive, poignant, and often amusing portrayal of the experiences of black teenagers growing up in Chicago.

emergence of teenagers as a separate group with ample leisure time and money to spend. Eager to tap the purchasing power of this new generation of Americans, postwar marketers and advertisers heavily promoted its singular status and social position, and the movie industry sought to fill its leisure time.

The expanding teenage market opened the way for new movie firms to emerge. The most successful was American International Pictures (AIP), founded as American Releasing Corporation in 1954 by James H. Nicholson and Samuel Z. Arkoff. With initial working capital of $3000, they churned out moldy melodramas and trendy shockers paired as double bills primarily for drive-ins. One of AIP's principal production units was run by the now legendary Roger Corman, who directed such lurid trifles as *It Conquered the World* (1956), *The Undead* (1957), *Teenage Caveman* (1958), and *The Wasp Women* (1959)—all reputedly produced in less than a week on bargain basement budgets. During the 1960s, Corman's cheaply made movies provided a showcase for such young actors as Jack Nicholson, Peter Fonda, and Dennis Hopper. Talented directors like Peter Bogdanovich, Jonathan Demme, Francis Ford Coppola, and Martin Scorsese all served apprenticeships with Corman as well.

Turning to Old Technologies

Cinerama

In an effort to boost sagging box office receipts at conventional movie outlets, some producers and exhibitors experimented with technology that had long been ignored by the movie industry. The process that achieved the most spectacular results was Cinerama, which had been invented in the late 1930s and used primarily for industrial and military purposes. The first commercial film venture employing this process was titled *This Is Cinerama*. This startling two-hour kaleidoscopic travelogue featured scenes such as a thrilling roller-coaster ride and a hair-raising plane trip. Its unveiling at the Broadway Theatre in New York City in September 1952 created a sensation. Audiences reportedly shrieked with terrified delight as they seemed to thunder down the chutes and around the curves of the Atom Smasher roller coaster at the Rockaways Playland amusement park or to zoom through the Grand Canyon.

Permitting spectators to make almost full use of their peripheral vision, this process created an intense sense of participation and involvement. On location, three synchronized cameras linked together, with their lenses set at 48-degree angles to one another, photographed panoramic vistas on three strips of film; in the theatre, three projectors threw crisscrossing images simultaneously on three screens that were joined and curved in an arc approximately 146 degrees wide and 55 degrees high. This semicircular screen, which was 51 feet wide and 25 feet high, encompassed almost the entire field of human vision.

The film's illusion of reality and dimension was enhanced by the use of a revolutionary stereophonic sound system. Sounds were recorded on seven tracks from microphones placed all over the setting. When the film was projected, speakers located throughout the theatre created the impression that each sound originated from its visual source. The clatter of roller coaster cars and the screech of airplane engines reverberated off the theatre's walls.

The film played to capacity crowds at the Broadway Theatre for over two years. It reaped record box office harvests as well at specially equipped theatres in such cities as Pittsburgh, Chicago, Detroit, and Los Angeles. Other successful Cinerama vehicles followed, but audience enthusiasm for the travelogue format soon diminished. M-G-M's use of the three-camera process in *How the West Was Won* (1962) and *The Wonderful World of the Brothers*

A schematic of the Cinerama process shows the evolution of the image from photography on location to projection in the theatre.

Grimm (1962) revealed its impracticality for dramatic narratives. Such key components of the Hollywood style as close-ups, camera pans, and expressive lighting patterns proved extremely difficult to implement. Both movies, which were costly and complicated to make, were quickly modified so they could be shown on standard screens.

Expensive and cumbersome, Cinerama was destined to remain a novelty attraction. By the late 1950s, only a handful of venues were equipped to show films made using this process. Few theatres were big enough to accommodate the huge screen and three projectors necessary for their presentation. And those exhibitors with sufficient space often had little financial incentive to make the changeover, because Cinerama-converted theatres seated fewer patrons than standard ones and were a lot more expensive to operate. Moreover, the projection system never proved wholly satisfactory. The three criss-crossing images did not always blend and synchronize convincingly, the two dividing lines separating the three images were often distractingly visible, and those sitting at the sides of the typical theatre could see only two of the images properly.

The 3-D Craze

A depth-producing process more fully exploited by mainstream moviemakers was Natural Vision, a system for producing the illusion of three dimensions rooted in the basic principles of binocular vision. Having antecedents in cinema's earliest days, it involved the use of two interlocking cameras whose lenses were positioned to approximate the distance between the left and right eyes of a human. The images captured by the two lenses were recorded on separate reels of film.

Two projectors, one for each eye, simultaneously cast slightly overlapping images on the screen. The projected images passed through special polarized filters. An automatic interlocking device kept the two films in synchronization as they went through the projectors. The viewer wore disposable spectacles with tinted lenses that fused the two images to form a single three-dimensional whole.

The African adventure *Bwana Devil* (1952), an independent production picked up by United Artists for national distribution, was the first movie to employ Natural Vision. Although poorly scripted and acted, and ineptly patched together from new 35-millimeter and old blown-up 16-millimeter footage shot in Africa, its special effects were nonetheless startling. The two man-eating lions stalking luckless railway workers appeared to leap out of the screen. Audience members are said to have dropped to the floor for cover as stray spears seemed to soar above them. *Bwana Devil* enjoyed a box office bonanza. (The Polaroid Company, sole manufacturer of the special spectacles, saw its stock rise by 30 percent in a matter of weeks.) Within months of its release, close to 5000 theatres were converted to show three-dimensional, or "3-D," movies—as they came to be called.

The 3-D rush was on. By the middle of 1953, nearly all the major studios were making movies in Natural Vision or some other similar stereoscopic process. Several of these projects enjoyed great popularity. Warner's *House of Wax* (1953), starring Vincent Price as a vengeful sculptor who makes wax figures out of his human victims, broke box office records just about everywhere it played. In 1953 and 1954, Hollywood made close to seventy 3-D movies. They included everything from M-G-M's extravagant *Kiss Me Kate* (1953), a film version of Cole Porter's musical adaptation of *The Taming of the Shrew,* to Universal's cheaply produced *Creature from the Black Lagoon* (1954), in which members of an Amazon expedition encounter a deadly gill-man. (The latter was the first 3-D feature to employ a single-strip process that required only one projector.)

The 3-D craze proved to be short-lived. By the close of 1953, it was clearly on the wane. When *Kiss Me Kate* initially bombed at the box office, M-G-M decided to release it nationally only in conventional form. Warner Bros. Pictures, which had once expected to produce most of its movies in Natural Vision, abandoned the process altogether after the release of *The Phantom*

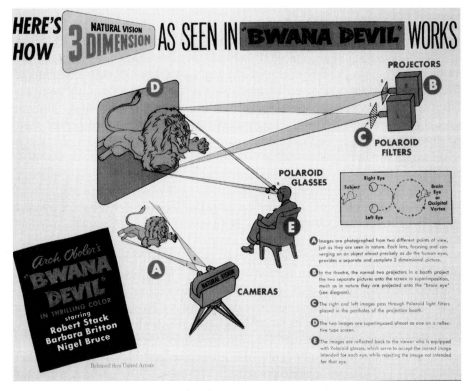

Promotional material for *Bwana Devil* (1952) explains the workings of Natural Vision, a stereo-scopic process based on the pioneering work of camera engineer Friend Baker. The prime mover in its development was Milton Gunzburg, a little-known writer, who had purchased the invention from Baker for a nominal fee and the promise of a small percentage of any accruing profits. Working with his brother Julian, an eye specialist, Gunzburg perfected the process.

of the Rue Morgue (1954) and *Dial M for Murder* (1954). The latter movie, directed by Alfred Hitchcock, was presented in two versions, but most people saw it in its conventional form. Hollywood's close encounter with the third dimension was ultimately undone by projection problems that produced eye-strain and headaches, the annoyance of having to wear special spectacles, and a glut of movies that relied more on gimmicks than plot and character.

Wide-Screen Formats

The initial success of stereoscopic cinema stimulated experimentation with less complicated and more versatile ways of enhancing the illusion of depth. Twentieth Century–Fox decided to gamble its future on a wide-screen format it christened CinemaScope. Based on a process developed during the First World War, it employed a special **anamorphic lens** to compress an image that was a bit more than two-and-a-half times as wide as it was high onto standard 35-millimeter film. This distorting compression was corrected during projection, again with an appropriate lens. One of the process's major advantages was the relatively low cost of converting theatres. The entire exhibition system—including the compensating lens (which could be screwed into an ordinary projector), an elongated and slightly curved screen, and a three-track stereophonic sound system—cost less than $20,000 to install. In the spring of 1953, in part to encourage exhibitors to make this investment, Fox announced that henceforth all its movies would be made in CinemaScope.

Its first feature employing the process was *The Robe* (1953), a biblical epic based on Lloyd C. Douglas's piously didactic novel about what happened to Christ's robe after his crucifixion. A little-known young Welsh-born English stage actor named Richard Burton was cast in the leading role of Marcellus, the soldier who wins the robe in a dice game. The dramatic sweep and power of the movie proved to be ideally suited for wide-screen presentation. Its premiere at New York's Roxy Theatre in September 1953 drew an enthusiastic public response (and carping from the critics). And when it opened in other major cities, the reaction was much the same.

In an effort to ensure widespread use, Fox decided to make CinemaScope available to its competitors. By the end of 1953, most of the major studios were licensed to use the process, and seventy-five CinemaScope features were in production. Some 5000 specially equipped theatres were able to accommodate this output, a figure that would triple within a year. Although providing somewhat greater depth than conventional procedures, CinemaScope was more panoramic than stereoscopic. In addition, it achieved width at the expense of clarity and definition; the projected image had a slightly blurred, grainy texture.

When it became increasingly apparent that standard 35-millimeter film stock was inadequate for wide-screen production, Paramount decided to experiment with a process called Vista Vision. This involved running the negative film through the camera horizontally, recording one image across two frames of 35-millimeter film. The doubled frame image was then optically reduced and printed on a 35-millimeter release print that could be shown with a special lens on standard projection equipment. The resulting image was sharper and clearer than that produced with CinemaScope. Alfred Hitchcock used this process for the chic and elegant *To Catch a Thief* (1955), with Cary Grant as a reformed cat burglar suspected of a wave of jewel robberies on the French Riviera.

Showman Mike Todd introduced a system in 1955 called Todd-AO that achieved even more spectacular results than Vista Vision. It employed the use of 65-millimeter film in the camera and a 70-millimeter print for projection. Among the early Todd-AO releases were *Oklahoma!* (1955) and *Around the World in Eighty Days* (1956). The process later came under the control of Twentieth Century–Fox.

Most of the major studios eventually adopted their own versions of wide-screen cinema. By the close of the 1950s, the dominant aspect ratios for 35-millimeter projection in the United States were standardized at 1.85:1 for nonanamorphic and 2.35:1 for anamorphic movies. Some wide-screen epics, however, have been filmed in aspect ratios as high as 2.75:1, meaning that the image is nearly three times as wide as it is tall.

Small-Screen Production

Even as they were trying to lure patrons back to the theatre, many movie firms began to turn out programs for the rival medium of television. By the end of the 1950s, Hollywood had become a hive of television producing activity. As early as 1952, Columbia Pictures' wholly owned subsidiary, Screen Gems, struck a $1-million deal with the Ford Motor Company to produce thirty-nine half-hour films for a television series called the *Ford Theatre.* Two years later, Disney and the ABC television network announced plans for a *Disneyland* series, a weekly potpourri of cartoons and films introduced by Walt Disney himself. It was designed to promote another Disney-ABC venture, Disneyland Park in Anaheim, California, as well as the studio's upcoming theatrical releases. Episodes were often devoted to behind-the-scenes glimpses of movies under production. An instant hit, the weekly Disney program was followed a year later by an even more successful series—a five-day-a-week afternoon program called *The Mickey Mouse Club.*

Disney's success served as a model for other movie studios. Warner took the plunge into television production in 1955 with an ABC offering called *Warner Brothers Presents.* The title was actually an umbrella for three separate one-hour programs that rotated weekly on Tuesday nights—*Casablanca, King's Row,* and *Cheyenne*—each based on a Warner movie of the same name. Most of the episodes were shot in five or so days, and studio sets were supplemented with old film footage to keep production costs low. After an unknown actor named Clint Walker clicked as Cheyenne Bodie, a laconic drifter of mixed ancestry, the other two shows were dropped. The series became simply *Cheyenne* and enjoyed a seven-year run on the network.

When the low-paid Walker held out for a new contract that provided for a larger percentage of residuals and merchandising profits, more time off between productions, and the right to make public appearances without having to return half the earnings to the studio, Warner replaced him with another actor. The studio apparently feared that meeting his demands would lead other rising television stars in its stable to follow suit. Others who tried to buck this new star system got much the same treatment. Within a few years, most of the major studios had turned to television as a way of putting sound-

Clint Walker was propelled from anonymity to stardom in the *Cheyenne* series. His salary had reached $1250 per week by the beginning of the 1958–1959 TV season, but his residual payments remained at the Screen Actors Guild minimum. Warner Bros. Television replaced him when he held out for a new contract.

stages and back lots into action, developing inexpensive contract players, and promoting new theatrical releases before a nationwide audience.

Studio Backlogs

Hollywood embraced television in other ways as well. All the studios had huge backlogs of movies collecting dust in their vaults. The profit potential from television sales could be substantial because the production costs of most of these movies had been fully amortized from theatrical revenues. (They were carried on company ledgers for tax purposes at the nominal value of $1 each.) Small firms specializing in low-budget series and formulaic features were the first to unload their film inventories. Monogram Pictures, which came into existence in the 1930s, released some 300 of its movies to television in 1951.

ANTHOLOGY TELEVISION DRAMA

Early television was oriented more toward New York than Los Angeles. A staple of the medium in the 1950s was the anthology drama series. By the middle of the decade, shows with such theatrical-sounding titles as *Kraft Television Theatre, Studio One, Philco Playhouse,* and *Armstrong Circle Theater* were presenting as many as a dozen original teleplays a week. The emphasis on originality stemmed from necessity. The movie studios owned the rights to most plays not in the public domain and refused to make them available to the rival medium.

This situation provided an extraordinary opportunity for talented young writers like Rod Serling, Paddy Chayefsky, and Reginald Rose to showcase their work on television. Tiny studio facilities put a premium on dialogue, psychological tension, and characterization. Writers were asked for scripts requiring small casts, a minimum of set constructions, few variations in lighting, and the most elementary of camera shots. Each production was self-contained. There were no continuing characters or situations to sustain audience interest from week to week.

With limited settings, movements, and camera work, directors tended to focus on the faces of the actors. This capitalized on television's unique intimacy, because a close view of a performer is roughly on a scale that approximates human contact. Actors enjoyed more control over the timing and intensity of their portrayals. In moviemaking, where everything is shot in fragments, the actor's concern with the perfection of the moment makes it difficult to grasp a role in its entirety. The anthology drama format permitted a unity of performance not possible in big-screen productions. But working conditions in live television were less than ideal. Actors had to learn their lines quickly, perform their roles

in hot and cramped quarters, and take orders from often inexperienced directors.

The technical tasks of an anthology director were quite complicated. Most shows were produced live, with all editing (camera switching, in this case) being done while the performance was in progress. In a typical production, three or four cameras were used. Each was equipped with a turret of several lenses so that the camera operator could switch from a long view to a close-up. Operators wore earphones through which they received instructions from the studio control room, where a bank of screens provided the director with the images being picked up by the cameras. A separate monitor showed the camera image on the air at any given moment.

While surveying the various monitors, the director issued supplementary instructions to the camera operators, who were already working from notes prepared in advance of the performance. Split-second decisions determined what went out over the air. Unlike moviemaking, a second or third take wasn't possible if somebody flubbed a line or a microphone came into view. These were the circumstances under which future film directors like Arthur Penn, George Roy Hill, and John Frankenheimer honed their skills.

More than any other television form, the anthology series provided insights into the fears, tensions, and anxieties of average people. Paddy Chayevsky's 1953 teleplay *Marty,* for instance, dealt with the mundane and lonely life of a burly Bronx butcher (Rod Steiger) who finds romance with a schoolteacher (Nancy Marchand). Neither character is conventionally attractive. "I didn't want my hero handsome, and I didn't want the girl to be pretty," explained Chayevsky. "I wanted to write a love story the way it would literally have happened to the kind of people I know.

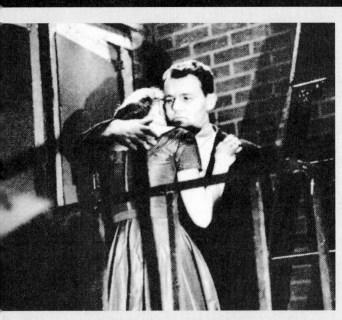

The title character of *Marty* (Rod Steiger, 1953) embraces Clara (Nancy Marchand, later of *The Sopranos*), a rather dowdy schoolteacher he met at a dance after she had been dumped by the man who brought her. This was the first teleplay bought by Hollywood and made into a theatrical feature. (Ernest Borgnine and Betsy Blair played the couple in the movie version.)

I was, in fact, determined to shatter the shallow and destructive illusion . . . that love is simply a matter of physical attraction."[2]

In the advertiser-supported environment of television, such intimate glimpses of reality may have played a part in the demise of this program format and hastened the entry of the Hollywood studios into the new medium. Advertisers have always been in the business of selling "magic." Commercials invariably provide, notes a broadcast historian, "a solution as clear-cut as a snap of a finger: the problem can be solved by a new pill, deodorant, toothpaste, shampoo, shaving lotion, hair tonic, car, girdle."[3] The

harsher realities depicted in the anthology dramas made such appeals seem fraudulent. Advertisers and television executives alike became increasingly wary of nuance and ambiguity, those shaded areas of complexity and doubt where the anthology dramas tended to dwell.

Many other factors contributed to the jettisoning of the anthology programs. As commercial television took hold in Japan, Europe, and Latin America, the possibility of expanding into these markets created a demand for programs that were easily transplantable to other cultures. The verbal shadings and subtleties in many anthology dramas were difficult to translate into other languages. In sharp contrast, the kinds of action-oriented television fare Hollywood produced could be dubbed with little difficulty. In addition, there was a growing dearth of quality scripts. Writers for the anthology format were poorly paid. Although they initially welcomed the chance to showcase their work, once they became established they moved on to more lucrative film endeavors. Producers, directors, and actors likewise sought work in Hollywood after having made their mark in the venturesome anthologies.

But more than any other factor, it was probably the changing size and composition of the television audience that ultimately doomed the anthology dramas. As the number of television households increased, the percentage of people watching these dramas decreased. As a result, advertisers shifted support to the quiz shows, sitcoms, westerns, and crime thrillers that were beginning to draw mass audiences. Such programs were also much less likely to offend social or political sensibilities — not a small concern given the prevailing Cold War climate.

Such cut-to-pattern pictures as *Smart Alecks* (1942), *Clancy Street Boys* (1943), and *Come Out Fighting* (1945), featuring the East Side Kids—Leo Gorcey, Huntz Hall, and Bobby Jordan, among others—became a staple of Saturday morning television.

That same year, Republic Pictures, organized in 1935 by former tobacco executive Herbert J. Yates, set up a subsidiary to distribute its low-budget westerns, melodramas, bucolic musicals, and serials to television. When it announced plans to release its westerns starring Gene Autry and Roy Rogers, the two cowboy crooners filed separate suits in federal court seeking an injunction against the transaction on the grounds that their contracts prohibited the use of their names, voices, or likenesses for advertising without their consent. A federal appeals court eventually ruled in favor of Republic, permitting it to release the westerns to television, where they could be edited for commercial inserts. The only stipulation was that the stars themselves should not appear to be endorsing specific products or services. Thus judicial sanction was given to the already common practice of chopping up movies into small bits to bracket product pitches.

The sale or lease of movies to television was complicated by a number of issues. The Screen Actors Guild (SAG), for instance, demanded recompense for the films shown on television. The studios were free to release pre-1948 movies without negotiation or payment because standard contracts prior to that year specifically gave producers the television performance rights. However, in his 1951 contract negotiations with producers, SAG president Ronald Reagan secured additional payments for actors appearing in all post-1948 movies played on television. The guilds for writers and directors soon negotiated added revenue for their members as well.

Fearful that they might be inviting their own destruction, the big studios initially refrained from tapping into their film vaults for television revenue. Fox and Paramount had sold a few of their low-budget features to television distributors, but this trickle was of little consequence. The cascade began in 1955 when industrialist Howard Hughes, who had purchased RKO outright a year earlier, decided to sell its assets, including its backlog of some 740 feature films and 1000 shorts, to General Teleradio. This broadcasting company, a subsidiary of General Tire and Rubber, quickly recouped some of its investment by selling the film library to a television distributor while retaining the rights for exclusive showings on its owned-and-operated stations in major cities. It also retained first-run television rights to 150 selected features. Within three years, it sold the studio's sprawling production facilities to Desilu, the television firm set up by two former RKO contract players, Lucille Ball and Desi Arnaz. (They purchased RKO's Hollywood and Culver City production facilities largely with the proceeds they had earned from selling the rerun rights to the 179 half-hour episodes in the *I Love Lucy* series, which ran on the CBS network from 1951 to 1957 and turned the married couple into household deities.)

The filming of *I Love Lucy.* The first sitcom to be shot on film, each episode was staged as a three-act play in front of a studio audience and photographed simultaneously with three 35-millimeter cameras from different angles. In postproduction, the best of the three different angles for every scene were edited together.

The sale of RKO's backlog of films to television was the vanguard of a large-scale merchandising of old movies. The rest of the majors were quick to join the rush to television, leasing or selling off their pre-1948 inventories. Feature films swiftly became a mainstay of local television programming. In the early 1960s, the three major television networks began to rent post-1950 color features for prime-time presentation. The movie industry soon came to regard television showings as an extension of the box office, part of the projected earnings of a picture.

The Collapse of the Studio System

During the war years, there had been a substantial increase in independent production. This trend was abetted by a strong market for movies that the big studios could not completely satisfy because of labor and material shortages and a new federal tax on income that could go as high as 91 percent.

High taxes had begun to swallow up so much of the salaries of actors, writers, and producers in the top income bracket that there seemed to be little incentive to remain a studio employee.

Many became independent producers to take advantage of the less onerous levy on capital gains (profit on the sale of goods or stocks), which were taxed at a fraction of the rate applied to earned income. A common scheme was to set up a corporation for the sole purpose of making a single motion picture. When the project was completed, the producer would dissolve this entity, receiving the picture in exchange for the stock. It could then be sold as a capital asset, which under the extant law was taxed at rates ranging up to 25 percent. (Congress modified the tax law in 1950 to prevent people from taking tax advantage through these "collapsible" corporations.)

The growth of independent production accelerated when the industry's system of vertical integration (the capacity to produce, distribute, and exhibit movies under a single corporate umbrella) began to break apart, and the big studios underwent retrenchment and reorganization. In 1944 the Justice Department reactivated its antitrust suit. The case eventually made its way to the U.S. Supreme Court, which ruled in 1948 that the vertical structure of the major companies violated federal antitrust laws. The high court remanded the question of theatre ownership to the federal district court in New York City where the case had originated. In 1949 this court decided that separation of production and distribution from exhibition was the appropriate remedy.

The five vertically integrated companies—beginning with RKO and continuing with Paramount, Warner Bros., Twentieth Century–Fox, and Loew's–M-G-M—signed consent decrees that broke the corporate chains linking production and distribution to exhibition. Although trumpeted as a major triumph for government trustbusters, this court-imposed dismantling did little to prevent the development of new concentrations of control. The theatre chains maintained their dominance in exhibition even though they were required to divest some of their holdings. But the distribution of movies, the key to controlling production, continued to be dominated by the established studios.

Foreshadowing the commercial practices prevalent today, the studios embarked on a policy of financing, marketing, and distributing movies made by independent producing units. The move to independent production gained impetus from United Artists, which by the 1950s had evolved into a company run by lawyers. It attracted major stars like John Wayne, Burt Lancaster, and Robert Mitchum to its fold by providing some financing, assisting in such particulars as renting studio space and preparing contracts, guaranteeing promotion and distribution, and allowing them to make movies with a minimum of front office interference. As actors, writers, directors, and producers increasingly turned to this form of production, the studio head was relegated to determining which of these people to sign to short-term contracts for picture deals.

By 1958 some 65 percent of Hollywood movies were being made by independent producers, although the major studios to varying degrees determined the character and quality of most of these projects. In return for their investment, most demanded the right of approval for the director, writers, actors, and anyone else integral to the production process. Those who sought financing outside the studio nexus ran the risk of not being able to get their movies widely distributed either at home or abroad. Under the typical distribution contract, a studio generally received 30 percent of a movie's gross receipts and was much more likely to show a profit than its producer—who may also have been required, as a condition for a release commitment, to rent the studio's equipment, technical services, and soundstages. (The "gross" refers to how much is left after the distributor splits the take of the movie with theatre owners.) The degree of independence enjoyed by producers depended primarily on the profitability of their pictures.

The Resurgence of Star Power

The status of screen stars changed during the postwar period as well. With the overhaul in production practices, the major studios reduced operating expenses by cutting loose contract players (along with other creative and technical personnel), a large number of whom had been with them since the 1930s. Many stars left on their own accord, dismayed at being forced into films they did not want to make and seeking greater remuneration for their services. (As early as 1942, James Cagney severed his ties with Warner Bros. Pictures to set up his own company in partnership with his brother William.)

The legal actions of Olivia de Havilland, under contract to Warner Bros. Pictures, strengthened the negotiating position of top stars. When her seven-year contract expired in 1943, the studio tacked on the months she had been suspended for turning down roles. Unhappy with her situation, de Havilland decided to challenge Warner's suspension polices. In a precedent-setting decision, the California courts ruled in her favor. No longer could Warner—or any other studio—add suspension time to the end of a long-term contract.

Freed from studio control, some stars were able to negotiate huge salaries and unprecedented participation deals. For his work in *The Bridge on the River Kwai* (1957), William Holden got 10 percent of the movie's gross receipts, with the understanding that his take would be paid to him at the rate of $50,000 a year. The movie's success at the box office ensured him of a steady income for the rest of his life. In his fabled deal with Universal in the late 1950s, Cary Grant, who had been a freelance actor since 1936, gained full ownership of his movies after seven years. To play the title role in *Cleopatra* (1963), Elizabeth Taylor wanted a cool million up front. She eventually signed

Elizabeth Taylor is seen here in a production still from Twentieth Century–Fox's trouble-ridden *Cleopatra* (1963), the capricious and imperious queen who brought a studio to its knees. Originally budgeted for $2 million, the movie's production costs escalated to more than $30 million.

a contract that called for her to get $125,000 per week for sixteen weeks, $50,000 a week after that if shooting continued, $3,000 weekly for living expenses, and 10 percent of the gross. Her total income for her work in the picture surpassed $7 million, this at a time when the highest paid American business executive was earning around $650,000 annually.

As production costs rose sharply, making projects much riskier, the number of major stars receiving a percentage of the gross for appearing in a movie increased steadily. By the 1980s, in any one season, some fifteen or so top stars, based on the strength of their recent track records, were able to negotiate gross participation deals. Needless to say, the bigger the star, the bigger the cut. For his supporting role as the Joker in *Batman* (1989), Jack Nicholson got $7 million up front plus 10 percent of the gross and 10 percent of the merchandising revenue from tie-in products. The deal put an estimated $60 million in his till. (According to trade press reports, retail tie-in sales reached some $1.5 billion worldwide, more than twice the movie's gross revenues.)

While providing no absolute box office assurances, a "big name" star's involvement in a costly project lends a certain semblance of stability. The media access movie stars enjoy can contribute greatly to public awareness of their new releases. In addition, the presence of familiar names helps to attract foreign investors and increase international sales. In today's marketplace, studio executives see star power as essential to getting movies global distribution.

Such established box office draws as Russell Crowe, Tom Cruise, Tom Hanks, Mel Gibson, Julia Roberts, Will Smith, Denzel Washington, and Bruce Willis can generally command $20 million or more against at least 10 percent of the gross. For example, Julia Roberts, one of the few females on Hollywood's unofficial "A+" list, was guaranteed a salary of $20 million for starring in *Erin Brockovich* (2000) regardless of how it did at the box office. Once the movie grossed $200 million—or ten times her fee—she started to make an additional 10¢ on every dollar it earned beyond that point. For the sleeper hit *The Sixth Sense* (1999), Bruce Willis reportedly earned $50 million, $20 million in salary combined with 17 percent of the gross. (Because such deals tend to be quite complicated, only the star's accountant is likely to know for sure just how much money was actually made.)

To move a risky or pet project from script to screen, an actor may forego any money up front in return for a larger cut of the gross. For his pivotal role in *Saving Private Ryan* (1998), for example, Tom Hanks waived his usual $20 million up-front fee. Instead, he agreed to split 35 percent of the movie's gross receipts with its director, Steven Spielberg. This financial arrangement proved to be extremely lucrative. Each earned as much as $50 million by the end of the theatrical run. (The cash generally continues to pour in when box office hits go to cable, network telecasts, DVD, and video.) Of course, if the movie had failed at the box office, they would have been working for free.

Hollywood and the Cold War

Adding to the breakdown of the old order, Hollywood was plagued by labor strife, rebellious exhibitors, restricted foreign markets, and anticommunist purges. Toward the close of the Second World War, a jurisdictional dispute involving the union affiliation of set decorators escalated into an industrywide strike. It dragged on for eight months, and strikers and studios alike acted brutally at times. A principal target of the strike action, the Warner studio used tear gas and water hoses to disrupt the picket lines. Many in the movie colony attributed the disruptions to communist agitation within the unions.

The Motion Picture Alliance for the Preservation of American Ideals, formed in 1944 to exorcise the communist demon from Hollywood, called for a government investigation of subversive activity in the movie industry. Along with producers, directors, writers, and set designers, its membership included such stars as Gary Cooper, Clark Gable, Robert Taylor, Barbara Stanwyck, and John Wayne. Principal funding for the group came from the heads of the major studios and press baron William Randolph Hearst. When postwar Soviet-American relations soured, it gained many new converts to its cause.

Congress Investigates Hollywood

In the ensuing Cold War, the House Committee on Un-American Activities (HUAC) launched an all-out, no-holds-barred assault against supposed subversive activities in the movie industry. In May 1947 a subcommittee of HUAC, which had half-heartedly investigated Hollywood twice before, held closed hearings at the Biltmore Hotel in Los Angeles to investigate the extent of the American Communist Party's influence in the movie industry. Most of the witnesses who testified were members of the Motion Picture Alliance for the Preservation of American Ideals.

The following October saw the beginning of public hearings in the Caucus Room of the old House of Representatives office building in the nation's capitol. Scores of reporters, many equipped with movie cameras, were on hand to cover the spectacle. Klieg lights hung in clusters from two massive chandeliers, providing illumination worthy of a studio soundstage. Uniformed police were on guard outside the hearing room to control the crowd that congregated in the corridors to catch a glimpse of the movie stars in attendance.

During the first week of the hearings, twenty-four "friendly" witnesses testified before the subcommittee. Among them were top studio heads, who tried to justify wartime movies, released mostly in 1943 when the Soviet-American alliance stood at its height, that depicted the former superpower in a favorable light while airbrushing out the insidious aspects of its repressive regime. An evasive Jack L. Warner contended that he knew of nothing in *Mission to Moscow* (1943) that could possibly be construed as deceptive or subversive. In support of M-G-M's much criticized *Song of Russia* (1943), in which Robert Taylor stars as a concert conductor on tour in the Soviet Union, Louis B. Mayer argued that it was merely a romance featuring a Russian setting and the music of Tchaikovsky. (All the same, the movie did tend to idealize everyday life in the Soviet Union. Sightseeing in Moscow, for example, Taylor's character enthuses, "I can't get over it. Everyone seems to be having such a good time.")

While revealing very little in the way of subversive screen content, the proceedings did provide some amusement. Staunchly anti-unionist Walt Disney, who had battled the Cartoonists Guild to the brink of bankruptcy, described attempts to subvert his studio and have Mickey Mouse follow the party line. Slow-speaking Gary Cooper said he disliked communism because "it isn't on the level." The dapper character actor Adolph Menjou, identifying himself as a close friend of FBI director J. Edgar Hoover, claimed that communistic messages could be injected into a movie by a look, an inflection, or a change in voice, but he could not provide any specific examples. SAG president Ronald Reagan, future leader of the free world, declared that Red threats had led him to pack a gun.

The following week, the "unfriendly" witnesses had their turn. Nineteen had been subpoenaed, but only eleven were called to testify. After denying

Robert Taylor appears before the subcommittee of HUAC that investigated communist infiltration of the movie industry. He testified that he had seen plenty of things "on the pink side" in Hollywood.

Communist Party affiliation, playwright Bertolt Brecht made a precipitous retreat to East Germany. The remaining ten included producer Adrian Scott, director Edward Dmytryk, and screenwriters Alva Bessie, Herbert Biberman, Lester Cole, Ring Lardner Jr., John Howard Lawson, Albert Maltz, Samuel Ornitz, and Dalton Trumbo. They all based their refusal to cooperate on the First Amendment, which states that Congress has no right to make any law restricting free speech or peaceful assembly, and therefore presumably no right to investigate anything involving these matters.

Each went to the stand; gave his name, address and occupation; attempted to read a prepared statement denouncing the subcommittee investigation; and then, after that had been ruled inadmissible, declined to answer the question as to whether he was, or ever had been, a member of the Communist Party. Only screenwriter Albert Maltz was permitted to read his entire statement. His credits included *Pride of the Marines* (1945), which criticized wartime profiteering, discrimination against Jews, and the harsh treatment of returning soldiers in the workplace.

Some of the so-called unfriendly witnesses were quite hostile when they appeared before the subcommittee. John Howard Lawson, founder and first president of the Screen Writers Guild, was especially unruly and arrogant. He was dragged shouting from the witness stand. After each witness left the

Humphrey Bogart and his wife Lauren Bacall lead a parade of performers in the nation's capital to protest the HUAC hearings.

stand, a subcommittee investigator read a lengthy dossier into the record detailing his alleged Communist Party affiliations. In November 1947, each was cited for contempt of Congress. Despite the First Amendment defense, they were indicted, arraigned, tried, and found guilty. In the spring of 1950, the U.S. Supreme Court refused to review their convictions. All went to federal prison to serve sentences of up to a year, thereby gaining a prominent place in the folklore of the left as the "Hollywood Ten."

Shortly before the hearings began, directors John Huston and William Wyler and screenwriter Philip Dunne organized a group that came to be called the Committee for the First Amendment. Among its members were such major stars as Lauren Bacall, Humphrey Bogart, Henry Fonda, John Garfield, Paulette Goddard, Katherine Hepburn, Myrna Loy, Groucho Marx, Gregory Peck, Edward G. Robinson, and Frank Sinatra. The group expressed its opposition to what it saw as HUAC's violation of civil liberties through two national radio broadcasts, several ads in the trade papers, and a highly publicized, star-studded trip to Washington, DC, on a chartered airplane.

In the aftermath of the hearings, however, the Committee for the First Amendment's facade of courage quickly collapsed. To save their careers, many of its star supporters disavowed political activism. Humphrey Bogart, for instance, wrote an article for the March 1948 issue of *Photoplay* magazine, titled "I'm No Communist," wherein he admitted being "duped." His trip to Washington, he conceded, had been "ill-advised." Such contrition, as a major study documents, proved to be "contagious and enduring."[4]

In November 1947, on the same day the ten unwilling witnesses were cited for contempt, some fifty movie industry leaders met at the Waldorf Astoria Hotel in New York City to discuss a uniform policy for dealing with them. In what has become known as the Waldorf Declaration of 1947, the major producers pledged that they would not "knowingly" hire any communists or other subversives, and they condemned the actions of the witnesses as a disservice to their employers.

Those among the ten still employed were either fired or suspended without pay. Except for director Edward Dmytryk, who was able to resume his career in the early 1950s by recanting his political beliefs in a "friendly" appearance before HUAC, they were unemployable under their own names for well over a decade. Thus the cornerstone of the infamous Hollywood **blacklist** had been firmly embedded. Many with leftist leanings soon experienced difficulty finding work in the movie industry.

Congressional Hearings Resume

After a long hiatus, the HUAC hearings resumed in 1951 with renewed vigor. In the interim, the political climate had become much more conducive to its investigation of subversives within the movie colony. A communist coup took place in the former Czechoslovakia; eleven leaders of the American Communist Party were indicted by a federal grand jury for conspiring to overthrow the U.S. government; China became a communist nation; the former Soviet Union detonated its first nuclear weapon; one-time high-ranking State Department official Alger Hiss was convicted of perjury (after denying passing confidential government documents to the communist underground); Julius and Ethel Rosenberg were arrested for espionage (they were later executed); the Korean War broke out; and Senator Joseph McCarthy launched a zealous campaign to root out subversives in high places.

During the course of the second set of hearings, nearly ninety witnesses testified; about a third of them provided the committee with the names of those they thought to be Communist Party members. The rest were "unfriendly" witnesses who sought refuge under the Fifth Amendment protection against self-incrimination. Among the most prominent of those providing names was Elia Kazan, who had directed such huge Broadway hits as *The Skin of Our Teeth* (1942), *All My Sons* (1947), *A Streetcar Named Desire* (1947), and *Death of a Salesman* (1949). His thriving career as a screen director was marked by the critical and commercial successes of *A Tree Grows in Brooklyn* (1945), *Boomerang* (1947), *Gentleman's Agreement* (1948), and a 1951 screen version of *Streetcar.* Few directors had a firmer footing in the popular arts.

Initially refusing to name names, Kazan changed his mind, claiming that secrecy only served the ignoble cause of the Communist Party—which he admitted belonging to for a few years in the mid-1930s. Having made this admission, he apparently had little choice but to give the committee the names it sought. In 1950 the U.S. Supreme Court had ruled in *Rogers v. United States* that, once witnesses had admitted their own party membership, they lost their immunity privilege under the Fifth Amendment and could not refuse to answer questions about other people's party membership.

In a lengthy affidavit, Kazan listed several fellow Group Theatre alumni from the 1930s who had been active in the Communist Party, and the next day he took out an ad in the *New York Times* justifying his actions. Although he professed patriotic motives, giving the names of friends and colleagues—names HUAC already had—seemed to serve no cause but his own. Whatever the case, the experience appears to have haunted him long after—as it did many others.

In an apparent attempt at exculpation, Kazan directed *On the Waterfront* (1954) from a screenplay by Budd Schulberg (who had also named names). In the movie, Marlon Brando plays a longshoreman faced with a choice about whether or not to blow the whistle on the corrupt and murderous mob boss running his union. His decision to testify before the Waterfront Crime Commission is portrayed as an act of courage, not cowardice—the unequivocally honorable thing to do given the circumstances.

Careers Are Destroyed

Scores saw their careers destroyed for refusing to testify. As paranoia and fear permeated the movie colony, producers rushed to rid their rolls of anyone who might cause embarrassment. The number of people blacklisted grew rapidly. All the creative guilds instituted their own loyalty oaths. A few directors of note, like Jules Dassin and Joseph Losey, chose exile in Europe. Actors were the hardest hit because they couldn't hide behind a false name. Many of those blacklisted turned to alcohol; a few, in despair, committed suicide.

Some blacklisted writers found work under pseudonyms for cut-rate salaries. The Oscar for the best screenplay of 1956 was awarded to Robert Rich for *The Brave One,* but it went unclaimed until 1975. The elusive Rich turned out to be a pseudonym for blacklisted writer Dalton Trumbo. Director Otto Preminger took the decisive step of breaching the blacklist in 1960 by announcing that Trumbo had scripted *Exodus* and that, as the movie's producer, he was making sure Trumbo's name appeared in the screen credits.

Blacklisting Spreads to Television

Writers, directors, and actors adversely affected by the HUAC hearings found themselves blacklisted from radio broadcasting and the fledgling medium of television as well. A widely circulated newsletter called *Counterattack: The Newsletter of Facts to Combat Communism,* created by three ex-FBI agents, endlessly warned of the dangers posed by communist infiltration into the entertainment field. Its publishers counted among their clients some of the country's most powerful corporations. In addition to issuing the newsletter, they also conducted "special investigations" into suspected subversive activities.

To expose those engaged in suspect pursuits, they issued a special edition of *Counterattack* in June 1950 called *Red Channels: The Report of Communist Influence in Radio and Television,* which suggested that 151 admired and talented people in the popular arts had engaged in activities helpful to the communist cause. Stella Adler, Leonard Bernstein, John Garfield, Lillian Hellman, Lena Horne, Howard Koch, Burl Ives, Arthur Miller, and Orson Welles were among those cited in the 215-page booklet (its cover showed a red hand closing on a microphone). Many of those listed were required to endure long clearance procedures before they were employable again.

Executives at the nascent television networks summarily dismissed anyone who might generate controversy or jeopardize advertising revenues. Once blacklisting was institutionalized, it expanded and soon went far beyond the names published in *Red Channels*. The practice was complicated by the unique structure of broadcasting. In the movie industry, most hiring was still concentrated in the major studios; in television, in contrast, networks, program packagers, advertising agencies, and sponsors all had a voice in deciding who was to be employed. The fear of reducing audience numbers or associating advertised products with causes or individuals that might be deemed offensive crippled creativity and impelled a retreat into formulaic programming.

Wounds Still Linger

Although blacklisting passed with the years, the wounds still fester today. Many in the creative community continue to harbor bitterness toward those who named names. Resentment over Elia Kazan's supposed betrayal of friends and colleagues remains especially strong. In 1999, for example, the decision by the Academy of Motion Picture Arts and Sciences to present an honorary Oscar to the ailing eighty-nine-year-old director for "lifetime achievement" was widely protested. A sore point has been Kazan's failure to apologize for testifying before the House committee. Those defending his reluctance to recant, however, are quick to point out that many of his critics have never expressed any remorse themselves for supporting the repressive Stalinist regime in Russia.

Corporate Upheaval

The 1960s witnessed a fundamental change in the control structure of the movie industry. The erratic earnings of the big studios, dating from the advent of television, made them highly susceptible to mergers and corporate takeovers. Those seeking to gain a hold in the movie industry were attracted by the potential profits from television production, large film libraries, real estate assets, and musical and literary copyrights. Because voting stock had become widely dispersed, executive cadres at the studios had only a tenuous hold on the corporate reins. This resulted in a constant ebb and flow of managerial personnel.

Disruptions at the once-mighty M-G-M were especially severe. Its production chief, Louis B. Mayer, had been forced to abdicate his throne in 1952 and had failed in a later bid to regain power. The production policies of his successors did little to boost revenues. The troubled operation was saved from ruin in 1959 by the release of a highly profitable remake of *Ben-Hur*, starring Charlton Heston in the title role, but its fortunes continued to decline steadily. Most of the revenues from *Ben-Hur* were squandered on a lavish remake of *Mutiny on the Bounty* (1962), with a miscast Marlon Brando playing an oddly foppish Fletcher Christian. During the decade, the studio underwent several stressful managerial changes, causing the ailing lion to become increasingly arthritic and enfeebled.

After being pursued by various corporate suitors, M-G-M was acquired in 1969 by Las Vegas–based financier and casino owner Kirk Kerkorian. The new management he put in place virtually liquidated the studio, selling thirty-eight acres of its Culver City back lot, as well as theatres in Australia, South Africa, and the United Kingdom. Movie projects were abruptly canceled, personnel were slashed, historic sets were leveled, and the company's collection of props, costumes, and other memorabilia was turned over to an auction house. Much of the money drained from the studio went into the construction of the M-G-M Grand Hotel in Las Vegas. The once-proud lion, although prosperous in his old age, now presided over roulette wheels, craps tables, and slot machines. Resuscitated several times over the years, the studio has yet to regain its position in the top ranks of the Hollywood hierarchy.

Most of the major studios, weakened by internal strife and disorder, were assimilated into complex corporate enterprises during the 1960s. Despite this breakdown and realignment of corporate structures, however, the dominant cinematic mode of expression in the United States remained largely intact. By retaining control over financing and distribution, the reconstituted studios continued to determine the stylistic and narrative norms of major releases. As in earlier eras, innovations were adapted to the conventions of the prevailing idiom. Moviemakers traversing from the margins to the mainstream invariably found that they had to sacrifice some aspects of their personal vision in return for bigger budgets and wider audiences.

The New Hollywood

The movie industry suffered a box office slump in the late 1960s, particularly for big-budget pictures. Laden with a large inventory of unmarketable movies, five of the major studios had a combined paper loss of $110 million in 1969 alone. One of the few companies not awash in red ink was Columbia Pictures, which enjoyed the biggest financial success in its history with the release of *Easy Rider* in 1969.

Coproduced by Bob Rafelson and Bert Schneider (whose father headed Columbia at the time), this saga about two cocaine dealers who motorcycle across the southern United States had been conceived by Peter Fonda and marked the directorial debut of Dennis Hopper. Fonda and Hopper also played the two lead roles, and Jack Nicholson appeared in a key supporting role as an alcoholic southern lawyer. Costing less than half a million dollars to make, *Easy Rider* grossed close to $20 million in North America alone. Its dazzling box office success at a time when many big-budget pictures were bombing made the movie industry much more inclined to gamble on young directors and innovative projects.

A New Generation of Directors

During the next decade, a new generation of talented moviemakers—among them Francis Ford Coppola, Brian de Palma, George Lucas, Martin Scorsese, and Steven Spielberg—gave Hollywood a fresh creative energy. Most of them had studied film history, aesthetics, and production as formal academic subjects in graduate programs in Los Angeles and New York. And all of them shared an abiding love of both old Hollywood movies and innovative European and Japanese cinema.

As might be expected, their directorial styles tended to mix the conventional with the experimental. While periodically pursuing personal projects with limited appeal, they derived strength and creative influence not by subverting the idiom of the Hollywood film but by expanding its stylistic parameters. Their movies often surged with ingenuity and creative vitality. By the same token, most of these movies manifested strong narrative structure, clear characterizations, careful camera work, tight editing techniques, and a superb command of dramatic action.

These young moviemakers initially enjoyed extraordinary autonomy and creative freedom. Pundits began to proclaim the advent of a "new Hollywood" dominated by directors rather than studio bosses. Some of the film school–educated directors themselves seemed to think they were in charge. "We are the guys who dig out the gold," boasted a cocky George Lucas. "The man in the executive tower cannot do that. The studios are corporations now, and the men who run them are bureaucrats. They know as much about making movies as a banker does. They know about making deals like a real estate agent. . . . But the real power lies with us—the ones who actually know how to make movies."[5]

Although the idea of a director-dominated movie industry was seductive and gained lots of media attention, shifts in creative control proved to be short-lived and superficial, and those pushing the parameters of movie conventions too hard soon found themselves marginalized. The big studios might have given a director with a proven track record some measure of creative freedom, but they relinquished little of their ultimate power over the production process. What is more, by allowing directors to assume greater responsibility for their own movies, executives were able to shift the blame for financial failure away from themselves. As a result, at the start of the 1980s, when big-budget movies made with a minimum of front office interference began to bomb at the box office, studio management was quick to chide director indulgence and assume closer control over the way movies were made.

The policy of giving directors substantial creative freedom fell into disrepute with the *Heaven's Gate* debacle in 1980. The financial failure of this visually stunning depiction of the conflict between immigrant settlers in nineteenth-century Wyoming and the ruthless empire builders who want to get rid of them virtually destroyed United Artists, the venerable studio that bankrolled the production. In his account of this project, Steven Bach places the blame squarely on the shoulders of writer-director Michael Cimino for indulging his aesthetic pretensions at the expense of narrative drive, character, and emotion. It failed, argues Bach, not because it went catastrophically over budget but because it didn't "engage audiences at the most basic and elemental human levels of sympathy and compassion."[6]

Of course, the actual reasons for any movie's inability to attract audiences large enough to justify its cost are difficult to discern. Bach's explanation can be seen as self-serving in that he was head of production at United Artists at the time *Heaven's Gate* was made. Whatever the merits of his argument, its acceptance in the movie industry made adherence to the established stylistic and narrative conventions all the more imperative.

Directorial Diversity

Over the past two decades, the movie industry has become more open to diverse directorial talent. Unlike in the old studio era, many minority group members have secured directing jobs. During the 1990s, nearly two dozen black directors were at work on a wide range of movie projects. Some, like Julie Dash, the first African American woman to direct a commercially distributed feature film, have specialized in personal pictures. Her quiet turn-of-the-century tale *Daughters of the Dust* (1991) focuses on the female descendants of slaves residing on the Sea Islands of Georgia. Originally made for public television, it first found a theatrical audience through a campaign of flyers and sermons in the black community. Others have worked in more popular cinematic forms. Carl Franklin, for example, has excelled in neo-*noir.* His directorial endeavors include the highly atmospheric *Devil in a Blue Dress* (1995), starring Denzel Washington as a novice private eye in post–World War II Los Angeles.

Asian American directors like Ang Lee, who first achieved acclaim with such understated movies as *Sense and Sensibility* (1995) and *The Ice Storm* (1997), have also flourished in Hollywood. To direct *Crouching Tiger, Hidden Dragon* (2000), featuring Chow Yun-Fat (*Anna and the King,* 1999), Michelle Yeoh (*Tomorrow Never Dies,* 1997), and Zhang Ziyi, one of Beijing's major young stars, the Taiwan-born Lee returned to his roots in China. Filmed in the Mandarin Chinese language and released in the West with subtitles, this highly choreographed martial arts movie earned both plaudits and substantial profits.

Hong Kong filmmaker Jackie Chan has likewise secured regular work in the American movie industry, although primarily as a comedic actor rather than as a director. The largest box office draw in Asia, with nearly seventy films to his credit, Chan finally broke into the orbit of Hollywood stars in 1996 with *Rumble in the Bronx.* Since then the engaging martial arts expert has starred in such hit movies as *Rush Hour* (1998), *Shanghai Noon* (2000), and *Rush Hour 2* (2001).

Directors from Bollywood, the center of Indian filmmaking in Bombay, are having an impact on American cinema as well. Bombay filmmaker Shekhar Kapur, for instance, directed *Elizabeth* (1998), a stunningly photographed epic of intrigue and divisiveness within the sixteenth-century British court. It was nominated for seven Academy Awards, including an Oscar for best picture.

Women moviemakers in general have made great inroads in Hollywood in recent years. Some female directors have dealt with distinctly "women's subjects." Recent examples include Amy Heckerling's *Clueless* (1995), Allison Anders's *Grace of My Heart* (1996), Jocelyn Moorhouse's *A Thousand Acres* (1997), Audrey Wells's *Guinevere* (1999), Karyn Kusama's *Girlfight,* (2000), and Joan Chen's *Autumn in New York* (2000). Others have displayed directing sensibilities that are difficult to categorize. Kathryn Bigelow, for example, directed *Strange Days* (1995), a dazzling but uneasy mix of socially relevant issues and futuristic action. Writer-director Mary Herron's movies include *American Psycho* (2000), a deliciously evil, perversely amusing look at the mind of a serial killer (Christian Bale) who seems to have stepped off the pages of *GQ*. It contains moments of lacerating violence that could repulse even the most ardent horror film fan.

Despite this increased diversity, directing in Hollywood is still dominated by white males. In the 1980s, for example, the number of women directing studio releases rose from zero to about 7 or 8 percent of the total. Over the next decade, however, those figures remained fairly flat. According to a 1998 study by the Directors Guild of America, female directors worked fewer than 5 percent of the total days guild members spent on theatrical movies in 1997—a 50 percent decline from the prior year. Although female membership in the guild has shot up to about 2000 of the 11,000 total, no more than 10 percent of the major movies made in any given year have a woman occupying the director's chair. As a recent article notes, this situation persists despite the fact that several studios are run by women.[7]

New Exhibition Outlets

Diversity has become the hallmark of viewing venues for movies. Beginning in the late 1960s, the old picture palaces gradually gave way to the **multiplex cinema**. Initially built in suburban shopping malls, these complexes, which now may have as many as thirty screens, allow moviegoers to choose from among several first-run movies at one location. Most multiplexes have both large and small showing rooms to accommodate audiences for pictures of varying popularity. Overhead costs are much lower than those for single-screen theatres. For example, one operator typically oversees a dozen or more automated projectors. A number of these facilities have become entertainment centers, boasting video game arcades and centralized concession stands that serve such snacks as gourmet popcorn and cappuccino.

Multiplexes made it possible for the big studios to release more potential "blockbuster" movies in more locations simultaneously during peak box office revenue periods (summertime, Christmas, and spring holidays). At the same time, however, the availability of a large number of screens during slack moviegoing periods proved a boom for some lower-budget films with smaller potential audiences. Innovative moviemakers like Spike Lee were able to get such unconventional pictures as *She's Gotta Have It* (1986) and *Do the Right Thing* (1989) channeled through the studio nexus to thousands of screens nationwide. Writer-director Jane Campion's *The Piano* (1993), a haunting tale of love and sex told from a woman's perspective, was likewise able to generate a large following in this manner.

Sometimes a movie designated exclusively for home viewing in the domestic market manages to make its way to the nation's multiplexes and other theatrical outlets. Among the most notable features to travel this route is director John Dahl's erotic and suspenseful *Red Rock West* (1994), which stars

Nicolas Cage as an honest drifter mistaken for a contract killer hired to murder a seductive adulterous (Lara Flynn Boyle). Convinced that this dour neo-*noir* thriller would not do well in theatres, Columbia Tri-Star executives quickly sold it to cable television and the home video market.

When *Red Rock West* proved popular in European theatres and fared well at the Toronto Film Festival, a small San Francisco theatre decided to book it. After it broke all box office records, Columbia arranged for a nationwide release in select theatres. The new strategy paid off. The movie won positive reviews and generated substantial revenues at the box office and from video rentals. Dahl's next picture, *The Last Seduction* (1994), was also released in theatres after it played on cable television. Its box office success gave a big career boost to Linda Fiorentino. The scheming, single-minded seductress she plays in this provocative picture makes the sexual predators of classic *film noir* seem like Snow White (see Chapter Eight).

Hollywood in the Home

Even with the continued growth of multiplexes, far more people now see movies on television than in theatres. In 1975, Home Box Office began to transmit recent releases, uncut and without commercial interruption, via satellite to the many cable television systems springing up across the country. Such competitors as Showtime soon joined in. In addition, cable channels like American Movie Classics, Bravo, and Turner Classic Movies provide a rich cinema repertory up to twenty-four hours a day. A wide range of film fare is also readily available through the rental or purchase of videocassettes and DVDs. The machines for these formats permit viewers to select their own show date and curtain time.

Altering Aspect Ratios

The standard television set found in the vast majority of American households today still has an aspect ratio of 4:3, meaning the image is only 1.33 as wide as it is high. (Most computer monitors have the same aspect ratio.) When movies made with wide-screen formats are prepared for telecasting or video release, they are typically modified to make them fit these dimensions. An enigmatic warning generally appears to announce this: "This film has been modified from its original version. It has been formatted to fit your TV."

Such modifications typically entail panning from one side of the frame to another (a computer-controlled scanner moves across the image—hence the term "panning and scanning"). In most instances, the outcome differs significantly from the original, and the process can drastically disrupt the carefully planned scene compositions of directors. Accepting the inevitable, many moviemakers try to keep all the important action within a central 4-by-3 box, called the "TV safe area," inscribed in the viewfinder of a film camera.

Altering the aspect ratio of movies can also compromise an actor's performance. In such wide-screen movies as *East of Eden* (1955), *Rebel Without a Cause* (1955), and *Giant* (1955), for example, James Dean uses his body with subtlety and nuance to convey character traits. "The *mise-en-scène* of a Dean film," as a study of wide-screen cinema notes, "relies on the careful positioning of his body in relationship to the other characters around him; he often turns his body slightly away from them so as to isolate himself in a somewhat private space of his own."[8] When panning-and-scanning techniques work to single out Dean, the affecting rhythms of this delicate spatial choreography can be lost altogether.

In recent years, a video format called **letterboxing** has become popular with film buffs. It more or less preserves the original aspect ratio of wide-screen movies by shrinking the overall size of images so that their edges can fit on a standard television screen—although wide black borders appear at the top and bottom. Many high-powered directors now insist that their movies be released on video in the letterbox format.

Some 80 percent of movies released on DVDs are in the letterbox format, but not everyone is happy with the practice. Although letterboxing preserves the original shape of a movie, it wastes at least 25 percent of the space on a standard television set. As recent surveys suggest, many viewers feel cheated by the empty space above and below the image. Some critics even assert that the letterbox movement is a conspiracy to force consumers to buy the wider, more expensive, big-screen digital TVs now on the market. In apparent response to growing complaints, many newer DVDs now include both "formatted" and wide-screen versions.

Movies in Cyberspace

Another potential means for viewing movies at home is the **Internet,** a vast network of tens of thousands of interconnected subnetworks with no single owner or controlling authority that links together millions of computers around the world. The **World Wide Web** organizes and standardizes the data flowing through these electronic pathways and lets individual computers tap into one another. Accessing the Internet has become so simple and straightforward that almost half of all Americans and millions more people throughout the world now make their way around the countless Web sites available. All kinds of data move across geographic, legal, and cultural boundaries more or less impervious to censorship controls.

The Web holds out the promise of creating a viable new venue of exhibition for movies because of its ability to present data as text, graphics, audio, and video. Already a variety of Web sites contain hundreds of independent shorts, student projects, and foreign films, as well as a growing number of classic Hollywood features. Although generally of poor quality, bootlegged copies of many new movies are also available on various Web sites.

In the mid-1990s, promotional Web sites for new theatrical releases began to emerge. Most have been little more than electronic press kits, providing plot summaries and publicity stills. But such ventures into cyberspace started to become more ambitious when *The Blair Witch Project* (1999) site, which offered background information and "found footage" not available elsewhere, was largely credited with building a groundswell of interest among young people around the country. Made by a team of University of Central Florida film school graduates for a mere $35,000 (over $300,000 more was spent for refinements), this faux documentary about the legend of the Blair Witch and the mysterious fate of the students who disappeared while investigating her was a resounding success at the box office. It grossed a reported $140 million in North America and perhaps another $50 million around the world.

When the amount of data that can be electronically transmitted via the Internet into people's homes expands, the major studios are likely to make most of their movies—new and old alike—available online for downloading. Under the prevailing distribution system, they typically release new movies in a series of so-called windows, starting with the theatrical release and followed by videos and DVDs, pay-per-view, pay-cable networks, and, eventually, broadcast networks. Access to the Web version of a recently released movie probably will be offered at the same time it enters the pay-per-view window.

This new form of electronic distribution, protected by encryption, will provide the movie industry with yet another potentially lucrative revenue stream. Moreover, if videos and DVDs are any indication, an additional home viewing option in all likelihood will not diminish the prestige or threaten the profitability of first-run theatrical releases. Millions of people will probably still opt for the experience of slipping into a darkened theatre, munching on some popcorn, and watching the drama unfold on a large screen in community with other moviegoers.

Future Directions

A new panoply of electronic marvels is waiting in the wings ready to take center stage. Assuming technical and economic hurdles can be overcome, the movie of the near future will no longer be made through a chemical film process and then projected using technology that hasn't changed much in the last hundred years. Instead, images will be captured using high-definition digital cameras, with fidelity akin to that of 35-millimeter film. And they will be presented by digital projectors without the degradation of visual quality that is inevitable when films are transferred from negatives to master prints and then to third-generation copies shown in theatres. Every run of a digital

TELEVISION NEWS HOLLYWOOD STYLE

Television is now a prime exemplar of the Hollywood style. The pervasiveness of feature films and other fictional forms is in itself sufficient evidence of Hollywood's hold on this electronic crucible. But television constructs the stuff of real life with the tools and techniques of moviemaking as well. Both national and local news programs are molded by dramatic and cinematic means of expression. As in movies, the emphasis is on personality, action, drama, and conflict.

The producers of television news deliberately design scene fragments to evoke emotional responses. Videotaped events are shaped into narrative-dramatic structures and edited in ways that heighten their emotional appeal. Action tends to be filtered through the personalities and personae of the key figures in the news story. Subjects who are frequently in the news are not unmindful of the medium's dramatic essence. Invariably their faces are made up, their wardrobes are carefully selected, and the backgrounds before which they appear are chosen or designed.

Stories unfold visually. News events are simplified, compressed, and structured to make them coherent to a mass audience. The conventional questions of the journalistic trade—who, what, when, where, and why—are answered with characters, events, settings, and morals. Issues are defined and presented in terms of personalities. As in westerns and crime thrillers, the focus tends to be on individual malefactors. Conflicts are presented as a struggle between good and evil or right and wrong, rather than between competing ideas and worldviews. Motives are reduced to self-interest. Lighting, camera placement, editing, and other cinematic techniques serve to intensify the spectacle and dramatic effect.

With prodding from Pentagon public relations personnel, television news producers even managed to give the 1991 Gulf War the dramatic shape and heady rush of a *Star Wars* movie. Each of the television networks in operation at the time introduced its war coverage with music, a logo, and a title— "War in the Gulf" on CBS, "America at War" on NBC, and "Crisis in the Gulf" on ABC and CNN. Impeccable casting contributed to the skein of cinematic melodrama. Allied commander General Norman Schwarzkopf seemed like a hero right out of an oversized Han Solo mold—manly, smart, sensitive, and resourceful. Iraqi leader Saddam Hussein, the evil villain of the small-screen drama, appeared to have about as much warmth and charm as Darth Vader. Coverage of the massive assault on Baghdad consisted largely of antiseptic images. Bombs and missiles appeared to strike their designated targets with the precision of laser swords.

Seasoned anchors give the dramatic slices of life distilled through television's national news outlets some semblance of continuity, cohesion, and congruence. Their mellifluous tones and pontifical manner create an aura of reasoned intellect. Whatever journalistic skills these performers may possess, their primary asset is the ability to remain composed in front of a camera under all circumstances. They are show business assets who enjoy much the same celebrity status as movie stars. We assess their thespian skills, comment on their appearance, and evaluate their phrasing and intonation. Even when the events they introduce are long forgotten, the characters they create—their screen personae— remain in our memory.

movie, whether in a large theatre or a small one, will provide pristine, flicker-free images devoid of lint, scratches, and torn sprockets.

In addition to enhancing the theatrical viewing experience, industrywide adoption of digital cinema will greatly reduce the amount of time and money it takes to distribute movies to exhibitors. Sending electronic copies of movies to theatre operators on disk or digital tape, or beaming them via satellite, will save a big chunk of the estimated $800 million the big studios spend each year making, insuring, and shipping bulky film prints. These new methods of distribution and exhibition could also create greater cinematic choice by opening up more avenues for smaller, independent works.

In the coming years, the advent of such glittering technologies will undoubtedly alter the whole character of the movie industry. Just how pervasive or how profound the changes will be, or how they will influence the culture in general, is impossible to predict. Who could have foretold, for instance, that a peep show machine would pave the way for the advent of a cinematic art form affecting the values, dreams, and aspirations of untold millions of people around the globe? To be sure, the mere existence of a new technology will not, in itself, alter social or artistic sensibilities. Who uses it, and what it is used for—these will be the decisive factors.

As the moguls of old either died off or were deposed, financiers, agents, and lawyers moved into Hollywood's top decision-making ranks. Over the past several decades, all the major studios have become or been absorbed by corporations that are conglomerate in orientation and transnational in size and scope. The same firms that turn out movies now also operate television networks and stations, cable TV systems, publishing houses, newspaper chains, and other media-related enterprises.

Concentration of control over both the content and conduits of popular art, information, and mass entertainment has reached unprecedented levels. Moreover, most media conglomerates have directors who also serve on the boards of the big banks, insurance companies, investment firms, and major industries that organize and manage much of the world's resources. Just what this situation portends for the future of the movie industry remains uncertain. The commercial imperatives of moviemaking still seem to work both for and against expanding the range of cinematic expression.

In many ways, the new Hollywood doesn't differ all that much from the old one. A surplus of ego and anxiety remains endemic to all aspects of movie production. Profit remains as the prime reason for producing, distributing, and exhibiting pictures. American movies continue to attract countless millions of people around the globe. And the Hollywood style still sets the principal standard against which competing forms of filmmaking must struggle. The next chapter analyzes the dramatic designs characteristic of the dominant mode of moviemaking in the United States.

Notes

1. See Thomas Hine, *The Rise and Fall of the American Teenager* (New York: Bard Books, 2000).
2. Paddy Chayefsky, *Television Plays* (New York: Simon & Schuster, 1955), p. 173.
3. Eric Barnouw, *The Image Empire: A History of Broadcasting in the United States, Volume III: From 1953* (New York: Oxford University Press, 1970), p. 33.
4. Larry Ceplair and Steven Englund, *The Inquisition in Hollywood: Politics in the Film Community, 1930–1960* (New York: Anchor Press/Doubleday, 1980), p. 291.
5. Quoted in Michael Pye and Lynda Myles, *The Movie Brats: How the Film Generation Took Over Hollywood* (New York: Holt, Rinehart and Winston, 1979), p. 9.
6. Steven Bach, *Dreams and Disaster in the Making of* Heaven's Gate (New York: New American Library, 1985), p. 416.
7. See Nancy Hass, "For Studios, 'Director' Is a Male Noun," *New York Times,* January 31, 1999, section 2, p.13.
8. John Belton, *Widescreen Cinema* (Cambridge, MA: Harvard University Press, 1992), p. 222.

Contents

ORSON
WELLES

CITIZEN
KANE

The Mercury Actors

JOSEPH COTTEN
DOROTHY COMINGORE

EVERETT SLOANE
RAY COLLINS
GEORGE COULOURIS
AGNES MOOREHEAD
PAUL STEWART
RUTH WARRICK
ERSKINE SANFORD
WILLIAM ALLAND

Genres and Designs

In contrast to the unpredictable patterns of everyday life, the typical movie is highly structured along specific paths of action designed to facilitate clarity of expression and heighten emotional involvement. At the most basic level, a causal chain of events is set in motion by the motives and conflicts of characters with whom we are encouraged to identify or empathize. Questions are raised about these characters that require answers. With few exceptions, at least two specific courses of action ordinarily emerge, one of which almost invariably involves heterosexual romance. To win or keep the love of a member of the opposite sex becomes a primary goal of the central characters.

Other lines of action are usually related to this romantic aspect, so that a small number of characters become involved in several interdependent developments. The subsequent conflicts and complications build to a climax and resolution. Although events may be presented out of chronological sequence, the enacted story has a clear beginning, middle, and end. Any remaining loose ends are likely to be tied up in a brief denouement or concluding scene. Such recurring patterns provide the promise of something new based on something familiar. Having a basic sense of what is likely to happen, we can direct our attention at how, when, and with what new twist it will happen. The specific dramatic designs typical of the Hollywood style provide the focus of this chapter.

Generic Categories

Most movies fall into some **genre,** or recognizable category, such as westerns, crime sagas, horror films, romantic comedies, musicals, and science fiction thrillers. Although the concept of genre enjoys wide currency, the actual basis for distinguishing between various kinds of movies is hardly clear or consistent. Genres have been categorized in various ways, but a dominant factor has been subject matter. For example, westerns deal with the historical American west; gangster films chronicle the rise and fall of criminal figures as they struggle against police and rival gangs; and war movies are concerned with battles, bloodshed, and behind-the-lines maneuvers. Other genres have been defined with regard to their rhetorical intentions. For example, spy thrillers offer suspense; comedies aim to amuse; and horror films seek to shock and disgust.

Another method of categorization is based on formal elements. For instance, musicals employ songs and dances; domestic melodramas involve strong expressions of emotion; *film noir* is marked by gloomy, low-key lighting, disorienting visual schemes, and unbalanced compositions; epics utilize wide-screen formats, vivid color, sweeping movement, elaborate costumes, and a "cast of thousands." Of course, such distinctions can be understood simply as ancillary to the central defining characteristic of subject matter. But delineating a class of films in terms of rhetorical intention or formal elements has implications for how it is approached.

From a critical standpoint, classifying movies into specific generic categories can best be viewed less in terms of particular and exclusive elements and more in terms of analytical usefulness. Many movies, in fact, don't fit easily into self-contained, consistent generic frameworks. For example, a romantic crime thriller like *Out of the Past* (1947) and a moody western such as *Pursued* (1947) both contain elements of *film noir.* Putting these two movies in the same analytical category, regardless of how it is labeled, focuses attention on the stylistic and narrative affinities they possess. It may also provoke interesting questions about the societal conditions under which they were produced. A lot of movies seem to fit more than one generic profile.

Hybrid Aspects of *Mildred Pierce*

Considerable scholarly attention has been given to the hybrid aspects of *Mildred Pierce,* whose autumn 1945 release coincided with the return of the troops and the transition to a postwar economy. The narrative structure, scene composition, camera work, and editing patterns of this unusual movie contain elements of both *film noir* and domestic melodrama. In some senses, the latter is a mirror image of the former. The family, so notably absent in *film noir,* is the focal point of domestic melodrama, whose emotional emphasis is on women in familial situations faced with crises.

In addition to its shadowy lighting and unbalanced scene compositions, *film noir* is characterized by an investigative narrative structure, frequent use of voiceover and flashback, and strong but unstable and often dangerous heroines. The *noir*ish scenes in *Mildred Pierce* constitute a small but essential part of the whole movie. Situated in the present and involving murder and the subsequent investigation, these scenes form the framework for the two lengthy flashbacks that tell the title character's own story.

In sharp contrast to the shadowy present-day settings, the *mise-en-scène* of these flashbacks adheres to the conventions of domestic melodrama. Interiors are evenly lit, and many scenes take place in daylight. There are also more group shots and fewer variations in camera angle. What is more, the stress is on familial discord and a frustrated housewife's career ambitions—the kind of overwrought emotional stuff studios promoted under the label "woman's picture" in the prewar and war years.

The downfall of the title character in *Mildred Pierce* is ostensibly caused by blind devotion to her innately evil daughter. On another level, however, the movie can be seen as a cautionary tale about the fate of women who stray too far from hearth and home—a message that certainly served the immediate interests of returning soldiers whose jobs had been occupied by women while they were away winning the war. Of course, with the unfailing wisdom of hindsight, we can see that nobody really benefits when a large segment of society becomes restless and resentful, as women pushed out of the workplace invariably did.

In the opening scene, director Michael Curtiz provides us with an overview of a beach house on a rainy night, establishing the location where the subsequent action will take place. This long shot dissolves into a closer view from the side of the beach house. A car is parked in front. We hear the snap of gunfire. In the next scene, we see the interior of the house. A man who is being shot looks almost directly at us; we are in the position of the killer. Two bullets hit the mirror behind the man, and two hit him in the chest. The camera follows him as he falls, and then it pulls back slightly along his body to reveal a gun being tossed on the floor as he rolls onto his back. A medium close-up of his face follows this as he utters "Mildred" and then expires. The camera tilts up to the mirror, in which we see a door close. We are denied a view of the murderer.

The scene shifts to an unidentified figure driving off in the car. This image slowly dissolves into a long shot of a pier on a rainy night. As the camera cranes down, we see a woman, whom we soon learn is Mildred Pierce (Joan Crawford). A policeman finds her standing alone on a pier, apparently contemplating suicide. She subsequently tries to pin the murder on her fast-talking business associate and admirer, Wally (Jack Carson), whom she lures

Murder victim Monty (Zachary Scott) looks almost directly at the camera. (*Mildred Pierce* [1945])

to the beach house where the killing occurred. How did this attractive, seemingly self-possessed woman end up in such desperate straits? At the police station, Mildred tells her story to the chief detective.

Through flashbacks, we learn how her first husband, Bert (Bruce Bennett), abandoned her because he resented the way she spoiled their elder daughter Veda (Ann Blyth). How she toiled as a waitress to give her two daughters a good education, piano lessons, and expensive clothes. How she began an affair with a profligate playboy, Monty Beragon (Zachary Scott). How her youngest daughter contracted pneumonia and died (the price Mildred pays for her illicit sexual activity?). How she worked her way up from waitress to owner of a lucrative chain of restaurants. How she deterred Veda from collecting damages in a breach of promise suit for which she had feigned pregnancy. How Veda left home to work in a nightclub. How Mildred married Monty, an aristocrat rich in real estate but poor in cash, in order to give Veda a proper pedigree. How a seemingly repentant Veda returned home. How Veda's debts and Monty's profligacy eventually forced her to sell her business. How she found out that Monty had been having an affair with Veda behind her back. How she confronted him with this sordid business.

After these lengthy segments, we return to the present. Mildred states that she killed her second husband. But the detective orchestrates Veda's surprise entrance and tricks her into confessing. A final flashback confirms that

A tearful Mildred (Joan Crawford) walks alone on the Santa Monica pier at night.
(*Mildred Pierce* [1945])

she actually shot Monty. The scene from the beginning of the movie in which we see Monty murdered is repeated. However, this time the shot of him looking almost directly at the camera is followed by a cut to a medium shot of Veda holding the gun. The causal chain has been capped. The detective opens the blinds to let the light of the new day into the interrogation room.

As she leaves the police station, Mildred is reunited with her first husband, Bert, who fully forgives the now-humbled heroine for her transgressions. In the dawn light, they walk away from the camera in a long shot toward a massive archway. In the foreground, we see two cleaning women scouring the steps of the Hall of Justice. All is in its proper place. Mildred has learned a painful lesson: Dire consequences await women who venture into the male world of commerce and enterprise. One is left with the distinct impression that she will no longer be wearing those pinstriped suits with padded shoulders.

As various film scholars have noted, this movie's structure and scene composition seem to raise questions about the credibility of the title character. The shot of Monty being murdered is not followed by the anticipated reverse shot showing the killer. Instead, a shot of an unidentified figure driving off in a car dissolves into an image of a distraught Mildred walking on a pier. The juxtaposition of these shots implicates her in the murder. Her tear-stained face further suggests that she might be the one who fired the gun.

A replay of Monty's murder reveals Veda (Ann Blyth) to be the killer. (*Mildred Pierce* [1945])

Throughout the events framing the flashbacks, diagonal shadows, dark interiors, and night exteriors suggest a *noir*ish world of intrigue and deception. A shadow is cast on Mildred, literally and figuratively. Like the typical *film noir* heroine, she seems at times to be cold and conniving. As she beguiles Wally in his nightclub, her masklike face is cut by a slanted shadow. Backlighting accentuates the massively padded shoulders of her overcoat. The beach house where she has locked Wally in with the murder victim is filled with enormous angular shadows. The environment overwhelms him, heightening our sense of his weakness and her duplicity. This contrasts sharply with the bright lighting of the two major flashbacks, in which Mildred presents herself as hard working, resourceful, and resilient. Following the second flashback, the detective undercuts her confession by insisting that she tell the truth. His maneuvers lead to the final flashback revealing what actually happened at the murder scene.

Just how women at the time of this movie's initial release reacted to Mildred's resumption of a restrictive gender role is impossible to say. But it is not hard to imagine that many female spectators exclaimed at the end: "I can't believe she's going back to that sad sack Bert!" In fact, none of the principal male characters has admirable qualities. Wally is a wily manipulator with few scruples, and Monty (especially as played by Zachary Scott) is an unmitigated cad.

The male chief detective unravels the mystery, but he is not on the screen long enough to elicit any viewer empathy or identification. Moreover, he doesn't discredit anything depicted in the flashbacks themselves. Mildred's false confession occurs in the present, and she's not seen committing the murder. Because the "truth" of flashbacks was a well-established movie convention, there was no reason for spectators to doubt those past events actually shown. Despite Mildred's regression to stultifying and humbling circumstances, this movie's representations probably did more to erode than support the male-dominated power structure that prevailed in the 1940s.

Mildred's face is cut by shadow. (*Mildred Pierce* [1945])

Wally (Jack Carson) frantically searches for Mildred in the shadowy beach house. (*Mildred Pierce* [1945])

The Western Genre

Issues, Elements, and Values

Of all the generic categories, the western has probably received the most scholarly scrutiny. In many ways, it is the movie idiom's most emblematic form of expression. Westerns emerged early in the history of cinema and were produced on a regular basis by the 1910s. The western's subject matter encompasses a broad chronological time frame and deals with a wide range of social issues stemming from attempts to establish settlements in hostile territory. Westerns feature epic cattle drives, range wars, rustlers, and encroaching homesteaders; covered wagon and stagecoach journeys; the building of the transcontinental railroad; prospectors in pursuit of gold and silver; gamblers, barmaids, and prostitutes plying their trades in saloons; post–Civil War outlaws seeking justice and retribution; legendary lawmen taming rough-and-tumble frontier towns; aging gunfighters facing down yet one more challenger; benevolent bandits pursued by unscrupulous lawmen; bounty hunters cleaning up the debris of civilized society; and rugged individualists trying to adjust to postfrontier society.

The latter scenario is effectively set up in the opening scene of *Ride the High Country* (1962). A somewhat haggard—but still dignified-looking— ex-marshal (Joel McCrea) rides down the crowded street of what seems at first to be a typical cinematic frontier town. He hears what he thinks are the cheers of the onlookers and tips his hat in response. A uniformed policeman abruptly interrupts his reverie, telling him to get out of the way because he is blocking the path of a race being run down the street. It turns out that what the aging lawman regarded as cheers are actually jeers for him to clear the road for a contest between a horse (that majestic symbol of the old west) and an ungainly-looking camel (the camel wins). Adding injury to insult, as he crosses the street he is nearly hit by an automobile. All of these elements of *mise-en-scène* suggest that the wild-and-wooly days of the old west are coming to an unceremonious close.

What unites the diverse elements of the western genre is its central focus on the continual problem of how to balance the interests of the individual and those of the community. The conflicts stemming from this problem are played out on the terrain of the "frontier," the region between civilization and wilderness. In the typical western, as Jim Kitses notes, this dichotomy between civilization and wilderness is transformed into east versus west and is structurally associated with such opposing values as freedom versus restriction, pragmatism versus idealism, tradition versus change, and self-interest versus social responsibility.[1]

These values take concrete form in such characters as the gunfighter, the marshal, the farmer, the Indian, the housewife, and the barmaid. They're also evident in such items as shoes and boots, tea and whiskey, trains and buckboards, aprons and gun belts, and hats and headdresses. The conflict of values inherent in frontier claims of both unlimited freedom and social conformity generally achieve dramatic resolution in ways that are emotionally satisfying. Depending on the particular movie and its oppositional structure, either civilization or wilderness may be deemed desirable or undesirable.

Frontier Protagonists

The values associated with the wilderness are typically manifested in a male protagonist who is self-reliant—a social outsider generally free of entangling relationships. Women usually mean trouble for this type. Even loving and loyal women are likely to challenge his way of life by posing the threat of marriage and the settled life. This man seems most comfortable with other males who share his disdain for domesticity. The standard-bearer of civilization's values, in contrast, is most often a male protagonist who is comfortable in society and enjoys being with women. He is likely to be married, to feel responsible for the welfare of the community at large, and to pursue collective action.

When these two character types appear in the same movie, they are often initially at odds but usually came to share a common purpose. The classic western *Shane* (1953) exemplifies the way they frequently unite to achieve some social goal. Homesteader Joe Starrett (Van Heflin) is at first wary of gunfighter Shane (Alan Ladd). He suspects that Shane is in the employ of the cattlemen who are trying to run him and his fellow homesteaders off the land they've settled. Although sympathetic to the plight of the homesteaders, Shane is initially reluctant to become involved in this conflict.

The bonding of the two characters is symbolized when they uproot a decayed tree stump that had resisted Starrett's solitary efforts. The incident also suggests certain similarities in their character traits when Starrett explains why he won't hitch the team to the stubborn old stump he strains to remove by hand: "Sometimes nothin' will do but your own sweat and muscle." They share other qualities as well. Shane shows signs of tenderness with Starrett's son Joey (Brandon de Wilde). Starrett is capable of violent action when the situation calls for it, which he demonstrates when he supports Shane in a barroom brawl with the cattlemen.

Although Starrett is an impressive figure, he is clearly not the equal of Shane. The conflict with the cattlemen isn't resolved until Shane alone faces down their hired gunslinger (Jack Palance). As the events unfold, most of what happens takes its logic from Shane's perspective (or that of Joey, who idolizes him), encouraging identification with and empathy for his actions. His viewpoint is privileged, his face and body are usually centered, and his lonely lifestyle is romanticized. It is also apparent that Starrett's wife, Marion (Jean Arthur), is sexually drawn to the wandering gunfighter, although her

Starrett (Van Heflin) and Shane (Alan Ladd) work together to uproot a stubborn old tree stump. (*Shane* [1953])

commitment to her husband and child makes any romantic entanglement with him a frustrating impossibility.

Melancholy pervades the final scene as Shane rides off alone toward the majestic Grand Tetons, with Joey crying after him, beseeching him to "Come back." The little boy's sexually naive plea—"Mother wants you!"—heightens our sense of Shane's sacrifice. But even if Marion were free, the prospect of marriage would be for Shane a metaphorical death of sorts. His values and way of life have no place in settled society. By removing the impediments to civilization, this imposing symbol of frontier freedom and autonomy has become an anachronism. So he drifts off to some unspecified land further into the wilderness, his life of solitude and self-determination only temporarily disrupted.

The classic plot formula of the lone gunfighter who rides in from the wilderness, enters a troubled frontier community, and leads a group of homesteaders in its struggle to prevail over the covetous cattlemen or hostile Indians who are holding back the advance of civilization reoccurred in a variety of movies in the fifteen or so years following World War II. There were also numerous westerns about ex-gunfighters who had taken up peaceful pursuits

Joe Starrett's "little woman" (Jean Arthur) seems drawn to the gentle gunfighter, whose values and way of life are so different from her husband's. (*Shane* [1953])

Joey (Brandon de Wilde) hollers "Mother wants you!" (*Shane* [1953])

THE WESTERN AS MYTH

Cultural historian Richard Slotkin argues that the frontier experience as amplified and refracted through post–World War II westerns helped to forge American political conceptions about the world in general.[2] Although he is vague about matters of cause and effect, the linkages Slotkin finds suggest that these westerns both reflected and reinforced an imperialist outlook. He notes, for example, that not long after President John F. Kennedy proclaimed the "New Frontier," government officials sent CIA agents they called "cowboys" to infiltrate Cuba. American troops fighting a "frontier" war in Vietnam were encouraged to think of South Vietnamese peasants as "settlers" who needed to be rescued from the "savagery" of communist "Indians."

It is in the western genre that Slotkin finds the clearest articulation of America's **myths**—those symbolic narratives that express the culture's central beliefs, political struggles, and social uncertainties. Myths contain the conceptual categories that inform words and practices, and provide a means of explaining problems that arise in the course of historical experience. Slotkin sees the frontier myth as the foundation of American thought and history, especially with regard to notions of democracy, heroic action, destiny, gender, and race. He outlines two conflicting variants of this myth, which competed with each other throughout most of the twentieth century.

The long-reigning "progressive" myth conceptualized westward expansion and the rise of the modern state in terms of a social Darwinian parable. It explained the emergence of a new managerial ruling class and justified the right to subordinate through violent means the "lesser" indigenous population to its purposes. Westerns made within this fundamentally antidemocratic mythical framework tended to reassert a vision of westward expansion in the nineteenth century that reflected and reinforced the notion that the North American continent belonged to the United States by a combination of divine right, practical need, and the assumed superiority of the American system of government. The frequent scenes of whooping war parties attacking

(lawyer, doctor, editor, storekeeper) being forced to resort to violence when their towns were threatened. Many new versions of stories about resourceful, self-sufficient outlaws and professional bounty hunters appeared as well.

Disguised Westerns

By the latter half of the 1960s, westerns involving self-reliant individualists seemed to have lost audience favor. The most popular westerns, such as *The Professionals* (1966) and *The Wild Bunch* (1969), revolved around a group of professionals who solve the problems of an organization like the railroad or the Mexican army rather than those of a community. Film analyst Will Wright attributes the popularity of such "professional westerns" to a growing disbelief in the efficacy of individual enterprise and an increasing faith in corporate power. He saw a new pattern emerging in these westerns "in which men wagon trains of peaceful pioneers can be seen in this context to explain, sanctify, and justify a long and bloody legacy of racism and deceit against Native Americans.

The "populist" myth, in contrast, celebrated westward expansion as the opportunity for equitable distribution of land and power. It developed in reaction to the emergence of the centralized corporate-industrial economy and the political claims of its proprietors and managerial elites. Primarily agrarian in outlook, it portrayed the modern state of the progressive myth as a belligerent challenge to democratic social organization and practice, and expressed apprehension about the concentrated power that accompanies modernization.

This myth found strong cinematic expression through the western genre soon after chilling reports appeared in the mass media of atrocities committed by American troops in Vietnam. Movies such as *Little Big Man* (1970), *Soldier Blue* (1970), and *Ulzana's Raid* (1972) depict savage whites massacring pure and hapless Native Americans. Overtly antiwar polemics permeate *Little Big Man*. Its plot structure hinges on the reminiscences of 121-year-old Jack Crabb (Dustin Hoffman), who survived Custer's last stand at the Battle of Little Big Horn. A bracing antidote to encrusted misconceptions, the blustering, egomaniacal George Armstrong Custer depicted here is a far cry from the heroic figure played by dashing Errol Flynn in *They Died with Their Boots On* (1941).

Whether this change in the western genre carries a broader cultural resonance is difficult to discern. Why were Native Americans now being shown in a sympathetic—if not pathetic—light? Were such depictions reflective of a growing disillusionment and disgust with the Vietnam War and the mythology that supported it, as Slotkin's analysis suggests? Efforts to determine how shifts in any genre's political orientation reflect changing perceptions of social and historical events or to assess the part such shifts play in shaping those perceptions necessarily result in conclusions that are tentative and speculative at best.

can work together for money yet through their work build a common bond of respect and affection that transcends any private desire for personal gain."[3]

Such death knells for the primacy of self-reliance and individual effort celebrated in the classical western proved premature. Although the western genre virtually disappeared from the screen in the late 1970s and 1980s, even a cursory glance at movies of this period suggests that the appeal of ad hoc individualism remained strong. Its enduring allure can be seen in the cinematic exploits of such "disguised" western heroes as Clint Eastwood's Dirty Harry, Charles Bronson's lone vigilante in *Death Wish* (and its sequels), and Sylvester Stallone's pumped-up ex-Green Beret, John Rambo.

These characters share a spiritual bond of sadness and solitude with the classical western hero, but they are far more resigned to the conditions imposed by contemporary circumstances. Whereas the gunfighter of the classic western strives to establish a pristine rule of order, these embittered loners simply seek to carve out a small space for themselves in which something like traditional justice can prevail. They have no expectation of ever quelling the forces of evil. In the harsh world they inhabit, the very social institutions the western heroes fought to establish have been suborned by greed and cupidity. A malefactor may be subdued, but society remains as sour as ever.

The basic structure and character types of the classic western reappear in various guises across many different genres and time periods. In such generically dissimilar movies as *Angels With Dirty Faces* (1938), *Casablanca* (1942), *Star Wars* (1977), and *Lethal Weapon* (1987), a self-reliant loner reluctant to become involved with others eventually joins forces with someone who has a strong sense of communal commitment and social responsibility. Paralleling the trajectory of the classical western, all of these movies tend to favor ad hoc individualism over the civilizing values of family and community. Most of what happens is pinned to the self-reliant loner's emotional point of view and takes its logic from his perspective.

Familiar Elements in *Schindler's List*

Despite its horrific subject matter, even a movie like *Schindler's List* (1993) follows a familiar path with familiar characters involved in familiar relationships. Its protagonist, Oskar Schindler (Liam Neeson), may be complex and enigmatic, but at heart he is Hollywood's most enduring male archetype: a self-reliant loner who reluctantly shifts from selfish isolation to social responsibility.

Like the owner of Casablanca's most popular gin joint, Schindler is a flawed hero—a drinker, a gambler, a womanizer, seemingly driven by little more than self-interest. He dresses expensively and frequents nightclubs, buying caviar and champagne for Nazi officers and their female companions, and prominently displaying a Nazi party emblem on his lapel (although the only cause he's interested in is his own). His impeccable black market contacts make him the right man to know.

When the Jews of Nazi-occupied Krakow are dispossessed of their businesses and herded into a squalid, walled ghetto, Schindler sees his chance to turn a huge profit. His plan is to persuade incarcerated Jews to lend him money so he can purchase a bankrupt enamelware factory and make cooking utensils for the Nazi war machine. He gets a perceptive Jewish businessman, Iztak Stern (Ben Kingsley), to recruit Jewish investors and workers for him and to run the business. While the self-serving Schindler charms and bribes the Nazi elite, Stern—a figure of unimpeachable integrity and rectitude—builds the company into a major supplier of mess kits and cookware for troops at the front.

The way these polar opposites come to share a common purpose is developed with singular subtlety. Stern sees the enamelware enterprise as a means of saving Jewish lives: factory employees, classified as essential workers, are exempt from "resettlement" in concentration camps. He persuades a reluctant Schindler to let him manipulate the company's payroll to protect unskilled laborers such as rabbis, old women, and children. The factory is soon seen as a haven, and Jews implore Schindler to bring their relatives into the work force. He grudgingly accedes to such requests—if only for his own selfish reasons. Through Stern's connivance and Schindler's acquiescence, hundreds are saved from labor camps and given jobs in the factory.

Within a year, the Final Solution is well underway. An odious Nazi commandant, Amon Goeth (Ralph Fiennes), ruthlessly razes the ghetto and ships the surviving Jews to a forced-labor camp. As Schindler watches the wholesale slaughter from a bluff above the city, he is mesmerized by the figure of a little girl weaving through this nightmare, her dusty red coat the only color in an otherwise monochromatic image. (Later, a smear of red in a handcart piled with corpses shows her fate.) It is at this point that the war profiteer seems to have an epiphany of sorts. He bribes the corrupt Goeth to permit reestablishment of his factory within camp walls, and business continues more or less as before. But Schindler has changed. As he witnesses the unrelenting cruelty and inhumanity of the Nazis toward the Jews, he's gradually transformed from an exploiter of slave labor to a savior who risks everything to keep his workers from Nazi gas chambers.

By the time the forced-labor camp is about to be shut down and the Jews sent to Auschwitz, the once-selfish Schindler has seemingly undergone a total conversion. He spends almost all of his ill-gotten gains bribing and paying off Nazi officials in order to be allowed to move some 1100 Jews out of Poland to the relative safety of a new factory in the former Czechoslovakia. The men arrive safely, but a trainload of women is mistakenly routed to Auschwitz through bureaucratic error. With chilling dispatch, they are stripped, shaved, and herded into showers. But before they can be gassed, Schindler walks into the death camp himself and brazenly persuades the authorities to relinquish their victims.

Through a combination of charm and chicanery, Schindler manages to shield his workers until the war is over and the death camps are liberated. During their entire campaign to save Jewish lives, Schindler and Stern never openly concede that they've come to share a common purpose. Near the end of the ordeal, however, they risk all to give each other one fleeting glance of mutual admiration. It's a look reminiscent of the visual exchange between Shane and Joe Starrett as they chop the rotten tree stump.

Recurrent Design Patterns

Beyond operating within certain generic conventions, moviemakers generally adhere to specific underlying design patterns that have roots in classical drama and literature. Although often revised, embellished, and challenged, these basic patterns of dramatic development tend to recur with remarkable regularity in American movies. They constitute an integral part of the overall cinematic mode of expression moviegoers and moviemakers alike have come to embrace.

Dramatic Conflict

As in all dramatic forms, conflict is the driving force of movies. A conflict near the beginning arising from obstacles preventing a character from achieving his or her desires or fulfilling his or her needs undergoes increasingly intense and suspenseful development before reaching a climactic conclusion. Such conflict can develop between characters with conflicting motives, between characters and their surrounding conditions, or through a single character's contradictory impulses.

In *The Godfather* (1972), a gangster film par excellence, there is conflict indigenous to the story as a whole, as well as the central character's internal conflict in dealing with contradictory impulses. The surface conflict concerns Don Vito Corleone's (Marlon Brando) refusal to join the four other ruling Mafia (here referred to as syndicate) "families" in the narcotics business. (When *The Godfather* was in preproduction, its producer, Al Ruddy, after meeting with the Italian-American Civil Rights League and its founder, Joseph Columbo, announced that all references to the Mafia and Cosa Nostra would be deleted from the script.) This sparks a brutal gang war and an attempt on his life. After the don is ambushed and critically wounded, his oldest son, Sonny (James Caan), enjoys a brief reign as family head.

The center of interest, however, shifts to the don's youngest son, Michael (Al Pacino), who has had nothing to do with his family's syndicate activities. Visiting his father at the hospital, Michael takes the first tentative steps toward a life of crime. In a clever subterfuge, he foils a second attempt on his father's life; he then has a violent confrontation with a corrupt police captain (Sterling Hayden). His fate is sealed after he kills to avenge his father and must hide out in Sicily. There he discovers his family heritage and falls in love and marries; but his wife, Apollonia (Simonetta Stefanelli), is soon killed by an explosion meant for him.

While Michael is sojourning in Sicily, older brother Sonny savagely beats their sister Connie's (Talia Shire) husband, Carlo Rizzi (Gianni Russo), who has been abusing her. In retaliation Carlo sets up Sonny. As Sonny races once again to his sister's rescue, he is brutally murdered. A now frail Don Corleone decides to capitulate with his archenemies in exchange for Michael's safe return to the United States. To shore up the family business, Michael moves into Las Vegas gambling. He also seeks out his old college sweetheart, Kay Adams (Diane Keaton), and marries her. When the old don dies of a stroke, the stage is set for Michael's ascendance to absolute power.

Ivy League–educated Michael's intense inner turmoil arises from his devotion to family and his doubts about its legacy of violence and power. He is the character who undergoes the most profound crisis, and the one on whom the basic dramatic design or plot structure most depends. Every plot twist opens a new door for him or closes an old one. Both the internal and external conflicts ultimately are resolved when Michael comes not only to join the family business but also to lead it.

His transformation from man of integrity to Mafia don is the stuff of a Shakespearean tragedy. Coarsened and turned cold by the blood that has been spilled, he has all the Corleone family's enemies systematically murdered. He is now the Godfather; the plot has come full circle. At the end, as at the beginning, the don is receiving his underlings with the authority and bearing of an all-powerful patriarch. As the door swings shut, closing out his wife, Michael haughtily holds out his hand to be kissed.

Irreconcilable Contradictions

Character conflict is typically built on an implicit foundation of irreconcilable contradictions, which are revealed through contrasting situations, action, and dialogue. In *The Godfather*, Don Vito Corleone is first seen holding court in his study, a dark, sealed, claustrophobic place. It is his daughter's wedding, and no Sicilian can refuse a request on that day. So the supplicants file through this exclusively male domain, and he dispenses favors and justice. An attack on a mortician's daughter will be met with violent reprisal. The impending deportation of a baker's prospective son-in-law will be prevented by payment to a corrupt immigration official. The procurement of a part in a movie for the don's pop singer godson will require ruthlessness. Meanwhile, outside the sun shines and the music plays on the veranda during the lavish wedding reception of the don's daughter, Connie. The activity is open, social, and inclusive. Men, women, children, and even rival Mafia members intermingle. Cutting between the two settings creates a stark contrast.

This pattern of stark contrasts persists throughout, with scenes appealing to one set of values followed by scenes appealing to their opposite. From the lyricism of Michael's old-world courtship ritual in Sicily, the scene shifts to New York, where Sonny hastily leaves an illicit tryst in order to beat his brutal brother-in-law to a pulp. At the don's funeral, a family confidant engages in an act of betrayal. The gangland killings ordered by Michael are juxtaposed with the christening of his godchild. This oppositional structure seems to suggest that a normal, secure family life and predatory business practices are ultimately irreconcilable. To the extent that the Mafia itself serves as a metaphor for the extremes of American enterprise, *The Godfather* can be seen as a scathing indictment of the capitalist ethos.

Rick (Humphrey Bogart) and Renault (Claude Rains) depart together for Brazzaville. Earlier Renault said of his companion, "He's the kind of man that, well, if I were a woman and I weren't around, I should be in love with Rick." (*Casablanca* [1942])

Interrogatory Patterns

The lines of action in most movies are commonly constructed in ways that put our minds in an interrogatory mode. As the drama unfolds, pressing questions invariably arise about the characters and situations. They may be implied through what happens or posed explicitly in the dialogue. Whatever the case, such questions serve to generate suspense and structure anticipation about possible outcomes. While some may be answered fairly quickly, others are intended to sustain interest until the closing scenes.

The sustaining questions in *Casablanca,* for example, center around what protagonist Rick Blaine (Humphrey Bogart) will do with two letters of transit that would allow the bearers to escape to freedom. Is he a secret idealist or simply a selfish saloonkeeper whose conduct is guided by practicalities? Will he give the letters to his former lover Ilsa (Ingrid Bergman) and her Resistance fighter husband Victor Laszlo (Paul Henreid)? Or will he leave with Ilsa himself? Perhaps he and his piano-playing sidekick Sam (Dooley Wilson) will depart together. Or maybe he'll develop another love interest. He seems drawn to the charmingly corrupt Captain Renault (Claude Rains). Could this be the beginning of a beautiful friendship? Or do more lustful desires lurk beneath their clever repartee? (Some critics cite Rick's decision to turn his back on heterosexual love in favor of male comradeship as evidence of the repressed homosexuality that underlies most American adventure stories. [4])

The interrogatory pattern of movies often hinges on what director Alfred Hitchcock whimsically called the **MacGuffin**—the documents, plans, secrets, or whatever that set the events in motion.[5] The plausibility of the MacGuffin is of little consequence, asserts Hitchcock, as long as the characters find it of vital importance. The letters of transit in *Casablanca* are a prime example. They are signed by Charles de Gaulle, leader of the Free French Forces, and supposedly cannot be rescinded or questioned. The ability to "suspend disbelief" while watching this well-crafted movie hardly seems adequate to explain audience acceptance of the assumption that, although the Nazis may not be squeamish about mass murder, they apparently develop ethics when it comes to even questioning two letters of transit. Moreover, the name itself affixed to the letters flies in the face of historical accuracy. The signature of General Maxime Weygand, Vichy governor of North Africa, would have been more accurate. De Gaulle had no authority in this region. (In the shooting script, the name attached to the letters is Weygand's, not de Gaulle's.)

Even a highly innovative movie like *Citizen Kane* (1941) has a dramatic design that hinges on a MacGuffin of sorts. The contrivance in this case is a dying man's final utterance, which none of the movie's other characters could possibly have heard. Just prior to expiring alone in the cavernous master bedroom of his Gothic mansion, Xanadu, the title character (Orson Welles) whispers the word "rosebud." We must assume a nurse heard him from behind a heavy door, because she doesn't enter the room until after he drops a snow globe and it crashes to the floor. A reporter tries to decipher the meaning of the enigmatic word by interviewing four people—an ex-wife, an old friend, a former business associate, and a butler—and reading a fifth person's private diary. However, nobody knows the answer. Those who saw Kane's childhood sled with the word Rosebud inscribed on it—Kane's parents, his guardian, Kane himself—are all dead. The survivors can offer only conjecture based on their own viewpoints, which are biased, selective, and incomplete.

In the final scene, which takes place at Xanadu, the reporter is asked what he has learned. He responds, "Not much." Like the jigsaw puzzle he fingers, a piece seems always to be missing. He has a question and no answer. In the furnace room below, the workman who tosses the sled into the fire has an answer. But he doesn't have the question. There are, in fact, no answers to be found here, "no trespassing" in the life of Charles Foster Kane.

What seems at first glance to be a movie about a man turns out instead to be one about the process of a personality's construction by the differing views of other people. Rather than presenting a story with a question and an answer, or several answers, *Citizen Kane* can be seen as holding up to scrutiny the entire process of question and answer. Despite the accumulation of details

Charles Foster Kane (Orson Welles) holds a snow globe. His dying utterance remains enigmatic. He is shown saying "Rosebud" twice. On both occasions he is holding the snow globe, which was originally in Susan Alexander's (Dorothy Comingore) possession (it can be seen in the background when Kane visits her apartment). (*Citizen Kane* [1941])

revealed about the title character as the enacted story unfolds, little more is known about the essential man at the end than at the beginning. From the opening newsreel, through the inquiries of the anonymous reporter and the conflicting recollections of the various people he interviews, to the final revelation of the camera, the movie is all clues and no conclusions.

Causal Connections

Clear cause-and-effect logic usually underlies a movie's structure. One event leads to another, which in turn leads to the next. Some need or desire in a central character usually sets the causal chain of events in motion. For example, the horror classic *Psycho* (1960) opens with an aerial view of a city, the camera hovering birdlike. As the camera glides toward a block of buildings in the shabbier part of town, titles converge at the bottom of the screen:

The sled with the name Rosebud burns along with the other effects left behind by Kane. (*Citizen Kane* [1941])

"PHOENIX, ARIZONA," followed by "FRIDAY, DECEMBER THE ELEVENTH," and then "TWO FORTY THREE PM." Why this precise date and time? (Director Alfred Hitchcock apparently chose December to justify a shot in which Christmas decorations inadvertently appear.[6]) Next comes a close view of a window, with the blinds drawn. Why this particular window? What's happening inside? A gruesome murder? An afternoon tryst?

The camera pauses to peer beneath the blinds. Cut to the interior. After scanning the drably furnished room, the camera comes to rest on a partly dressed woman (Janet Leigh) lying on a bed. She is looking up at a man (John Gavin) who is dressing himself. The framing of the image focuses our attention on her because we can't see his face. What is her relationship to this man? Is she a prostitute? No, it seems they are lovers. A lack of money prevents them from marrying—she's a low-paid secretary in a real estate office, while he toils in a hardware store to pay off alimony and other debts. As a consequence, they are reduced to furtive assignations in seedy hotel rooms during the middle of the day. Troubled by these trysts, she yearns for respectability.

Back at her office, a client brandishes $40,000 in front of the troubled secretary. She's entrusted to take the money to the bank but goes to her apartment instead. Inside the apartment, her image is reflected in a mirror. Is this a visual metaphor for her divided state of mind? Has she decided to steal the

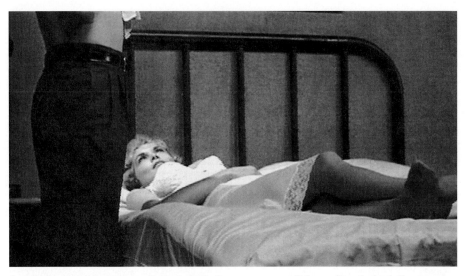

Sam (John Gavin) and Marion (Janet Leigh) after an apparent liaison. (*Psycho* [1960])

money? She turns her head. There is a close-up of the envelope containing the money on a bed near a half-packed suitcase. The angle of the camera suggests her point of view. As she dresses and packs, the camera cuts back to the envelope a few more times. She snaps the suitcase closed and slips the envelope into her purse. The links of the causal chain that will lead to her last shower have been set in place.

Causal connections may to varying degrees be explicit or implicit. On occasion, music as well as imagery may point to possible causal connections. The ululating violins strings in composer Bernard Hermann's score for *Psycho* suggest bird noises. Birds are closely associated with the intense young proprietor (Anthony Perkins) of the isolated motel where the secretary stops for the night. Not only is his hobby avian taxidermy, but low-angle views in his shadowy parlor give him a hawkish appearance. Moreover, when he shares supper with the secretary, the room features a large stuffed owl mounted high on one wall. During her brutal stabbing, the sound track throbs with screeching, birdlike music. The attacker's attire suggests that the young man's unseen mother may be the murderer, but birds have been associated with him rather than her.

The Detective Genre

Classic Versus Hard-Boiled

To arouse curiosity and create suspense, causes are often withheld in the detective film—a genre that traces its roots to Edgar Allan Poe's "The Murders in the Rue Morgue," which first appeared in the April 1841 issue of *Graham's Maga-*

Real estate client Cassidy (Frank Albertson) unwittingly offers Marion a possible solution to her problem. Her decision to steal the $40,000 marks the movie's first major turning point. (*Psycho* [1960])

zine. Applying his extraordinary intellectual powers, Poe's erudite and aristocratic Parisian detective, C. Auguste Dupin, solves the a hideous double murder of a mother and daughter without leaving the comfortable quarters he shares with the anonymous narrator of his exploits. His literary and cinematic descendants include such dabblers in detection as Sherlock Holmes, Jane Marple, Hercule Poirot, and Philo Vance, among many others. These "classic" sleuths possess a seemingly indefatigable interest in any complex detective problem, and they solve their cases through acute observation and deductive reasoning.

By far the most famous of the classic detectives is Sherlock Holmes, introduced by Arthur Conan Doyle in *A Study in Scarlet* (1887). Abrupt in manner, master of a dozen obscure sciences, and doggedly persistent in his puzzle-solving efforts, Holmes uses his brilliant analytical faculties to solve crimes that have the authorities baffled. Once the culprit is caught, Holmes retreats to his cozy Baker Street lodgings to play the violin and indulge his cocaine habit, struggling to overcome ennui until his special skills are once again required.

Some measure of this character's popularity is indicated by the fact that more different actors have portrayed him on screen than any other fictional creation. The most inspired casting had Basil Rathbone as Holmes and Nigel Bruce as Dr. Watson, his loyal sidekick. Starting with *The Hound of the Baskervilles* (1939), Rathbone and Bruce played these roles in fourteen movies (and dozens of radio programs).

Classic detectives like Holmes reside in an essentially orderly and rational universe that yields its mysteries to science and logic. Murder and malfeasance tend to be isolated incidents of moral and social aberration. But the genre took a new turn in 1929 with the appearance of Dashiell Hammett's novel *The Maltese Falcon,* whose "hard-boiled" private eye protagonist Sam Spade relies on instinct rather than intellect to solve his cases. His seedy downtown office, shared with a faithful and efficient secretary (whose devotion he shamelessly exploits), functions as a refuge from the cruel outside world in which crime is endemic and solutions tend to be tentative and incomplete.

The novel was adapted for the screen as early as 1931, and reworked five years later as *Satan Met a Lady* (1936), but it was writer-director John Huston's carefully crafted 1941 version of *The Maltese Falcon* that established the defining qualities of Hollywood's hard-boiled formula. As embodied by Humphrey Bogart, Sam Spade is a complex character, a curious blend of toughness, honor, wry wit, and cynical idealism. The rogues he mingles with deceive him and each other, and are revealed in the end to be as phony as the coveted bird they pursue. The movie's critical and commercial success ensured that hard-boiled private eyes would enjoy a privileged place alongside their classic counterparts in the pantheon of screen detectives.

Causal Threads in *Chinatown*

In most detective films, whether classic or hard-boiled, the unfolding drama depends on events, usually brutal, about which we have incomplete knowledge: What happened? Why? Who is responsible? The past holds the answers. All the detective has to do is dig in the right place to find them. Typically there's a mystery involving a murder. We know an effect but not the causal factors. Part of the fun comes from matching wits with the detective trying to uncover clues that will lead to the culprit. The dull-witted police are baffled, and the detective's confidant lacks his associate's acumen but asks the questions that help clarify the situation. Along the way, we are led astray by circumstantial evidence. A suspect appears guilty but is later proved innocent. In the denouement, the detective discloses the missing causes—who killed whom, how, and why.

While generally adhering to this basic formula, *Chinatown* (1974) contains an intricate weave of causal threads that cannot be readily unraveled. Its hard-boiled protagonist is private eye J. J. "Jake" Gittes (Jack Nicholson), a former policeman who was once on the Chinatown beat, where "you can't always tell what's goin' on." He quit the force after he had tried to keep someone from being hurt but inadvertantly made sure that she would be.

Now Gittes runs a successful detective agency specializing in messy divorce cases and extramarital affairs. He is hired to investigate the illicit love life of Los Angeles Water Commissioner Hollis Mulwray (Darrell Swirling). As he works his way through an intricate maze of deception, flippantly offering explanations for the corruption he unravels, the increasingly perplexed pri-

A cuckolded husband (Burt Young) sees photographs of his wife fornicating in the woods. What initially sounds like sexual moaning turns out to be his groans of dismay. (*Chinatown* [1974])

vate eye finds that he must continually revise his inaccurate judgments after uncovering further evidence. What started out as an ostensibly simple matter turns out to involve incest, pedophilia, murder, and high-level political tampering with the city water supply.

Set in Los Angeles in 1937, the movie opens with a series of black-and-white photographs of a couple in the woods locked in sexual intercourse. On the soundtrack are disembodied groans. The groans continue as the camera pulls back to reveal Gittes's cuckolded client (Burt Young) looking at a picture of his wife on all fours, her dress bunched above her waist. Her partner is mounting her from behind, his hat still secure on his head. The client is so upset by the incriminating evidence that he tosses the pictures into the air and grabs the venetian blinds. Gittes understands his misery but coolly and detachedly cautions him to stop gnawing on the newly installed fixtures.

This salacious start implies that we are headed for uncharted cinematic waters, but the overall design stays well within the mainstream of the movie idiom. The dramatic elements begin to take form about five minutes into the movie. Jake is introduced to a new client by his associates, "operatives" Walsh and Duffy, who assist him in gathering evidence, taking photographs, and snooping on the sexual indiscretions of wayward spouses. The client calls herself "Mrs. Mulwray" (Diane Ladd) and asks Gates to investigate her husband Hollis's involvement with another woman. Although the detective attempts to dissuade her from pursuing the matter, she insists that he investigate the alleged extramarital affair.

Looking into the matter, Jake thinks he has discovered Hollis Mulwray with his mistress, but the young woman in question (Belinda Palmer) is something else altogether. After this alleged sexual escapade is reported in the newspapers, the plot spins in another direction with the arrival of the real

The first major turning point. Private eye Jake Gittes (Jack Nicholson) is about to meet the real Mrs. Evelyn Mulwray (Faye Dunaway). (*Chinatown* [1974])

Mrs. Evelyn Mulwray (Faye Dunaway). Her attorney, who threatens to sue Gittes and have his license revoked, accompanies her. But who was the woman who hired Gittes, if she is the real Mrs. Mulwray? Why did that woman hire him? Did someone hire her? For what reason?

Gittes's initial motivation for pursuing answers to these questions is clear. He must get to the bottom of who duped him, and why, because he can't earn his living without a license. But he persists in his investigation even after Mrs. Mulwray abruptly drops the lawsuit—"quicker than the wind from a duck's ass," as Jake colloquially puts it. His suspicions about her reversal are reinforced after Hollis Mulwray's drowned body is found in a remote, empty reservoir outside Los Angeles during the middle of a drought. To add to the mystery, it turns out that the victim has salt water in his lungs.

A prototypical private eye, Jake Gittes is motivated by his own peculiar code of honor and justice. The obstacles he encounters and overcomes dictate the dramatic action. When he gets too close to the truth about an irrigation swindle, a knife-wielding thug (director Roman Polanski) tries to scare him off by viciously cutting his nostril. But the detective is undeterred in his efforts to piece together the causal connections and unravel the mystery. About eighty-five minutes into the movie, a clear causal pattern begins to take shape. Jake finds a pair of horn-rim bifocals in the saltwater pond at the Mulwray mansion. He knows they belong to Hollis Mulwray or to the person who murdered him. This realization leads to the resolution of the story.

Detective fiction ordinarily ends in restoration of the social order, with subversive elements at least temporarily subdued. But in a perverse twist on the established form, in *Chinatown* violence and deviant desire prevail. When all the key characters improbably converge on a street in the Chinatown section of Los Angeles, the only scene that actually takes place there, the private

The second major turning point. Jake spots the eyeglasses in the pond. (*Chinatown* [1974])

eye's efforts to save the good and punish the evil end in failure. "Forget it, Jake," says one of his operatives in an enigmatic (albeit ethnically insensitive) closing line. "It's Chinatown!"

Thematic Tendencies

Meaning in any movie is conveyed from moment to moment. Every shot, scene, and sequence is pregnant with potential significance. Over and above momentary meanings, certain ideas and feelings may be developed over the course of a movie. These pivotal concepts and sentiments constitute a movie's unifying **theme,** the central concern or focus around which it is structured.

Thematic analysis is a way of answering such questions as, What is the movie about? What's its message? What statement, if any, does it make as a whole? What repeated elements or **motifs** reinforce the central concern? Is there some single primary mood or feeling that pervades throughout? Do the internal or external conflicts that drive the drama have significance beyond the context of the movie itself? Are insights into some aspect of life, experience, or the human condition in general provided by the resolution of this conflict?

Any technique, image, gesture, or event in a movie may have thematic implications. In *Schindler's List,* for instance, the intricate composition of the images, coupled with the eerily harmonized performances of Liam Neeson and Ralph Fiennes, creates cinematic doubles of Oskar Schindler and Amon Goeth. At first the two seem to be cut from similar cloth. They even look very much alike, which is emphasized by matching images of them shaving their fair Aryan faces.

As we learn more about each of them, however, we discover that despite their apparent similarities they manifest marked differences. Goeth is a Third Reich Caligula who kills for sport and sees Jews as abstractions. He likes to begin his morning with a little target practice. Standing on the balcony of his villa overlooking the camp, he shoots Jews in the head with an insouciant air of indifference for the lives he's taking. Schindler, in contrast, is someone who looks at people as individuals and tries to figure out which of those can benefit him. These differences are suggested in a scene showing the two men talking and drinking together; a thin vertical shadow in the center of the frame serves as a line of demarcation between them.

Near the end of the movie, we get another image of Schindler and Goeth in profile. This time, however, the line of demarcation between them is not a thin shadow but a thick wall that—whether intentionally or otherwise—functions as a visual analogue for how much Schindler has become distanced from Goeth and from Nazi ideology. Such recurrent images lend support to the thematic contention that the potential for both heroism and villainy reside in all of us—and that, in times of moral crisis, we realize that potential through the exercise of choice.

Thematic Structure of *It's a Wonderful Life*

Themes in movies tend to be structured around such dynamic polarities as dark versus light, city versus country, migration versus settlement, competition versus cooperation, and urbanity versus provincialism. A survey of movies from 1930 to 1980 suggests that the thematic developments made in the idiom of the Hollywood film often turn on the incompatible values and beliefs associated with the individual and the community.[7] The strong psychological pull these polar opposites exert is poignantly presented in the often darkly romantic comedy *It's a Wonderful Life* (1946), for many years the king of Christmas perennials on television.

Since childhood, protagonist George Bailey (James Stewart) has been torn between devotion to family and community and vague yearnings for freedom and the intrigues of the outside world. The revelation of his internal conflicts as the action unfolds suggests several implicit questions we all face at one time or another in our own lives: How can we be involved with others and still maintain a high degree of autonomy and independence? Are both an adventurous life and domestic tranquility possible? Are the values of a stable family situation and ambitious careerism reconcilable? As we all invariably do, George comes to realize that there are no easy choices. A lifestyle that promises adventure and freedom also offers the possibility of loneliness and anonymity. In devotion to family and community lingers the potential for predictability, boredom, and frustrated desire.

At the start of the movie, George's mounting personal and financial problems have plunged him into deep despair. In a flashback sequence, we see his life from boyhood and learn that he often paid a price for helping others. He rescues his younger brother after a fall through the ice, but goes deaf in one

Young George Bailey (Bobby Anderson) plans to go exploring and "have a couple of harems and maybe three or four wives." (*It's a Wonderful Life* [1946])

ear as a result. While working at the local drugstore, he stops the pharmacist Mr. Gower (H. B. Warner) from inadvertently sending a poisonous prescription to a patient and gets a slap in the head for his good deed.

At the drugstore soda fountain, young George (Bobby Anderson) waits on a sweet girl named Mary (Jean Gale). When she declines a coconut topping on her chocolate sundae, he explains to her that this exotic fruit comes from far off places like Tahiti and shows her his copy of *National Geographic*. ("Only us explorers can get it," he brags. "I've been nominated for membership in the National Geographic Society.") There's a soft-focus close-up of Mary as George talks enthusiastically about exploration and the adventures he expects to have. Indifferent to his wanderlust, she whispers in his deaf ear that she will love him until the day she dies. "Did he ever marry the girl? Did he go exploring?" asks his guardian angel, Clarence Oddbody (Henry Travers). The question seems to imply that one can't do both.

By the time George reaches adulthood, he can't wait to get out of his quiet birthplace of Bedford Falls and away from his father's building and loan association. He wants to shake "the dust of this crummy little town" off and see the world. But he can never quite break loose from the constraints of social

Symbols of domesticity and adventure. (*It's a Wonderful Life* [1946])

responsibility. Each time he plans to go away, some new crisis arises that re-quires his continued presence. He's also reluctantly drawn to Mary (now played by Donna Reed), who has come back home after college because she misses Bedford Falls. (As they look at each other longingly and begin to kiss, he protests, "Now you listen to me. . . . I don't want to get married . . . ever . . . to anyone. . . . You understand that?") Of course, they marry and eventually have four children. Another soft-focus close-up of Mary signals that George's fate is sealed.

The thematic undercurrents of any movie tend to reside in its *mise-en-scène*. In George and Mary's wedding-night scene, for example, symbols of domesticity and adventure seemingly blend together harmoniously. Their friends have put together a makeshift honeymoon cottage for the newlyweds. As George enters and looks around in amazement, a series of shots follow from his point of view: a bouquet of daisies and chrysanthemums to the front left of a South Seas travel poster; a bathing beauty poster behind a table con-taining candles, a wedding cake, champagne, and cheap china; an old Vic-trola situated in front of chickens turning over an open fire; a tight view of the turntable as the fire roars; and yet another soft-focus close-up of Mary's smiling face. The images are accompanied by Hawaiian music (signifying an exotic, distant land for a 1940s audience?).

Garish Pottersville. Like an alienated *film noir* protagonist, George Bailey (James Stewart) frantically searches for someone who will confirm his identity in this nightmarish parallel universe. (*It's a Wonderful Life* [1946])

But kids, debts, and a failing business soon shatter the illusion that one can have both domestic bliss and a life of adventure. George finds himself overwhelmed by his obligations—especially his responsibility for the family savings and loan association, which is the only thing protecting the people of Bedford Falls from greedy, miserly, mean local banker Potter (Lionel Barrymore). When his absent-minded Uncle Billy (Thomas Mitchell) misplaces $8000 in bank funds during the Christmas season, and Potter finds the money but says nothing, George is without any hope for the future. A bank examiner is scheduled to go over the books, and because of the mishap George faces possible imprisonment.

On the brink of suicide, he is given a vision by his guardian angel of what life would be like for his family and his town if he had never been born. In this parallel universe, the pastoral village of Bedford Falls has become the garish Pottersville, a dark and foreboding place filled with burlesque houses, peep shows, and pawnshops. As George wanders through this bleak landscape of neon signs, hardened hearts, and shattered dreams, he discovers that virtually no one he had known has fared well in life.

Moreover, neither Mary nor anyone else in town seems to recognize him, including his old buddies Ernie (Frank Faylen) the cab driver and Bert (Ward

Bond) the policeman (the *Sesame Street* duo of Bert and Ernie reportedly got their names from these two characters). More than anything else, this agonizing anonymity seems to convince him of the essential goodness of his ordinary life. He begins to weep, begging for some semblance of normalcy. His supplications find a sympathetic divine ear, and things return to the way they were before he began his nightmarish odyssey.

Cut to George's house. As his loving wife and children stand beside him, depositors, friends, and relatives flood into the parlor and begin to fill a large basket with money in gratitude for his life of self-sacrifice and generosity. A wire from an old friend, now a millionaire manufacturer, states that he has made $25,000 available to George if he needs it. The sheriff tears up the warrant for his arrest, and even the dour bank examiner makes a financial contribution. George's war hero brother arrives and makes a toast: "To my big brother George—the richest man in Bedford Falls." All burst into "Auld Lang Syne."

Typical of most movies, the thematic structure of *It's a Wonderful Life* serves to dissolve dilemmas. On reflection, however, an unsettling sense that all is not well may remain. In the final scene, friendship is equated with money. No one has accounted for the missing $8000. The Pottersville vision itself lingers as a powerful reminder of the precariousness of personal relationships, family bonds, love, friendship, and neighborly and community ties. What is more, this vision serves to discredit just about everyone in town. It suggests that without George, whose own despair was subdued only by divine intervention, they would have become drunkards, prostitutes, and old maids.

Despite the upbeat ending, George's agonizingly conflicting desires and needs, so clearly in evidence throughout the unfolding action, are hardly fully resolved by his Christmas Eve conversion to the settled life. It is not difficult to imagine how the young George, assuming the gift of augury, would have recoiled from his later self, as from an image of acquiescence to the status quo. Every arrangement in life, the movie seems to suggest, invariably carries with it the shadow of not being something else.

The Family Man's Linchpin

Much the same thematic linchpin is at the core of the 2000 Christmas season release *The Family Man.* Protagonist Jack Campbell (Nicolas Cage) enjoys the kind of existence young George Bailey would have envied. He is the high-rolling president of a New York City mergers-and-acquisitions firm, has a penthouse in Manhattan, wears well-cut Zegna suits, drives a shiny new Ferrari, and cavorts with a bevy of beautiful women, any one of whom is bound to show up at his door ready to be unwrapped. Even though it is Christmas Eve, and his staff would like to spend time with their families, this seemingly content corporate wheeler-dealer prefers to work through the holiday to close a multibillion-dollar merger deal. Is it possible that he has nothing better to do? Could something conceivably be lacking in his life?

During a quick trip to the grocery store for some eggnog, Jack defuses what appears to be robbery. The would-be holdup man, a taxi driver named Cash (Don Cheadle), turns out to possess supernatural powers. When Jack smugly claims to have everything in life he ever wanted, this street-tough Clarence Oddbody gives him a cryptic warning before disappearing into the night. Shrugging off this peculiar incident, he retreats to his plush penthouse and goes to bed alone. The next morning he is shocked to wake up and find himself in a four-bedroom New Jersey suburban home, apparently married to Kate (Téa Leoni), the college sweetheart he had left at JFK Airport thirteen years earlier when he chose to pursue adventure and career advancement abroad.

In a state of panic, he runs out of the house and returns to New York City, where he discovers that nobody from his "real" life recognizes him. Moreover, someone else occupies his penthouse, and he is no longer the president of his company. Completely perplexed, he once again encounters Cash, who explains to him that he has been given an opportunity to glimpse what life might have been like had he not left Kate and traveled a different path. Returning distraught to the suburban home in New Jersey, he gradually settles into the domestic disorder and occasional bliss of his "new" life, struggling to raise two kids and meet mortgage payments by working for his blustering father-in-law (Harve Presnell) as a tire salesman.

This yuletide confection's thematic structure provides a springboard for further reflections on the inherent trade-offs that are inevitably involved in any significant choice. Like George Bailey, Jack finds himself grappling with the conflicting appeals of an independent, prosperous existence with the supposed trappings of happiness and a more mundane life in which the intangible joys of family and friends are leavened by a seemingly unending cycle of domestic routine. He can't have one way of life without sacrificing much of the other.

Story/Plot Distinctions

In most Hollywood films, familiar character types and conventional design patterns guide us smoothly to a more or less satisfying denouement. But in more convoluted screen dramas like *Pulp Fiction* (1994), events are altered through a logic that defies easy detection. Its driving creative force, writer-director Quentin Tarantino, revises, embellishes, and contests the prevailing patterns of the movie idiom in ways that make them seem born of the moment.

The movie's highly fractured narrative structure contains three vignettes, framed by opening and closing diner scenes that turn out to dovetail. They are juggled around out of chronological order (without the aid of character-generated flashbacks), and many of the same characters move in and out of them. To add to the compelling confusion, the repetition of the holdup in the diner scene has slight variations in the language. In the opening version, when Honey Bunny (Amanda Plummer) orders the customers not to move, she combines the word 'mother' with the ancient Anglo-Saxonism for the sex act as part of a participial phrase ("mother----ing"). When this scene is replayed, she uses this Oedipal allusion in plural form ("mother----ers").

To sort out the unusual way events have been abbreviated, reordered, and even repeated in an unconventionally structured movie like *Pulp Fiction,* it is useful to distinguish between plot time and story time—categories adapted by film analysts from the literary criticism of the "Russian formalists," a group of scholars active in the years immediately preceding the 1917 revolution and in the decade or so that followed.[8] The **plot** is the way the events, characters, and settings of a story are represented in terms of temporal order, duration and frequency. This differs from the **story** itself, which refers to the events—both implicitly and explicitly presented—in chronological order and linked by cause and effect.

Simply put, the story is what happened and the plot is how what happened is presented. For creators and viewers alike, the story is a mental construct that is manifested in the plot presentation. The creators of a movie start with a story in mind and out of it construct a plot. Viewers, in turn, construct a story from the aural and visual cues in the plot in order to understand the whole causal, chronological course of events.

Within this conceptual scheme, the plot of *Pulp Fiction* appears carefully constructed rather than simply a shapeless mass of matter. Jumping from one vignette to another and then back generates a great deal of suspense about what is going to happen next. The clothing changes of Vincent Vega (John Travolta) and Jules Winnfield (Samuel L. Jackson), who float in and out of all three vignettes, as well as the replay of the diner scene, serve as a temporal signpost of sorts, providing a key for reorganizing plot events into chronological order.

The way their outfits switch back and forth from dark suits to more casual clothes suggests that, in story time chronology, the postcredits Prologue in which Jules and Vincent converse before killing the three young men comes first. Next comes the "Bonnie Situation" (vignette 3), in which these killings are repeated and a fourth man is murdered, Winston Wolf (Harvey Keitel) disposes of a fifth man Vincent accidentally shot, and the two killers change out of their blood-soaked business attire into T-shirts and shorts. Then the interlinking precredits Prologue and Epilogue, set during the diner holdup, take place. Next comes "Vincent Vega and Marsellus's Wife" (vignette 1), which includes boxer Butch Coolidge (Bruce Willis) being bribed by Marsellus Wallace (Ving Rhames) to throw a fight and Vincent and Mia Wallace

(Uma Thurman) twisting together at Jack Rabbit Slim's before she overdoses on his heroin. Finally, we have "The Gold Watch" (vignette 2), in which Butch kills Vincent and rescues Marsellus from the redneck rapists. The flashback preceding this latter vignette, in which the military officer (Christopher Walken) gives young Butch (Chandler Lindauer) the gold watch, occurs about twenty-five years prior to all the other events in the movie.

Although each vignette has a beginning, middle, and end, the overall impression is of one story about a community of characters. The basic plot structure is circular in that the action begins and ends in the same coffee shop. But about midway through, plot time has advanced beyond story time, telegraphing what will happen. As a result, the climax resonates eerily into the future.

Incomplete Closure

The closure in most movies is not complete. Characters often seem to continue on after the denouement. Rick Blaine and Captain Renault walk off together into the Moroccan mist to *begin* a beautiful friendship. Michael Corleone's ascent to power foreshadows *The Godfather, Part II* (and *III*). In textbooks, as in movies, the end of one chapter often signals the start of another. The next chapter focuses on the interaction of character constructions, actors' personae, and stereotypical representations.

Notes

1. See Jim Kitses, *Horizons West: Anthony Mann, Budd Boetticher, Sam Peckinpah: Studies of Authorship Within the Western* (Bloomington: Indiana University Press, 1970), p. 11.
2. Richard Slotkin, *Gunfighter Nation: The Myth of the Frontier in Twentieth Century America* (New York: Atheneum, 1992).
3. Will Wright, *Sixguns and Society: A Structural Study of the Western* (Berkeley: University of California Press, 1975), p. 104.
4. See William Donelley, "Love and Death in *Casablanca*," in Joseph McBride, ed. *Persistence of Vision: A Collection of Criticism* (Madison: Wisconsin Film Society Press, 1968), p. 103.
5. Alfred Hitchcock, "Rear Window," in Albert J. LaValley, ed. *Focus on Hitchcock* (Englewood Cliffs, NJ: Prentice-Hall, 1972) pp. 43–44.
6. See Stephen Rebello, *Alfred Hitchcock and the Making of* Psycho (New York: Harper Perennial, 1991), p. 90.
7. See Robert B. Ray, *A Certain Tendency of the Hollywood Cinema, 1930–1980* (Princeton, NJ: Princeton University Press, 1985), pp. 55–69.
8. See Boris Tomashevsky, "Thematics," in *Russian Formalist Criticism: Four Essays,* trans. Lee T. Lemon and Marion J. Reis (Lincoln: University of Nebraska Press, 1965).

Characters and Stereotypes

"We had faces, then!" cries Norma Desmond, the dethroned and deranged silent-screen star played by Gloria Swanson in *Sunset Boulevard* (1950). Stars and lesser lights still do, and voices and physiques, as well, capable of providing a great deal of pleasure to viewers simply by being memorable, interesting, or beautiful. Characters are given life through the physiognomy, vocal attributes, and bodies of actors. Because actors portray them, characters in movies may seem like real people. But they are actually constructions designed to serve some narrative or dramatic purpose. Often these constructions involve stereotypical representations. This chapter looks at character constructions, screen acting, actors' personae, and prevalent stereotypes in movies.

Character Constructions

The various characters in a movie are each generally endowed with a limited number of specific traits that contribute to the unfolding drama. In *The Godfather* (1972), for example, Don Vito Corleone (Marlon Brando) is thoughtful, shrewd, and lethal. Eldest son Sonny (James Caan) is brash and hot-tempered. Second son Fredo (John Cazale) is inept and weak-willed. Daughter Connie (Talia Shire) is jealous and volatile. Her husband Carlo Rizzi's (Gianni Russo) flagrant womanizing and abuse of her serve as a source of family dissension. Michael (Al Pacino) is the

Michael (Al Pacino) explains to outsider Kay (Diane Keaton) how his father conducts business. Had Michael hooked up with someone within the family circle, such explanations would not have been necessary or plausible. (*The Godfather* [1972])

most sensitive and perceptive of the don's offspring. The don's adopted son and legal counselor, Tom Hagen (Robert Duvall), is level-headed and quick-witted.

Michael's non-Italian college sweetheart, Kay Adams (Diane Keaton), is naive and diffident. Her questions in the opening segment about family customs, the wedding celebration, and the nature of Don Corleone's business serve an expository function. During the opening wedding scene, Michael's explanation to her of the way his father gets things done also provides an implicit causal link to the later "horse head" sequence. She is curious to know how Michael's father helped singing idol Johnny Fontaine (Al Martino) with his career.

While the singer croons "I Have But One Heart" in the background, Michael tells her that when Fontaine was first starting out he was signed to a personal service contract with a big band leader. As his career took off, Fontaine wanted to get out of his contract. Don Corleone, the singer's godfather, went to see the bandleader and offered him $10,000 to let the singer go. But the bandleader refused. So, the next day, the don went to see him again, this time accompanied by his enforcer, Luca Brasi (Lenny Montana). Within an hour, the bandleader signed a release, for a certified check for $1000. An astounded Kay wants to know how he did it. Michael responds that his father "made him an offer he couldn't refuse." As Luca Brasi held a gun to the bandleader's head, explains Michael, his father assured him that either his brains or his signature would be on the contract. From this brief anecdote, which functions as a kind of verbal flashback, we are able to garner a great deal early on about the head of the Corleone family and the way he conducts business.

Central Characters

Central characters or protagonists invariably have positive qualities such as compassion, probity, or loyalty. These serve to justify their triumphs over enemies and to ensure audience sympathy and support. Such values may be relative, however, when a story is limited to the hermetic world and points of view of its principal characters. The activities of the Corleones, for example, are isolated in a moral vacuum. In the absence of an efficacious law enforcement system, they appear to be forces of justice and protectors of the weak. Their victims are limited to characters embodying traits society frowns upon: an unprincipled Hollywood producer, a crooked police captain, family traitors, and other gangsters willing to deal in drugs (which the old don regards as a "dirty business").

What is more, there are no strong characters with competing values to provide a meaningful counterpoint to the Corleone family's moral outlook. The only character to take issue with their morality is Kay, and she is too reserved and diffident (especially as played by Diane Keaton) to mount much of a challenge. Even with their brutal crimes and trafficking in prostitution, the Corleones are, in fact, made to seem in many ways quite admirable. They give primacy to familial kinship ties, extended through the sacred practice of serving as godparents; operate with a strict code of honor; and have a strong sense of communal solidarity.

Supporting Characters

Supporting characters are an integral part of most movies. Their human weaknesses and foibles often complicate the protagonist's problems and provide insight into his or her personality. Several supporting characters help to establish the seemingly contradictory traits of Rick Blaine (Humphrey Bogart), the protagonist of *Casablanca* (1942). Near the beginning of the movie, he's approached by his occasional mistress Yvonne (Madeleine LeBeau). She's drunk and distraught and wants to know where he was last night. He responds with casual disdain that it's so long ago he doesn't remember. "Will I see you tonight?" she inquires. He tells her that he never plans that far ahead. Before she can make any more trouble, he hustles her out, directing his bartender (Leonid Kinskey) to take her home. "What a fool I was to fall in love with a man like you!" she shouts after him.

Other interactions further suggest that Rick is impassive, disengaged, and generally dispirited. While he is seated on the terrace with Captain Louis Renault (Claude Rains), who attempts without success to probe his past, a

Rick (Humphrey Bogart) brushes off his occasional mistress Yvonne (Madeleine LeBeau) with the indifference of a man who casually uses women. (*Casablanca* [1942])

croupier informs him that the cashier needs money to cover a patron's winnings. Rick seems cavalier about the loss. When Renault later cautions him not to interfere in an arrest at the cafe that evening, Rick assures him that he sticks his neck out for nobody. Although his place is a powder keg of intrigue, Rick's paramount concern seems to be the preservation of privacy.

Rick's initial reluctance to become involved in the schemes and subterfuge around him places the responsibility for the narrative progress of *Casablanca* onto other, more goal-oriented supporting characters, such as Ugarte (Peter Lorre), an unctuous seller of ill-gotten exit visas. His murder of two German couriers to obtain letters of transit sets the action in motion. When he feigns sympathy for the couriers, Rick responds cynically, "They got a break. Yesterday they were just two German clerks; today they're the honored dead."

Rick's progression from selfish isolation to social responsibility, a psychological transformation that occurs in countless movie protagonists, is revealed in several incidents involving minor characters. In one such incident, a newly married young Bulgarian woman (Joy Page) tells him that her husband (Helmut Dantine) is at the roulette table, where he has been unsuccessfully trying to raise the money for their exit visas. Because they have no money, Captain Renault will give them exit visas only if she does a "bad thing" with him, sacrificing herself for her husband. Rick initially seems indifferent to her plight and with offhanded cynicism tells her to go back to Bulgaria. But a

Joel Cairo (Peter Lorre), Wilmer (Elisha Cook Jr.), and Kasper Gutman (Sidney Greenstreet). Oddball supporting characters endowed with unique traits greatly enhance the screen drama. (*The Maltese Falcon* [1941])

short time later he quietly instructs his croupier (Marcel Dalio) to let her husband win at roulette.

Odd or Curious Traits

Like the central figures, supporting characters generally have the number and kind of traits necessary to function effectively in the unfolding drama. Because such characters are not the principal focus of interest, however, they are often endowed with certain peculiar distinguishing features. In *The Maltese Falcon* (1941), for example, private eye Sam Spade (Humphrey Bogart) encounters an odd array of seedily raffish characters as he investigates the murder of his partner and searches for the gem-encrusted bird of the title. Among the comic opera villains he confronts are Kasper Gutman (Sidney Greenstreet), a greedy "fat man" with a mirthless laugh and a propensity for pomposity ("I'll tell you straight out, sir, I'm a man who likes talking to a man who likes to talk"); Joel Cairo (Peter Lorre), a slight, prissy man with a nasal voice and strange accent, a gardenia scent on his calling card, and a tendency to launch into spasms of fury and fear (when the falcon turns out to be fake,

Sam (Humphrey Bogart) admires Brigid's (Mary Astor) seemingly knowing, somewhat flirtatious feigning of innocence—the slightly exaggerated way she casts demure glances down at the floor, wringing her hands and touching her brow. (*The Maltese Falcon* [1941])

he screams at Gutman; "You—*imbecile!* . . . you—*bloated idiot!* . . . you—*stupid fat-head,* you!!!"); and Wilmer (Elisha Cook Jr.), a boyish-looking "gunsel"— underworld slang for a young homosexual used by an older man—with a cold, demented look in his eyes.

The most deceitful and deadly of this movie's assemblage of more than slightly askew characters is Brigid O'Shaughnessy (Mary Astor), an artful schemer whose predatory tendencies are concealed behind her good looks and an aura of cloying helplessness. ("You won't need much of anybody's help," Spade says admiringly when she beseeches him to help her. "You're good—chiefly your eyes, I think, and that throb you get in your voice when you say things like 'Be—*generous,* Mr. Spade.'") Her chameleonlike personality changes almost as frequently as her name. She is, in turn, the refined Miss Wonderly, the chimerical Miss Le Blanc, and the worldly Miss O'Shaughnessy. The hard-boiled private eye is not taken in by any of her guises, but she has clearly aroused his curiosity and his lust.

Although drawn to her strong allure, Spade resolves to turn her over to the police when he eventually realizes she murdered his partner. ("I hope they don't hang you, precious, by that sweet neck," he says icily.) As she is taken away, we see the bars of the elevator door close in front of her tear-stained

The bars of an elevator door serve as a presage of Brigid's impending imprisonment. (*The Maltese Falcon* [1941])

face, presaging the bars of the prison cell that awaits her. The cynically idealistic Spade once again is alone. And the gem-encrusted golden falcon has once again proved to be elusive, "the stuff that dreams are made of," as the private detective observes with grim satisfaction near the close of the movie.

The line is adapted from the epilogue to William Shakespeare's *The Tempest*. Toward the end of the play, when the magician Prospero stops his pretense, he declares that all that has gone before has been an illusion: "Our revels now are ended. These our actors, / As I foretold you, were all spirits and / Are melted into air, into thin air." Human lives, he says, are just as frail as make-believe: "We are such stuff / As dreams are made on, and our little life / Is rounded with a sleep." Because none of the characters in this movie is who or what he or she claims to be, this reference provides an especially appropriate way to round it out.

Unconventional Protagonists

Central characters in most movies generally adhere to certain established conventions and expectations. In recent years, however, some moviemakers have been pushing the parameters of characterization to entirely new dimen-

Vincent (John Travolta) and Jules (Samuel L. Jackson) discuss European eating habits with an easy intimacy. The engaging conversation takes on bizarre aspects following a fade when we see them (the point of view is from inside the car truck) unloading their weapons. (*Pulp Fiction* [1994])

sions. Part of what makes *Pulp Fiction* (1994) so audacious, for instance, is the way writer-director Quentin Tarantino drastically departs from the standard practice of making the speech traits of protagonists consistent with their function in the unfolding screen drama.

Vincent Vega (John Travolta) and Jules Winnfield (Samuel L. Jackson), the two hired killers at the center of this innovative reworking of the crime genre, talk about everything from foot massages and the definition of a television pilot to such matters as the French names for American fast food. While driving to a hit, for instance, Vincent, who has recently returned from Europe, explains to Jules that in Paris they call a Quarter Pounder with Cheese a Royale with Cheese. When Jules wants to know what they call a Whopper, he responds, "I dunno. I didn't go into Burger King." He then goes on to tell his incredulous companion that in Holland they actually put mayonnaise instead of ketchup on french fries. What makes this so odd is that hit men in movies never talk about such mundane things because they have nothing to do with the story at hand. The engaging vernacular style in which Jules and Vincent discuss a wide range of topics makes them not only charming and witty but actually likable.

Jules engages in a bit of biblical embellishment: "The path of a righteous man is beset on all sides by inequities of the selfish and the tyranny of evil men." (*Pulp Fiction* [1994])

These cold-blooded killers are on their way to retrieve a briefcase that contains some mysterious glowing substance. It belongs to feared crime boss Marsellus Wallace (Ving Rhames). Before leaving town, he instructed Vincent to take his new wife Mia (Uma Thurman) out for a night of fun, with strict orders not to touch her. Vincent is nervous because Marsellus is rumored to have had a man thrown out of a fourth-story window for massaging Mia's feet. He shares his concerns with Jules, and they debate the degrees of intimacy with respect to the female anatomy. Their amusing assessment of the erotic status of a foot massage precedes the brutal killing of the wayward yuppies who have stolen the briefcase. This sets a pattern of conversation and situation that persists throughout the movie in which comedy and violence are intricately intertwined.

Virtually all of the dialogue contains surprises of one sort or another. The psychopathically religious Jules likes to recite a contrived version of Ezekiel's prophecy against the Philistines to scare those who are about to die, which he does just before he and Vincent open fire on the terrified young men who were preparing to dig into their breakfast from a local Hawaiian burger bar. The cold professionalism of this powerful soliloquy of menace and madness, coupled with the sadistic way Jules humiliates the most vocal member of the group and playfully samples his specialty hamburger before the bloodbath begins, provide a stunning prelude for the many violent ironies to come.

The often crude language of the characters conceals a certain rhyme, rhythm, and even subtle eloquence. What they say and do frequently involves the buttocks. In one scene, for example, a military officer (Christopher Walken) delivers a lengthy monologue explaining how he happened to come by a gold watch, which he is now presenting to a little boy named Butch (Chandler Lindauer). The watch was passed down by the boy's great-grandfather, a

Captain Koons (Christopher Walken) explains, "He hid it in the one place he knew he could hide something." (*Pulp Fiction* [1994])

World War I veteran, and was concealed in the rectum of his father (a POW of the Vietcong who died in captivity). Intent on bringing the watch home to little Butch, the military officer hid it up his own rear end.

This scene turns out to be a flashback to boxer Butch Coolidge's (Bruce Willis) childhood. In a room off a boxing arena, the adult Butch snaps awake from his reverie, apparently deciding that family honor prevents him from throwing a fight. Again, the action veers off in an unexpected direction related to anal activity. Butch not only crosses paths with crime boss Marsellus Wallace (Ving Rhames), whom he cheated by winning the fight, but they are subsequently imprisoned in the dungeonlike basement of a pawnshop by a pair of rednecks prone to sadomasochistic sexual practices. After managing to untie himself, Butch comes upon the two of them engaging in the anal rape of a bound Marsellus. When he's once again in command, the crime boss tells the redneck who just violated him, "I'm gonna git medieval on your ass."

The delightfully dense Vincent often misses out on major developments in the unfolding drama because he's in the toilet. That's where he is, for instance, when the two small-time thieves (Amanda Plummer and Tim Roth), referring to each other as Honey Bunny and Pumpkin, decide to hold up the diner in which they're chatting about crime prospects (liquor stores entail too much risk and provide too little profit, and banks are slightly beyond their capacity). While Vincent is in the toilet at Mia's place, she mistakes his bag of heroin for cocaine, overdoses, and goes into an opened-eyed coma. And he's literally caught with his pants down sitting on the commode in Butch's apartment when the boxer returns and shoots him as he's coming out of the bathroom. (He uses the submachine gun left behind by Marsellus, who joins Vincent in the stakeout because—as we will later learn—Jules has found salvation and resigned from a life of crime.)

Creating Characters

Actors bring screen characters to life. A skilled actor can draw upon an extraordinarily detailed visual vocabulary to reveal subtle changes in the feelings of a character. Variations in eyebrow position, mouth shape, and nostril size, and even slight shifts in levels of body tension or relaxation can provide clues to a character's frame of mind. Arm motions and hands gestures, as well as ways of sitting, standing, and lying, can signal a wide range of feelings—from friendliness, hostility, and superiority to weakness, inferiority, and lack of resolve. Vocal pitch, stress, tone, accent, rate of speech, and pronunciation can convey a character's emotional state, personality, and social-class status.

Elements Beyond the Actor's Control

A few noteworthy efforts notwithstanding, until fairly recently screen acting was largely a dark continent on the map of film scholarship.[1] The small number of explorations into this mostly uncharted terrain may stem in part from the difficulty of separating what actors actually do from the way they are presented. Because they are ordinarily before the camera for only a minute or two at a time, film actors are not required to give sustained, consistent performances. Moreover, they typically work in small segments that are often completely out of sequence. This means that emotionally charged or otherwise significant moments must often be performed isolated from the emotional context of scenes that in the completed picture will appear earlier.

The screen actor must learn how to break performances into small bits, how to work without the direct response of an audience, and how to adjust expressions and gestures for the intimate framing of the close-up. A false move, phony gesture, or facial expression lacking conviction will not escape the camera's probing eye. Close-ups can catch even the tiniest hint of feeling, regardless of whether it is appropriate to the situation or the character's state of mind. (The pitiless demands of the close-up dashed the professional aspirations of many accomplished stage actors when they turned to movies.)

Even under the best of circumstances, the independence of screen actors as interpretive artists is limited. In the theatre, the stage director does extensive work and is in charge during rehearsals; but after the curtain rises, the actors are in control, and the production succeeds or fails with them. While the play is in progress, an actor has the freedom to explore a variety of character nuances. In sharp contrast, in movies, others determine the final pace and rhythm of a performance. Such things as camera placement and the choice of a long shot or a close-up are matters that greatly influence the effect of an actor's performance but over which he or she has no control.

Much of a performance is created in the moviemaking process itself. By working separately on small segments of a scene, and by making judicious cuts and camera placements, a talented director can coax a convincing performance from even an inexperienced or limited actor. Close reaction shots at the right moment can create the impression that an actor is responding subtly and with deep emotion when, in fact, he or she is not doing anything. A wide range of meanings or nuances, none of them intended by the actor, can be nurtured through careful lighting, camera work, and cutting, and through the emotional cues of music.

Interplay Between Actor and Character

Working within the limiting context of cinema, some actors are nonetheless able to "inhabit" the characters they play, as Marlon Brando does in *The Godfather*. In creating the character of Don Vito Corleone, he affected a wheezing, aspirate voice seemingly cracked with age (later to be mimicked by a host of impersonators, including Brando himself in *The Freshman* [1990]). His voice has an eccentric, slightly ethnic sound, redolent of the character's Sicilian origins. His vocal patterns are supplemented by subtle movements of his fingertips in front of his mouth and the way he raises his eyebrow at times instead of speaking.

With his raspy voice, deliberate gestures, and penetrating stare, Brando manages to invest the aging but still powerful don with an air of wisdom and even nobility. By the time he dies in his garden, he has become such a real person that we feel upset; this is someone we have known. Our sadness over the old don's death, however, is assuaged by appreciation for how the actor has aroused our emotions.

A great deal of our enjoyment at the movies undoubtedly comes from this interplay between actor and character. A sort of "double consciousness" seems to kick in when we get caught up in a performance. French psychiatrist Octave Mannoni provides useful insights into how the acceptance of an illusion as reality always rests on a delicate balance of belief and denial, of faith and disavowal. His work suggests that behind every incredulous moviegoer lies a credulous one. There seems to be a split in our consciousness as we watch a movie between "*je sais bien . . .*" and "*mais quand meme . . .*"—that is, "I know very well this illusion is only an illusion, but nevertheless some part of me still believes in it."[2]

Actors' Personae

Most enduring screen players develop a persona or public image that lends a wealth of connotative meaning to any character they play. The kind of isolated figure Clint Eastwood cuts, for instance, in role after role seems to tap into some deep strain in Western culture and history. For over three decades, he has infused a sense of solitariness into even stock and two-dimensional

John Wayne as the Ringo Kid in *Stagecoach* (1939), his springboard to stardom. Between 1930 and 1938, Wayne had appeared in nearly sixty movies, mainly low-budget westerns.

characters in a way that resonates with audiences across generations and national boundaries. From the squinty-eyed gunslinger who rides into town to exact his own brand of retribution, to the renegade police detective who defies bureaucratic procedure in pursuit of malefactors, to the craggy-faced former killer of terrifying repute who regresses into rage to right a wrong, the lean, laconic actor has always specialized in playing social outsiders cut off from other people by inclination and circumstance.

Many stars cement a persona by settling into a particular set of mannerisms and vocal characteristics, exhibiting a version of themselves so carefully crafted that acting and being become one. John Wayne, for instance, essentially shaped his screen persona in front of the camera during the 1930s. Under his original name of Marion Morrison, the inexperienced actor secured the leading role in the 1930 western epic *The Big Trail*. But stardom proved elusive, and he spent much of the decade stomping the sagebrush in Saturday-morning serials and cheap action pictures, gradually honing his natural attributes into a distinctive screen persona. His role as the Ringo Kid in *Stagecoach* (1939) propelled him into the top ranks of box office stars—a position he maintained for the next several decades.

During the 1940s and 1950s, as a recent study of the star suggests, Wayne's screen persona came to symbolize the popular conception of American manhood and individualism as it had evolved in the first half of the century.[3] In such diverse roles as a heroic U.S. military officer leading Filipino guerillas to victory in *Back to Bataan* (1945), a ruthless empire builder in *Red River* (1948), a memory-haunted ex-boxer in *The Quiet Man* (1952), and a relentless ex-Confederate soldier in *The Searchers* (1956), his rough features and granite-like demeanor conveyed a sense of inner strength, the quality that arguably cuts closest to the secret of his enduring screen success. In combination with other qualities, such as sensitivity and amiability beneath a hard exterior, this proved to be magic for many moviegoers.

In the old studio era, stars typically adapted essentially the same speech and phrasing patterns, facial expressions, gestures, and physical movements to meet the requirements of each new role. Scripts were often tailored to fit what studio management saw as their special talents and personalities. Casting contract players in roles tailored to their own qualities and traits had a decidedly practical dimension. With so many scripts to develop, so many movies to make, so many actors to assign, so many projects to monitor, and so much output to move into theatres, pigeonholing players in their established personae helped to alleviate the pressures of studio production schedules.

In most instances, studios refined and polished specific personality traits of their players using comments in fan mail, sneak previews, exhibitor preferences, and box office grosses as guides. Early in Bette Davis's career, for instance, Warner Bros. Pictures, for whom she spent two decades under contract, developed her persona around the performances that seemed to yield the most favorable audience response. She was initially cast in a diverse variety of parts, appearing as an ingenue in *The Man Who Played God* (1932), a sophisticate in *The Rich Are Always with Us* (1932), a spoiled flirt in *Cabin in the Cotton* (1932), a free spirit in *Ex-Lady* (1933), an urban toughie in *Jimmy the Gent* (1934), and a playgirl in *Fog Over Frisco* (1934). In its efforts to match role and actor, the studio seemed unable to establish a stable and appealing screen identity for her.

When Davis appeared as the vulgar and vicious waitress who seduces and destroys an infatuated doctor (Leslie Howard) in a screen adaptation of W. Somerset Maugham's *Of Human Bondage* (1934), which she made on loan to RKO Radio Pictures, the latent fire-and-ice potential apparent in some of her previous roles finally came to the fore. Playing this part at full throttle, she ripped into the famous "wipe my mouth" speech near the end of the film. ("It made me sick when I had to let you kiss me," her character tells the now disgusted doctor, noting that she consented only because he begged and hounded her. "And when you kissed me, I always used to wipe my mouth!

Wipe my mouth.") Her saucer eyes, high-strung manner, staccato speech, and emotional intensity combined to produce something unique. Like other enduring stars, she became her own type, which Warner Bros. exploited through casting and publicity as soon as she was back on the lot.

Some stars developed distinct screen personae soon after they were signed to a contract. Clark Gable, who joined M-G-M in 1930, quickly garnered favorable public attention after appearing in 1931 with several of the studio's top female stars, among them Norma Shearer (*A Free Soul*), Greta Garbo (*Susan Lenox: Her Rise and Fall*), and Joan Crawford (*Possessed*). His role in the latter movie as an unhappily married attorney who sets up a love nest with the Crawford character firmly fixed his persona as a romantic leading man. And his next picture, *Hell's Divers* (1932), in which he and Wallace Beery played boisterous rivals in the Naval Air Force, showed him to be equally comfortable as a rugged he-man type.

In sharp contrast, Humphrey Bogart's screen persona only became fully molded only after he had appeared in more than forty films. He scored his first screen triumph as the unregenerate killer Duke Mantee in *The Petrified Forest* (1936), a role he originated on Broadway. But during the latter half of the 1930s, he ground out eight to twelve movies a year primarily playing such characters as the crooked lawyer, bootlegger, or racketeer who winds up either dead or maimed before the last reel.

All that began to change when he won the role of the hard-boiled private eye Sam Spade in *The Maltese Falcon*. His persona of a reluctant hero whose moral core is encrusted in cynicism took clearer shape in *Across the Pacific* (1942) and became firmly fixed in *Casablanca*. Through some curious cinematic alchemy, he used his voice, facial expressions, and general demeanor and mannerisms—the distinctive lisp, the squint, the grimace, the meditative tugging of an earlobe, the tightening of the lower lip over the teeth—to create a vivid screen persona. By the time he appeared in *To Have and Have Not* (1944) and *The Big Sleep* (1946), Bogart stood as an archetypal figure, tough on the outside and compassionate within, capable of romantic and personal commitments without compromising his autonomy.

A sharp disparity often exists between a star's background and screen persona. Although Humphrey Bogart's gravelly voice and tough-guy stance suggest working-class roots, he was actually the son of a society doctor and nationally famous magazine illustrator. His childhood was one of both privilege and emotional turmoil. Educated at the Delancey and Trinity schools in New York, he spent an additional year at Philips Academy in Andover, Massachusetts, a move intended to prepare him for the Ivy League. But he soon veered off the prep school track. Flunking out of Philips, he joined the navy near the close of World War I. He then drifted to Broadway where, as a young stage actor, he played a series of country-club juveniles and charming wastrels, giving little hint of the screen persona that would inspire several generations.

Although Bogart himself never made it to the Ivy League, his movies developed a strong cult following among many students who did. Beginning in the late 1950s, the Brattle Theatre in Cambridge, Massachusetts, put on festivals featuring his movies each semester during Harvard's final-exam period. When *Casablanca* was shown, students commonly chanted lines of memorized dialogue as the actors spoke them on the screen. The popular Club Casablanca in the Brattle's basement was only the first of many memorabilia-filled watering holes the Bogart persona inspired.

Several of *Casablanca*'s other key players had completely reinvented themselves as well, molding screen masks that hid very different upbringings. Claude Rains, who portrayed the urbane, witty Captain Louis Renault, didn't go to school beyond the second grade. With shades of Pygmalion, he transformed himself with elocution books and voice lessons from a cockney lad with a speech impediment into a young man of seeming refinement and elegance. During the First World War, he actually rose in rank from private to captain—accomplishing the almost impossible in the class-bound British society. With his stage-honed demeanor and upper-class accent, he had apparently acted himself into the role of officer and gentleman.

When stars undergo a major shift in persona, perceptions of a character they have played in the past can change in significant ways. In the late 1940s, for example, Ingrid Bergman deserted her husband and young daughter and ran off to Italy with director Roberto Rossellini, bearing his child out of wedlock. She had long been depicted in the media as the ideal wife and mother. This revelation of marital infidelity and parental dereliction severely tarnished her saintly image and left many feeling betrayed. In the light of Bergman's fall from grace, Ilsa Lund, the character she played so compellingly in *Casablanca,* may seem even more of a riddle, incapable of committing to one man—either to her husband or her lover.

Screen Stereotypes

Screen characterizations draw heavily on stereotypical representations circulating in society at large. As applied to people, **stereotype**s reflect fixed ideas about how members of a particular group think or behave, and tend to be organized around such factors as age, race, ethnicity, gender, religion, vocation, and nationality. Although not utterly false, nor necessarily negative, stereotypes are utterly shallow. They always entail a high degree of simplification and inhibit the recognition of individuality and personal uniqueness.

Stereotypes are apparently the natural outcome of human **perception**— the mental activity of organizing the input of the senses (sight, hearing, touch,

METHOD ACTING

An innovative acting approach achieved prominence in the post–World War II period. In 1947 several alumni of the Group Theatre, a prewar acting ensemble, formed the Actors Studio, a workshop for talented actors to hone their craft between engagements. The new studio drew heavily on the ideas of Konstantin Stanislavsky, who had developed his approach to acting at the Moscow Art Theatre, which he cofounded in 1898 in reaction to the highly stylized and artificial techniques prevalent at the end of the nineteenth century. He had encouraged actors to build an inner identification with the characters they portrayed by drawing on their own past experiences and emotional histories.

Lee Strasberg, who emerged as the New York studio's principal teacher and theorist, had transformed Stanislavsky's theories and techniques into **the Method**—elaborate psychoanalytic strategies to help actors delve into their own unconscious motives, trigger actual emotions, and transfer them to the characters they are playing. But Strasberg deviated from the Russian master's tenets by fostering an approach that emphasized the actor's personality over the character's and that gave little attention to such matters as movement and diction. Through introspection the appropriate vocal and physical responses would supposedly come without conscious effort. Spoken dialogue, in fact, became secondary. Lines were thrown away, choked on, and often mumbled.

Hailed as the Method's high priest, Strasberg devised a series of rigorous exercises to release intense emotions within an actor. They demanded great discipline and depths of concentration. (One especially controversial element of his teaching was called "private moments," in which actors sang, stripped, fondled themselves, or thought about dead loved ones in order to break

down inhibitions.) Many of the thespians who sat at his feet went on to invigorate the nascent television industry and to establish a new order of acting intensity on the Broadway stage.

The Method is often cited as a major catalyst in changing movie acting and characterization as well. Although many Method-trained actors became formidable figures in the movie industry, among them Paul Newman, Joanne Woodward, Jane Fonda, Dustin Hoffman, Robert DeNiro, and Al Pacino, just how this approach is manifested on the screen is difficult to discern. The stress on the player's personality over the character's was easily assimilated into the invisible form of acting that developed within the idiom of the Hollywood film. An intuitive Method of sorts was, in fact, at work almost from the inception of movies, as directors like D. W. Griffith sought to erase artificiality from acting by having screen players wholly project themselves into their characters.

An added problem in assessing the extent of the Method's impact on screen acting is that actors chiefly trained elsewhere are often linked with the Actors Studio. Marlon Brando's name, for instance, is frequently invoked to denote the Method style of acting. Although a member of the studio since its inception in 1947, Brando was trained primarily at Erwin Piscator's Dramatic Workshop at the New School for Social Research in New York City. His principal teacher and mentor was the eclectic Stella Adler, who strongly opposed Strasberg's insistence on the unraveling of unconscious feelings in the quest for inner truth. Director Elia Kazan, one of the founders of the Actors Studio, recalled that, whenever people later associated Brando with Strasberg, the actor would correct them by saying, "No, I went to school with Stella."[4] Like Stanislavsky, with whom she studied during a sojourn in Paris, Adler stressed the given circumstances of the script and logical action for the character in developing a role.

The brooding inarticulateness and halting speech patterns often associated with the Method probably owe as much to Marlon Brando's interpretations of the characters he played as they do to Strasberg's strategies. Brando established not only a style of screen acting but a standard as well. Undoubtedly the most original actor of his time, his macho demeanor and muscular physique belied an oddly delicate sensibility. Few virile male leads before him lent such a strangely erotic, almost androgynous quality to even violent characters. His characterizations in such movies as *A Streetcar Named Desire* (1951), *The Wild One* (1953), and *On the Waterfront* (1954) spawned a host of imitators—most notably James Dean, who assumed many of the young Brando's screen mannerisms.

Production still of Marlon Brando as Stanley Kowalski. *A Streetcar Named Desire* (1951) was one of several films in the 1950s that made Brando the most influential actor of his generation.

Dean's amorphous, seemingly real-life, rhythms in the movies *East of Eden* (1955), *Rebel Without a Cause* (1955), and *Giant* (1955) struck an especially strong emotional chord with teenagers of the 1950s. He seemed to become a personification of restless American youths, an embodiment of all their anguish and alienation. The adulation of his fans grew posthumously to legendary proportions after he was killed in a highway crash in 1955. Dean achieved cult status of a kind that surrounded no other star since Rudolph Valentino. Of course, yesterday's authenticity often appears artificial to later generations. By today's standards, Dean's strangled speech and tortured facial configurations may seem more stylized than naturalistic.

Although Dean's portrayal of mumbling, angry, introverted characters came to epito-

mize popular conceptions of the Method-trained actor, he was not one of the more active members of the Actors Studio. After passing his audition in 1952, the twenty-one-year-old aspiring actor performed a scene for evaluation that Lee Strasberg critically and publicly lambasted. Afterward, Dean refused to attend classes at the studio for a while. When he finally did return, according to a study of the Actors Studio, he merely audited class sessions and did not participate.[5]

The intense, self-referential style stressed by Strasberg, who died in 1982, is no longer central to the training of actors in the United States. His idiosyncratic interpretation of Stanislavsky gradually receded before an imposing array of acting approaches that include non-Western movement and performance techniques. Although the Russian master's spirit still remains, the Actors Studio long ago discarded the dogma of its early years. Classes in movement, voice, textual analysis, and theatrical styles are now integral to the curriculum.

taste, smell) into interpretations that make sense in relation to past experience and cultural orientation. In stereotyping, people or social situations are categorized or mentally arranged on the basis of a small number of similar superficial traits or distinctive identifying features, particularly such visual cues as skin color, eye shape, and nose width. (These are the kinds of traits most commonly used to define what has come to be called race, a social category with little basis in biology given that external appearance is controlled by only a tiny percentage of a person's genetic makeup.) The supposed attributes of a category are taken as the basis of evaluation of everyone assigned to it. In many instances, not even a fragmentary basis in personal experience is necessary for a stereotype to take hold. The culture at large provides ready-made categories in the absence of direct contact. Given the heavy emotional freight stereotypes often carry, they may be highly resistant to contradictory evidence or logical argument.

Once identified and dissected, cinematic stereotypes can provide a revealing expression of otherwise hidden beliefs and values. This makes them an effective means of tracing how prevailing feelings and attitudes associated with some specific social category of people can change over time. Steeped as they are in stereotypes, movies made in the idiom of the Hollywood film may play a major role in shaping, reinforcing, and altering perceptions about women and members of socially dispossessed minority groups.

Female Stereotypes in Movies

The common gender stereotypes of the Hollywood film become more apparent when characters, situations, and actions are removed from the narrative flow and their relations of similarity and difference are analyzed. Within the typical movie, such analysis suggests, men and women are generally represented as extreme opposites. Female characters tend to be defined in terms of what male characters are not. That is, if the male is strong, then the female must be weak; if the male is rational, then the female must be emotional; and so on. These divisions are transformed into a number of oppositions, such as masculine versus feminine, public versus private, active versus passive, and productive versus consumptive.

A masculine man is likely to be depicted as active in the public sphere, socially and sexually assertive, and a prime producer of essential goods and services. A feminine woman, in contrast, is more likely to be portrayed as involved primarily in the private domain, passive in societal and sexual matters, and a consumer rather than a producer. Female characters deviating from these established categories, especially with regard to sexual assertiveness, serve as sources of both anxiety and intense erotic excitement. And they are generally shown to be unstable, dangerous, and even deadly.

Although notable exceptions exist, until fairly recently, these gender divisions were fairly consistent. The plot dynamics of most movies revolve around

Rick (Humphrey Bogart) tells Ilsa (Ingrid Bergman) she belongs with her husband. (Bergman was about two inches taller than Bogart, who stood on blocks for this shot.) (*Casablanca* [1942])

male heroes who are the active agents. Unless they are temptresses or are at the center of such domestic melodramas as *Mildred Pierce* (1945), in which their successes are invariably compromised, female characters tend to be secondary to the male protagonist's objectives in the public sphere of work, war, missions, or expeditions. In *Casablanca,* for instance, Ilsa's subordinate status is firmly fixed in the finale when Rick decides to take up the Allied cause. He explains to her that he has a job to do, that she can't follow where he is going, and that she can't be any part of what he's got to do. "Ilsa," he says patronizingly, "I'm no good at being noble, but it doesn't take much to see that the problems of three little people don't amount to a hill of beans in this crazy world. Someday you'll understand that. Not now. Here's looking at you, kid." (How many men of a certain age, like the Woody Allen character in *Play It Again, Sam* [1972], have yearned furtively to deliver these lines?) He then sends her off with her remarkably patient and tolerant husband.

Most female characters are little more than male fantasies, suggests critic Molly Haskell, stereotypes of what men want to believe about women. She charted screen depictions of women from the trembling virgins and footloose flappers of the 1920s to the demeaned and dehumanized "chicks, kooks, groupies, and cartoon pinup girls" of the 1960s and 1970s. "Audiences for the most part were not interested in seeing, and Hollywood was not interested in sponsoring, a smart, ambitious woman as a popular heroine," she concludes, "A woman who could compete and conceivably win in a man's world would defy emotional gravity, would go against the grain of prevailing notions about the female sex. A woman's intelligence was the equivalent of a man's penis: something to be kept out of sight."[6] (Both have received cinematic exposure in recent years.)

The Bond Barometer

The perennially popular James Bond movies provide a rough barometer for gauging changes in gender relations on the big screen. The basic plot formula, initially based on the novels of Ian Fleming, has remained more or less the same for almost four decades. After flirting with his supervisor's secretary, Miss Moneypenny, and ably assisted by the ingenious devices of "Q," the eccentric equipment officer, British special agent James Bond (who has been portrayed by several actors—most notably, Sean Connery) defies attempts on his life, penetrates the domain of a comic-strip villain intent on world domination, and brings him to an ignoble end. Along the way, Bond seduces—or is seduced by—one or more female characters. In the concluding scene, he is typically seen drifting in a boat with a sexual conquest cradled in the crook of his arm or at least engaging in sexual foreplay somewhere in the vicinity of a body of water.

From the outset, the bed-hopping Bond's female companions were themselves not tethered by constraints of family, marriage, and domesticity. Nor were they necessarily punished for their sexual desires, as had been the standard Hollywood practice in the old studio era. They did tend nonetheless to be somehow hormonally "deviant," overly aggressive, frigid, or of uncertain sexual orientation, and generally on the "wrong side" politically in being in the service of the villain. After becoming involved with the rakish secret agent, they were often "repositioned," as it were, both within the political sphere (recruited in the service of "good" instead of evil) and the traditional order of gender difference (put back into place beneath Bond, both literally and in terms of the social hierarchy).

Although the irresistible Bond's mere touch could still no doubt soften even the most hostile woman, this series has seen some shifts in recent years in the way women are represented. In *Tomorrow Never Dies* (1997), for example, Bond (Pierce Brosnan) is paired with a female Chinese communist agent named Wai Lin (Michelle Yeoh, the foremost female star of Hong Kong kung fu movies), who has martial arts skills equal or superior to his. In one fight scene, she defeats a whole gang of villians on her own. More progressive than any of her predecessors, she doesn't succumb to Bond's sexual charm until the very end of the movie, after the mission has been accomplished.

Cinematic *Femme Fatales*

One of most prevalent female stereotypes in movies has been the *femme fatale*—an unscrupulous, seductive woman who uses her wiles to entrap and exploit unwitting men with the promise of unbridled passion. Appearing in many guises, this she-monster carries echoes of the mythical sirens who lured ancient mariners to their deaths. She is commonly contrasted to a woman who is domestic, devoted, and decidedly dull, with the two acting as magnetic poles between which the male protagonist gravitates.

Highly desirable but dangerous female predators leading unsuspecting males into trouble have been a screen staple since at least 1915, when Theda Bara made her debut in *A Fool There Was* playing a character designated only as "the Vampire." The *femme fatale* was central to many crime thrillers of the 1940s, with plots commonly revolving around her challenge to the values of the male-dominated society and the authority of male characters. During the Cold War, female sexual predators on the big screen frequently took on a distinct reddish hue. They could often be found using sexual wiles to dupe some politically naive male into toeing the party line. The slip straps showing beneath the transparent blouse of this scarlet temptress typically signaled her communist affinity.

More recent movies featuring *femme fatales* include *Fatal Attraction* (1987), *Basic Instinct* (1992), and *Disclosure* (1995)—the trilogy that made Michael Douglas the poster boy of male paranoia about clever career women. The basic storyline of *Fatal Attraction* centers on an emotionally disturbed single woman's obsessive pursuit of a happily married man. While his wife and six-year-old daughter are out of town visiting his in-laws, lawyer Dan Gallagher (Michael Douglas) spends an illicit weekend with book editor Alex Forrest (Glenn Close), whose wild locks trigger images of a modern Medusa (the terrifying woman of Greek myth with hair of serpents).

During their heated tryst, Dan and Alex (note the gender-neutral name) have sex in a freight elevator, on a kitchen sink, and even in a bed. He makes it clear that he's happily married (albeit sexually restless) and that they can't see each other again; but she doesn't quite see it that way. His adulterous interlude becomes a nightmare when she turns out to be a psychopath who threatens him and his family (even the household pet isn't safe from this knife-wielding predator). In the concluding scene, after Dan has apparently drowned her, she rises up from the bathtub water with seemingly supernatural powers to strike again. Protecting her domestic domain, his virtuous wife (Ann Archer) finally slays this monster.

The kinky seductress at the center of *Basic Instinct,* Catherine Tramell (Sharon Stone), has a live-in lesbian lover who slashed two younger brothers to death with a razor. Another close companion carved up her own husband and three children. A writer of gruesome murder mysteries, Catherine claims

Sitting on a raised, spotlighted platform, Catherine Tramell (Sharon Stone) tantalizes a group of male detectives. (*Basic Instinct* [1992])

to need these perverted people for inspiration. Her latest novel is about the brutal ice pick stabbing of a fading rock singer who resembles one of her male sex partners. She becomes a suspect when this paramour is killed in precisely the same way as the character in her story.

As a group of male detectives try to interrogate her, Catherine flirts with them shamelessly, even uncrossing her legs so they (and the audience) can look directly up her dress. One of the detectives assigned to the case, Nick Curran (Michael Douglas), a recovering alcohol and cocaine abuser, seems mesmerized by her sexual brazenness. Although she delights in teasing male libidos and may even be a cold-blooded killer, he nevertheless heeds the call of his hormones. As they engage in amorous acrobatics, the dead bodies begin to pile up.

While conducting his investigation, Nick finds out that his ex-lover, police psychologist Beth Garner (Jeanne Tripplehorn), became obsessed with Catherine after they had a one-night stand in college. Finding Beth near the savagely bludgeoned body of his partner (George Dzundza), Nick screams at her to "freeze." As she moves toward him, holding something in her pocket, he shoots her squarely in the chest. Before dying, she murmurs, "I love you." In her pocket is a key chain, not a weapon of any kind.

During the final scene, Nick and Catherine have sex in his bedroom (as usual, she straddles him). As they are relaxing afterward, she curls away from him. Her right arm reaches over the side of the bed. In a split second, she seemingly decides not to punctuate their postcoital rapture with the ice pick lying nearby on the floor (the camera descends down her side of the bed and comes to rest with a close-up of the implement).

The female predator in *Disclosure* not only can talk knowledgeably about "new compression algorithms" but also mouth such double entendres as "You know, I like all the boys under me to be happy." In an ironic twist, plot developments center around principal male character Tom Sander's (Michael Douglas) claims of sexual harassment by his former lover Meredith Johnson (Demi Moore), who has supplanted him at the high-tech offices of Digicom.

At the end of her first day on the job, in a heated sex scene that sets up the central plot line, this dressed-to-kill, lusty, and heartless woman plies the now-married Tom with wine and tries to seduce him. Protests to the contrary, he's obviously excited by her teasing, haughty aggression. Soon he's kissing her, and then pulling off her jet-black designer outfit and allowing her to perform oral sex on him. After gaining control of himself, he beats a precipitous retreat. She charges out of her office after him yelling, "You get back here and finish what you started!" The two are soon squaring off against each other, creating factions within the organization and gradually revealing ulterior motives. In the denouement, her duplicity and deception are revealed.

These three fantasies of threatened masculinity touched a lot of nerves. The linkage of brutality with bisexuality in *Basic Instinct* earned the wrath of both feminists and gay activists. Letter-writing campaigns and organized protests were in motion even during preproduction. In San Francisco, after filming started, members of Queer Nation took their anger to the streets. On at least one occasion, they managed to disrupt the filmmaking process completely. When the movie opened nationwide, such groups as the Gay and Lesbian Alliance Against Defamation (GLAAD) and the National Organization of Women (NOW) expressed their outrage over its damaging stereotypes by staging demonstrations in front of theatres in New York, Washington, DC, Seattle, San Francisco, Los Angeles, and other cities. Despite such protests, which were widely reported in the media, the movie was a box office smash.

Sexual Power in *The Last Seduction*

The cinematic *femme fatale* is pushed to new extremes in *The Last Seduction* (1994). Directed by John Dahl from Steve Baranick's script, almost everything in this movie revolves around protagonist Bridget Gregory (Linda Fiorentino). Her movements and her motivations propel the narrative trajectory forward. As the action unfolds, she is revealed to be intelligent and ruthless, and to lack moral qualms. What is more, her strong sexual drive is unburdened by romantic attachment or sentimentality. She has no weak spots for anyone or anything.

All the other characters in this tangled web of murder, sex, and money revolve within the orbit of her intricate schemes, including her medical student husband Clay (Bill Pullman), whom she has induced to sell pharmaceutical cocaine on the black market for extra cash. We first see him enduring a tense meeting with a couple of toughs. In exchange for a suitcase filled with cocaine, they hand over $700,000 in laundered cash, but not before having a

THE CAMERA'S GAZE

Beginning in 1975 with the publication of Laura Mulvey's highly influential essay "Visual Pleasure and the Narrative Cinema," the notion that the "look" or "gaze" of the camera in the filming situation is masculine in character has been central to a great deal of film theory.[7] In the typical Hollywood film, according to Mulvey and the many writers who followed in her wake, scenes are broken down, blocked, staged, and photographed in ways designed to put female figures on erotic display, turning them into passive objects for the pleasure and gratification of men. Drawing upon psychoanalytic concepts, Mulvey hypothesizes that, although most males find such displays highly pleasurable, viewing the female anatomy threatens to reawaken unconscious castration anxieties formed when sexual difference was first perceived during childhood. The mainstream cinema, she claims, provides two basic psychic mechanisms to assuage this threat: Women are either "fetishized" or "investigated."

The process of fetishization involves substituting another part of the anatomy (breasts, hair, face, legs, shoulders, backside) and making it important enough to compensate for the arousal of castration fears. Investing such body parts with power and significance supposedly exorcises the threat posed by the female anatomy, allowing heterosexual male viewers to derive pleasure from lingering close-ups, glamorous costumes, and other techniques employed in the erotic display of women. The elaborate visual compositions and stunning chiaroscuro effects director Josef von Sternberg creates with Berlin-born actress Marlene Dietrich in such movies as *Morocco* (1930) and *Dishonored* (1931), in Mulvey's view, stand as an extreme example of the general strategy of containing castration anxiety by fetishization.

The abatement of anxiety depends on ascertaining the guilt of a female character (invariably associated with castration) and asserting control over her through devaluation, punishment, or forgiveness. This strategy is typified by the concerns of classic *film noir*, in which a *femme fatale* seemingly intent on symbolically castrating or otherwise destroying the male protagonist is either killed, imprisoned, or saved if found to have redeeming qualities. Through some unconscious process, this "demystifying" of her mystery serves to contain castration anxiety by reenacting the original traumatic discovery of presumed female castration. (Just why such a psychic reenactment should alleviate rather than exacerbate emasculation fears is left unexplained.)

The kind of psychoanalytic probing Mulvey's model of spectatorship set in motion has produced an extensive literature about the possible unconscious motivations operating in the cinema and about why people go to the movies and how that experience may be organized to provide pleasure and

little fun scaring him. He is easily rendered helpless and squats on the ground and cries.

The naive and ineffectual Clay makes the drug deal so that he and his wife can pay off loan sharks and purchase a penthouse. Back at their apartment, she is delighted when he walks through the door with the money. But he makes the fatal mistake of slapping her when she berates him for having reduce anxiety. At the same time, however, this orientation has caused much consternation and debate among film scholars. Over the past fifteen years or so, its limitations and shortcomings have come under increasingly strong attack. Among other things, critics have noted that analytical frameworks stressing the male gaze tend to neglect such key factors as class status, age, race, ethnicity, and sexual preference—all of which doubtless exert a strong influence on the cinematic experience. The issue of heterosexual female pleasure at the cinema also gets short shift. After all, women not only go to the movies often but also seem to enjoy the experience.

Although movies indisputably provide plenty of opportunities for the erotic contemplation of the female face and form, even a cursory consideration of the camera's gaze confirms that it is decidedly bisexual. Male as well as female anatomy is often the focus of amatory display. Entire categories of movies, such as biblical epics, jungle adventures, and boxing films, are practically devoted to the display of the male body. In holding sway over the African jungle, Tarzan, whose first screen appearance dates back to 1918, rarely wore more than a loincloth. Former Olympic swimmer Johnny Weissmuller portrayed the legendary apeman in the movies more often than anyone else. Few opportunities were missed to show off his muscular physique. The Hollywood film, in fact, has a long history of intimate close-

A lingering close-up of Brad Pitt's "ripped abs."
(*Thelma and Louise* [1991])

ups of male facial and bodily parts—from Rudolph Valentino's smoldering stare, to Paul Newman's washboard midriff, to Sylvester Stallone's bulging biceps.

As current research makes apparent, the visually pleasurable process of watching a movie is far more complex than the simple association of male or female spectators with "masculine" or "feminine" gender positions. Assuming a more cultural and historical perspective, gender scholarship in general has veered away from a narrow psychoanalytic account and is far more concerned with issues involving genre, stardom, and censorship. In recent years, the whole penchant for psychoanalyzing cinematic expression has been subject to a great deal of criticism from various quarters. A growing number of critics and skeptics have expressed alarm that these probes into the psychic aspects of the movie experience are turning the fertile field of film studies into a barren branch of psychology.

stuffed the bank notes in his shirt. While he is taking a shower, to wash off the "stink of fear," she absconds with the ill-gotten cash.

Stopping for gas in a town in upstate New York, she decides to imbibe a bit at a local bar, where her brazenness beguiles a hick named Mike Swale (Peter Berg). Although she initially rebuffs him, he keeps her attention by boasting about his substantial male endowment. After reaching into his pants for verification, she goes back to his place. Later when she phones her lawyer, Frank Griffith (J. T. Walsh), for advice about how to handle her husband, he suggests that she encamp in the town under the cover of a new identity until things settle down. (Later sensing what she has in mind for her husband, he wonders, "Anyone check you for a heartbeat lately?")

During Bridget's sexual couplings with Mike, he assumes the "feminine" role—he is emotional, wants to talk afterwards, and longs for greater intimacy and commitment. When he begins to complain about being a sex object, she brusquely completes his sentence, telling him to "live it up." As she struts away from the bed in her stilettos, her dominating demeanor seems to dare both Mike and the viewer to desire her. This obvious flaunting of the female form, as Stella Bruzzi notes, argues against any interpretation of the scene that "would emphasize how Bridget's legs are exposed and framed with the tireless male gaze in mind."[8]

On the surface, the beguiling Bridget's goal is money and power. At heart, however, she is pure evil. Operating with perverse panache, she will engage in any subterfuge to accomplish her aims. Her most valuable asset is that nobody quite catches on to the full depth of her duplicity and deception until it is too late. This enables her to manipulate men when they are at their most vulnerable. After a private investigator (Bill Nunn) hired by Clay tracks her down, for example, she appeals to his male vanity, asking him to confirm whether the rumors about black men are true. When he foolishly obliges by releasing his seat belt to unzip his pants, she smashes her car directly into a telephone pole. The airbag protects her, while he goes head first through the windshield.

Although having told Mike in no uncertain terms that she only wants sex from their relationship, she neglects to add that he is also to be her patsy in her nefarious schemes. Deciding to dispose of her hapless husband, she persuades the malleable Mike to murder him. When he fails to follow through, she kills Clay herself by spraying mace in his mouth. She then sets up Mike to take the rap, threatening to reveal that in a drunken stupor he married a man in drag. While he vents his anger on her in exactly the manner she intended, she surreptitiously dials 911 so that his sexual assault will be recorded and verified as a rape by the authorities. This is literally the last "seduction" of Mike, the one that seals his fate. As she leaves town in a chauffeur-driven limousine, unpunished and impenitent, a sly little smile begins to curl around the corners of her sensual lips.

Minorities in Movies

For much of the twentieth century, racial and ethnic minorities were marginalized in movies, treated as comic relief or represented as villains. And when they were central to plot developments, their portrayals tended toward the negative. Native Americans were commonly characterized as little more than savages intent on massacring peaceful white settlers. Mexicans were invariably depicted either as brutal bandits or endearingly lazy cowards with comic accents. Those of eastern or southern European background were more often than not presented as simple-minded, scheming, or innately criminal. The scheming Jewish merchant, for example, appears in many early screen comedies. And movies like *Little Caesar* (1930) and *Scarface* (1932) crystallized the still prevalent stereotype of the Italian-American gangster.

Stereotyping Asians and Asian Americans

Who gets stereotyped, and how they get stereotyped, tends to reflect tensions, anxieties, or conflicts in society at large. The way east Asians tended to be represented on the screen, for example, may have helped to alleviate the fears of miscegenation reflected in such legislation as the Immigration Act of 1924, which barred Japanese and Chinese—as members of the "yellow race"— from immigrating and from becoming naturalized citizens. Sexually passive Oriental sleuths who sublimated their energies into solving mysteries enjoyed particular popularity on movie screens across the country.

Asexual Oriental Sleuths

The Charlie Chan film series of the 1930s and 1940s featured the affable Chinese American detective created in 1926 by Ohio-born pulp fiction writer Earl Derr Biggers for a *Saturday Evening Post* serial. Although his first few screen appearances were mainly peripheral (two Japanese actors initially portrayed him), the Fox Film studio soon put him front and center with *Charlie Chan Carries On* (1931), and the series took off. Swedish-born actor Warner Oland played the role seventeen times before his death in 1938. Sidney Toler, a Missourian of Scottish decent, succeeded Oland and made eleven more films in the Fox series.

In the basic formula, followed fairly strictly, Charlie Chan of the Honolulu Police Force, master detective and worldwide celebrity, happened upon a puzzling murder in an interesting or exotic locale, usually not Hawaii. Relying on brains rather than brawn, he gradually turned up incriminating clues, although his phlegmatic meanderings sometimes allowed for another murder or two to occur. At the climax, he would either set a trap using himself as the bait or, more commonly, gather the suspects together and reenact the crime in the invariably correct expectation that the culprit would be revealed through a rash act or slip of the tongue.

The redoubtable sleuth spoke stilted English with a singsong cadence ("May I extend courteous greeting?") and frequently rattled off faux-Confucian aphorisms ("Bad alibi like dead fish—can't stand the test of time").

One of his bumbling sons, who usually prefaced sentences with a "Gee, Pop," often accompanied him as he traveled the globe—from London, Egypt, Paris, Shanghai, and Monte Carlo to Reno, Panama, and Rio. Keye Luke appeared as Charlie's "number-one son" Lee eleven times. When Toler assumed the Chan mantle, "number-two son" Jimmy, played by Victor Sen Yung, usually joined him on murder investigations. Desiring to be detectives themselves, they generally got in the way and provided comic relief until their father solved the case in spite of them. Lest there be any hint of miscegenation, the libidos of these otherwise Americanized youths seemed to shut down in the presence of white women.

The greatest mystery of the series was how old Charlie himself ever managed to have children in the first place, given that he showed no signs of sexuality, let alone lust. His slow gait, drowsy manner, and halting speech patterns suggest he spent private moments with an opium pipe rather than a sex partner. In 1937, while the Charlie Chan series was still going strong, a diminutive Japanese detective named Mr. Moto, played by Hungarian-born Peter Lorre in eight films through 1939, made his screen debut. First penned by Pulitzer Prize–winning novelist J. P. Marquand in 1935, this seemingly timid but cunning character apparently sublimated his energies into crime fighting as well, because he, too, was essentially asexual.

The Nefarious Fu Manchu

When represented on the screen at all, Asian male sexuality was generally associated with the villainy of such fictional characters as the diabolical Dr. Fu Manchu. Created by Fleet Street reporter Sax Rohmer in 1911, he was featured in a series of silent British two-reelers during the 1920s starring Harry Agar Lyon. Paramount ushered him into the talkies era with *The Mysterious Dr. Fu Manchu* (1929), followed by *The Return of Dr. Fu Manchu* (1930) and *Daughter of the Dragon* (1931). None other than faux Oriental Warner Oland played the fiendish megalomaniac in all three Paramount productions. Concurrent with the latter movie's appearance in theatres across the country, the Bell Syndicate came out with a daily newspaper-strip adaptation of Rohmer's lurid tales about this Far East menace. His infamy soon spread to other venues as well, including radio and eventually television.

In all his various incarnations, the wily and nefarious Fu Manchu's singular obsession was to wipe out the " whole accursed white race" with his countless Asian hordes and win world domination. In M-G-M's *The Mask of Fu Manchu* (1932), with gaunt British-born character actor Boris Karloff (who had lately played Dr. Frankenstein's monster) as Fu Manchu, an English expedition rushes to the edge of the Gobi Desert to get the legendary golden mask and scimitar of the thirteenth-century conqueror Genghis Khan before Fu Manchu can use these relics to proclaim himself the new Khan and lead his

Fah Lo See (Myrna Loy) exhorts, "Faster! Faster!" (*The Mask of Fu Manchu* [1932])

Pan-Asian allies on a massive jihad. He plans to baptize the scimitar in the blood of an English maiden (Karen Morley), who has been dressed in a slinky white nightgown and placed supine on a stone slab in preparation for the sacrifice. "Would you like to have maidens like this for your wives?" he asks his frenzied followers. "Then conquer and breed! Kill the white man and take his women."

His equally perverse daughter, Fah Lo See (Myrna Loy), has sexual designs on a captive young Englishman (Charles Starrett). She seems especially aroused watching him, stripped to the waist, getting repeatedly whipped by her Nubian slaves. Apparently relishing every lash, she exhorts excitedly, "Faster! Faster!" Little wonder the stalwart Sir Nayland Smith (Lewis Stone)—Fu Manchu's Anglo-Saxon adversary from the British Secret Service—asks "Will we ever understand these Eastern races?"

Exquisitely conceived torture devices are one of the diabolical doctor's specialties. In *The Mask of Fu Manchu,* he has one victim tied to a table underneath a huge bell whose pealing begins to drive him mad and another strapped between converging dagger-covered walls. Even Sir Nayland Smith is bound to a pendulum for a slow descent into a pit of ravenous crocodiles. And the fifteen-episode Republic Pictures serial *Drums of Fu Manchu* (1940), with Henry Brandon as Fu Manchu, contains several devilishly devised tortures. In one episode, for instance, Fu drops the hero through a trap door into a pool where a giant octopus waits to squeeze him to death. The evil doctor's infliction of acute mental and physical pain is made all the more cruel and cold-blooded by the deference, courtesy, and decorum with which he treats his victims.

Ming the Merciless

In the mid-1930s, another fiendish Asian villain, Ming the Merciless, emerged on the silver screen. Appearing in three *Flash Gordon* serials during the decade, this despotic emperor (Charles Middleton) wanted nothing less than to take over the entire universe. His name left little doubt about his methods for achieving this grandiose goal. He likewise lusted after beautiful white women, and Flash (Buster Crabbe) repeatedly warned him to "keep his slimy hands off" companion Dale Arden (Jean Rogers). To have his way with Dale, who screamed and fainted with alarming regularity, Ming even tried putting her into a trance. Such cunning and sinister characters, representing Eastern evil and treachery incarnate, could only have intensified racial prejudice and exacerbated long-existing American anxiety about the "yellow peril"—the alleged danger that Western societies could be overwhelmed by numerically superior Oriental peoples.

Stereotyping African Americans

Almost from the time movies were first made, people of West African origin were represented as servile, ridiculous, or downright dangerous. A screen version of Harriet Beecher Stowe's 1852 novel *Uncle Tom's Cabin* appeared as early as 1903. An anonymous white actor made up in "blackface" played the obsequious Uncle Tom who, despite unspeakably cruel treatment, never wavers in his devotion to the young daughter of his white master. A buffoonish black couple's romance is played strictly for laughs in *Wooing and Wedding of a Coon* (1905). The foolish black protagonist of *The Masher* (1907) fancies himself a white ladies' man. He is rebuffed by all but a mysterious veiled woman who, much to his chagrin, turns out to be black.

Bestial Blacks in *The Birth of a Nation*

Bestial black characterizations reached an apotheosis of sorts in *The Birth of a Nation* (1915). The focus of the movie is on two white families—the abolitionist Stonemans of Pennsylvania and the slave-owning Camerons of South Carolina—whose lives are torn apart by the war and its aftermath. At their modest Piedmont plantation, the genteel Cameron family is terrorized by a troop of black raiders, and the once idyllic South undergoes "ruin, devastation, rapine, and pillage," according to the narrative subtitles. Both families lose sons on the battlefield while the daughters face the new black menace to white maidenhood. (In reality white men posed a far greater threat to black maidenhood in the antebellum South. Because slaves were denied any rights, a black woman molested by a white man had no legal recourse. Virtually every plantation produced children of mixed race, most of whom were simply worked and sold like all other slaves.)

Fervid racism and fear of miscegenation permeate the section dealing with the Reconstruction period and the rise of the Ku Klux Klan. We see blacks "drunk with wine and power" and "crazy with joy" engaged in a reign of terror, shoving and taunting white people and flogging "faithful colored servants" senseless. We also see them holding placards promoting "equal marriage." (In the aftermath of the Civil War, and well into the twentieth century, anxieties about white women coupling with black men touched as nothing else the raw nerve of racism. A black man in the South who merely whistled at a white woman ran the risk of being lynched.)

No white woman apparently is safe from this black onslaught. Pursued by an emancipated house slave (Walter Long), young Flora Cameron (Mae Marsh) leaps from a precipice, carrying her honor through "the opal gates of death." This leads her anguished brother Ben (Henry B. Walthall), an organizer of the white-garbed vigilante group (actually started in Pulaski, Tennessee), to avenge her death and punish the despoilers of the antebellum Southern way of life.

A particularly nasty scene opens with a still photograph of an empty South Carolina state legislature. This image slowly dissolves as the chamber comes to life full of raucous black lawmakers, bare feet on desks, swilling liquor and eating fried chicken. After these legislators enact a statute providing for interracial marriage, a group of blacks on the assembly floor is shown ogling something above them. The camera then cuts to reveal the object of this leering: a group of frightened-looking white women in the gallery.

Blacks are represented as faithful servants, slothful boors, or sex-crazed savages. As an added insult, white actors in blackface played all the major black roles. Actual blacks appear in only a few scenes: when the Stoneman boys, visiting the Camerons, are taken out to the plantation to see contented field hands picking cotton and dancing merrily in the slave quarters, and during the boisterous session of the postwar South Carolina legislature. Strapping Elmo Lincoln, soon to achieve fame as the first screen Tarzan, played White Arm Joe, the stalwart village blacksmith's (Wallace Reid) chief opponent when he takes on a barroom full of lawless blacks.

The really vile characters are "mulatto," from the Spanish word for a young mule, seeming to suggest that interracial coupling invariably produces inferior progeny. Paterfamilias Austin Stoneman (Ralph Lewis), a radical Republican leader in the U.S. House of Representatives, is shown to be sexually obsessed with his vengeful mulatto housekeeper, Lydia Brown (Mary Alden). Acting under her diabolical influence, he brings his henchman, mulatto Silas Lynch (George Siegmann), to political power. Filled with whiskey and lustful craving,

The slaves on the Cameron family's Piedmont plantation apparently couldn't be happier. (*The Birth of a Nation* [1915])

the malicious Lynch later tries to force the congressman's blond, virginal daughter Elsie (Lillian Gish) into marriage as the barbarous troops of his "black empire" run amok in the streets, indiscriminately assaulting and killing whites.

In scenes building toward the suspense-filled climax, an inflamed black militia pursues kindly Dr. Cameron (Spottiswoode Aitken), patriarch of the much-put-upon clan, who has been rescued from arrest by two loyal black servants (referred to as "faithful souls"). He and his group seek shelter in a cabin with two ex-Union soldiers. While the black militia surrounds them, other blacks continue rioting at Piedmont. Meanwhile, Elsie Stoneman has been bound and gagged after resisting Lynch's advances. Things look bleak until the noble knights of the Ku Klux Klan, "the organization that saved the South from the anarchy of black rule," ride to the rescue under the leadership of Ben Cameron. Elsie is saved, and the renegade ex-slaves are pushed back, beaten, and killed. Northern and Southern whites are once again united "in defense of their Aryan birthright."

Asexual Black Servants of the Studio Era

After this movie's depiction of feral and frenzied blacks lusting for white female flesh provoked widespread protests and calls for increased censorship, Hollywood tended to eschew such brutal portrayals in subsequent produc-

Stepin Fetchit in a publicity shot. His off-screen existence apparently was nothing like that of the characters he played. Stories abound about his flamboyant lifestyle—the lavish parties, the six houses attended by sixteen Chinese servants, the $2000 cashmere suits imported from India, and the twelve luxury automobiles.

tions. During the 1920s and 1930s, black characters were typically kindly souls, slow moving (except when they danced), adept at only menial tasks, and happy to let the white folks manage the world. They rarely showed any signs of sexual desire.

When black actors sought work in Hollywood, they were commonly cast in such roles as maid, mammy, manservant, and comic sidekick. The best-known black movie performer of the early 1930s was Lincoln Perry, who adopted the professional name Stepin Fetchit. From 1929 to 1935, his career peak, he appeared in some twenty-six movies, often working on as many as three or four at a time. In such pictures as *The Ghost Talks* (1929), *David Harum* (1934), *Stand Up and Cheer* (1934), and *Charlie Chan in Egypt* (1935), he lent life to stylized characters who were invariably dim-witted, tongue-tied, slow gaited, and lackadaisical. These depictions were all the more damaging because he was able to do them so convincingly. His success spawned a bevy of black imitators who found steady screen work at a time when his career was on the wane.

Some black actors were able to bring quiet strength and sensitivity to even stereotypical roles. Former drummer and bandleader Dooley Wilson, for example, managed to invest Rick Blaine's sidekick Sam in *Casablanca* with a

Dooley Wilson as Sam in *Casablanca* (1942). At the time he tested for this part, Wilson (his nickname came from singing Irish songs in "whiteface") was under contract to Paramount, where he made $350 a week primarily playing porters. To borrow him, Warner Bros. paid Paramount $500 a week for a guaranteed seven weeks. (As was standard practice, Wilson saw nothing of the extra $150 a week).

high degree of dignity. But this character is only a slightly enhanced version of the asexual black servant so prevalent in this era. There's more than a touch of Uncle Tom in his self-effacing service to "Mister Richard" and his humble demeanor around "Miss Ilsa." His subservience is reinforced by remarks like Ilsa's slighting reference to the "boy at the piano."

Reinforcing Stereotypes Across Media

Stereotypes are usually reinforced across popular art forms. One of the most popular radio shows of the 1930s and 1940s was *Amos 'n' Andy,* which featured two white ex-vaudevillians, Freeman Gosden and Charles Correll, in blackface. (The motif composed for Lillian Gish's character in *The Birth of a Nation* became the radio program's theme music.) All of the characters were direct descendants of the burnt-cork comics of the antebellum minstrel shows. Amos was depicted as trusting, simple, and unsophisticated, while Andy was slow and shiftless. The two owned and operated the Fresh-Air Taxi-

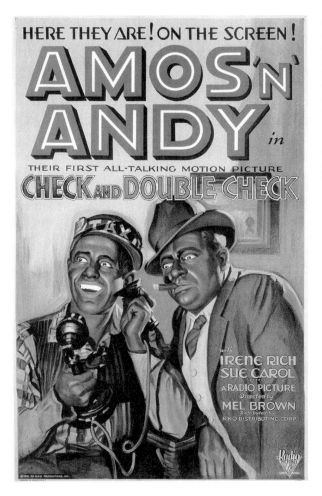

A poster for *Check and Double Check* (1930). This Amos 'n' Andy film featured musical numbers by Duke Ellington's orchestra. At the time, the black bandleader and composer called the movie a "crowning point" in his career. Although this was hardly the case, the association with Amos 'n' Andy did greatly expand the audience for his music.

cab Company, whose assets included one broken-down topless automobile, one desk, and one swivel chair for the president to "rest his brains." The action often took place at a lodge presided over by a scheming fellow called "the Kingfish," who was prone to malapropisms and syntactical mishaps.

In *Check and Double Check* (1930), Gosden and Correll brought their blackface characterizations to the silver screen, but they failed to match their radio success. Perhaps the characters they created were more appealing when audiences could imagine them as actually being black. The imaginary world of Amos, Andy, Kingfish, and the other characters was a far cry from the harsh reality of ghetto life. In the segregated society of the period, however, many people were doubtlessly unaware of the disparity. From our perspective, it is not hard to see how such black stereotypes served to legitimate segregation and discrimination.

Positive Black Stereotypes

Disruptions in society can bring about major shifts in stereotypes. The screen image of blacks, for instance, began to change during the Second World War. The war's emotional intensity seemed to exacerbate long-existing prejudices and racial tensions. The summer of 1943 saw the eruption of violent race riots in Detroit and other cities, which not only hindered war production but also provided fodder for Nazi propaganda mills. Such racial confrontations put a national spotlight on the bigotry still plaguing the land. Not only were blacks denied decent housing and high-paying wartime civilian jobs, they were discriminated against in the armed forces as well. Although the United States was purportedly fighting against the racist doctrines of the Nazis, the American military itself was racially segregated.

Despite this harsh reality, the wartime screen image of racial relations was mostly of an America whose citizens respected one another's differences and worked together to defeat a common enemy. In the ethnically diverse military units depicted in such pictures as *Bataan* (1943), bigotry, racism, and discrimination were—if not totally absent—at least easily negotiable. This movie's rag-tag fighting team consists of a black, a Latino, and two Filipinos, as well as a West Pointer, an air force officer, a working-class sergeant, and a young sailor—all four of whom are white. The black demolitions expert (Kenneth Spencer) is shown as an especially committed fighter who willingly sacrifices his life for God and country. He not only leads the group in a prayer service for their fallen captain but also later saves one of his white comrades from walking into enemy fire. All die valiantly in their attempt to delay faceless hordes of cruel Japanese from crossing a key bridge.

Harmonious racial relations were presented in wartime radio as well. In 1942 the popular daytime serial *Our Gal Sunday* added the character of a black soldier. Returning intermittently during furloughs, he functioned primarily to provoke conversations between Sunday and her husband about the loyalty of black servicemen to the United States. That same year, another daytime serial, *The Romance of Helen Trent,* contained an extended episode involving the heroine of the title, who was gravely injured while attempting to save a truck loaded with war goods. She was rescued and treated by "a Negro doctor." In gratitude, she later found the doctor a job as a physician in a war plant. This plot development opened the way for several more discussions among the characters about the competency, loyalty, and patience of black Americans.

Super Sidney

The wartime plotline of a noble black person winning over whites and making them feel better for the experience continued well into the postwar period. Few actors played this new stereotype of black nobility with greater success than Sidney Poitier, who made his screen debut in *No Way Out* (1950) as a dedicated doctor (gifted black actors Ruby Dee and Ossie Davis debuted as well). In the final scene, his character even seems to gain grudging respect from the sniveling white gangster (Richard Widmark) who had been baiting him mercilessly and stirring up racial conflict.

During the next two decades, Poitier played so many noble and ingratiating characters that the media dubbed him "Super Sidney." His role in *The Defiant Ones* (1958) as a convict on the run chained to a racist redneck (Tony Curtis) earned him his first Academy Award nomination for best actor. In the final reel, as might be expected, Poitier's character sacrifices his last chance of escaping to assist his now-crippled fellow fugitive. Cradling him his arms, he sings W. C. Handy's "Long Gone" as the sheriff and his posse approach. Five years later, Poitier won an Oscar for *Lilies of the Field* (1963), the sentimental tale of a kindly itinerant handyman who helps a group of East German nuns build a chapel in Arizona. By 1968 the talented thespian had become the number-one box office star in the country.

For the most part, Poitier was cast in movies that revolved around racial issues. In the racially charged *In the Heat of the Night* (1967), he played Philadelphia homicide detective Virgil Tibbs, whose core anger is contained by considerable reason and intellect. In the course of investigating a murder in a southern town, Tibbs is constantly confronted with virulent racism. After the local police chief (Rod Steiger) treats him condescendingly, he responds with a line that doubtlessly resonated well beyond movie theatres: "They call me MISTER Tibbs." Of course, the manifestly decent Tibbs ultimately triumphs. He not only uncovers the murderer's identity but also wins the friendship and admiration of the bigoted police chief. A huge box office success, *In the Heat of the Night* paved the way for many more movies with strong black characters.

In the latter half of the 1960s, rioting erupted in the nation's inner-city ghettos, slain leader Malcolm X assumed almost mythic status, and a black power movement gained great momentum. In this context, the kind of brotherly-love pictures Poitier specialized in came under increasing attack for being out of tune with the racial tenor of times. Black and white critics alike took the actor to task for his role in *Guess Who's Coming to Dinner,* which practically parodies his saintly screen persona.

Released in 1967, the same year the U.S. Supreme Court struck down anti-miscegenation laws, this saccharine saga gingerly tackled the still touchy topic of interracial romance. An idealistic young white woman (Katharine Houghton) shocks her affluent suburban parents (Spencer Tracy and Katharine Hepburn) by bringing home the black man (Poitier) she wants to marry. Although everything is thrown into turmoil, the cards are clearly stacked in favor of easy resolution. As if good looks, courtly charm, and impeccable

Young Joey Drayton (Katharine Houghton) brings her thirty-seven-year-old fiancé, John Wade Prentice (Sidney Poitier), home to meet her parents. Will the sharp disparity in their ages be a cause for concern? (*Guess Who's Coming to Dinner* [1967])

manners were not enough, Poitier's prospective son-in-law character is also a brilliant doctor in line for a Nobel Prize. All is worked out after a meeting of the interracial couple's perplexed parents. (The peculiarly passionless couple's single kiss is shown reflected in a taxicab's rearview mirror.)

Although often overly contrived and idealistic, Poitier's screen characters nonetheless provided a strong challenge to the negative black stereotypes that had prevailed in the movie industry since its inception. Moreover, the extraordinary box office success of his movies helped to break down racial barriers in Hollywood and broaden the range of roles open to black actors of succeeding generations. Beginning in the 1970s, as a successful producer and director, he also provided greater opportunities for blacks behind the scenes.

Intergalactic Stereotypes: *The Phantom Menace*

The old negative stereotypes still enjoy some cinematic currency. Among the digital denizens of the faraway galaxy in *Star Wars: Episode I—The Phantom Menace* (1999) are several familiar racial and ethnic representations. The dim-witted, computer-animated amphibian Jar Jar Binks, with his big lips, bulging eyes and a wide nose, comes right out of Hollywood's bag of black caricatures. His ineptness and cowardice in the face of danger is a running joke throughout the movie. He steps in animal dung, gets his tongue stuck in an electrical socket, lards his speech with malapropisms, and says things like "Yousa Jedi not all yousa cracked up to be" and "Why mesa always da one?" (The way he

The widely reviled Jar Jar Binks. Of all the negative stereotypes that permeate *The Phantom Menace* (1999), none has caused more consternation than Binks. The stupidest, most servile character in the movie, he is a computer-generated throwback to the demeaning Stepin Fetchit roles of the 1930s.

says "mesa" sounds suspiciously like "master.") His floppy ears resemble dreadlocks, and his vocal inflections suggest a West Indian patois (black stage performer Ahmed Best provided the voice of this Rastafarian amalgam of negative screen stereotypes).

Other negative stereotypes are also evident in this movie. A fat, buffoonish character named Boss Nass, seemingly a caricature of a stereotypical African chieftain, rules the Gungan tribe to which Jar Jar Binks belongs. (Commenting on his planetary neighbors, the Naboo, Nass notes: "Dey tink dey so smartee, dey tink dey brains so big.") Most Gungans wear flared trousers and share Jar Jar's bouncing lope. Few ethnicities escape heavy-handed stereotyping. An intergalactic "yellow peril" is conjured up by the slit-eyed, faux-Asian-accented Neimoidians. These cunning and duplicitous hive-dwellers have exceptional organizing abilities and command a labyrinthine organization of bureaucrats and trade officials.

When the Jedi knights attempt to repair their broken spaceship, an insectlike junk dealer named Watto stymies them. He has a hooked nose that curves to his chin, speaks with an accent that carries distinct echoes of Yiddish, and has acquired a small fortune in currency, slaves, and other possessions through shrewd deal making and well-placed wagers. Only through the bravery of young Anakin Skywalker (Jake Lloyd) do the Jedi get the parts they need. The towheaded youngster is emancipated but separated from his mother, who still belongs to the money-grubbing Watto.

The Last Act

A wide range of factors shapes screen content and character types. For much of the twentieth century, the motion picture medium was not fully protected by the free speech and free press provisions of the First Amendment to the U.S. Constitution. As a result, moviemakers had to be especially attentive to the protectors of public morality—government agencies, civic and religious groups, and segments of the mainstream press. In the final chapter, the focus is on how public demands for censorship, and the private constraints instituted to accommodate them, influenced virtually every aspect of the Hollywood style.

Notes

1. For example, see James Naremore, *Acting in the Cinema* (Berkeley: University of California Press, 1988).
2. Octave Mannoni, *Clefs pour l'Imaginaire ou l'Autre Scene* (Paris: Eds. le Seuil, 1969), pp. 163–164.
3. See Garry Wills, *John Wayne's America: The Politics of Celebrity* (New York: Simon & Schuster, 1997).
4. Cited in Peter Manso, *Brando: The Biography* (New York: Hyperion, 1994), p. 105.
5. See David Garfield, *A Player's Place: The Story of the Actors Studio* (New York: Macmillan, 1980), pp. 94–95.
6. Molly Haskell, *From Reverence to Rape: The Treatment of Women in the Movies,* 2nd ed. (Chicago: University of Chicago Press, 1987), p. 4.
7. Laura Mulvey "Visual Pleasure and the Narrative Cinema," *Screen* 16, 3, Autumn 1975, pp. 6–18; reprinted in Mulvey, *Visual and Other Pleasures* (Bloomington: Indiana University Press, 1989). This volume also contains two reconsiderations of her original essay.
8. Stella Bruzzi, *Undressing Cinema: Clothing and Identity in the Movies* (New York: Routledge, 1997), p. 128.

Censoring Screen Content

More than for any other art form, the creation of movies is rooted in the realism of dollars and cents. Merely to recoup the huge expense involved in its production, let alone achieve what the trade paper *Variety* calls a "boffo" box office, the typical movie must attract millions of people. This economic reality, coupled with a lack of full constitutional protection for freedom of expression in movies, caused Hollywood to tread cautiously throughout much of the twentieth century. This final chapter traces the growing demands for official censorship of screen content, the self-regulatory measures taken to stave them off, and the virtual collapse of most legal strictures over movies in the emerging electronic environment.

Early Efforts at Content Control

Moving pictures were a source of moral concern from the outset. As early as 1896, the presentation of a short film titled *The May Irwin–John C. Rice Kiss* (1896) caused outrage in many locales. It featured middle-aged actors May Irwin and John C. Rice performing the climactic kissing scene from their Broadway hit, *The Widow Jones*. Their kiss was done in a close-up, creating a sense of intimacy not possible on the stage, where actors remain relatively remote from the audience. (Even at this early time, there seemed to be an awareness that an essential part of the

May Irwin and John C. Rice kiss for the camera. (*The May Irwin–John C. Rice Kiss* [1896])

cinema's appeal has to do, in a certain sense, with voyeurism.) For an irate observer in Chicago, this "prolonged pasturing" came "near to being indecent in its emphasized vulgarity." In a letter to the editor of the New Orleans *Daily Item,* another angry citizen called it "repulsive to the clean of mind."[1]

Despite such protestations, or perhaps because of them, this film was in big demand across the nation. Its profitability prompted the production of scores of risqué and titillating trifles, a situation that raised the wrath of would-be censors concerned about the presumed power of such depictions to arouse impure thoughts and provoke immoral activity. In New York City in 1897, a showing of the short film *Orange Blossoms,* which featured a pantomime of a young bride preparing for her wedding night by deftly disrobing yet revealing very little flesh, was halted by a court order. The presiding judge denounced the film as an "outrage on public decency."[2]

Adding to the agitation of government agencies, early films sometimes attacked authority. For example, Edwin Porter's provocative little film *The Kleptomaniac* (1905) dwelt on the unfairness of the American judicial system. It contrasts the actions and fates of two women of very different economic status. We see first a wealthy woman shoplifting a few trinkets from a department store and then see a poor woman impulsively filching some bread to feed her family. Both are caught and arrested. In the final courtroom scene, the poor woman is sentenced as a criminal while the wealthy women is discharged as a victim of kleptomania. An epilogue comments ironically on these events: A blindfolded figure of justice is shown holding up a scale. On one side of the balance is a bag of gold; on the other, a loaf of bread. The balance moves in favor of the gold. The blindfold is removed, and the figure of the justice is revealed as having only one eye, which is fixed firmly on the gold.

Some moviemakers even suggested a connection between poverty and capitalist greed. In director D. W. Griffith's *A Corner in Wheat* (1909), for example, a grain speculator hoards wheat to elevate its price while workers, farmers, and shopkeepers go hungry. This inequity is punctuated in a stunning shot juxtaposition of the wheat tycoon gorging himself at a sumptuous banquet and the other characters waiting on a long bread line. Such social injustices, experienced by many moviegoers, must have carried a potent cultural charge when they were magnified and dramatized on movie screens around the country.

Pressure on Exhibitors

When movies moved to storefront nickelodeons and larger theatres, the growing agitation they caused was intensified by the fact that many of the key players in this industry were Jews with eastern European roots. For the largely Protestant establishment, threatened by the convulsive sociocultural changes associated with immigration, industrialization and urbanization underway at the turn of the century, movie houses and the people running them became a symbol of all the forces eroding the country's moral values. Theatre operators were especially inviting targets. Unlike many other perceived social dangers, they could be subject to direct pressure by the authorities.

A massive assault was mounted against exhibitors by agents of social control (politicians, police, religious leaders, and the like). On Christmas Day 1908, New York City's mayor closed the more than 600 movie houses under his jurisdiction. The stated purpose of this order was to inspect the dwellings for safety hazards. But under pressure from local church leaders, the mayor announced that he would issue new licenses only on the condition that exhibitors agreed in writing to remain closed on Sundays. He also threatened to revoke the licenses of exhibitors who showed films that tended to degrade the morals of the community. Led by nickelodeon operator William Fox, exhibitors swiftly challenged the closings in court. The mayor was enjoined from imposing more stringent controls, and the movie houses were allowed to reopen. But many more confrontations followed.

Industry Self-Censorship

In an effort to forestall official censorship, the Motion Picture Patents Company (MPPC) joined forces in 1909 with the People's Institute, a reform organization led by Protestant upper-middle-class New Yorkers. The result was the National Board of Censorship (changed in 1915 to the less foreboding National Board of Review). The board comprised social workers, educators, church people, and the like. Authority rested in a General Committee of twenty members chosen from civic and educational organizations. Several subcommittees, selected by the General Committee, previewed and evaluated movies to determine their suitability for public viewing.

Judgment of a particular movie was based on the presumed effects its contents would have on a large, heterogeneous audience. The MPPC producers agreed to submit all their movies (about two-thirds of total industry output) to the board for approval prior to releasing them, and to excise any footage found to be objectionable, subject to a right of appeal to the General Committee. Reviewed movies were listed in the board's weekly bulletin and classified as "Passed" or "Passed with changes as specified" or "Condemned." Mayors, police chiefs, and civic groups from all over the nation became bulletin subscribers. In various cities, local censorship authorities used the board's ratings as a guide for their own evaluation of movies.

By 1914 the board claimed to be reviewing 95 percent of the total film output in the country. Producers who gained its seal of approval—an open pair of scissors superimposed on a four-point star—were generally assured that their movies would be shown in most locales without official censorship boards. But the voluntary review board came under increasing attack for its allegedly liberal policies and opposition to official censorship. Many observers began to question whether its function was to oversee or overlook.

Pressure for official censorship mounted following the release of D. W. Griffith's epic *The Birth of a Nation* (1915). Although it was a huge success at the box office, the movie's glorification of the Ku Klux Klan and ridicule of the desire of blacks to attain political rights riled many spectators and brought bitter protests from groups like the fledgling National Association for the Advancement of Colored People (NAACP). Riots and interracial strife followed its release in several cities, thus strengthening calls for greater control over what could be shown on the screen.

In an effort to appease his critics, Griffith grudgingly excised over 500 feet of film from the movie, reducing its total number of shots to 1375. This footage has never been recovered, but it reportedly includes a scene of white women being sexually assaulted by blacks and an epilogue advocating the deportation of blacks to Africa. Despite such cuts, protests and censorship action followed the movie around the country. A number of states and cities decided to ban it altogether.

THE PROVOCATIVE MOVIES OF OSCAR MICHEAUX

Beyond the bans and the protests, D. W. Griffith's racist representations in *The Birth of a Nation* contributed to the creation of a separate industry that produced movies aimed at black audiences. By the mid-1920s, film companies run by blacks (often bankrolled by whites) had sprung up in such diverse locations as Jacksonville, St. Louis, Omaha, Philadelphia, Chicago, New York, and Los Angeles. One of the most prolific of these filmmakers was Oscar Micheaux. Between 1918 and 1948, he made over forty feature films.

Like other black filmmakers of the day, the multitalented Micheaux toiled on the tightest of budgets. In many of his surviving films, the acting is amateurish, the lighting and editing crude, and the dramatic structure disjointed. Nonetheless, he was sometimes able to present racial issues and social conflicts in powerfully graphic ways that aroused anger and anxiety among both blacks and whites. As a recent study suggests, his most provocative work was done in the era of speechless cinema.[3] And many of the pictures he made during this period regularly ran into censorship difficulties.

In addition to depicting the Ku Klux Klan's intimidation techniques, Micheaux's early movies dealt with such sensitive topics as white squeamishness about interracial romance and the rampant lynching in the South. Moreover, he presented not only blacks as heroes but also whites as villains. He even had black actors performing in "whiteface" makeup. At the same time, a number of his black characters were far from admirable. Working within the confines of melodrama, he exposed such problems in the black community as the behavior of dishonest politicians and hypocritical ministers.

As a study of Micheaux's conflicts with censors documents, from the outset the content of his movies troubled the agents of social control.[4] To meet the demands of Chicago's biracial censor board, he had to make multiple changes in *The Symbol of the Unconquered* (1920), which presents a scathing portrayal of the Ku Klux Klan as a greedy mob of thieving misfits. (An incomplete print of this thought-to-be-lost film was repatriated in 1992 from Belgium's national film archives.) Impenetrably intricate at times, perhaps owing to missing sections, it features a diligent black prospector (Walker Thompson) who discovers oil on his property. His good fortune draws the resentment of a self-loathing, lighter-skinned black man (Lawrence Chenault). Passing himself off as white, he conspires with members of the night-riding vigilante group to secure the oil-rich land through vicious intimidation.

Censors were especially concerned about the film's interracial elements. Exploring artificial color barriers, its romantic line of action involves a fair-skinned black woman (Iris Hall) who has moved to the northwest to occupy a cabin on land inherited from her dying grandfather. Amid efforts to locate the place, she meets and falls in love with the honest and heroic prospector. However, he is afraid to admit his feelings for her because he wrongly thinks she's white. In an upbeat ending, he and his beloved wind up rich and happy, and the hooded terrorists are subdued.

In concessions to censors and cautious exhibitors, Micheaux often reworked his movies, sometimes even adding elaborate and confusing scenes to win approval. A bogus black preacher, played by the great Paul Robeson (making his screen debut),

(continued on next page)

THE PROVOCATIVE MOVIES OF OSCAR MICHEAUX (*CONTINUED*)

Posters promote movies that present very different versions of the Ku Klux Klan's vigilante justice.

is the central character in *Body and Soul* (1925). He extorts payoffs from the local gambling house and watering hole, exploits the generosity of the devoted women in his congregation, and even rapes a young female member of his flock (Julia Theresa Russell). In the surviving print, undoubtedly shaped by the sensibilities of censors, the apparent sexual assault improbably proves

State-Imposed Constraints

At the very time the cinema was becoming an agent of ideas and a source of social controversy, government officials were subjecting it to increasingly intense scrutiny. Movie censorship boards in the United States had begun to spring up soon after the turn of the century. The first municipal ordinance, passed in Chicago in 1907, empowered the chief of police to issue permits for

The bogus preacher (Paul Robeson) grins lasciviously in the rape scene from *Body and Soul* (1925).

to be part of a nightmarish dream sequence. This allows for a happy and uplifting ending in which the still inviolate young woman marries the minister's high-minded twin brother (also played by Robeson).

One of Micheaux's most controversial films was *Within Our Gates* (1920). The principal focus is on an idealistic young schoolteacher (Evelyn Preer) with a scarred past striving to bring education to disadvantaged children and find romantic fulfillment. (No copies of this movie were believed to survive until a print was discovered in 1988 at the National Film Archive in Madrid, Spain.) The events depicted in the first two-thirds of the story are overshadowed by a lengthy flashback revealing the shocking details of what happened to her and her family as a result of virulent racism.

Her adoptive father (William Stark), a sharecropper struggling to free himself from economic bondage, is falsely accused of killing a white plantation owner (Ralph Johnson). A lynch mob of ordinary townspeople—men, women, and even children—organizes to exact vigilante justice on him and his family. The young woman's little brother manages to escape on horseback, but her parents are brutally beaten and then hanged for a crime they didn't commit. In the intervening time, the plantation owner's brother (Grant Gorman) comes upon her in a nearby cabin. He tries to rape her only to recoil in shock when a mark on her chest reveals that she is his own offspring. The use of parallel editing effectively links the lynching and the sexual attack, suggesting that both are employed as instruments of terror against the black community.

Black and white church and community leaders alike tried to prevent showings of *Within Our Gates,* fearing that its graphic scenes of lynching and attempted rape would rekindle the racial violence that had erupted in dozens of American cities in the summer of 1919. (In Chicago, where some of the worst rioting occurred, some 6000 federal troops were called in to stop the bloodshed.) In the heated racial climate of the post–World War I period, fueled by fierce rivalry among whites and blacks for jobs, the movie was subject to severe censorship and even banned outright in some cities.

the exhibition of movies. He was invested with the right to withhold permission for those movies deemed immoral or obscene. State censorship boards began to appear beginning in 1911. The first state to pass a censorship law was Pennsylvania; Ohio and Kansas followed suit in 1913, and Maryland did so in 1916. The personal predilections of state and local authorities frequently provided standards for judgment. A confrontation with a censor could be costly, resulting in mutilated prints, adverse publicity, and lost revenue.

Censors had a lot of latitude in the area of obscenity, a legal category that is ill defined to the present day. In an 1896 decision, the U.S. Supreme Court accepted a trial judge's use of the British "*Hicklin* rule" for determining whether a work is obscene.[5] In the 1868 case from which this rule emerged, the British court defined obscenity as that which has the *tendency* "to deprave and corrupt those whose minds are open to such immoral influences, and into whose hands a publication of this sort may fall." Under this standard, an entire work could be suppressed even if only a few of its passages were found to be obscene. The U.S. Supreme Court's recognition of the *Hicklin* rule made the "most susceptible person" criterion for determining obscenity the accepted one in both federal and state courts in the early twentieth century. (The high court didn't officially abandon this standard until 1957, when it declared in *Butler v. Michigan* that it unconstitutionally restricted adults to only those materials suitable for children.[6])

Early in 1915, the Detroit-based Mutual Film Corporation challenged the constitutionality of the state censorship commissions of Ohio and Kansas in a trio of cases that went all the way to the U.S. Supreme Court.[7] Among other things, Mutual claimed that the statutes under which these commissions operated infringed on the liberties of speech, opinion, and press guaranteed by both the state constitutions and the First Amendment to the U.S. Constitution. In the lead case, from Ohio, the high court ignored Mutual's reliance on the federal Constitution (the First Amendment didn't become applicable to the states until 1925) and concentrated instead on the pertinent provision of the Ohio constitution guaranteeing freedom of speech and press.

Although acknowledging the importance of freedom of expression, the justices found little that linked movies to the traditions of the print media. Movies, they noted, "may be used for evil," that "a prurient interest may be excited and appealed to," and that some things "should not have pictorial representation in public places to all audiences." They conceded that movies were "mediums of thought," but then so were many other things, such as "the theater, the circus and all other shows and spectacles." After explaining that a long history of precedent permitted extending police power over such forms of entertainment, the nine justices unanimously concluded: "It cannot be put out of view that the exhibition of moving pictures is a business pure and simple, originated and conducted for profit, like other spectacles, not to be regarded, nor intended to be regarded by the Ohio constitution, we think, as part of the press of the country or as organs of public opinion."

In the Kansas case, the outcome was the same. To the argument that the statute "violates the Bill of Rights of the United States and the State of Kansas," the high court responded that censorship of movies did not "abridge the liberty of opinion." Movies were mere entertainment, and therefore not entitled to legal protection. If censors didn't like what they saw, they could cut a movie to death. These decisions served as the rule of law for the next thirty-seven years and had a profound effect on the moral parameters of the emerging idiom of cinematic expression that came to characterize moviemaking in the United States.

Domestic Discord

The Red Scare

During the First World War, the National Association of the Motion Picture Industry (NAMPI), which had garnered lots of government goodwill, averted most state and all federal attempts at movie censorship. In the postwar period, however, its attempts at self-regulation did little to diminish demands for greater government control of screen content. This was a politically turbulent time in American life. The success of the Bolshevik Revolution in Russia, in which a small political party had seized control of a backward, despotic country in the name of the proletariat, impelled anarchists, communists, and other radical factions in the United States to create their own revolutionary movement. Although disputes and differences negated any possibility of unified action, the "Red menace" was nevertheless blamed for race riots, mob violence, worker walkouts, and a host of other domestic problems stemming from complex causes.

Rumors of a radical conspiracy to overthrow the U.S. government became rampant after brown-paper packages containing bombs addressed to prominent citizens were discovered in U.S. post offices. State legislatures, patriotic organizations, and business groups demanded that the federal government take decisive action. The attorney general of the United States, whose own home was damaged by a bomb, launched a series of raids and roundups in which thousands of suspected revolutionaries were arrested and held behind bars for days or weeks—often without any specific indication of the charges against them.

Fear fed prejudice and intolerance. Blacks, Jews, Catholics, and other minorities of all sorts came under suspicion for not being "100 percent American." The Ku Klux Klan, whose membership had swelled to well over 4 million by 1924, was in the vanguard of the assault on ethnic and religious diversity. When first reorganized in 1915, the group's chief goal was white supremacy, but over time, as it grew and spread from the Deep South to the Midwest and the Pacific coast, Jews and especially Roman Catholics became a principal target in most localities. It drew into its white-sheeted fold mostly the poorly educated and less disciplined elements of the white Protestant community. D. W. Griffith's *The Birth of a Nation* often served as a recruiting tool.

Movies commonly conformed to the strongest currents in society. At the height of the Red scare, Hollywood turned out several anticommunist features. On screens across the country, revolting Reds replaced hideous Huns as arch villains. Typical of this output is *Dangerous Hours* (1920), whose young, university-educated hero is inspired by the Russian revolutionaries he has read. In his zeal, he supports a strike at a silk mill and is recruited into a ring intent on sabotaging American industry. The odious Red Army officer who commands the conspirators is, a title card tells us, "carried away with a wild dream of planting the scarlet seed of Terrorism in American soil." The idealistic young man eventually realizes that he has been duped and exposes the plotters.

Shifting Sexual Mores

Even as civil strife and suspicion spread, an incongruously impatient and in-decorous spirit seemed to possess the population—especially the young. F. Scott Fitzgerald, oracle of what came to be called the Jazz Age, saw the whole of society going hedonistic. The "flapper" with her short skirt and hair and her painted face competed with the virginal girl next door as the feminine ideal. Although Prohibition was the law of the land, bathtub gin flowed freely, and speakeasies sprang up everywhere. The saxophone replaced the violin as the dominant instrument at dances. Young and old alike intimately embraced as they moved in syncopation to the sensual sounds. The roar of automobile engines sounded a clarion call to the libido as well. Many affluent young people apparently thought nothing of jumping into the car and driving off—away from the prying eyes of parents, chaperons, and neighbors.

Most moviemakers were more concerned about shifting sexual mores than communist-inspired subversion. The 1920s saw the production of hundreds of movies that flaunted sex, condoned the pursuit of pleasure, and ridiculed the Victorian-era virtues of chastity and fidelity. The movie titles alone from this period suggest lasciviousness: *Red Hot Romance* (1922), *Virgin Paradise* (1921), *The Way Women Love* (1920), *Scrambled Wives* (1921), *The Fourteenth Lover* (1921), *A Shocking Night* (1921), and many others. Seldom did these movies provide anywhere near as much as their titles promised, but there was enough moral turpitude in evidence on screen to prompt calls for increased censorship from press and pulpit alike.

Director Cecil B. DeMille set the standard for cinematic salaciousness. In such confections as *Old Wives for New* (1918), *Don't Change Your Husband* (1919), *Male and Female* (1919), *Why Change Your Wife?* (1920), *Forbidden Fruit* (1921), and *The Affairs of Anatol* (1922), he dramatized stories of infidelity and illicit passion in an atmosphere of scanty costumes, lavish sets, and bathrooms of rich vulgarity. In the typical DeMille movie of this era, the action commonly comes to a halt as the heroine (usually Gloria Swanson) deftly disrobes to wash and anoint herself in preparation for a festive occasion or perhaps for some more private pleasure. Bathing itself is an elaborate ceremony rather than merely a sanitary necessity. Dressing and undressing takes place in and out of bedrooms. Both male and female attire suggest a world of sybaritic opulence. By the final reel of DeMille's domestic melodramas, straying spouses and errant youths invariably regret their moral transgressions. However, the hypocrisy of this ultimate triumph of virtue over vice was not lost on the censors, who often demanded that he trim depictions of hedonistic pleasure.

Hollywood Hedonism

The lifestyles of many screen players contributed to the growing concern about declining moral standards. There has always been a certain amount of opprobrium attached to the acting profession. The Athenian ruler Solon (c. 594 B.C.) denounced Thespis, regarded as the inventor of drama, on the grounds that playing roles is a form of public deception. Uneasiness about role-playing persisted into the twentieth century. Successful screen actors were hardly seen as Horatio Alger types who rose from rags to riches through virtue and hard work. A profession in which a former plumber's helper could make a million dollars a year was bound to arouse resentment as well as adulation, especially when the misdeeds and malfeasances of the stars started to spill into the spotlight.

The idolized Mary Pickford caused a mild stir early in 1920 when she set up residence in Nevada and secured a divorce from her husband, actor Owen Moore. A short time later, after denying rumors of romance, she and swashbuckling star Douglas Fairbanks Sr. (himself recently divorced) were married in California. The attorney general in Nevada made headlines when he filed suit to set aside Pickford's divorce decree, charging she had not been a bona fide resident of the state. The Nevada Supreme Court eventually upheld the divorce, but the revelations about the star's private life clouded her screen aura of girlish innocence.

A far more scandalous light was cast on the movie colony in September 1920 when a valet at the Ritz Hotel in Paris found the nude dead body of Olive Thomas lying on a sable cape. In her hand was a bottle of mercury bichloride solution. The sprightly Hollywood screen star had been visiting the capital of France on a "second honeymoon" with her husband, Jack Pickford, Mary's brother and a major star in his own right. Although the tragic death from poison was ruled accidental, revelations of carousing and cocaine consumption made for good press copy for months.

Hollywood was a magnet for all sorts of characters in search of an offer. The comedians were among the raunchiest of the lot. The bacchanals of Mack Sennett, head of the Keystone Studio, became legendary for their free-flowing alcohol and uninhibited sex. Crimes were bound to occur in this kind of environment, and when they did the popular press was quick to report them.

Twenty-year-old Olive Thomas. Investigations into her death revealed a lurid private life that did not tally at all with her screen persona of sweetness and innocence.

The most serious allegations of moral dereliction and degeneracy involved former Keystone comedian Roscoe "Fatty" Arbuckle.

On Labor Day weekend in 1921, Arbuckle hosted a party at a San Francisco hotel to celebrate his recently signed three-year, $3-million contract with Famous Players–Lasky's distributing arm, Paramount. During this orgiastic revel, a movie aspirant named Virginia Rappe suffered severe convulsions. When she later died from peritonitis caused by a ruptured bladder, Arbuckle was indicted for manslaughter. Newspapers across the country played up the sensational aspects of the case, suggesting that her death was caused by a combination of his great weight and perverse sexual practices.

Fatty Arbuckle in a production still from *The Sheriff* (1918). The corpulent screen comic's embroilment in scandal did much to deplete the store of goodwill the movie industry had built up during the First World War.

Two trials ended in hung juries, and in a third he was acquitted for lack of evidence. The jury in that final trial even wished him well. But the stench of scandal remained with the corpulent screen comic. Even prison wardens refused to show his pictures. Protests from civic organizations and members of the clergy caused his earlier movies to be withdrawn from distribution, and three pictures completed just before his arrest were not released. Paramount had to write off a million-dollar loss from the unreleased pictures.

During Arbuckle's second trial, prominent director William Desmond Taylor was shot in the back at his Hollywood bungalow. A team from Famous Players–Lasky, where he had been under contract, got to the murder scene before the Los Angeles police and began scooping up anything that might seem scandalous. Despite this effort to avoid scandal, the police managed to confiscate more than enough material to further tarnish the image of the movie capital. Among the more salacious items reportedly found at the crime scene were a hidden cache of pornographic photographs featuring a number of easily recognizable female players and lots of lacy lingerie tagged with initials and dates, presumably souvenirs from sexual encounters. There were also letters linking the middle-aged Taylor romantically with ingenue Mary Miles Minter. Another of his paramours, popular Keystone comedienne Mabel Normand, was revealed to be a drug addict. The murder was never solved, and although Minter and Normand were eventually cleared of suspicion, their careers were ruined.

Within a year of Taylor's unsolved murder, all-American matinee idol Wallace Reid died in a sanitorium where he had sought a cure for his morphine addiction. Drug dissipation and the agonies of withdrawal had weakened his resistance, and he contracted a fatal case of influenza. Reid had been injured in a train crash on location making *Valley of the Giants* (1919). Because there was no way to shoot around the star, a studio doctor gave him morphine to ease the pain. He was supplied with the drug while making other pictures as well. By the time he played opposite Gloria Swanson in *The Affairs of Anatol,* his addiction was an open secret in Hollywood.

Even such beloved stars as Charlie Chaplin became mired in scandal. His poignant tramp character had made him an almost mythic figure. But the comic actor's propensity for females barely beyond pubescence raised eyebrows as early as 1918 when, at the age of twenty-nine, he married a sixteen-year-old girl. Two years later the couple divorced, and in 1924 he married another sixteen-year-old. Gossip columns wallowed in the revelation that Chaplin's teenage bride was pregnant at the time she took her marriage vows. Without the wedding, he might have faced charges of statutory rape for having sex with a minor. His behavior further contributed to the already strong impression that Hollywood was synonymous with the unsavory life.

New Self-Regulatory Measures

Increased sexual explicitness of screen content, coupled with the scandals that hit Hollywood in the early 1920s, gave new impetus to the legislative locomotive. Despite intense lobbying efforts, a new thirteen-point code of screen propriety unveiled by NAMPI in March 1921, and a parade of witnesses pledging that the industry would effectively regulate itself, the state legislature in Albany, New York, passed a bill permitting prior restraint of movies. Entreaties and supplications to the state's governor also met with failure. In the summer of 1921, not long after he signed the bill into law, New York's new licensing board began its work. By year's end, some three dozen states were considering censorship legislation, and movies had became a focal point for the fury of those who felt the nation was sinking into a moral abyss.

The campaign for federal censorship of movies also grew in intensity. The movie capital kept coming up in speeches highly critical of it. One irate senator described Hollywood as a place "where debauchery, riotous living, drunk-

ardness, ribaldry, [and] free love seem to be conspicuous."[8] Some of the calls
for federal regulation of movies revealed strong anti-Semitic sentiments. The
nationally prominent rector of the Christ Church in Brooklyn, for instance,
railed against the Jewish heads of the movie industry in no uncertain terms,
accusing them of being "vile corrupters" of American morals.[9] He demanded
that the federal government use its regulatory power to censor their movies.

The Hays Office

With the movie colony's mishaps and malfeasances making front-page news,
frightened industry leaders hired Will H. Hays, elder in the Presbyterian
Church, former chairman of the Republican National Committee, and current postmaster general, to head the Motion Picture Producers and Distributors of America (MPPDA)—a new trade association created to supersede previous, less effective attempts. Under his leadership, this mouthful of an
organization quickly launched a successful public relations campaign to defeat a Massachusetts censorship bill subject to a referendum.

Publicized by press agents as "movie czar," Hays was, in fact, no more than
an employee of the studio heads whose job was to promote probity and generate profits in the movie industry. As part of its public relations campaign,
the Hays Office—as the MPPDA came to be called—initiated a number of
measures. A "morals clause" was written into all contracts permitting studios
to discharge an employee at the first premonition of "moral turpitude." Central Casting, incorporated to regulate the employment of extras, purged its
rolls of prostitutes, people with criminal records, and those who pursued their
calling on the casting couch.

Other measures included the production of publicity shorts showing stars
as regular folks whose lives were not terribly different from those of their fans.
Industry insiders knew better. One short looked in on gaminlike Marion
Davies as she cleaned her modest apartment. There was no hint that she was
press magnate William Randolph Hearst's mistress and lived with him in medieval splendor at Hearst Castle in San Simeon, California. Another presented
leading lady Alma Rubens at home with her mother. She was, in fact, a heroin
addict and in a few years would be dead. The industry also launched a publicity campaign to discourage young women from migrating to the movie capital, and it sponsored a Studio Club to house female aspirants already in
Hollywood.

Director Cecil B. DeMille's *The Ten Commandments* (1923) must have
seemed to many observers to be an allegory of recent Hollywood behavior. It
depicts the bacchanalian revels around the golden calf in gleeful detail and
then shows the divine retribution. The studio heads followed a similar pattern when they hired Will Hays to halt Hollywood's worship of false gods. This
mail order Moses took several steps to dissuade producers from making pictures that might provoke censure. He got them to submit synopses of all plays,

novels, and stories for scrutiny before filming, and he set up a Studio Relations Committee to keep them informed about the kinds of material various states considered censorable.

This agency codified a list of "Don'ts and Be Carefuls" in 1927 based on a study of the specific rejections and deletions made by municipal and state censorship boards. The list of "Don'ts" contained eleven items that could not be depicted on the screen: profanity (either by title or lip); licentious or suggestive nudity; illegal drug trafficking; any inference of sexual perversion; "white slavery" (the interstate transportation of women for immoral purposes); sex hygiene and venereal diseases; childbirth; children's sexual organs; ridicule of the clergy; willful offense to any nation, race, or creed; and "miscegenation" or interracial coupling. (Cohabitation, sexual relations, and marriage involving persons of different racial classification were illegal at one time or another in thirty-one states, including every state in the South.)

The list of "Be Carefuls" comprised twenty-five subjects. Areas in which special care needed to be exercised included such things as the use of the flag, international relations, arson, firearms, theft, robbery, brutality, murder techniques, methods of smuggling, hangings or executions, sympathy for criminals, sedition, cruelty to children or animals, the sale of women, rape or attempted rape, "first-night" or honeymoon scenes, a man and woman in bed together, deliberate seduction of girls, the institution of marriage, surgical operations, the use of drugs, and excessive or lustful kissing. These two lists of admonitions were based on precedent, not principle, and provided little immunity from what promised to be enduring and worsening censorship problems for the movie industry.

With the general introduction of sound in 1929, criticism of movie content magnified. Some of the loudest complaints about immorality in talkies came from Catholics, who were 20 million strong in the late 1920s, roughly 17 percent of the population. Because the Catholic Church wasn't divided into diverse denominations, it was far more capable of unified action than were Protestant groups. When movie dialogue began to offend this ecclesiastical giant, the Hays Office swiftly took action to placate it. Early in 1930, industry leaders adopted a revamped and expanded version of the "Don'ts and Be Carefuls" by a Jesuit priest and a lay Catholic publisher of a trade journal for movie exhibitors.

The 1930 Production Code

Officially called the Motion Picture Production Code, this new set of guidelines detailed various offenses that could not be committed against middle-class morality. For example, the audience was never to be enticed into sympathizing with crime, wrongdoing, evil, or sin. No aspect of the law—divine, natural, or human—was ever to be ridiculed. Vulgarity, obscenity, and profanity were to be avoided. The sanctity of marriage and the home was to be upheld. Although adultery and illicit sex were recognized as occasionally necessary plot devices, they were not to be explicitly treated or justified, or attractively presented. Sexual relationships, even within marriage, were to be downplayed. Any display of excessive or lustful kissing and embracing was prohibited.

Hays hailed the new self-regulatory rules for moviemaking as a clear indication of the industry's ability to police itself responsibly in the era of talking pictures. But enforcement mechanisms once again proved to be weak. The major companies agreed to submit each movie they produced to the Studio Relations Committee before sending it to the laboratory for printing. If a movie was found to violate any provision, it could not be released until necessary changes were made. A panel of three members, selected on a rotation basis from the principal producers, served as an appeals board with the power to overrule the decisions of the committee. Because they knew that their own movies might come under scrutiny, the members of the rotating panel were often reluctant to support deletions in rival productions.

Transgressions of the Code

The novelty of sound had helped bolster movie attendance during the first years of the Great Depression, but the vicissitudes of the 1930s soon took a toll on the entire movie industry. By the summer of 1932, a sharp drop in attendance had caused roughly a third of the movie houses around the country to go dark. As box office receipts dwindled, violations of the industry's self-imposed moral prescriptions multiplied. They were violated, as a recent study reminds us, "with impunity and inventiveness in a series of wildly eccentric films. More unbridled, salacious, subversive, and just plain bizarre than what came afterwards, they look like Hollywood cinema but the moral terrain is so off-kilter they seem to be imported from a parallel universe."[10]

Although such blatant deviations from the strict provisions on matters of sex, vice, violence, and morality constituted only a small percentage of the movie industry's overall output, they provided ample ammunition for the growing ranks of the reform minded. A major source of concern was Hollywood's renewed interest in crime figures. Sporadically popular in the speechless era, the gangster movie came into its own with the staccato speech patterns and evocative sound effects—screeching tires, screaming sirens, and clattering submachine guns—made possible by the advent of talkies in the late 1920s. Although short on subtlety and depth, and restricted by inflexible sound equipment, such movies as *Little Caesar* (1930), *The Public Enemy* (1931), and *Scarface* (1932) were attractively cast and surged with vigor and excitement. The obligatory retribution the central characters invariably sustained in the final reel did little to diminish the demands for stricter screen censorship.

Cinematic depictions of illicit love affairs, risqué situations, off-color conversations, and frisky "fallen" women caused even greater consternation. A raucous Roman orgy, highlighted by a lesbian dance of seduction, is featured in the religious spectacle *Sign of the Cross* (1932). Several major female stars portrayed prostitutes, among them Helen Hayes in *The Sin of Madelon Claudet* (1931), Joan Crawford in *Rain* (1932), and Marlene Dietrich in *Blonde Venus* (1932). In *The Story of Temple Drake* (1933), an adaptation of William Faulkner's sensational novel *Sanctuary,* Miriam Hopkins appears as a thrill-seeking Southern belle who slips into degradation after she is raped by a gangster (Jack LaRue) and deposited in a New Orleans brothel. The smart-aleck stenographer played by Jean Harlow in *Red-Headed Woman* (1932) seduces her married boss on his own living room sofa. Running an automobile plant with an iron hand, Ruth Chatterton's character in *Female* (1933) satisfies her sex drive with a succession of young men in her employ. Her love nest is equipped with a buzzer system so that the staff will know which room requires cocktails.

Few movies at the time dealt with sexual matters more blatantly than *Baby Face* (1933), a Warner Bros. Pictures release starring sultry Barbara Stanwyck. Using her body to bargain for favors, the working-class predator she plays moves up floor by floor, sexual conquest by sexual conquest, into the upper reaches of a banking firm. Everyone from a junior clerk to the top executives falls under her erotic spell.

Her seductions culminate with the exploitation of the recently appointed president (George Brent). Upping the ante with a new stratagem, she withholds her sexual favors to cajole him into proposing marriage. After she gets him to the altar, he keeps her in luxury by skimming money from the bank. When the shortages surface, she initially refuses to hock her jewels to aid him. Facing embezzlement charges, he shoots himself before she can tell him of her change in heart. Although losing the one man she ever loved, she still has her jewels as consolation.

As with most movies likely to encounter censorship problems, *Baby Face* was toned down considerably during the self-regulatory process. In deference to the Studio Relations Committee, as a study of the "fallen woman" film points out, Warners trimmed several scenes to obscure the sexual transactions, relying more on camera work and the musical score to suggest what was happening.[11] (After each of the title character's sexual conquests, the camera tilts a few floors farther up the side of the bank building, usually accompanied by a honky-tonk rendition of "St. Louis Woman.") These alterations did little to impress New York's licensing board, which rejected the movie entirely, finding the story's viewpoint untenable under the state's censorship statute.

The majority of big studio movies opened with a gala premiere at one of Manhattan's Broadway picture palaces before going into general release. This well-established practice made the New York censorship board especially influential, because an outright rejection affected potential box office revenues

Production still of Mae West and Cary Grant in *She Done Him Wrong* (1933), based on her play *Diamond Lil*. Sizing up Grant, West drawls, "You can be had." Such assertive sexuality made the self-parodying star a lightning rod for moral crusaders.

nationwide. To win approval, the studio made several additional changes designed to reduce *Baby Face*'s stress on sexual exploitation.

Among other measures, Warner reworked an early scene in which the title character's mentor, a cynical old cobbler (Alphonse Ethier), urges her to capitalize on her beauty by exploiting men. "All life, no matter how we idealize it," he asserts, quoting Friedrich Nietzsche's *The Will to Power*, "is nothing more than exploitation." In the revised version, this perverse philosophy lesson is replaced with a more morally uplifting message. The studio also hastily shot a new ending in which she not only repents but also sacrifices her wealth to prevent her miraculously recovered husband from going to prison. The two of them then retreat to a life of hard work and poverty in a steel town. (The morally redeemed sexual predator's return to hard times is simply suggested by stock footage of steel mills.) Despite such modifications, the movie's raciness remained largely intact. It got a green light from the New York censors with only a few cuts but was banned outright in Ohio and Virginia (which had passed a censorship law in 1922).

The movies featuring Mae West left little doubt in the minds of reformers that the new code was merely a layer of camouflage to permit producers to test the limits of public taste. West had been a highly successful and controversial vaudeville performer, playwright, and stage performer before she brought her oversized hourglass figure and ribald ripostes to the silver screen in the early 1930s. In such movies as *Night After Night* (1932), *She Done Him Wrong* (1933), and *I'm No Angel* (1933), her double entendres, leering looks, and swinging hips made a mockery of the code's moral strictures.

Typical of West's repartee is her response when asked if she's ever met a man who could make her happy. She retorts, "Sure, lots of times." This line itself, of course, cannot account for the erotic enticement of her drawling voice. Almost everything she said sounded sexually suggestive. As a recent study shows, her screen persona of an aggressive female—one who initiates seductions and who relishes sexual power and independence from male control—challenged traditional gender relationships and earned the wrath of the reform crusaders to new levels.[12] Although clergy and women's clubs condemned her as immoral, customers flocked to her movies. And she seemed to be as popular in small towns as she was in urban centers.

The Payne Fund Studies

Agencies of social control were especially concerned about the possible effects of the slackening of screen standards on young people. By the end of the 1920s, an estimated 28 million minors, including more than 11 million children under the age of fourteen, went to the movies weekly.[13] The results of a four-year study published in 1933—initiated by the Motion Picture Research Council, which was composed principally of conservative Protestants, and financed by the Payne Study and Experiment Fund, a private philanthropic foundation—seemed to confirm the strong influence of movies on this segment of the audience.

Under the direction of W. W. Charters of the Bureau of Educational Research at the Ohio State University, social scientists from seven universities conducted a series of twelve studies. Most of this research drew heavily on the traditional methodology of the social sciences, particularly the experimental method and the survey technique, through which data about what movies do *to* or *for* patrons could be quantified and generalized. Attitude change, imitation, emotional arousal, and other such concepts amendable to the tools of the trade were emphasized.

One of the most sweeping studies relied on recollections of experiences that occurred years earlier to provide a general picture of how movies influenced a youngster's dress, mannerisms, speech, emotions, moods, ideas about romance, ambitions, temptations, career plans, and the like.[14] Over a thousand young people were asked to report on of how they thought movies had influenced them. Most were college and high school students, but a small number of office and factory workers were included in the sample as well. Additional information was derived from interviews with 135 of the subjects and from conversations among groups of students as they discussed movies. Data were also collected from questionnaires administered to 1200 grade school children.

No attempt was made to quantify this mass of material. Rather, the facts were allowed to "speak for themselves." Extensive quotes from the recorded recollections and other data culled and analyzed provided support for the general conclusion that movies were a source of imitation, unintentional learning, and emotional influence for young people. One male college student, for instance, was quoted as saying that it was directly through movies that he "learned to kiss a girl on the ears, neck, and cheeks, as well as on the mouth." Several subjects reported that while watching such movies as *The Phantom of the Opera* (1925) they experienced an extreme sense of shock and fear, which stayed with them long after they left the theatre. Others indicated that movies generated intense feelings of sorrow, excitement, or romantic passion.

This imaginative study suggested that movies played a significant part in shaping young people's conceptions of the world and in providing them with patterns of conduct to emulate. However, much the same could probably be said for the novels, comic strips, newspapers, magazines, and radio programs of the time. Because movies were studied in isolation, there is no indication of the relative strength of the various popular art forms. Nor do we have any way of knowing to what degree the subjects who provided the autobiographical data were representative of youths in general, because they were not chosen through techniques of "random sampling" in which each and every member of the population to be assessed has an equal chance of being selected. The autobiographical material itself is also of limited value. Such anecdotal and retrospective reports can hardly be expected to yield reliable or representative evidence about the general effects of movie experiences that occurred years earlier.

Whereas most of the researchers themselves were careful to qualify their findings, the common preface to each of the volumes in which Payne Fund studies appeared reflected a subtle hostility toward movies. Professor Charters, who seemed determined to show that movies were having a harmful effect on the youth of America, wrote it. In his volume summarizing the main findings, Charters concluded, "The commercial movies are an unsavory mess."[15] His motives became even more suspect when he cooperated fully with a journalist in the publication of a highly biased book based on the studies called *Our Movie Made Children*.[16] This distillation distorted the research findings in ways that served to confirm the worst fears of the self-appointed guardians of the public welfare and provided strong support for the growing movement to bring the moviemakers to redemption.

The Legion of Decency

The most vigorous reform campaign was initiated by the Catholic Church, which apparently had become disillusioned with the Hays Office's failure to enforce the new code for screen conduct. At their annual convention in 1933, Catholic bishops decided to organize a national Legion of Decency. Catholics in the 104 dioceses nationwide were entreated to repeat or sign a pledge condemning the corrupting effect of salacious movies on public morals. A Catholic boycott of movie theatres in Philadelphia brought national attention to the ecclesiastical crusade. Theatre boycotts were threatened in other locales as well. Box office receipts tumbled in heavily Catholic neighborhoods, especially in the big cities, and the message went out to the movie industry that it was time to seek salvation.

With remarkable alacrity, the Catholic Church obtained what reform-minded groups had sought since the nickelodeon era—the power to exert a strong moral influence over movies. In this regard, it has often been criticized for imposing sectarian principles on a pluralistic society. But the Catholic moral posture wasn't very different from that of other major religious, civic, and educational groups at the time. The Legion of Decency campaign to reform the movie industry, in fact, quickly garnered support from major Protestant and Jewish groups. It also received ringing editorial endorsements from newspapers across the country. The marshaling of such a large and solid body of highly influential groups and institutions strongly and actively opposed to prevailing production practices could not be ignored by the movie industry without dire economic consequences. The big studios, already caught in the throes of the depression, heeded the call to repent.

Industry Censorship Under Breen

The Production Code Administration

In the summer of 1934, less than three months after the formation of the Legion of Decency, the Hays Office disbanded the Studio Relations Committee and replaced it with the more formidable Production Code Administration (PCA). The rotating appeals panel was also eliminated, leaving only the possibility of an appeal directly from the PCA to the board of directors of the MPPDA. The members of this parent organization agreed not to release or distribute any movie unless it received a certificate of approval signed by the director of the PCA.

To keep this new enforcement machinery well oiled, producers were charged a fee based on the total production cost of each picture submitted for approval. The PCA was empowered to impose a $25,000-per-day fine against any defiant MPPDA member who sold, distributed, or exhibited a movie not bearing the seal of approval. An advertising code became binding the following year, with a fine ranging from $1000 to $5000 for failure to honor its dictates. In addition, the MPPDA's Title Registration Bureau, which had been established in 1925 to eliminate duplication of movie titles, was now given authority to prohibit the use of salacious, indecent, or obscene titles.

Will Hays placed Joseph Ignatius Breen, a devout Catholic and father of six, in charge of the new self-regulatory apparatus. The rotund Breen's hail-fellow manner hid a deep-seated obsession with Jewish influence in the movie industry. By the 1930s, Jews were represented in the upper reaches of Hollywood far out of proportion to their numbers in the general population. The heads of the major studios were mainly Jewish immigrants or the sons of Jewish immigrants from central and eastern Europe. Of the eight leading companies, six were run by men of orthodox Jewish parentage, and Jews played important roles at most stages in the development of the other two. The operators of the major theatre chains and most powerful talent agencies were Jewish as well. So were the lawyers who transacted most of the movie industry's business.

Aside from basic bigotry, the reasons for Breen's preoccupation with this strong Jewish presence in the movie colony are far from clear. A recent study suggests that Jews had a conservative and even anti-Semitic influence on the making of movies. [17] The studio heads hesitated to hire Jewish actors and made them change their names when they did employ them. They also discouraged the use of Jewish themes and characters. Their ethnicity supposedly made them so insecure that they hungered for esteem, respectability, and, most of all, assimilation. The principal way to achieve this, they believed, was to have their movies reflect an understanding and acceptance of broadly shared American values.

The new director of the PCA didn't see it this way at all. Breen attributed almost everything he didn't like about the movie industry to the Jewishness of its leaders, whom he referred to at various times as "dirty lice," "the scum of the earth," a "foul bunch, crazed with sex . . . and ignorant in all matters having to do with sound morals." [18] His correspondence is replete with such offensive remarks and reveals a great deal about his attitudes toward the studio heads during his long tenure as industry watchdog. He seemingly saw himself as the one man who could bring the Hebrews of Hollywood to their knees, and he was quick to notify them if he felt they were circumventing the code's moral mandates.

For all his bigotry, Breen was not indifferent to the box office. Producers could—and often did—finagle and maneuver. Moreover, despite what he said behind their backs, Breen was polite if not deferential in his dealings with industry leaders. Men whose benediction could bestow fame and fortune, and whose disfavor could bring banishment, were not about to tolerate ethnic epithets from an employee—even if an entire legion came to his support.

To a considerable extent, Breen was successful in alleviating licensing tensions. In the process, however, the PCA became more restrictive than many of the state and municipal censorship boards. One of Breen's first tasks in his new post was to review the script for Mae West's *It Ain't No Sin*. By the time he finished bowdlerizing this movie project, West was a changed woman. It was not a change for the better. The sexually suggestive title metamorphosed into the bland *Belle of the Nineties* (1934), all references to her character's past as a prostitute were removed, her sexual innuendos were toned down, and she even ended up married in the final reel.

Platinum blonde sex siren Jean Harlow suffered much the same fate. Her newest picture went through several title changes before it was released—from *One-Hundred Per Cent Pure* to *Born to Be Kissed* to, finally, *The Girl From Missouri* (1934). And her movie *Reckless* (1935), about a chorus girl who messes up various people's lives, had to be reworked several times before it received Breen's seal of moral approval. Loose morals, exposed female flesh, and bedroom antics were soon in scant supply on screens across the country.

From Stage to Screen

In his dealings with producers, Joseph Breen pressed politely but firmly for strict adherence to PCA provisions. Although most movie projects caused few problems, adaptations of provocative Broadway plays often resulted in especially difficult negotiations. He was likely to return such treatments and script proposals with extensive comments and a long list of items his office found objectionable. In response to Breen's concerns, moviemakers invariably toned scenes down in the screen adaptation.

When producer Samuel Goldwyn bought the movie rights to Sidney Kingsley's long-running Broadway hit *Dead End*, a scathing indictment of slum life, he anticipated having to make major changes in the dialogue and setting to secure PCA approval. The focal point of the play is a gang of foul-mouthed street urchins who wile away their days skipping school, getting into fights, stealing, gambling, and swimming in New York City's garbage-strewn East River. The camaraderie of the street gang is the fulcrum of their lives, the only security and happiness they know in an otherwise oppressive environment.

Although sympathetic to *Dead End*'s social message, Breen suggested several specific changes for code compliance. Among other things, he wanted the language of the street kids cleaned up and a scene expunged in which wanted killer Baby Face Martin (Humphrey Bogart), who has returned to the slum that spawned him, shoots a policeman. He also preferred that the contrasts between the living conditions of the poor in the slum tenements and those of the rich in the abutting luxury apartment building not be drawn too

Leo Gorcey in a scene from *Dead End* (1937). After a stint at Warner Bros.
Pictures, he settled in at the tiny Monogram studio as the leader of the "East
Side Kids" in a series of cheaply made movies. In this street gang, his character's
major offense is fracturing the English language.

sharply. In this regard, he recommended avoidance of any emphasis on the
presence of filth or smelly garbage cans or debris floating in the river where
the boys swam.

To comply with the code authority's expectations, Goldwyn had the play's
depiction of slum life softened considerably. His screenwriter, Lillian Hellman, toned down a scene in which the street punks pull off a rich kid's clothes
and rub dirt into his genitals, sanitized the salty street language, reduced the
inflammatory rhetoric about social injustice, and even cured Baby Face Martin's former girlfriend Francey of acute syphilis. (In the movie, Francey [Claire
Trevor] appears to suffer from little more than a bad cough.) In addition, most
likely more for Hollywood sheen than PCA approval, Hellman transformed
the play's impoverished protagonist Gimpty, so-called because he suffered
from rickets as a child, into the healthier, handsomer Dave (Joel McCrea), a
painter decorating the exterior of a small restaurant in exchange for food.

Despite these modifications, *Dead End* (1937) can be seen as a strong cinematic condemnation of conditions conducive to poverty, crime, and despair.
But some segments of the audience may well have found the movie's milieu
inviting, especially given the presence of the "Dead End Kids"—as the actors
playing the street urchins came to be called. Reprising their roles from the
Broadway stage production, Billy Halop (Tommy), Leo Gorcey (Spit, whose
expectorating was minimized), Huntz Hall (Dippy), Bobby Jordan (Angel),

Gabriel Dell (T. B.), and Bernard Punsley (Milty) delivered strikingly effective screen performances. Although adults may have been appalled by their antics, many youngsters probably found them fascinating and even worthy of emulation. The appealing actors won so much popular favor that they were featured in such serious social melodramas as *Angels with Dirty Faces* (1938), *Crime School* (1938), *Hell's Kitchen* (1939), and *They Made Me a Criminal* (1939). In these pictures, and many others, being a Dead End Kid seems like a great deal of fun.

Concern with Catholic Classifications

The PCA's interpretations of the code's provisions were not always restrictive enough to satisfy the decency legionnaires. Early in 1936, the Catholic Church initiated its own system of review and classification of movies. The International Federation of Catholic Alumnae, whose evaluation staff was made up mostly of older women with a conservative bent, undertook the task of assigning ratings. Movies were placed in one of four categories: A1, morally unobjectionable for general patronage; A2, morally unobjectionable for adults; B, morally objectionable in part for all; and C, condemned. Catholics were exhorted to avoid B-rated movies although they were not compelled to do so. The weekly lists of ratings for movies were circulated to the faithful by the offices of the church's 104 dioceses nationwide.

Studios sometimes went to ludicrous lengths to avoid receiving a "condemned" rating. M-G-M's 1941 release of *Two-Faced Woman,* a comedy of errors in which Greta Garbo played identical twins, was branded with a C even though the PCA, under the direction of Geoffrey Shurlock, an English-born Episcopalian, had given it a seal of approval. (Breen had resigned as head of the agency early in 1941 and become production chief at RKO; he returned to his old post in May 1942, apparently having been unhappy supervising studio budgets and personnel.) The picture's plotline revolves around a plain-looking wife's attempt to entice her indifferent husband by impersonating her own glamorous, somewhat promiscuous sister. To win Catholic approval, M-G-M agreed to shoot a completely new scene in which the husband receives a telephone call apprising him of the masquerade. But the rest of the movie is nonsensical in that the husband acts as though he doesn't know that the blond beauty he is pursuing is actually his wife. The revised version received a B classification.

Foreign Regulators

Movies were shaped almost as much by the economic exigencies and censorship constraints in the international market as by efforts to appease pressure groups at home. Almost from the outset, those who forged the conventions of the movie idiom had an eye toward American hegemony abroad. However,

Hollywood's domination of European and other foreign markets was not simply a matter of the universal appeal of its evolving idiom of cinematic expression. In addition to the First World War's disruption of Europe's film production, the American movie industry's incursion into foreign markets was aided by the rising costs of production following the advent of talkies. At the same time, the major studios' use of inexpensive foreign filmmaking facilities allowed them to infiltrate into local movie production and to rake off government subsidies designed to support indigenous industries.

The great wave of American movie exportation after the First World War resulted in retaliatory quotas designed to protect domestic production and foster indigenous cultural expression. Hollywood sought to counter these measures through the Foreign Department of the Hays Office, which advocated free enterprise, open competition, and unhindered trade abroad. It largely worked to eliminate restrictions on the importation and circulation of American movies and to keep the major studios informed about national censorship policies. A great deal was at stake in these activities because Hollywood derived more than a third of its revenue from foreign markets.

The regulatory practices of the PCA often reflected foreign censorship concerns. Joseph Breen was especially sensitive to the idiosyncrasies of the British Board of Film Censors (BBFC), an industry self-regulatory agency set up by exhibitors in 1912 to deal with the many censor boards that had sprung up in Britain. Unlike its American counterpart, the BBFC never developed a written code stating what could and could not be done on screen. Nonetheless, the standards it developed over the years were consistent enough to allow producers to anticipate its expectations. Some of its taboos bordered on the absurd.

The PCA has often been ridiculed for the stipulation that even married couples should sleep in separate beds. According to a former official of the self-regulatory agency, this silly mandate came from the BBFC, and not Breen's office. [19] The matter first became an issue with the 1938 RKO comedy *The Mad Miss Manton,* in which an elderly caretaker and his wife are shown waking up in a double bed. When the BBFC balked at this invasion of the "sacred intimacies of married life," the studio darkened the offending scene so that the sleeping arrangements were barely discernible. After that incident, whenever a bedroom scene appeared in a script submitted to the PCA for consideration, an agency official would simply remind the producer that twin beds would be needed for England. For the sake of British distribution, American moviemakers complied with a wide range of restrictions.

Wartime Restrictions

During the Second World War, while the Office of War Information attended to politics on the screen, the PCA continued to focus on flesh, not fascism. The entire social fabric of American society seemed to unravel during the war

THE KANE/HEARST CONTROVERSY

Expostulations against the movie industry came from many quarters. A major controversy swirled around *Citizen Kane* (1941), whose title character—heir to millions, newspaper publisher and art collector, a man long on ability but short on principle and driven by unbounded political ambition—bears more than a passing resemblance to press baron William Randolph Hearst. By most accounts, Hearst hardly became anything like the hollow and embittered Charles Foster Kane, but rather was a generous, gracious host who loved a good time even in his declining years. But the movie does capture the sweep of his life, the intensity of his drive, his consuming ego, his deep disappointments, and his promiscuous pursuit of artworks and artifacts.

Perhaps the cruelest aspect of the movie was its thinly veiled portrait of Hearst's long-time mistress Marion Davies, a former chorus girl who proved to be a talented screen comedienne but never achieved the kind of stardom he had envisioned for her. In the guise of Susan Alexander (Dorothy Comingore), she is presented as a dim-witted and inept operatic singer who becomes a nagging, quarrelsome drunk with a gratingly shrill speaking voice. Adding to the insult and injury, Kane died with the word "Rosebud" on his lips, which was widely rumored to be Hearst's pet name for Davies's private parts.

Apparently incensed by the way Davies was represented, the seventy-eight-year-old publisher launched a no-holds-barred effort to stop the movie's release or at least diminish its box office potential. Among other things, publicity for all RKO features was banned in all Hearst newspapers, and an announced serialization of the novel *Kitty Foyle,* originally to be linked with the release of the RKO movie version, was dropped from the publication schedule.

Many movie theatres, fearing retaliation from the Hearst newspapers, refused to book *Citizen Kane*. Even the Rockefeller-controlled Radio City Music Hall, where most of RKO's major features premiered, declined to present the picture after Hearst's syndicated gossip columnist Louella Parsons reportedly threatened Nelson Rockefeller with a family exposé. To appease the powerful publisher, the head of the M-G-M studio, Louis B. Mayer, offered to pay RKO in excess of $800,000 to destroy the negative and all the prints.

The offer was rejected. RKO corporate president George Schaefer, who fostered such acclaimed movies as *Gunga Din* (1939) and *The Hunchback of Notre Dame* (1939), was determined to release *Citizen Kane* nationwide. Toward this end, he threatened the major theatre chains with a suit charging conspiracy. The theatres owned by the Warner Bros. studio gave in and booked the movie, and the other chains soon followed. The Hearst forces, however, were undeterred.

Rumors soon began to circulate in the movie industry that those doing business with Schaefer and RKO could expect to feel the wrath of the Hearst empire as well. A smear campaign among RKO stockholders suggested that the studio wasn't prospering because Schaefer's alleged anti-Semitism made it difficult for him to get along with the Jewish movie executives who dominated the industry. As RKO's stock began to drop in price, the Atlas Corporation's Floyd Odlum, who was already a major shareholder and an outspoken opponent of Schaefer's policies, bought controlling interest in the movie company. By mid-1942 Schaefer was finished at RKO. Within two weeks of his departure, Orson Welles and his Mercury Theatre Company were summarily ordered off the studio lot. Other Schaefer-inspired production units suffered much the same fate.

years. Millions of young people, cut loose from community ties, experienced much greater sexual freedom. Marriage, birth, and divorce rates soared. Many women working in factories and war plants enjoyed unprecedented social mobility and personal and economic freedom. The general surge in war-related employment was accompanied by growing labor strife, racial and ethnic discord, and struggles for women's rights. Juvenile violence and vandalism also became a major problem, especially in the urban war centers with their crowded conditions and general lack of parental supervision.

In the face of this wartime social upheaval, the PCA remained steadfast in its efforts to maintain cinematic morality. When reviewing a feature film for code approval, Joseph Breen did not simply demand deletions; he also worked to effect changes in the entire moral outlook of the screen drama. His handling of the wartime romantic melodrama *Casablanca* (1942) is typical of the way he tried to infuse morality into movie projects.

The industry censor objected to the scene in which protagonist Rick Blaine (Humphrey Bogart) encounters his former lover, Ilsa Lund (Ingrid Bergman), in a marketplace the day after his drunken denunciation of her supposed unfaithfulness. He fumbles an apology, but she wants to put their entire relationship behind her. Soon she'll leave, never to see him again. The rejection triggers his cynicism, and he disparages her romance with current companion Victor Laszlo (Paul Henreid). Someday she'll lie to Laszlo as she lied to him, he says caustically, and then he'll be waiting for her. Never, she rejoins; Laszlo is my husband and was "even when I knew you in Paris." She walks away abruptly, leaving him dejected. Breen found it unacceptable that Ilsa was married when she fell in love with Rick in Paris.

Because the marriage of Ilsa and Victor was an essential element in the dramatic design of the movie, the studio was reluctant to remove Ilsa's remark to Rick. In a compromise, Ilsa revealed that throughout most of the Paris interlude she thought her husband was dead (although she clearly remains intimate with Rick for a brief time after it is apparent he's alive). This seemed to satisfy Breen. What is more, the reference to Victor returning just as she was preparing to leave Paris actually gave her a stronger reason for abandoning Rick and made the impossibility of their love all the more poignant.

Excerpts of memos culled from the PCA's archives, which were open to the public in the early 1980s, indicate that Breen objected to a number of lines in the incomplete script of *Casablanca*.[20] Among those he found unacceptably sexually suggestive included "Of course, a beautiful young girl for M'sieur Renault [Claude Rains], the Prefect of Police," "The girl will be released in the morning," and "It used to take a villa at Cannes, or at the very least, a string of pearls—now all I ask is an exit visa." The studio acceded to minor changes in the lines involving Renault's lechery, and the character willing to prostitute herself for an exit visa was eliminated altogether.

However, Warner refused to alter a line from the scene in which Ilsa, having returned to Rick's cafe, explains to him that as a young girl from Oslo,

Ilsa (Ingrid Bergman) threatens to shoot Rick (Humphrey Bogart). Unable to pull the trigger, she drops the gun and comes into his arms. What happens during the dissolve following their passionate kiss is left to the imagination. (*Casablanca* [1942])

freshly arrived in Paris, she met Victor Laszlo at the home of some friends. He opened her eyes to a new world of ideas and ideals, and she worshipped him with feelings she interpreted as love. Rick rudely cuts her off, obviously imagining a more sordid story than the one intended because he's heard it all before, to the tune of "a tinny piano in the parlor downstairs." Breen saw this remark as a definite reference to a bawdy house but allowed it to remain in the script anyway.

Breen's guiding hand was felt even at the subtle level of camera work and editing. One of the changes he demanded in *Casablanca* concerned the scene in Rick's private quarters above the cafe, when Ilsa beseeches him to overcome his hurt feelings and remember the "Cause." He responds sardonically, "I'm the only cause I'm interested in!" Desperate to secure an exit visa for her husband, Ilsa threatens him at gunpoint but quickly loses her resolve. She begins sobbing, and they embrace.

In the original scenario, as they kissed, there was a fade out and then a fade back in to the interior of the apartment. Breen thought that the time interval suggested by fading the image out and in implied that their physical contact had gone far beyond mere kissing. He insisted that replacing this effect with the blurring of one image into another and shooting the return to the interior without any evidence of a bed in sight would remedy this impression. In the completed movie, whether time passed during the dissolve to a view of the airport tower, and if so what occurred, is left to the imagination.

As the war years took their toll on the moral fabric of America, Breen occasionally deviated from his earlier standards. Prior to the war, for instance, he had warned studios away from James M. Cain's sharp, brooding novella of adultery and murder, *Double Indemnity,* because of its "low tone and sordid flavor." In the fall of 1943, however, he approved a somewhat sanitized screenplay of the story with hardly a murmur. He also gave the green light to *Mildred Pierce* (1945), another Cain book he had previously cautioned against adapting for the screen even though he still found it "sordid and repellent."[21] Such concessions inspired other filmmakers to push the moral parameters of the prevailing idiom.

Industry regulatory controls were loosened in other ways as well. In March 1942 the MPPDA rescinded its threat of a $25,000 levy for exhibitors showing movies without PCA approval because the fine was thought to be in violation of the antitrust laws. (The penalty for recalcitrant producers and distributors remained in effect until 1956.) The change had little immediate effect because the integrated structure and distribution practices of the movie industry assured continued adherence to the provisions of the production code. It was intended primarily to protect the trade association from lawsuits by disgruntled producers who had been denied the seal of approval. But this crack in the regulatory machinery would ultimately contribute to its collapse.

Code Authority in Decline

The postwar period witnessed the gradual abandonment of the production code, precipitated by the adverse antitrust rulings, the rise of independent production, the importation of foreign films, and the dramatic drop in box office receipts as people moved to the new suburbs and turned to television and other divertissements. An aging Will Hays retired from the fray at the end of the war. In September 1945 Eric Johnson, then president of the United States Chamber of Commerce, succeeded him as head of the MPPDA. Three months after assuming his new post, Johnson changed the name of the organization to the more succinct Motion Picture Association of America (MPAA).

Joseph Breen remained in charge of the PCA, but he was clearly out of touch with the increasingly popular films from abroad in the postwar period. In Europe, in the closing days of the war, there was a dramatic shift in filmmaking techniques. A movement in Italy, later labeled **neo-realism,** introduced a new kind of motion picture to world screens characterized by realistic and socially committed plots, nonprofessional acting, and location shooting. The critically acclaimed films made by directors from the neorealist school include Luchino Visconti's *Ossessione* (1942), Roberto Rossellini's *Open City* (1945) and *Paisan* (1946), Vittorio De Sica's *Shoeshine* (1946) and *The Bicycle Thief* (1948), and Guiseppe DeSantis's *Bitter Rice* (1949), all of which played to enthusiastic crowds at burgeoning American **art houses**—small theatres devoted primarily to showing foreign films.

The PCA suffered a storm of protest from the press when Breen denied the seal of approval to *The Bicycle Thief,* a poignant tale scripted by Cesare Zavattini of a destitute family man who desperately attempts to recover the stolen bicycle he needs to keep his new job as a billboard plasterer. Although the film had already won an Academy Award, along with many other accolades, the industry watchdog had withheld his benediction because its distributor refused to delete two scenes. In one, during a frantic day of searching the streets for the bicycle, the man's son (his back to the camera) tries to urinate against a wall, only to be forced to zip his pants back up when his father calls him to continue the search. In the other, the father finds the thief and chases him into a local bordello, from which both men are forcibly ejected.

Although not outright violations of the production code, the two scenes did fly in the face of several prior decisions involving similar matters. (For example, *Open City* won a seal of approval only after a brief scene showing a child sitting on a chamber pot was trimmed.) The MPAA's board upheld Breen's ruling, but many theatres booked the film even though it lacked a seal. This marked just one of many damaging blows during the postwar period to the PCA's enforcement machinery.

Cleavage Concerns

One of the most prolonged challenges to Breen's conservatism came from aeronautical industrialist Howard Hughes, who had produced and directed *The Outlaw* (1943), a fictional account of the exploits of Billy the Kid. In making the movie, Hughes frequently focused the camera on the ample bosom of his female lead, Jane Russell, a former dental office receptionist and part-time model. In one scene, Russell's character, Rio, is tied between two trees with leather thongs. Using his engineering expertise, Hughes designed a special brassiere for the screen novice to accentuate her bust as she writhes in feigned agony. In several other scenes, the camera lingers on her loosely fitting blouse as she leans over, bends, stoops, or kneels for one contrived reason or another.

In the spring of 1941, after reviewing a print of the finished picture, Breen fired off a missive to Hughes demanding dozens of cuts before a seal of approval would be granted. Refusing to accede to these demands, the multimillionaire moviemaker appealed to the MPPDA board. At the hearing, his publicist displayed stills of several female stars from other movies. A mathematician used calipers to show that proportionately the amount of anatomical exposure in the objectionable shots of Russell was no greater than that shown in the frame enlargements taken from those other PCA-approved movies. As a result of this demonstration, the board decided that far fewer cuts would be necessary for code compliance.

After removing some footage, Hughes received a certificate of approval. By the time he was ready to release *The Outlaw*, however, Twentieth Century–Fox, the company scheduled to distribute it, had canceled its agreement. Hughes opened the movie early in 1943 at a single theatre in San Francisco. Promotional posters of Russell displayed throughout the Bay Area caused an uproar. When arrests were threatened, the posters were promptly withdrawn. But the publicity campaign proved to be a resounding success. The movie played to record-breaking numbers for ten straight weeks. Hughes then withdrew it and concerned himself with the war effort.

At war's end, Hughes again made plans to bring his pet movie project before the public. Early in 1946, United Artists, which at the time was not a member of the recently renamed Motion Picture Association of America, agreed to release *The Outlaw* nationwide. Once again, Hughes orchestrated a lurid and vulgar advertising campaign. Newspapers, magazines, billboards, and even skywriting proclaimed the robust proportions of the movie's female lead. An airplane wrote the words "The Outlaw" in the sky over Pasadena and then made two enormous circles with a dot in the middle of each. Newspapers ads for the movie asked such questions as "How would you like to tussle with Russell?" and "What are the two main reasons for Jane Russell's rise to stardom?" Some of the advertisements contained the false and misleading statement "Exactly as filmed—not a scene cut," and many ads had not been submitted to the code authority for approval or had been rejected after being submitted.

The code authority responded by revoking its certificate of approval. Hughes, in turn, brought suit against the MPAA in federal court charging violation of the antitrust laws, restraint of trade, and infringement of the First Amendment guarantee of freedom of expression.[22] After considering the merits of the case, the presiding judge ruled in favor of the MPAA, finding no evidence that its policies tended to reduce or destroy competition in the production, distribution, or exhibition of movies. He also criticized the salacious promotional campaign for the picture, holding that the industry can be hurt as much from indecent advertising as from indecent movies. When his appeal of this ruling was denied, Hughes had to return the certificate of approval for *The Outlaw* and remove the association's seal from all prints of the movie.

Because the association's $25,000 fine no longer applied to exhibition, a number of theatres were willing to show *The Outlaw* even though it lacked a

A poster for *The Outlaw* (1943) stresses Jane Russell's anatomy. Howard Hughes launched an unprecedented publicity campaign to promote the robustly proportioned nineteen-year-old. Soon after shooting began in 1940, his publicist papered the United States with Russell's pictures, distributing to newspapers and magazines thousands of photographs highlighting her ample bosom. She became familiar to most adult Americans well before they saw her on screen.

seal of approval. However, before permitting it to be exhibited, both state and municipal licensing boards demanded cuts and changes. Once again, the main concern was just how much cleavage could be shown on the screen. In some locales, the demanded deletions were so extensive that Hughes turned to the courts for relief. But judges usually sided with the censors. Massachusetts prohibited Sunday showings, and Ohio and Maryland banned it entirely. A Baltimore judge upheld the ban, claiming that Russell's breasts "hung over the picture like a thunderstorm spread out over a summer landscape."[23] The Legion of Decency gave it a condemned rating, and many religious groups protested local showings throughout the country. The notoriety surrounding the movie had a salutary effect at the box office. Wherever it played, large crowds lined up for tickets.

The financial success of *The Outlaw* undoubtedly weakened the PCA's self-regulatory mechanisms. United Artists again defied the code authority in 1953 when it released an innocuous comedy called *The Moon Is Blue*—essentially a lighthearted look at seduction and adultery—even though it had been denied a seal of approval and had also been condemned by the Legion of Decency. Its box office success dispelled the prevailing belief that defiance of the dictates of the PCA and Catholic Church would result in financial ruin for a movie. By the time the ailing Joseph Breen retired in 1954, the entire self-regulatory structure was on the verge of collapse. That year he received a special Oscar for "his conscientious, open-minded and dignified management of the Motion Picture Production Code."[24]

A New Catholic Campaign

Early in 1956, Catholic bishops launched a new campaign against what they perceived to be the rising tide of moral laxity in movies. This effort intensified in the winter of that year when the PCA, now headed by Geoffrey Shurlock, approved the release by Warner Bros. of *Baby Doll* (1956). Based on two short plays by Tennessee Williams, who also wrote the screenplay, the movie features Carroll Baker as a childlike wife who, though nearly twenty years old, sleeps in a crib, sucks her thumb, and has yet to consummate her marriage with her lustful, middle-aged husband (Karl Malden). His desperation is such that every time she takes a bath he peeks at her through the keyhole in the bathroom door. Much of the action revolves around a smarmy business rival's (Eli Wallach) attempts to seduce the nubile wife and bring the husband to justice for setting fire to his cotton gin.

The movie's director, Elia Kazan, thought it was "a lark from beginning to end" and "not to be taken seriously."[25] Church leadership, however, did take it seriously. *Baby Doll* was promptly condemned by the Legion of Decency and personally denounced by the archbishop of New York from the towering stone pulpit of St. Patrick's Cathedral. The outraged prelate's stinging denunciation sparked protests against the picture throughout the nation. In some dioceses, bishops imposed a six-month boycott of theatres where it was playing. Due in large part to the Catholic campaign, the movie secured only an estimated 25 percent of its potential bookings.

Although Catholic crusaders succeeded in limiting *Baby Doll*'s national exposure, this proved to be their last major victory at the box office. The fragile link between religious groups and the movie industry came under increasing strain in the 1950s as Hollywood's disaffection with ecclesiastical dictates of any sort intensified. At the same time, American Catholicism itself was becoming less monolithic and hierarchical. By the end of the decade, the Legion of Decency was in retreat. In late 1957, and again in 1963, it expanded its classification system in an ongoing effort to develop a more adaptive approach to

Production still of Carroll Baker in the title role of *Baby Doll* (1956). Her character lounges about the house in her lingerie, seductively sucks her thumb, and sleeps in a crib surrounded by a litter of soft-drink bottles, pulp magazines, and other symbols of her arrested mental state.

movies. Three years later, the organization metamorphosed into the less militant sounding National Catholic Office of Motion Pictures.

Supreme Court Rulings

The Miracle and "Sacrilegious" Expression

Movies began to enjoy greater legal freedom in 1952, following New York's attempt to ban the Italian-made film *The Miracle* because state officials considered it sacrilegious. Written and directed by Roberto Rossellini, it dramatizes the story of a simple-minded peasant woman (Anna Magnani) who is impregnated by a bearded stranger she believes to be Saint Joseph. She considers her pregnancy a miraculous gift from God. However, after apprising her fellow villagers of this "miracle," she is subject to derision and ridicule. To escape this treatment, she hides out in a nearby cave until she is about to give birth. She then goes to the town church, where her baby boy is born. The forty-minute movie ends with the new mother reaching for her child while murmuring, "My son! My love! My flesh!"

The motion picture division of the New York State Education Department, that since 1927 had been vested with full authority to preview all movies shown in the state, licensed *The Miracle* first without English subtitles and then with them, in 1949 and 1950, respectively. The movie opened at the Paris Theatre in New York City late in 1950 with two French films, as part of a trilogy called *The Ways of Love*. Within two weeks, the city's Catholic commissioner of licensing declared *The Miracle* "officially and personally blasphemous" and ordered it removed from the screen.[26] In the meantime, the Legion of Decency had condemned the movie as a "sacrilegious and blasphemous mockery of Christian and religious truth."[27] New York's archbishop also denounced the movie and enjoined Catholics not to patronize the theatres where it was being shown. Following this denunciation, members of the Catholic War Veterans picketed the Paris Theatre. The manager of this little art house even received bomb threats.

Claiming to have been deluged with hundreds of letters, postcards, and telegrams protesting the showing of *The Miracle*, the New York Board of Regents ordered a special three-member subcommittee to review the movie. When this group found it to be sacrilegious, and therefore in violation of state law, its American distributor, Joseph Burstyn, was ordered to appear before the board to show cause why his license should not be rescinded. Burstyn refused to appear on the grounds that the board lacked the authority to revoke a license once it had been granted. After reviewing the movie, the full board unanimously agreed that it was sacrilegious and revoked his license. Burstyn appealed in the New York courts, which upheld the board's decision.

Late in May 1952, a unanimous U.S. Supreme Court, in reversing the appellate court's decision, ruled that the New York law prohibiting sacrilegious expression was an unconstitutional abridgment of free speech and free press.[28] The high court stated that the standard of sacrilegious was "far from the kind of narrow exception to freedom of expression which a state may carve out to satisfy the adverse demands of other interests in society." The broad, all-inclusive definition of sacrilegious given by the New York courts, said the high court, sets the censor "adrift upon a boundless sea amid a myriad of conflicting currents of religious views, with no charts but those provided by the most vocal and powerful orthodoxies." The court further held that the state had no legitimate interest in protecting the various religions from distasteful views sufficient to justify prior restraint.

Although the Supreme Court put the moving picture within the pale of constitutional protection, explicitly reversing the 1915 *Mutual* decision, those working in this medium were not afforded the same safeguards as print practitioners. Noting that each method of expression tends to present its own peculiar problems, the justices permitted a variable standard. Moreover, the issue of whether all prior licensing of movies is in itself unconstitutional was left unresolved.

Lady Chatterley's Lover and "Immoral" Ideas

Still, throughout the decade, the high court, in a series of cases, continued to erode the powers of licensing boards. One of the major foreign films to run afoul of the censors was a British-French coproduction of *Lady Chatterley's Lover,* imported to the United States in 1959 by Kingsley International Pictures. Although this movie version of D. H. Lawrence's controversial novel contained no explicit sex scenes, it was clear in revealing that Constance Chatterley—in despair over the emptiness of her life—had an adulterous relationship with her husband's gamekeeper.

The licensing board of the state of New York refused to grant a permit for the film. In support of its position, it cited a state law that made it illegal to show a movie "which portrays acts of sexual immorality, perversion, or lewdness, or which expressly or impliedly presents such acts as desirable, acceptable or proper patterns of behavior." Rather than make any cuts, Kingsley appealed to the New York Board of Regents. Its decision to support the censors was later annulled by an appellate court, upheld by the Court of Appeals of New York, and eventually considered by the nation's court of last resort.

The U.S. Supreme Court was unanimous in ruling against the New York censors, though the justices were not in agreement on the reasons for doing so.[29] A five-member majority focused on the position of the state's highest court of appeals that the law under which the licensing board acted requires "denial of a license to any motion picture which approvingly portrays an adulterous relationship, quite without reference to the manner of the portrayal." What New York had done, in effect, was to prevent the exhibition of a movie because it advocated the *idea* that adultery under certain circumstances may be appropriate. For the majority of the court, this construction could not be allowed to stand because the Constitution "protects advocacy of the opinion that adultery may sometimes be proper, no less than advocacy of socialism or the single tax."

Restrictions on State Censorship

By the end of the 1950s, the constitutionality of prior restraint of movies was in doubt. The highest courts in Ohio and Massachusetts had invalidated the licensing laws in their respective states. Only four states continued to maintain censorship boards—Kansas, Maryland, New York, and Virginia. Finally, in 1961 the U.S. Supreme Court ruled on the constitutional status of licensing per se in a case involving *Don Juan,* a film version of Mozart's opera *Don Giovanni.* Its distributor, Times Film Corporation, had decided to challenge Chicago's censorship ordinance. After paying the licensing fee, the distributor refused to submit the movie to Chicago's superintendent of police for previewing. When the city, in turn, refused to grant a license for exhibition, Times appealed the decision in the federal courts, charging that Chicago's licensing system and prior restraint of movies in general were unconstitutional. Both the federal district court and court of appeals dismissed the complaint.

In a five-to-four decision, the U.S. Supreme Court upheld Chicago's power to license movies, ruling that such prior restraint was not in itself necessarily unconstitutional.[30] The majority stressed that neither the specific standards nor the stipulations of the Chicago ordinance was at issue in this case. The Court also took care to limit the scope of its ruling, stating that no "unreasonable strictures on individual liberty" should result from licensing movies before they are exhibited. After citing historical examples of abuses of prior restraint, the dissenting minority concluded that the majority's decision "officially unleashes the censor and permits him to roam at will, limited only by an ordinance which contains some standards that, although concededly not before us in this case, are patently imprecise."

The *Times* ruling left open the question of what standards may be employed by censorship boards in judging the acceptability of movies. The high court moved toward clarifying this matter four years later, when it unanimously reversed the conviction of a Baltimore theatre owner for showing the movie *Revenge at Daybreak* (1952) without a license.[31] It threw out the Maryland censorship statute, stating that it did not provide adequate procedural safeguards "against undue inhibition of expression." Henceforth, said the Court, censors must make licensing decisions expeditiously, provide proof that a movie is illegal before rejecting it, and allow for prompt judicial review.

With these stipulations spelled out, movie censorship boards around the nation began to collapse. The one state that persisted in licensing movies was Maryland, which rewrote its censorship statute to comply with the high court's new requirements. Among other provisions, the revised law required licensing decisions to be made in fifteen days. This narrowly drawn statute was found to be constitutional by the federal courts.[32] But the legal climate for movies had clearly changed. In 1981 even Maryland decided to get out of the censorship business. For all practical purposes, this marked the end of governmental attempts at prior restraint of movies in the United States.

From Codes to Ratings

The greater legal freedom accorded to movies eventually led to a major overhaul of the movie industry's self-regulatory mechanisms. Modifications were made in the industry's code for screen conduct in 1956 and again a decade later to allow moviemakers greater latitude in the representation of human experience. In the fall of 1968, the MPAA—in conjunction with the International Film Importers and Distributors of America (IFIDA) and the National Association of Theatre Owners (NATO)—scrapped the old production code system and adopted a national system of voluntary classification. Most mainstream producers and distributors agreed to submit their pictures for rating prior to commercial release.

The impetus for this industry-operated rating system came from the U.S. Supreme Court's ruling in two cases, handed down on the same day, that state and local authorities have the right to protect minors from exposure to subject matter deemed permissable for adults.[33] In one decision, the high court upheld the constitutionality of a New York criminal statute prohibiting the sale of sexually explicit material to minors under age seventeen, even though the material in question (magazines depicting female nudity) would not be considered obscene for adults. In the other ruling, while striking down a municipal movie-rating scheme as to vague, the high court did not preclude the acceptance of a more carefully drafted age classification system for proscribing minors from viewing certain movies.

With the introduction of an industry rating system, a newly created Code and Rating Administration (CARA)—now referred to simply as "the rating board"—replaced the old PCA. Located in Los Angeles, it currently has eleven members, who serve for a two- or three-year term. The MPAA's president, who selects the board's chair, does not participate in, nor may he or she overrule, its decisions. (Texas-born Jack Valenti, onetime presidential assistant to Lyndon Johnson, has headed the MPAA since 1966.) The appointed chair, in turn, selects the other members of the panel, who are not expected to possess any special knowledge of movies. They are chosen on the basis of such vague criteria as a shared parenthood experience, intelligent maturity, and the capacity to put themselves in the role of most parents when they make their decisions. The composition of this panel at any given time is a closely guarded secret, lest moviemakers try to influence the outcome of the classification process.

Movies were initially classified into one of four designations: G, suggested for general audiences; M, suggested for adults and mature young people; R, restricted—persons under sixteen not admitted unless accompanied by a parent or adult guardian; and X, persons under sixteen not admitted. Early in 1970 the M rating (which was thought to be confusing) was changed to GP, all ages admitted—parental guidance suggested. At the same time, the R and X age limits were increased to seventeen. Two years later, GP was changed to the current designation: PG, parental guidance suggested—some material may not be suitable for preteenagers. The MPAA's seal—which validates the rating—was withheld from any film that received an X designation.

Moviemakers were able to avoid the formal classification procedure by applying an X on their own rather than having the rating board do so. The board received a great deal of flack for the X rating for the critically acclaimed

A poster promotes the X-rated *Midnight Cowboy* (1969). The film became the only movie with this rating to win the Oscar for Best Picture.

Midnight Cowboy (1969), whose title character, a hayseed hustler (Jon Voight), engages in homosexual activity to support himself. When United Artists first submitted the movie, however, the board actually gave it an R rating. After consultation with a psychiatrist, who felt that the movie's "homosexual frame of reference" would give naive teenagers a damaging view of sexuality, company executives decided to impose the more restrictive X rating themselves.[34] (It was finally rerated R late in 1970.)

If a company desires a less restrictive classification, it may resubmit a reedited version of its movie or request a change from an appeals board consisting of representatives of the MPAA, IFIDA, and NATO. The president of the MPAA presides over this board, which is the final arbiter for ratings.

Classification is supposedly based on careful consideration of thematic content, visual treatment, and the use of such elements as language, violence, sex, and nudity. But producers are sometimes able to negotiate a less restrictive rating with only one or two minor cuts.

With the new rating system and more permissive legal climate, nude scenes, simulated sex, and explicit language became commonplace in American cinema. The makers of mainstream movies now had the latitude to deal with a wide range of adult matters that had earlier been denied cinematic expression altogether. For example, *Last Tango in Paris,* a 1973 United Artists release, gave serious treatment to the theme of sexual aberration. Marlon Brando plays a character so emotionally damaged after his wife's suicide that he can express his anguish only through aggressive acts of crude sex. His sexual encounters with a compliant but indifferent chance female acquaintance (Maria Schneider) involve frontal nudity, masturbation, and even sodomy.

United Artists applied an X to the feature on its own, because it was clearly intended for adult audiences. For those regions where an X-rated film could not be shown, an R version was made available. The movie proved to be a resounding critical and commercial success. It earned many enthusiastic reviews and raked in over $100 million at the box office. The Motion Picture Academy nominated Brando and director Bernardo Bertolucci for Oscars.

Obscenity at Issue

When the U.S. Supreme Court began to build a bulwark against prior restraint of movies, those seeking to curtail screen content turned to the nation's obscenity laws. Beginning in 1957, the high court attempted to define obscenity and set standards for applying its definition. That year, in a five-to-four decision, it defined obscene material as that which "deals with sex in a manner appealing to prurient interest."[35] At the same time, it included within the sphere of constitutional protection "all ideas having even the slightest redeeming social importance." In establishing guidelines for determining obscenity, it reaffirmed its rejection of the *Hicklin* test, which allowed material to be judged by the assumed effect of an isolated excerpt on particularly susceptible persons. It also sanctioned the test that had been evolving in state and federal courts: "whether to the average person, applying contemporary community standards, the dominant theme of the work taken as a whole appeals to the prurient interest."

A footnote in the majority opinion explains that material of a prurient (from a Latin word meaning "to itch") nature has "a tendency to excite lustful thoughts." What do such thoughts entail? Most dictionaries define *lust* in terms of intense or unrestrained sexual craving. What specific depictions of sex, which the court itself noted is "a great and mysterious motive force in human life," are likely to evoke such unrestrained cravings? How is that judgment to be made? By what standard? And whatever criteria are applied, why should the government have the right to exercise any control over the moral content of a person's thoughts?

As a result of the high court's 1957 decision, the issues of what kinds of materials were actually obscene and how they could be controlled soon became one of the most recurrent matters taken to the courts for resolution. The elderly, erudite members of the country's highest tribunal found themselves devoting an inordinate amount of time to sexually explicit materials of all sorts. When movies were among the exhibits in obscenity cases, several of the justices and most of the clerks went either to a basement storeroom or to one of the larger conference rooms to see firsthand the source of the alleged prurience. One aged justice, whose eyesight was failing, watched from the front row, able to make out only the general outlines. His clerk or another justice would describe the action on the screen. "By Jove," he would exclaim. "Extraordinary."[36]

The justices tried on a number of occasions to clarify the concept of obscenity but found themselves sharply divided over its meaning. By the dawn of the 1970s, even hardcore sex films were receiving nationwide exposure. One of the most successful releases of this sort was the sexual smorgasbord *Deep Throat* (1972). Featuring close-ups of actual copulation, fellatio, and cunnilingus, its satirical storyline revolves around a woman (Linda Lovelace) who's unable to achieve sexual satisfaction until her deranged doctor (Harry Reams) discovers that her clitoris is not in the usual place. According to the trade paper *Variety*, it ranked eleventh in box office grosses in 1973 among all movies released in the United States. What is more, such diverse communities as Binghamton (New York), Cincinnati (Ohio), Houston (Texas), and Sioux Falls (South Dakota) decided it had redeeming social value under the prevailing definition of obscenity. In this climate, prosecutors around the nation found it extremely difficult to persuade juries to ban the exhibition of any hardcore pornographic film fare.

Those advocating legal restrictions on the rights of adults to read or see sexually explicit material gained support for their cause in June 1973 when a five-member majority of the U.S. Supreme Court, which by then included four Nixon appointees, rendered five major decisions concerning obscenity legislation and control. The lead case, *Miller v. California*, was the most significant. [37] The majority opinion set forth revised guidelines for determining obscene material: "(1) whether the average person, applying contemporary community standards, would find that the work taken as a whole appeals to the prurient interest; (2) whether the work depicts or describes in a patently offensive way, sexual conduct specifically defined by the applicable state law; (3) whether the work taken as a whole lacks serious literary, artistic, political or scientific value." At the same time, the Court noted that states are not required to adopt these guidelines and that they are free to establish other standards so long as they are no more restrictive than those outlined in this decision. Further, although legislatures could seek to suppress obscenity, the same majority noted that nothing in the Constitution required them to do so.

Prior to this ruling, many lower courts had decided that the First Amendment required that a national community standard be employed. The majority's opinion rejects this standard for judging if something appeals to the "prurient interest" or is "patently offensive," and specifically permits statewide standards and implies that even local communities can make their own determinations regarding whether a work is obscene. (A 1987 ruling placed the ultimate assessment of "serious value" in the hands of judges rather than juries.[38])

For all the efforts at greater specificity, the high court was still resorting to such indefinite concepts as prurient interest, patent offensiveness, and serious literary value—the meanings of which will necessarily vary depending on the experiences, outlooks, and predilections of the persons defining them. In fact, the new guidelines proved to be no more definitive in practical terms than those they replaced. Only eleven days after the *Miller* decision, the Georgia Supreme Court upheld the conviction of an Albany, Georgia, theatre manager for exhibiting *Carnal Knowledge* (1971), an R-rated movie about the sexual attitudes and obsessions of two male friends from college through middle age that a jury had found to be in violation of the state's antiobscenity laws. The Georgia court's decision was appealed by the MPAA to the U.S. Supreme Court in the hope that the justices would reconsider their position allowing varying community standards of judgment.

In June 1974 the high court unanimously ruled that the movie did not meet the *Miller* standard for obscenity.[39] At the same time, the majority opinion confirmed that, although the various states may establish the whole state as the relevant community, they are not required to do so. In the absence of statewide standards, it allowed jurors to determine prurient appeal by drawing on their own knowledge of the views of the average person prevailing in the community from which they were selected.

The Court did stress that local juries do not have "unbridled discretion in determining what is 'patently offensive'" and noted that the Georgia courts in this case misunderstood the second part of the *Miller* test. The kind of material that is patently offensive, it explained, includes representations or descriptions of such things as "ultimate sex acts, normal or perverted, actual or simulated" and "masturbation, excretory functions, and lewd exhibition of genitals." With regard to *Carnal Knowledge,* the Court noted that, although "ultimate sexual acts" are understood to be taking place, there is "no exhibition whatsoever of the actors' genitals, lewd or otherwise, during these scenes," and "nudity alone is not enough to make material legally obscene under the *Miller* standards."

Despite various attempts at refinement, the high court's current guidelines have caused the same confusion and uncertainty, and led to the same waste of law enforcement and judicial resources that were experienced under the previous standards. Apparently a concept as elusive as obscenity—especially when it is considered in the context of artistic or social worth—defies legal definition or meaningful enforcement. The task of devising legal mechanisms that suit the demands of one segment of society without limiting the freedom of other segments remains as intractable as ever. Although some law enforcement agencies continue to pursue purveyors of sexually explicit material, a great many more have decided that, when weighed against such pressing problems as murder, rape, and robbery, the prosecution of obscenity cases involving forewarned, consenting adults is simply not a high priority.

The New Moral Order

The old trinity of forces—industry-employed censors, organized religious groups, and governmental licensing boards—has long passed from power. In the delicate process of protecting children without limiting what adults may watch, only the MPAA's rating board remains as a regulator of mainstream theatrical releases. In the summer of 1984, its classification system was modified, primarily in response to an outcry over the assignment of a PG rating to *Indiana Jones and the Temple of Doom* (in which a mad Hindu priest rips the heart from a human sacrifice). The PG-13 rating was added—parents are strongly cautioned to give special guidance for attendance of children under thirteen.

The rating board has been able to exert influence over producers through its power to impose restrictive designations. The major studios were particularly sensitive to the stigma of an X rating, and in their contracts with independent producers, they usually stipulated that all movies must receive either an R or a less restrictive rating. As a consequence, the X rating eventually fell into disrepute, becoming identified in the public mind with pornographic films. The nicer-sounding NC-17—no one under seventeen admitted—replaced it in 1990.

This new rating was first applied to *Henry and June* (1990), a movie about a *ménage a trois* involving the writer Henry Miller that includes several fairly explicit sex scenes. It played in only a handful of theatres and wound up in the red. Most NC-17-rated movies have suffered a similar fate. Because many major exhibition chains refuse to show anything labeled NC-17, and most theatres in malls are forbidden by contract with mall owners to present such pictures, the chances of movies with this rating being profitable are greatly reduced. To exacerbate matters, many of the big video store chains will not handle NC-17 titles either. As with the dreaded X before it, the NC-17 rating is a stigma for mainstream movies to avoid at all costs.

Sometimes the difference between an NC-17 and an R is a matter of mere seconds. In *Eyes Wide Shut* (1999), about an upper-class doctor whose sexual fantasies and frustrations lead him on a strange and protracted odyssey, some sixty-five seconds of an eighteen-minute ritualized and moribund orgy scene were digitally altered so that the movie could carry an R rating instead of the far more restrictive NC-17. In the altered version of this ghoulish gathering, acts of solemn copulation are partially shielded at three points by shrouded digital figures.

As American society's mores have changed, so have the meanings of the ratings. Digital alterations notwithstanding, *Eyes Wide Shut* contains frontal nudity, explicit sex talk, and vivid scenes of simulated sex that would have been branded X in another era. Mass exposure to news stories about such things as oral sex in the Oval Office and cigars as sex toys seems to have de-sensitized a large segment of the population to the depiction of sexual matters, even in movies aimed at adolescents.

Box office receipts over the past few years for "summer movies" replete with crude language, scatological humor, and adolescent sex scenes (including one that involves the defiling of an apple pie) seem to confirm that youngsters have had little problem gaining access to R-rated fare. Theater owners across the country make periodic vows to enforce the rating system more vigorously, checking photo identification and taking other such measures. But any crackdown seems doomed to failure, especially at the large multiplex cinemas where teenagers apparently have little trouble getting around restrictions.

One major enforcement hurdle involves the economics of the exhibition business. Theatres earn most of their profits not from movies but from concession sales. As much as eighty cents of every dollar spent on candy, popcorn, soft drinks, and hot dogs is pure profit for the theatres. Because theatre managers generally get a share of this money, they can hardly be expected to expend much energy in dissuading teenagers from hanging out in lobbies all day, playing video games, buying food and drinks, and drifting from screen to screen.

The pursuit of profits will undoubtedly continue to expand the movie idiom's parameters of propriety. The trend toward ever more explicit sex, scatology, and coarse language has already spread to a broad swath of American popular culture. The publication of confessional memoirs is commonplace. Participants on television talk shows regularly reveal the most sordid details of their lives. Pornographic images proliferate in cyberspace. And on cable TV shows like *Sex and the City*, the sex talk is down and dirty.

The graphic language and depictions dominating the mass media these days suggest radical changes in the sexual mores and customs of large segments of American society—a trend that would seem to preclude any possibility of a return to the moral strictures of the past. Moreover, experience has shown that efforts by censors—whether public or private—to coerce the taste of others, to restrict adults to only those materials suitable for adolescents, or to inhibit artistic exploration of even the most sordid aspects of human experience, have invariably been inimical to the preservation of a free society and a creative culture.

Notes

1. Quoted in Terry Ramsaye, *A Million and One Nights* (New York: Simon & Schuster, 1926), pp. 259, 271.
2. Quoted in Richard S. Randall, *Censorship of the Movies: The Social and Political Control of a Mass Medium* (Madison: University of Wisconsin Press, 1968), p. 11.
3. See Pearl Bowser and Louise Spence, *Writing Himself into History: Oscar Micheaux, His Silent Films, and His Audiences* (New Brunswick, NJ: Rutgers University Press, 2000).
4. See Charlene Regester, "Black Films, White Censors: Oscar Micheaux Confronts Censorship in New York, Virginia and Chicago," in Francis G. Couvares, ed., *Movie Censorship and American Culture* (Washington, DC: Smithsonian Institution Press, 1996), pp. 170–171.
5. See *Rosen v. United States,* 161 U.S. 29 (1896).
6. See *Butler v. Michigan,* 352 U.S. 380 (1957).
7. *Mutual Film Corp. v. Ohio Industrial Commission,* 236 U.S. 230 (1915); *Mutual Film Corp. v. Ohio Industrial Commission,* 236 U.S. 236 (1915); *Mutual Film Corp. v. Kansas,* 236 U.S. 248 (1915). These cases were heard in the federal courts because they involved disputes between parties from different states.
8. Senator Henry L. Myers, *Congressional Record,* 67th Congress, 2nd Session, 1922, LXII, Part 9, 9657.
9. See William Chase, *Catechism on Motion Pictures in Interstate Commerce* (New York: New York Civic League, 1921).
10. Thomas Doherty, *Pre-Code Hollywood: Sex, Immorality, and Insurrection in American Cinema, 1930–1934* (New York: Columbia University Press, 1999), p. 2.
11. See Lea Jacobs, *The Wages of Sin: Censorship and the Fallen Woman Film, 1928–1942* (Berkeley: University of California Press, 1997), pp. 69–81.
12. See Ramona Curry, *Too Much of a Good Thing: Mae West as a Cultural Icon* (Minneapolis: University of Minnesota Press, 1996).
13. Edgar Dale, *Children's Attendance at Motion Pictures* (New York: Macmillan, 1935), p. 73.
14. Herbert Blumer, *Movies and Conduct* (New York: Macmillan, 1933).
15. W. W. Charters, *Motion Pictures and Youth: A Summary* (New York: Macmillan, 1933). p. 54.
16. Henry James Forman, *Our Movie Made Children* (New York: Macmillan, 1935).
17. See Neal Gabler, *An Empire of Their Own: How the Jews Invented Hollywood* (New York: Crown, 1988).
18. Quoted in Gregory Black, *Hollywood Censored: Morality Codes, Catholics, and the Movies* (New York: Cambridge University Press, 1994), p. 170.
19. Jack Vizzard, *See No Evil: Life Inside a Hollywood Censor* (New York: Simon & Schuster, 1970), pp. 113–115.
20. See Gerald Gardner, *The Censorship Papers: Movie Censorship Letters from the Hays Office 1934 to 1968* (New York: Dodd, Mead, 1987), pp. 1–4.
21. See Leonard J. Leff and Jerold L. Simmons, *The Dame in the Kimono: Hollywood, Censorship, and the Production Code from the 1920s to the 1960s* (New York: Anchor Books, 1990), pp. 127–128.
22. *Hughes Tool Company v. Motion Picture Association of America,* 66 F. Supp. 1006 (S.D.N.Y., 1946).

23. Quoted in Murray Schumach, *The Face on the Cutting Room Floor: The Story of Movie and Television Censorship* (New York: William Morrow, 1964), p. 59.
24. Quoted in Anthony Holden, *Behind the Oscar: The Secret History of the Academy Awards* (New York: Simon & Schuster, 1993), p. 408.
25. Elia Kazan, *A Life* (New York: Knopf, 1988), pp. 561-562.
26. Quoted in E. Giglio, "The Decade of *The Miracle* 1952–1962: A Study in the Censorship of the American Motion Picture" (Ph.D. dissertation, Syracuse University, 1964), p. 53.
27. *Motion Pictures Classified by National Legion of Decency,* February 1936–October 1959 (New York: National Legion of Decency, 1959), p. 260.
28. *Burstyn v. Wilson,* 343 U.S. 495 (1952).
29. *Kingsley International Pictures v. Regents,* 360 U.S. 684 (1959).
30. *Times Film Corporation v. Chicago,* 365 U.S. 43 (1961).
31. *Freedman v. Maryland,* 380 U.S. 51 (1965).
32. *Star v. Preller,* 419 U.S. 955 (1974), sustained the federal courts below, which had declared the revised statute constitutional.
33. *Ginsberg v. New York,* 390 U.S. 629 (1968); *Interstate Circuit v. Dallas,* 390 U.S. 676 (1968).
34. See Steven Farber, *The Movie Rating Game* (Washington, DC: Public Affairs Press, 1972), pp. 85–86. *Midnight Cowboy* became the only X-rated movie to win the Oscar for best picture.
35. *Roth v. United States* and *Alberts v. California,* 354 U.S. 476 (1957). The appeals in these cases, which involved, respectively, violations of federal and state obscenity statutes, were heard by the high court together.
36. Bob Woodward and Scott Armstrong describe "movie day" at the high court in *The Brethren: Inside the Supreme Court* (New York: Simon & Schuster, 1979), p. 198.
37. *Miller v. California,* 413 U.S. 15 (1973).
38. *Pope v. Illinois,* 481 U.S. 497 (1987).
39. *Jenkins v. Georgia,* 418 U.S. 153 (1974).

Glossary

actor These days, an appellation applied to both male and female players. The actor is at the heart of moviemaking, although this is not without a certain irony. As a rule, actors put in a full workday on the set to create perhaps two or three minutes of usable footage. Most of the time, they simply stand or sit around, waiting for the technical staff to do its work, trying to keep their energy levels up for those few key moments, and grappling with the inevitable ennui that results from inactivity.

ADR editor Short for automatic dialogue replacement editor. This person is responsible for replacing—or "looping"—dialogue recorded on the set. The actors are brought in to re-record their lines. Microphones are set up in front of a large screen. The movie is cut so actors see only that portion they have to work on, which usually involves one or two lines at a time. The lines to be replaced are played back so that the actors can get an idea of the rhythm. This technique is generally employed to replace dialogue marred by such things as on-set noise, previously undetected flubs, and inappropriate inflections.

anamorphic lens (Greek "form anew") A specially designed camera lens that compresses a wide image to conform to the dimensions of standard 35-millimeter film. This distorting compression is corrected during projection, again with an appropriate lens.

art director A title whose meaning depends on the era and the studio (or independent production company). During the studio era, a supervising art director generally fashioned the overall look of a movie, but now that responsibility is often given to a **production designer,** who then oversees one or more art directors who assist in designing and creating sets.

art house A small theatre devoted primarily to showing foreign films.

aspect ratio The ratio of the width to the height of a film or television image. Almost every movie through the early 1950s was shot in a format of 1.33:1—that is, there are roughly four units of width for every three units of height. This is generally referred to as the Academy ratio because it was mandated by the Academy of Motion Picture Arts and Sciences to provide a uniform standard for exhibitors. After some experimentation during the 1950s, the movie industry settled on a standardized aspect ratio of 1.85:1 for 35-millimeter projection. However, ratios may range up to 2.75:1 in certain formats.

assistant director The person who handles many of the more menial or routine (albeit still essential) tasks, such as calling for quiet on the set, rounding up necessary staff for filming a scene, and maintaining an efficient working atmosphere.

audience previews Special screenings conducted for demographically targeted groups who fill out cards and answer questions concerning aspects of the movie they watched.

auteur **theory** (French "author") The position that cinema is an art of personal expression and that its great directors are to be as much esteemed as the authors of their works as any writer, composer, or painter. The director is seen as the primary creative force in movies, the one who synthesizes, orchestrates, and helps guide the contributions of other production personnel.

backlight Lighting placed above and on the opposite side of the subject from the camera. It ordinarily functions to define depth by sharply distinguishing actors or objects from the background, and it can produce a bright edge or halo on an actor's head and shoulders. When such lighting predominates, and no light falls on the camera side of the subject, it often serves to heighten a sense of mystery or fear by producing shadowy, spectral-like figures.

barn doors The shutterlike black metal flaps that reduce the spread of a beam from a lamp.

best boy The **gaffer**'s top electrician. (The key **grip** has a best boy as well.) Responsibilities may include ordering necessary lighting equipment, keeping track of employee time cards, and doing other basic paperwork.

bird's-eye view A **shot** taken from directly above a subject.

blacklist A roster of persons who have incurred disapproval or suspicion because of their supposed political beliefs. Those listed are considered unemployable or are otherwise penalized.

blind bidding The practice of requiring exhibitors to contract for the rental of movies without seeing them.

block booking The practice of requiring exhibitors to book a package of several movies, often including one or two they want and many they don't.

blue-screen photography The technique of filming a subject in front of a blue (sometimes green) background. This background is then removed through optical or digital processes, allowing the subject to be isolated so that it can be integrated into a new setting. Actors are often filmed against a blue-screen background in order to place them in a different scene or on a miniature set. A blue or green background is commonly used because there is only a tiny amount of these colors in human flesh tones.

camera angle The point of view from which the camera surveys a subject.

camera obscura (Italian "dark chamber") One of the earliest antecedents of the photographic camera. It consisted of a sealed box with a pinhole in one side that acted as a **lens** to focus light on the opposite side.

camera setup The arrangement of a **scene** in preparation for shooting. Each new setup may involve changes in the lighting scheme, the deployment and movement of actors, the angle and position of the camera (and possibly lenses and filters), and the placement of microphones. Because of the amount of time and organization entailed in these activities, **shots** requiring the same basic setup are typically filmed together even though they may appear in different parts of the scene.

casting director The person who auditions **actors** and makes suggestions for the various roles in a movie.

chiaroscuro (Italian *chiaro,* "clear or light," and *obscuro,* "obscure or dark") The moody interplay of light and shadow.

cinematographer Often referred to as the **director of photography,** the person responsible for such matters as the planning and execution of lighting, **film stock** and **lens** selection, and camera placement and angle.

close-up A **shot** whose field of view is very narrow. In terms of the human figure, a face might fill the frame.

codes of meaning The implicit or explicit rules or social agreements in a **culture** about what stands for what, what goes with what, and what behavior is appropriate in what situation. See **semiotics** and **sign.**

color timer The person who adjusts the final print, working closely with the **cinematographer** to ensure that the look and mood of the movie are consistent with the director's intentions from shot to shot. Image contrast, density, and color balance are among the variables adjusted.

composite Two or more individual images combined onto one piece of film by photographic or digital means.

computer-generated imagery Images created in a computer. Also called computer graphics, computer animation, and digital animation.

continuity editing A range of shooting and editing procedures for creating apparent continuity of space, time, and action so that there is a smooth, logical flow of action from **shot** to shot within a **scene.**

costume designer The person who creates a costume plan for an entire movie, selecting or designing the clothing worn by the actors with due regard for details such as setting, place and time, weather conditions, social class status, and overall tone and mood.

crane A vehicle equipped with a mechanical arm or boom at whose end is a camera platform that can be lifted and moved fluidly through space. It makes possible otherwise unobtainable camera angles and distances. The camera can be moved in and out or up and down, or some combination thereof. Depending on the speed of movement and the specific context, the effect of **shots** taken from a crane can be soothing, exhilarating, or tension producing. A shot taken from a crane is generally referred to as a crane or boom shot.

culture The way a particular society makes sense of daily life: its recurring patterns of interpretation, **meaning,** and social awareness. See **codes of meaning** and **perception.**

cut An instantaneous change from one **shot** to another.

dailies The prints of what was photographed the day before. See **rushes.**

deep-focus photography Technique yielding an image in which the foreground, middle ground, and background of a scene are in sharp focus.

depth of field The area in which objects located at different distances from the camera remain in focus.

dialogue All the words spoken within **scenes.**

dialogue coach During rehearsals and just before **takes,** the person who commonly goes over the **script** with actors, making sure they know their lines and sometimes assisting with delivery.

diegesis (ancient Greek "recounted story") Everything that belongs to the fictional world of the movie—that nonexistent place fabricated out of temporal and spatial fragments. It is frequently applied in its adjective form "diegetic." Characters, action, and dialogue are diegetic, whereas music, **voice-over narration,** and other such devices are usually nondiegetic.

director The person in charge of the day-to-day process of translating a script into images and sounds. Directors attend to the preparation, staging, and enactment of scenes; the inflections, pace, and mood of the **dialogue** and action; and such matters as camera placement and movement, lighting patterns, focus, and framing. In some cases, their role is limited to these activities. In other instances, their dominion may extend to every aspect of production, from scripting to casting to final editing.

director of photography See **cinematographer.**

director's cut The final edited version of a movie that has the director's approval. This may or may not become the version released to theatres, although it may be made available on videotape or **DVD.**

dissolve A fluid form of shot transition between scenes involving the blurring of one image into another. For a brief moment, as one shot is gradually vanishing while another is gradually appearing, both images are visible on the screen at the same time. Sometimes called a lap dissolve.

distribution The marketing and delivering of movies to theatres.

dolly A small, wheeled platform or flatbed on which the camera can be mounted to give it mobility. A dolly-in usually generates a sense of curiosity gratified, but if may also evoke a sense of spatial intrusion as the camera enters an area only previously observed. A dolly-out, in contrast, often suggests a sense of leave-taking, escape, or abandonment.

drive-in theatre A venue specifically designed for the showing of movies on an outdoor screen for viewing by patrons from within their motor vehicles.

dubbing The process of matching voice with the lip movements of an actor on the screen; also called lip-syncing.

DVD Originally, short for digital video disc. The designation subsequently changed to the more general digital versatile disc. More recently still, the expansion was dropped altogether; the official name is now simply DVD.

establishing shot A **long** or **extreme long shot** that sets up the spatial parameters of the dramatic situation and locale or otherwise introduces the **scene** within which the subsequent action takes place. Closer and more particularized shots usually follow, with an occasional return to a long shot to reestablish the context. This pattern may be repeated for each new scene.

exhibition The business of presenting movies to the public.

exposure time The length of time that light is allowed to fall on the strip of film passing through the movie camera.

expressionism An artistic movement that began in Europe around the turn of the twentieth century. In theatre, film, and the visual arts, this rather imprecise but useful category incorporates works that entail the use of violent distortion to represent intense emotions—especially terror, pathos, or agony.

extra A player who adds to the background or atmosphere of a scene. Such players are hired on a daily or weekly basis and usually have no lines of dialogue. Under union rules, however, they must be paid at a higher rate if they speak more than five lines in a movie.

extreme close-up A shot with a very narrow field of view. In terms of the human figure, a small part of the face, such as the lips or an eye, may fill the frame.

extreme long shot A shot with a very broad field of view. A person or object might be visible, but the setting clearly dominates.

eye-level shot A shot in which the camera is pointed directly at a subject.

eyeline match A technique of **continuity editing** involving two **shots**. The first shows a character looking at something. The second, taken roughly from the angle of vision established in the first shot, shows what the character is looking at, but the vantage point is more or less neutral. See **over-the-shoulder shot, objective point of view, reverse-angle cutting,** and **subjective point of view.**

fade An optical effect used as a transitional device in which the image on the screen takes form from black (fade-in) or gradually goes to black (fade-out). Fades may vary in duration, depending on the desired dramatic effect. They generally suggest a greater time interval than **dissolves.**

femme fatale An unscrupulous, seductive woman who uses her wiles to entrap and exploit unwitting men with the promise of unbridled passion.

fill light A light used to minimize the shadows cast by the **key light.** See **three-point lighting.**

film editor The person who monitors the work of the various departments in the postproduction stage to see that all visual and aural values are uniform and consistent. Once these things are assured, this editor's primary responsibility is to select, arrange, trim, and splice together the separate film shots into a credible and coherent **rough cut.**

film noir (French "black film" or "dark cinema") American crime thrillers of the 1940s and 1950s marked by **low-key lighting,** disorienting visual schemes, an investigative narrative structure, frequent use of **voice-over narration** and **flashback,** and strong but unstable and often dangerous heroines. The appellation "neo-*noir*" is often applied to more recent downbeat crime thrillers like *Chinatown* (1974), *Body Heat* (1981), and *The Last Seduction* (1994).

film stock A plastic strip coated with a light-sensitive substance called an emulsion.

final cut The sequence of shots in a movie as it will be released to the public. This term also refers to the contractually guaranteed right to approve a particular edited version of a movie for release without further revision. See **rough cut** and **director's cut.**

flashback The disruption of the chronological sequence of events to recall earlier occurrences.

floodlight A light with a soft, diffuse quality. It casts an even beam over a fairly large area.

focal length A measurement of the distance from the center of the outside surface of a camera lens to the film plane.

focus puller The person who adjusts the focus on the camera lens during any shot that requires it.

Foley artist An expert in creating all sorts of sound simulations, such as footsteps approaching, doors closing, guns firing, glass breaking, clothes rustling, or wind blowing.

footage A specific length of film that has been exposed to light.

frame The rectangular form that marks off the edges of each image.

frame enlargement A magnified reproduction of a single film frame or video image taken directly from a movie or television program.

front projection A system that utilizes a highly reflective screen against which live action is filmed. An image from a slide or movie projector is transmitted to this screen using a half-silvered mirror set at a forty-five-degree angle in front of the camera so that the live actors and objects in the foreground cast no visible shadows on the projected background. The overall lighting is adjusted so that it is just bright enough to wash out traces of the transmitted image that falls on the actors and set.

f-stop setting A device on the camera that controls the size or diameter of the lens aperture or opening. In order of the widest to the narrowest aperture, the standard range of f-numbers are f1, f1.4, f2, f2.8, f4, f5.6, f8, f11, f16, f22, and f32. Each stop lets in twice (or half) as much light as the next (or previous) setting. Thus, a setting of f8 will let in twice as much light as one of f11. Adjusting to a smaller aperture, called "stopping down" the f-number, increases the degree of **depth of field.**

full shot A shot of a subject that includes the entire body but not much else.

gaffer The chief electrician who implements the lighting setups and who oversees a crew that may number in the dozens.

gauge A term that refers to the width of **film stock.** The most common gauge used in moviemaking is 35 millimeter, but a movie on occasion may be shot in 65-millimeter stock and then copied to 70-millimeter stock for theatrical showings. This results in projected images that are generally sharper because a wider gauge permits a wider frame, which requires less magnification to fill up the screen. For budgetary or aesthetic reasons, a director sometimes chooses to shoot in a 16-millimeter format or on videotape, and then blows up the print or transfers the tape to 35-millimeter stock for distribution to theatres.

genre A way of categorizing movies in terms of subject matter or common cinematic treatment. Westerns, crime sagas, horror films, romantic comedies, musicals, and science fiction thrillers are common generic categories.

glass shot A technique whereby background scenery painted on glass is positioned in front of the camera and filmed so that it appears to be part of a **scene.**

graphic artist The person who typically prepares a **storyboard,** or series of sketches, to visualize the look of each **shot** or **scene** fragment.

graphic match Actors, objects, and other compositional factors that retain their approximate positions in the frame from shot to shot.

greensman The person in charge of dressing sets and locations with plants.

grip The all-purpose person on the set, equivalent to a stagehand on a theatrical production, who does odd jobs and various small but essential tasks.

hairstylist The person who fashions coiffures consistent with the traits of each **actor**'s character. To create a specific effect, a hairstylist might work with the actor's own hair or with wigs, toupees, falls, switches, and the like.

high-angle shot A shot in which the camera is pointed down at a subject.

high-key lighting A style of lighting in which the **fill light** reduces or eliminates the shadows cast by the **key light,** producing a more or less brightly lit image with little contrast between the darks and lights. This effect often implies cheerfulness and gaiety, and is generally employed in musicals and comedies.

Hollywood style The character types, dramatic designs, shooting strategies, and editing techniques characteristic of mainstream American movies. Though by no means static or rigid, this style sets a standard against which competing modes of filmmaking must contend. Also called the movie idiom and the idiom of the Hollywood film.

Internet A vast network of tens of thousands of interconnected subnetworks, with no single owner or controlling authority, that link together millions of computers throughout the world.

iris An old transitional device, rarely used these days, in which an image appears as an expanding circle or disappears as a contracting circle.

iris diaphragm A mechanical device made of overlapping blades that controls the amount of light passing through the camera lens. As the blades of the **iris** open, allowing more light to pass through, the **depth of field** decreases; conversely, as they close, the depth of field increases.

jump cut A **cut** from one shot to another that creates abrupt spatial and temporal changes.

key light The chief or brightest source of light in a scene. See **three-point lighting.**

kick light A spotlight moved behind and to one side of a subject, which often makes a face look sinister or mysterious.

Kinetograph An unwieldy battery-driven camera that weighed about five hundred pounds and resembled an upright piano in size and shape. It was for all practical purposes immobile.

Kinetoscope A viewing machine consisting of a large cabinet containing batteries, a light, and a motor that turned a fifty-foot loop of film at about forty-six frames per second. There was an eyepiece at the top of the cabinet through which one spectator at a time could peer or "peep" at the flickering shadows on the strip as it moved in rapid succession along the sprockets. Except for the groans of the machinery, the film passed before the spectator's eyes in silence.

Kuleshov effect A concept that describes the way impressions of characters and situations can be strongly influenced through the combination of essentially unrelated images. The name comes from Russian filmmaker and teacher Lev Kuleshov, who reportedly demonstrated this effect in one of his many experiments during the early 1920s at the film college in Moscow.

leadman Assistant to the **set decorator,** the person responsible for finding and acquiring the needed furnishings for a set.

lens A piece or several pieces of transparent glass whose outside edges may be curved in order to cause light waves to converge or diverge.

letterboxing A process that more or less preserves the original **aspect ratio** of wide-screen movies by shrinking the overall size of images so that their edges can fit on a standard television screen—although wide black borders appear at the top and bottom.

location scout The person who searches for places that have the feel and atmosphere the director or producer wants to create for the movie.

long shot A shot that gives a wide view of the visible field. A person or object may be about half the height of the frame, but the setting receives the strongest emphasis. See **establishing shot.**

long take A lengthy or extended **shot** uninterrupted by editing.

looping A process whereby actors are brought into a sound studio to redo their lines while watching repeating loops of those portions of the movie that require revision. See **ADR editor.**

low-angle shot A **shot** in which the camera is pointed up at a subject.

low-key lighting A style of lighting in which there is little **fill light,** resulting in a dark or shadow-filled image. This effect often serves to heighten tension and contribute to a sense of despair or mystery.

MacGuffin A term coined by director Alfred Hitchcock for the documents, plans, secrets, or whatever sets events in motion, especially in suspenseful films. The plausibility of the MacGuffin is of little consequence as long as the characters find it of vital importance.

makeup artist The person responsible for the way actors appear in a wide range of lighting situations. Makeup effects can range from the cosmetic to the prosthetic, in which a player's appearance is temporarily transformed.

match on action A cut from one shot to another that continues a physical action without any disorienting jumps.

matte shot A technique in which a portion of an image is matted or blanked out, with another picture substituted for that part of the frame. With in-camera matting, the film is exposed twice, once with the first matte and then with a second matte that obscures the area covered by the first. When projected, the two separate shots appear to be one. By the 1920s, matting most often was done in a lab using an **optical printer.** Multiple film images are now commonly scanned into a computer, combined digitally, and then transferred to a single piece of film.

meaning A person's inner response to someone or something—the internal experiences that are evoked, including images, interpretations, and feelings. Such responses are invariably shaped by past memories and expectations, as well as the current social and **cultural** context.

medium shot A shot showing a subject from roughly the waist up, with only incidental background in view. A medium close-up shows a subject from the shoulders up. A medium long shot reveals about three-fourths of a subject.

Method (the) Elaborate psychoanalytic strategies to help actors delve into their own unconscious motives, trigger actual emotions, and transfer them to the characters they are playing.

miniature A small-scale model used to simulate aircraft, buildings, ships, and gigantic creatures. In the original *King Kong* (1933), for example, the seemingly huge ape perched defiantly atop a model of the Empire State Building was a mere eighteen inches in height.

minor player An actor who has a small speaking role or, at least, portrays a character who has a name.

mise-en-scène (French "staging" or "putting in the scene") The meaningful elements—such as setting, scenery, props, lighting, costumes, makeup, and character behavior—placed before the camera and in relation to it.

montage (French "to assemble") A term virtually synonymous with editing but one that connotes an act of "creation" more than simply one of "combination." It also refers to specific editing principles developed by Russian filmmakers in the 1920s.

montage editing In American movies, a term generally used to describe the piecing together of snippets of action to convey a great deal of information in a short period. Slavko Vorkapitch, a Yugoslavian writer who came to Hollywood in 1922, perfected this editing technique.

morphing A term adapted from "metamorphosis." The process involves altering the shape and general appearance of images by scanning filmed frames into a computer and manipulating **pixels,** or individual picture units.

motif A repeated element that reinforces a movie's **theme** or central concern.

multiplex cinema Initially found in suburban shopping malls, complexes with as many as thirty or more screens, allowing moviegoers to choose from among several first-run movies at one location.

musical composer The person who, normally during the late stages of editing, writes the score for the movie but ordinarily does not orchestrate it personally.

myth A symbolic narrative that expresses a **culture's** central beliefs, political struggles, and deep social uncertainties. This concept also refers to stories that serve to reduce anxiety by dealing with irreconcilable contradictions in a culture and providing imaginative ways of living with them. These contradictions are usually expressed in terms of extreme oppositions. The **thematic** structures of many movies appear to turn on such oppositions as migratory and sedentary, competitive and cooperative, and individual and community.

negative cutter The person who matches the actual camera negative with the cut of the film provided by the editor, who assembles a temporary work print that's usually full of scratches and splices. A positive print is then struck from this negative. It is used to make a handful of negative prints. Hundreds of positive prints are made from these negatives for distribution to theatres.

neo-realism A film movement that originated in Italy during the last stages of the Second World War. Realistic and socially committed plots, nonprofessional acting, and location shoots are among its key elements.

nickelodeon A makeshift movie house that for a brief period charged a nickel for admission. The term combines the price of admission with the Greek word for "theatre."

normal lens A lens that closely approximates the scope of human vision. Also referred to as a medium-length lens, its horizontal field of view and image magnification are about the same as if the spectator were standing where the camera is located. Relative sizes look in proportion, and relationships appear free from distortion. Movement toward or away from the camera is reproduced more or less faithfully.

Nouvelle Vague (French "New Wave") A movement of sorts begun in France in the late 1950s by a group of young filmmakers who were interested in exploring new potentials of cinematic art. Often associated exclusively with the young critics of the influential film journal *Cahiers du Cinema* (film notebooks), this movement actually involved a wide range of new

French directors who challenged dominant cinematic practices.

objective point of view A **shot** suggesting that individuals, events, and locations are being shown neutrally rather than from any character's vantage point. Of course, all shots are the outcome of choices made by moviemakers to achieve a specific purpose.

180-degree system A strategy of shooting and editing that entails keeping the camera on one side of the dramatic action, creating an imaginary line that divides the set or location in half. This facilitates the breakdown of the overall space of the scene into smaller units without confusing the audience about the spatial relationships of what is being depicted at any given moment. Any shots obtained from the same side of the imaginary line will be consistent with one another. If the camera were to cross this line, **actors** and objects would reverse positions when the combined shots are projected on the screen. See **graphic match.**

on location A shooting site other than a **soundstage** or similarly controlled, artificial environment.

optical printer A device used to integrate the images of one film into those of another through direct photography. It consists of a projector and a camera with lenses facing each other. Two or more pieces of film with elements of a scene are placed in the projector and photographed together onto a new piece of film in the camera. Until the advent of computerized image processing in the 1990s, optical printers were used in countless movies to blend together aspects of scenes shot separately.

option A common practice in the movie business that involves securing the rights to some work for a specified period of time by paying a percentage of its agreed-on total cost. Although the amount of the initial payment is ordinarily subject to negotiation, as a general rule it approximates 10 percent of the full purchase price.

over-the-shoulder shot A shot commonly employed in conversation scenes in which a speaker is seen from the perspective of a person standing just behind and a little to one side of the listener, so that the head and shoulder of the listener are in the frame, along with the head of the speaker.

pan A rotation of the camera from left to right (or the reverse) on its vertical axis in varying degrees to reveal what lies on either side.

parallel editing A style of editing that involves cutting back and forth between two or more separate scenes to suggest that the action depicted is occurring simultaneously; also called crosscutting.

perception The mental activity of organizing the input of the senses (sight, hearing, touch, taste, smell) into interpretations that make sense in relation to past experience and cultural orientation.

persona An ancient Greek theatrical term referring to the masks actors wore to convey various emotions. In contemporary film analysis, it is used to focus attention on the "mask," or public personality, of a screen player or other performer.

perspective The representation of three-dimensional objects and depth relationships on a two-dimensional surface. Various techniques are used to create the illusion of depth or distance. Closer objects and figures can be shown in greater detail and sharper focus than distant ones (called aerial or atmospheric perspective). Sometimes objects and figures are placed in overlapping planes so that the closer ones partially block the distant ones from view. In another technique, called linear perspective, attention is directed to a vanishing point, the spot at which parallel lines receding from the eye of the observer seem to converge.

pixels Individual picture units that can be manipulated in a computer.

plot In formal analysis, the way in which what happened in a **story** is related—how the events, characters, and settings are represented in terms of temporal order, duration, and frequency.

postproduction The final stage of moviemaking. It includes such things as cutting and combining what has been photographed, recording the musical score, **dubbing** poorly reproduced dialogue, and adding sound effects.

preproduction The first of the three overlapping stages of moviemaking. It involves all the work preparatory to the camera rolling—scriptwriting, set design and construction, location scouting, makeup testing, costume selection, and scores of other tasks.

principal cinematography The shooting phase of moviemaking. It brings the director, the talent, and the technicians together on the set or on location.

principals The **actors** in a movie who have the most significant speaking parts, of which two or three might be lead roles and the others supporting ones.

producer A title that can signify a great deal or mean very little. When the title is accurate and deserved, it designates the prime mover behind a movie project—the person who acquires the rights to the **script,** hires creative and technical talent, secures funding from a movie company, and gets a guarantee that its distributing arm will place the finished product in theatres and allot enough money to promote it properly. A powerful producer's guiding hand may be felt in all three stages of the moviemaking process.

production The phase of making a movie in which most of the staging and shooting takes place; the period of principal cinematography. This term also refers to the entire process of making a movie.

production designer The person who is primarily responsible for fashioning the overall look of a movie. See **art director.**

production manager The person in charge of budgeting and preparing the script "breakdown"—that is, estimating the most efficient way of scheduling and shooting each scene. Now often called an associate or a line producer, this person is on the set every day attending to the technical and administrative aspects of making a movie, arranging for locales and transportation, and ensuring that **extras** needed for **scenes** are available and ready.

production still An image captured by a still photographer on the set of a movie or television program. Although sometimes useful for studying details of setting or costume, such stills can be misleading because actors and objects are typically arranged, lighted, and photographed in ways different from how they appear in the finished film.

prop A physical item that is used in a scene, such as a chair, a table, eyeglasses, or a book.

propaganda Messages deliberately designed to influence attitudes and beliefs toward some predetermined end. The term itself has religious roots. It comes from Latin and originally referred to propagating the Roman Catholic faith. In modern usage, propaganda has acquired derogatory connotations, suggesting something simplistic and one-sided that appeals to emotion rather than reason. It generally entails the use of distortion, exaggeration, and deception.

property master The person who gets the "action" props—everything that moves, is held, or is handled.

rack focus A technique in which the **lens** is adjusted during shooting so that the sharpness of the focus shifts from the foreground to the background, or vice versa; also known as selective framing.

rear projection A technique that ordinarily entails staging action in front of a translucent screen behind which a filmed background is projected. The camera then records the combined image of the foreground and background. Reversing this process, miniature rear projection allows full-sized actors to appear on a miniature set. To create the scene in *King Kong* (1933) in which the giant ape gropes for the character played by Bruce Cabot, for example, images of the actor filmed earlier in a full-sized cave set were porjected from the rear onto a small screen just beyond the mouth of the cave on the miniature set. As each frame of the eighteen-inch Kong model's actions was photographed, the film of Cabot was moved ahead one frame.

reflector A broad sheet of reflecting material strategically placed to cast either natural or artificial light into the shadowed areas of a **scene.**

residuals Compensation for the reuse of one's work.

reverse-angle cutting The joining of separate shots so that the second shot reverses the field of view of the first by more than 90 degrees. Such shot combinations typically are connected visually by an **eyeline match** and adhere to the **180-degree rule.** See **shot/reverse shot.**

revoicing A procedure whereby all of an actor's lines are redone. See **ADR editor.**

rough cut The preliminary assembly of a movie's **shots** that does not ordinarily include any added sound. It is prepared by an editor from selected **takes,** which are combined according to the order indicated in the script.

rushes Quickly processed footage from the previous day's shooting viewed before the next working day to check the quality of the photography and performances; also referred to as **dailies.**

scene The smallest dramatic unit of a screenplay. It presents a situation that appears to be spatially and temporally continuous.

score A movie's musical accompaniment.

screenplay A blueprint of sorts for the making of a movie. It consists of the basic idea, the characterizations, the dialogue, the creation and assembly of scenes, and the specific structure of each scene in visual and aural detail. The term is commonly used interchangeably with **script.**

screen test An evaluation for a part in a movie that entails making a short film or videotape of an actor reading a section of a **scene** in character.

scrim A circular wire mesh screen placed in front of some lamps to soften the light and reduce its intensity.

script Any full-length **screenplay,** from the final submission of the screenwriters to the detailed **shooting script** prepared by the director.

script doctor A rewrite specialist brought in to mend, repair, or revise part or all of a screenplay written by others.

script supervisor Someone whose job is to ensure that everything in a scene matches from **shot** to shot—from the **actors'** hair, makeup, and costumes to the arrangement of props on the set.

second unit director The person who supervises the shooting of crowd scenes, action footage, and the like that don't require the main players (who may actually do all their work on a studio **soundstage**).

semiotics (from a Greek root meaning "sign") An analytical approach whose principles are derived from the scholarly writings of Charles Sanders Peirce (1839–1914), an American philosopher and physicist, and the recorded lectures of Ferdinand de Saussure (1857–1913), a Swiss linguist. Originally concerned with spoken and written language, the semiotic enterprise now embraces such nonverbal forms of expression as dress, gestures, and facial expressions. The seminal idea underpinning semiotics is that **mean-** ings are based on relationships of similarity and difference. See **sign** and **codes of meaning.**

sequence A somewhat slippery concept that generally refers to a group of **scenes** linked together or unified by some common theme, time, idea, location, or action.

set decorator The person responsible for things that don't move and for arranging them for shooting.

set designer The person who supervises actual set construction and carpentry.

set lights The lighting sources that create all the shadows and highlights in the background of a shot. In addition to increasing visual interest, this layer of illumination can give a sense of time and place that adds to the mood and meaning of a setting. It can also simulate realistic elements, such as the stark patterns formed by shafts of daylight piercing Venetian blinds.

shooting script The final version of a screenplay, used on the set or on location, from which the movie is actually made. In addition to scene headings, descriptive material, and dialogue, it contains the breakdown of the settings, characters, dialogue, and action into the specific **shots** with the particular camera angles, movements, or positions the director expects to execute.

shot Some aspect of a scene that has been captured by the camera in a single, uninterrupted run. Also, the pieces of film that are joined together in the edited print. The typical movie comprises 700–800 separate shots, each of which was selected from one or more **takes.**

shot/reverse shot A type of **reverse-angle cutting** commonly employed in conversation scenes involving two people in which an initial shot, from an angle focusing one participant, is followed by another shot from a complementary angle focusing the other participant. A scene might begin, for example, with a **two-shot** of a man and woman talking to each other. This would be followed by a medium **over-the-shoulder shot** of the man alone and then a similar shot of the woman. This pattern allows long conversation scenes to be broken down so that we see the significant facial expressions and reactions of the actors as they speak.

shutter A mechanical device that opens or closes the aperture on a camera or projector. In a camera, it alternately closes while fresh film is pulled into the gate and then opens for a set length of time (usually measured in fractions of a second) to control the exposure of the given film. In a projector, it controls the length of time the light passing through the film remains on the screen.

sign Anything from which people can generate **meaning.** For purposes of analysis, a sign may be separated into two components, the signifier and the signified. The signifier is the physical bearer of meaning; the signified is the meaning itself. See **semiotics** and **codes of meaning.**

slow motion Movements on the screen that appear slower than they would in actual life. This effect is achieved during shooting by running film through the camera at a speed faster than the standard twenty-four frames per second; subsequent projection at standard speed slows down the action depicted.

soft focus A slightly blurred effect achieved by using a special filter or **lens,** or by filming with a standard lens slightly out of focus.

sound effects Any sounds in a movie, excluding music, **dialogue,** and **voice-over narration.**

sound mixer The person who combines the separate voice, music, and effects tracks into a single master track.

soundstage A windowless, soundproofed, professional shooting environment, approximately the size of large barn.

special effects Techniques for achieving unusual or striking photographic results during production.

speed A term that refers to various sensitivities to light of film stock. A film's speed is determined by the fineness, density, and size of its grain—the light-sensitive particles in the film emulsion.

spotlight A light with a harsh, focused beam. It is usually used to illuminate small, concentrated areas.

star lighting A special lighting system that singles out chief figures in a scene. During the old studio era, stars were usually lit in ways that made their faces appear to emanate rather than reflect light. This effect was reinforced by the fact that such facial lighting usually had no identifiable source in a **scene.**

Steadicam A device consisting of a lightweight frame, torsion arm, movie camera, and small video monitor that can be attached by harness to the body, making possible movements similar to those of a dolly. The operator is able to walk or even run up stairs with the camera while maintaining an extremely smooth, steady image.

stereotype As applied to people, the fixed ideas about how a particular group thinks or behaves. Such conceptions tend to be organized around factors like age, race, ethnicity, gender, religion, vocation, and nationality. Although not utterly false, nor necessarily negative, stereotypes are utterly shallow. They always entail a high degree of simplification and inhibit the recognition of individual, personal uniqueness.

stop-motion animation A technique in which a **miniature** figure is moved incrementally through a range of motions and photographed one **frame** at time with each movement. When the filmed scene is run at the standard speed of twenty-four frames per second, the illusion that the figure is actually moving of its own volition is created. **Computer-generated imagery** has now replaced this method in almost every application in which the intention is to create a realistic effect. Constructed within the memory of the computer, the model or figure can be made much more detailed and versatile.

story In formal analysis, a mental construct that is manifested in the **plot** presentation. It consists of events—both implicitly and explicitly presented—in their chronological order, linked by cause and effect. The creators of a movie start with a story in mind and out of it construct a plot.

story analyst A person at the base of a movie studio's hierarchical structure, whose job is to read books, plays, scripts, and the like, and to prepare a synopsis of the story.

storyboard A series of sketches used to visualize the look of each **shot.** The end result looks somewhat like a cartoon strip. For all practical purposes, storyboards are the equivalent of a script in visual, graphic form.

story editor A person who supervises **story analysts** and appraises their recommendations in light of studio and industry standards for success.

studio system The systematic manufacture of a large number of movies in huge studio complexes that operate with an elaborate division of labor and standardized production procedures. The old Hollywood studio system operated from the 1920s to the 1950s.

subjective point of view A combination of **shots** that suggests the angle of vision or psychological state of one of the characters in a scene.

supervising sound editor The person who oversees such matters as **revoicing** and the placement of music.

swing gang Personnel who actually bring all the objects back to the set; also referred to as the set-dressing crew.

swish pan A quick horizontal movement from one position to another caused by spinning the camera on its vertical axis. It results in a blurring of details between the two points. Also called whip pan, zip pan, and wipe.

take A version of a particular shot. It begins each time the camera motor is turned on and ends when the motor stops.

talent agency A firm that secures employment for writers, directors, actors, and other creative talent. Larger firms may also represent prominent production companies and packagers, and assemble talent packages. Few movie deals are put together without the involvement of a talent agency. These agencies are franchised by the various professional guilds and licensed by the states in which they operate. In compensation for services performed on behalf of individual clients, they receive a state-authorized maximum of 10 percent of their gross income. Packaging fees are negotiated separately and are a source of substantial revenue, especially in television.

telephoto lens A lens that flattens or compresses space. Also referred to as a long lens, it provides a narrow horizontal field of view but magnifies and enlarges objects from long distances, making them appear the same size and quite close together. See **normal** and **wide-angle lens.**

temporal ellipsis A break in time designed to compress narrative duration and heighten drama.

theme The central concern or focus around which a movie is structured. See **myth.**

thirty-degree rule A principle applied in **continuity editing** stipulating that camera angles must vary between adjacent shots by at least thirty degrees. This serves to suggest that a cut from one shot to another has dramatic purpose. Joining two discontinuous pieces of footage photographed from the same camera angle creates a noticeable glitch—slight differences in the positions of the performers.

three-point lighting The standard lighting setup employed in Hollywood productions. Although it entails dozens of actual lights, and not just three, they are situated in ways to suggest three basic sources. The main source of illumination is the **key light,** which creates the effect of light falling from a specific direction. To soften the hard edge of the shadows cast by key light, more diffuse **fill light** is used. **Backlight** is usually placed above and on the opposite side of the subject from the camera. It ordinarily functions to define depth by sharply distinguishing actors or objects from the background, and can produce a bright edge or halo on an actor's head and shoulders.

tilt A movement of the camera up or down on its horizontal axis.

top lighting Illumination from directly above a subject that outlines its upper areas and separates it from the background. Such lighting can also be employed to make eyes look like dark sockets—inscrutable, unnatural, and a little frightening.

tracking shot A shot in which the camera travels through space forward, backward, or laterally while mounted on any one of a variety of mobile supports. In some instances, it literally moves along tracks laid on the floor or built into the ceiling.

treatment A brief outline describing the action of a movie project but containing little or no dialogue. For many writers, this is a first step before they begin the **screenplay** proper.

turning point An incident or event that spins the action into another direction; also referred to as plot point or curtain.

two-shot A shot that contains two people. A "three-shot" contains three people, and so forth.

under lighting Lighting that comes from below a subject, casting shadows upward and lending it a ghoulish look.

visual effects Those effects achieved with the aid of photographic or digital technology in the postproduction stage; also called optical or photographic effects.

voice-over narration Any spoken material that is separate from the scene depicted on the screen (including internal monologues). It can be from an anonymous source or a character in the story. Such narration, which is generally limited to information not supplied directly in the action or dialogue, may stress a particular viewpoint or provide impartial commentary.

wide-angle lens A lens that produces a wide horizontal field of view and creates a feeling of great size and scope by making things appear smaller and farther apart from each other. Moving objects seem to travel faster than normal if they are approaching or receding from the camera position. Objects situated close to the camera lens are enlarged and distorted. Also referred to as a short lens.

wipe A transitional device in which one image slowly replaces another by seeming to push it off the screen.

World Wide Web A software system that organizes and standardizes the data flowing through the electronic pathways of the **Internet,** and lets individual computers tap into one another. It holds out the potential of creating a new venue of exhibition for movies because of its ability to present information as text, graphics, audio, and video.

worm's-eye view A shot taken from directly below a subject.

zoom lens A lens whose focal length can be varied while shooting is in progress, permitting instantaneous "zooming in" on a detail (magnifying and flattening it as a telephoto lens does) or "zooming back" from it (demagnifying it and giving the space more volume).

Index